Groundbreakers

The Key 100 Growth Companies in the UK

Nightingale MultiMedia

JOHN WILEY & SONS
Chichester • New York • Weinheim • Brisbane • Singapore • Toronto

This publication is designed to provide up-to-date and impartial information in regard to the subject matter covered. It is sold on the understanding that the publisher is not engaged in rendering investment or financial advice and does not accept any liability for the use of financial information in the book. If guidance on investment is required, the services of a competent professional person should be sought.

Other Wiley Editorial Offices

New York • Weinheim • Brisbane • Singapore • Toronto

Library of Congress Cataloging-in-Publication Data

Groundbreakers / Nightingale MultiMedia (firm)
    p. cm.
  Includes bibliographical references and index.
  ISBN 0-471-96453-0
    1. Corporations — Great Britain — Growth.   2. Small business — Great Britain.
  3. Growth companies.   I. Nightingale MultiMedia (firm)
  HD2845.G76 1997
  338.6'42'0941—dc21
                                             97–21293
                                             CIP

British Library Cataloguing in Publication Data

A catalogue record for this book is available from the British Library

ISBN 0–471–96453–0

Typeset in 11/13pt Times from the editor's disks by York House Typographic Ltd, London

Contents

CONTENTS

Introduction

The idea for *Groundbreakers* came about when a group of Nightingale MultiMedia journalists were conducting interviews with CEOs and strategy directors of blue chip multinationals. One of the key points which emerged was the extent to which these companies had retreated from unfamiliar markets to return to core activities. One of the implications of this strategic move was that yet greater areas of formerly core operation would be outsourced to other blue chips, but also to specialist and emerging businesses.

Many purchasing directors were familiar with the coterie of growth companies in their own sector but choosing between the new businesses outside the scope of their own experience was difficult. The material supplied by directories of new businesses offers no discrimination. Several suggested that we track down the really promising businesses in the £50 million to £250 million annual turnover bracket.

The definition of 'really promising' was crucial and we sought the guidance of leading advisers, Business Links, Enterprise Agencies, the Department of Trade and Industry, small business brokers and business journalists to help us define the selection criteria. The parameters would include a general stipulation that the companies must fall in the turnover bracket mentioned above – although some highly technological research-based businesses with particular promise would be included. In addition there should be some provable element of success, preferably financial growth. For some groundbreaking companies there is no doubt that they will be significant forces in years to come but profits have yet to be outstanding. This may be because the company is investing in research or new products and services. Some biotechnology companies fall into this category. The task with biotechs is not identifying them but having sufficient evidence to decide which will be the real high fliers.

The selection criteria for *Groundbreakers*

The future of the UK economy lies with its growth businesses. This is a sentiment which is often advanced by government, consultants, research agencies and professional services organisations. Protagonists argue that the future top 100 companies will be drawn from the ranks of the small but rapidly growing enterprises. The vast majority of businesses in Britain – around 90 per cent – report annual sales of less than £1 million. Many are steady and form the backbone of the economy. They include high street retailers, workshops and offices with a handful of people. These are quintessential small businesses, but they are not growth companies.

Growth companies are businesses that by dint of exceptional performance regularly transcend their previous best standards. In many cases their management are motivated by a passionate desire to succeed which they imbue into their workforce. Many fast growing enterprises have identified an outstanding market opportunity which can be met cost-effectively with an original product or service. In this book there are many examples of entrepreneurs who have seized the moment to meet an identified market demand which is poorly served or not addressed at all. A large slice of our companies fall into the industrial sectors which are experiencing – and forecast to enjoy – rapid expansion: IT, media, healthcare, telephony and leisure.

But to win inclusion in *Groundbreakers* companies need to show more than energy and market intelligence. We have examined more than 500 growing companies nominated by an extensive range of authoritative sources from journalists specialising in growth companies, through professional advisers, consultants and service organisations to industry representative bodies and academic departments. More than 50 blue chip organisations were contacted and many supplied lists of their preferred suppliers in the growth companies sector.

Our cover sponsor Beeson Gregory gave helpful advice in drawing up our list of companies worth considering and guided us in refining our selection criteria. In addition Techinvest, the *Holway Report*, Merrill Lynch, FININVEST, Durham University, the National Federation of Enterprise Agencies and the consultant James Warhurst were exceptionally helpful in screening candidates. A special thank you to the small business guru Brian Winterflood who kindly examined our early – and extensive – list of potential candidates, and gave his views. I would like to add a special thank you to everyone at Duncan Lawrie for their guidance.

When any leading commentator is asked what distinguishes one business – of any size – from another, the answer is usually: management. So it is with growth companies. The quality of management certainly dictates the longevity of companies which aspire to be among the world beaters. For many founders of businesses in the emerging companies sector the eye is firmly fixed on the daily operational realities. But the test comes in balancing the exigencies and demands of operational issues, with ensuring that the company has a strategic future, understanding in which direction it must go to build and expand. One-product companies may grow for a sustained period but they can only have ambitions to be real players if demand for their product or service will mushroom or it is capable of significant development or variation. If the business is going places, eventually the senior management will be obliged to leave the operational management to more junior personnel and concentrate on the planning and future of the company.

Management – however it is defined – is the cardinal standard for assessing the quality of businesses and is chief among our selection criteria. Our journalists and researchers needed to be convinced that candidate companies showed sufficient calibre of management to warrant inclusion in our short-list. Every company is different but the achievements of the business were a strong indicator as to the strength of its management. In addition their commercial, professional and academic backgrounds contribute to a complete picture.

There are other litmus tests which define the potential of emerging companies. Many of the companies in this book speak about market leadership; it is a phrase to view with some scepticism. Genuine market leadership suggests that the company has a significant advantage over competitors. Generally analysts, commentators and even businesses refer to national, regional or global leadership in a given sector or niche. But the phrase is bandied about with such carelessness. Businesses often remain vague about where and in which sector. A software company may for example proclaim its market leadership for accounting packages. The fact that its market is Peterborough and its leadership is limited to packages under its own proprietary brand is, apparently, neither here nor there.

Genuine market leadership in a sector which is important enough to be an ongoing source of fruitful business is extremely important. It shows flair, originality and the capacity to meet customer demand. It also demonstrates a talent to read the market and provide something more applicable to the needs of the markets than competitors. This could be a product which is more cost-effective than those of rivals or one which is better quality or more multi-faceted. These days it usually means that it does more, better and cheaper than anyone else.

One crucial criterion for enterprises with ambitions to enter the international market is the ability to form alliances with blue chip operators. The reputation of a new business is key in winning orders and a major contributor to building a name is to form partnerships with the likes of IBM, Sony,

Hewlett-Packard, BP, Intel, or Microsoft. This gives instant credibility. It shows that a principal player has recognised the emerging company as one with which to do business. The spin-off benefits are immense for a new company on that demanding stage. There's nothing like experience to give a grounding in how to meet customer expectation at that level. In some cases these smaller companies are so good at managing multi-layer international partnerships that it could almost be a second career for them. Advanced Risc Machines (ARM) is a case in point. The quality and cost-effectiveness of its design of new chips is so attractive that it has semiconductor, electronics and telephony companies queuing up on the doorstep to strike new partnerships.

Some 90 per cent of our choice do not make anything. They either design, create, consult, sell or provide services. We have several pure distribution companies in our list. Companies like Ideal, Azlan, Abacus Polar and Morse are pure distributors. Businesses like FI Group, Capita, Admiral, CMG and Logica are the outstanding outsourcing companies of their day and pure service companies. In the leisure field GWR Group, VideoLogic, Probe and J.D. Wetherspoon are prime examples of companies which have lighted on an idea and run with it. The research for *Groundbreakers* also showed that our companies did not need to be new businesses, *per se*. They could be older established companies which were unremarkable until new management realised what could be done and suddenly the face, composition and results of the enterprise were radically changed. Companies like Eldridge Pope, Critchley Group and Chernikeeff are obvious examples.

Some of the companies chosen for inclusion have taken a simple and straightforward concept, and discovered new and stimulating ways to present the idea to its markets. Demon Internet, DCS Group, Cranswick, and Epitaxial Products International are all companies which proved that they could do business in a more effective and innovative way than competitors. Taking a simple and direct idea and doing it well is an undercurrent of the research. Bluebird Toys, Tinsley Robor and TrafficMaster are all classic companies which established expertise through a dedicated focus, on toys, CD packages and in-car traffic systems in these cases.

The quality of strategic planning will always be vital to groundbreaking companies. Sage, MAID, Vanguard Medica and Biocompatibles International typify a quality of vision and planning which distinguishes these enterprises as well-constructed and well-designed.

Sage is often cited as a classic growth company. It has built on the early vision of David Goldman through processes of organic growth and international acquisition to be a genuine market leader which is astutely managed financially. Its products are created with flair and industry, and it is an arbiter of enlightened human resources practice.

Summary

We looked for a combination of these qualities and attributes in all of our companies, while being sensitive to the peculiarities of each sector and the rapidly changing demands of the global economy. The vast majority of our companies are already active in international markets, through direct sales, external agencies, alliances or their own offices in countries abroad. The resilience of these companies will be determined by their capacity to provide quality, cost-effective goods and services which consistently outstrip market demand. The challenge for their management having reached dominant positions in their industries is to stay there through flexibility of approach, innovation in products and service and receptiveness to customers.

Journalists

Chris Calder
Guy Campos
Lucy Clarke
Helen Elias
Nick Hills
Chris Mellor
Terry Neale
Kay Reynolds
Andrew Sangster
Mark Taylor
Liz Unsworth
Keith Walker
Peter Welbourn
Frazer Wright

Listing Options for Growth Businesses

Graham Cole is a director of corporate finance at Beeson Gregory, corporate advisors, stockbrokers and nominated advisors. He specialises in advising companies on their capital raising and development strategy. He is chairman of the CISCO (City Group for Smaller Companies) sub-committee on corporate governance. Cole is also a non-executive director of a UK public company. He analyses the merits of the diverse listing options available to growing companies.

There are many sources of finance for growing companies, from private investors, development capitalists, through to a public flotation on a recognised stock market. Many companies will gravitate towards a public offering for some or all of the following reasons:

- direct access to capital now and in the future;
- the flexibility offered by the quoted paper, especially for future acquisitions;
- the objectivity established by an external price;
- enhanced public profile and credibility.

Until recently, the board of a UK company contemplating flotation would probably have only considered the main market of the London Stock Exchange. Now, however, there is a range of options available. The choice of which market is applicable in different corporate circumstances will be key in deciding where to list. these new markets include the Alternative Investment Market in London, NASDAQ in New York and the pan-European EASDAQ.

AIM

In June 1995 the London Stock exchange started the Alternative Investment Market (AIM). This was introduced as a replacement to the very successful Unlisted Securities Market (USM). Both markets are designed for the smaller, entrepreneurial company, which, by virtue of size, or other regulatory barrier, would not be suitable for the main market.

The Exchange defined the objectives of AIM as having:

- a distinctive identity;
- wide accessibility;
- appropriate regulation;
- competitive costs;
- access to capital;
- a trading mechanism.

There was considerable apprehension, not to say cynicism, when AIM started. The institutional investors especially did not look with any great enthusiasm at this potential flood of new, very small companies seeking public capital. The situation was exacerbated by the specific nature of AIM. The Exchange made a virtue out of the fact that it would not itself be reviewing companies for suitability, nor reviewing the offer documents; in this way it hoped it would be able to contain the costs.

The responsibility for the filtering of AIM candidates was passed to a new professional introduced by the AIM rules, the nominated advisor. It was *his* responsibility to provide the judgement as to whether the company was suitable for flotation, and to provide the quality control over the offer document and the whole flotation process. The Exchange is the final arbiter of who could be a nominated advisor, and indeed, has allowed only some 60 professional firms to be approved nominated advisors (having rejected a similar number). The Exchange will also be policing the policemen, as they will be reviewing each nominated advisor's performance on an annual basis, and can censure, fine or even disqualify an advisor.

So, after its first year, has AIM been successful?

I believe the answer is a firm yes. Many institutions are now extremely interested in new AIM flotations. In the first year or so, AIM has seen around 180 entrants, with a market capitalisation of around £3.7M, at the end of June 1996, having raised new money of around £420M.

NASDAQ

This is not a new option for companies, as the market itself started in 1971. However, the potential attractions of an offering on NASDAQ are becoming more obvious to UK and mainland European companies. The National Association of Securities Dealers Automated Quotation system (NASDAQ) is based in the United States. It is regulated by the Securities and Exchange Commission, and has been regarded as a market which has appealed more to high tech and life science companies, although other industrial sectors as well represented.

It has in recent years been spectacularly successful in the new issue market in the USA, especially in comparison with other main US markets, the New York Stock Exchange, and the American Stock Exchange. NASDAQ itself ascribes its success to:

- its screen based technology and efficiency; there is no trading floor, and dealers trade over their terminals;
- the quality (and spread) of its market makers and sponsors;
- sound regulation;
- its realistic listing standards;
- willing investors and satisfied issuers.

Have these assertions been borne out? Among the many NASDAQ stocks are companies such as Microsoft, Sun Microsystems and US Healthcare. In 1995, NASDAQ had a total market capitalisation of $1,159.9bn, and 476 new companies raised a total of $18.6bn. The market itself has more than 370 non-US companies.

EASDAQ

Building on the avowed success of NASDAQ a group of European banks, sponsors, development capitalists and other professionals launched a European equivalent, EASDAQ in November 1996.

It is the intention this will be the first pan-European stock market. Access will be through traditional institutions in each of the member states of the European Union. There will not be a single base – London, Frankfurt or Paris for example – but it will operate across the EU.

It will be a complete market, covering:

- admissions;
- trading;
- settlement;
- regulation.

It has been registered in Belgium, as this was the first country to implement the EC Investment Services Directive. It is intended to be profitable, with a small cost base. Although it is obviously designed for European stocks, it will progress to dual listings by US stocks on EASDAQ, and EASDAQ stocks on NASDAQ, so widening the investor base. This is further underlined by the fact that, although the market will be well regulated out of Brussels, its rules are based on those of NASDAQ. It is intended the market will be well regulated, and certainly not a loose, easy admission market. The process of admission will involve:

A qualitative review

The EASDAQ board will look at

- the good standing of the company and its management, as well as their integrity, and relevant experience;
- the intended use of the proceeds;
- the adequacy of financial information;
- the company's future development plans.

A quantitative review

The applicant must have

- a sponsor;
- two market makers;
- assets of ECU 3.5m;
- capital and reserves of ECU 2m;
- an adequate spread of shareholders;
- its documentation in at least English;
- a published prospectus.

The admission process will take the form of:

- informal discussions with EASDAQ;
- informal review by EASDAQ;
- final drafting of the prospectus;
- formal application to EASDAQ;
- formal review/approval by the company's own local competent authority (e.g. the Stock Exchange in the UK);
- admission to EASDAQ;
- commencement of trading.

There is no doubt the creation of this new pan-European market has created considerable interest; by the time the next edition of *Groundbreakers* is published, we may know whether this interest has translated itself into a successful market.

Which market?

With these increased options, how should the board choose the right direction? Obviously, various objectives and subjective factors will be relevant, but the following points should not be overlooked:

- Where is the company's principal area of operation? If the UK is the only base, and is likely to continue to be so, then it is unlikely that there will be an enthusiastic reception for a float on NASDAQ.

If however, the company's activities take it either to the USA, or across Europe, then NASDAQ and EASDAQ could be considered.

- Does the management have the desire (and ability) to expand overseas – this may be as relevant for any second round financing, when the company is established and known in, e.g. the USA, as for the initial offering.

Whereas some markets may initially be attractive because they offer better valuations, the relative costs and time involved in the issue should not be overlooked.

There is no doubt that the increase in the number of stock markets opening up will increase interest and awareness in those public markets as a source of capital.

Marketing for Growth

Simon Jones, account director at Harvard Public Relations, is a specialist in marketing for growth businesses. His clients all operate within the high technology sector. In this article, he discusses the principle marketing issues which confront emerging companies.

'Business has only two basic functions – marketing and innovation.' (Peter F. Drucker)

Increasingly businesses acknowledge the crucial role which marketing plays in assisting and managing growth. It is the task of marketing to identify which audiences need to be addressed; which opinions need to be changed and what tools are available given the probable budgetary constraints. What all businesses should recognise is that beliefs, attitudes and behaviour can be influenced and changed, and that the most powerful route to eliciting change is marketing.

More often than not the sales and marketing business plans run in parallel, with the marketing campaign playing a supporting role in the sales process. Most growth businesses are yet to achieve 'household name' status, but still need to generate recognition and a positive perception among its target audiences, which are often other businesses. Being perceived as a leader and a respected spokesperson in the business-to-business environment is seldom an accident. It is usually a result of a planned and sustained marketing effort.

Many companies feel that they can define their markets to a high degree – sometimes even name all their customers and potential customers. But does this mean that there is not a role for marketing? On the contrary, practitioners talk about the *marketing mix* – a generic term for using a variety of marketing tools such as advertising, public relations, direct mail, and exhibitions – but what counts is using the most appropriate and effective tools to suit a business's specific requirements – inevitably in accordance with assigned budgets. For those companies with a small, clearly defined target customer group there are usually some excellent direct communications tools that can be deployed – marketing does not always mean generating mass awareness.

At the beginning of each financial year a budget should be set aside for marketing activities. This should be reviewed quarterly and reflect the aspirations and sales targets of the company. Advertising expenditure should be monitored closely as there is no finite level of expenditure relating to this discipline – space is always there to be bought – but with other marketing activities such as direct mail, exhibitions and media relations there is usually a ceiling to what can practically be achieved.

For the majority of growing businesses the primary aim of all marketing activity will be to generate sales leads. Image, awareness and education all support this process but what matters ultimately are good, quality sales leads. If leads are to be generated and wastage avoided clear targeting is an essential starting point – for example there is little point at aiming a meat product at a vegetarian group. With target audiences carefully defined the marketing process can commence.

Choosing the most appropriate elements of the marketing mix to be used is the next step – and this can be facilitated by seeking advice from an independent marketing or communications consultant. Ensure that before any campaign is embarked upon, an effective means of evaluation is put in place, because all expenditure needs to be justified against objectives (usually sales achieved, but sometimes a change in awareness or attitudes).

Advertising, even if it is extremely focused, is by no means cheap but it can certainly generate wide awareness and appeal to a wide audience. It is good for imparting short, sharp messages or conveying a visual identity but not so good for communicating complex arguments or propositions. But remember, image-based advertising by its very nature requires a continuous presence; awareness decays very quickly. Direct mail is an ideal support activity but can also incur some hefty production charges up front and requires comprehensive follow-up to ensure any kind of quality returns.

One of the most important influencers is the editorial sector of the media and it is the job of every marketeer to ensure that a media relations campaign, no matter how small, is initiated. Co-ordinating a media relations campaign alongside sales brings the two disciplines together and ensures that they feed off each other. In devising a strategy, businesses need to explore every possible avenue to gain an edge over competitors. And remember people are much more likely to believe editorial or 'independent commentary' than an advertisement.

Medial relations transcends the familiar and overworked press release by providing numerous opportunities for editorial exposure within the media –

news stories, articles, case studies, letters, competitions and sponsorship should be considered within the staple diet of every marketing campaign. Companies can really make a difference to their campaigns by introducing creative flair and understanding the way the way the media works. The media receives mountains of information and therefore it is important that considered judgements are made on what businesses are communicating to newspapers, magazines or broadcasters. As a general rule, look at how interesting and relevant the story will be to the publication's readers: a new sales assistant's appointment may be of interest to you, but it is hardly likely to be of interest to the press. If a publication does not run new product stories, then do not waste time and effort trying to persuade journalists to include a piece on your new product.

The ultimate objective of media relations is to achieve beneficial editorial coverage in the media, but remember that editorial cannot be bought. A variety of different approaches to the media are available to businesses. For example if the aim is to raise product awareness, one may want to run a competition in association with the publication. Obviously the prize should be of interest to the readers as well as relevant to your business.

If you believe that you have something important or interesting to say, then consider writing a letter to the editor for publication. It is also worth approaching the editor to see if the publication would take a full length article on the subject.

What matters in marketing is vision, planning and measurement of results – start from the premise that marketing will make a difference, put it into practice and then reap the rewards.

The Importance of Intellectual Property Protection to the Small Business

The success of many growing businesses is based around the development of innovative technologies and designs. However, these advantages can be eroded if the company does not take sufficient steps to protect them. In this article, Mark Green, of Urquhart-Dykes & Lord, one of the UK's leading firms of Patent and Trade Marks Agents, explains the importance of intellectual property protection, the steps small businesses can take to obtain it and some of the pitfalls for the unwary.

The rapid pace of technology, the increasingly litigious nature of society, the need to place valuation on intangible assets: all of these are current issues in the global business environment. The pressure on businesses and individuals to protect their intellectual property rights has never been greater and the cost of failure to protect never been higher.

Intellectual property rights are only worth while if there is something a business has to sell, be it goods, services or expertise. The rights give legal recognition to the ownership of new ideas or brand names and give the proprietor the right to stop other people exploiting his property. The innovator can benefit from his ingenuity – be it the invention of a new electrical connector, the design of a chair, the marketing of a drink under a new brand name or the authorship of a novel. The rights will be sold or licensed to others or can be used to safeguard investment in new ventures and developments.

Intellectual property comes in many forms – patents, trade marks and service marks, designs and copyright Some intellectual property accrues naturally, such as the copyright in a literary work or software programme, while other forms require registration, such as patents and trade marks. All intellectual property must be expressed in some suitable form that transactions can occur as with any other form of property. The limits of ownership of the property can be identified, as with the walls around a piece of land.

example, a patent comprises a description which defines the scope of the invention. A trade mark registration will be the mark itself, also protects against competitors who offer similar goods or services.

Businesses – in all circumstances – should have a business plan and the plan should have realistically obtainable objectives. If an enterprise is centred around innovation, the development, protection and exploitation of the innovation should form part of this plan. If the full possibilities of various intellectual property rights are used as appropriate, then the enterprise will have a far stronger wall of protection than if these possibilities are left to chance or are ignored altogether. As with any wall, the bricks of different intellectual property rights should interlock as far as possible, in order to strengthen the construction. It is important that small developments are protected as appropriate since a competing enterprise will find it much harder to break through an interlocked structure of intellectual property rights. British businesses in the past have been less aggressive than their counterparts in Germany, Japan and the US in filing applications for intellectual protection. The advent of the single European market is improving matters, but statistics still show Britain lagging behind, putting inventors at a disadvantage in the competitive marketplace.

In a technologically-innovative company, patents can be seen as the most appropriate form of protection. However, patents may not be the most appropriate route. Thus rather than patent a process an inventor may prefer to keep his process entirely secret and exploit it either alone or in conjunction with others under confidentiality agreements. Whether such secrecy is the best form of protection will depend upon the process. Agreements have a tendency to be broken Furthermore someone else may invent the same process independently.

A common error which is made by those who are new to the complexities of patents and registered designs is disclosure of the invention or design before an application has been made for its protection. Confidentiality is extremely important. No disclosure of the invention or design should be made to anyone who is not under a legal obligation, by contract or otherwise, to keep it confidential.

Most forms of intellectual property are local to individual countries. When considering protection abroad it is advisable to consider the potential markets. If one has no intention of actively marketing in another country, nor knows of a third party to whom one could sell or licence the relevant intellectual property rights, then it is probably not worth bothering with obtaining protection in that country. A properly-constructed business plan should take foreign markets into account. If protection is not obtained abroad, others will be free to exploit it, but in those countries where intellectual property rights do exist, these can be infringed by importation.

Obtaining registered rights such as patents, designs and trade marks is complex. Great care should be exercised before deciding to tend to the procedures oneself. The registered rights are legal documents and the text of these documents must be able to stand up to legal attack. This is especially true in patents. It can be a false economy to not employ the services of a patent agent in drafting the specification for prosecuting the application, particularly if applications are to be made worldwide. The costs can be brought down by working as closely as possible with the agent. Of course, no patent agent can guarantee the commercial success of an invention. If the idea has no commercial basis at the outset, then the money spent using a patent agent will be an added loss. These costs may seem high, but when viewed as a percentage of total expenditure on R&D, launch, advertising, and promotion, they are not usually significant.

There is no point having intellectual property rights unless you are prepared to use them. It is up to the owner of the property at all times to ensure that his interest and rights are protected. Litigation is, without doubt, expensive. However. the amount of intellectual property litigation which reaches the courts is very small. Usually an agreement between parties can be reached. It is also possible to ensure all forms of intellectual property rights against the cost of litigation, although such insurances are usuallv only available if an application has been prosecuted by a qualified practitioner, such as a patent agent or trade mark agent.

The boot can, of course, be on the other foot. It is important that before launching a new product or embarking on a new project, infringement clearance search is carried out to ensure that there are no conflicts with patents, trade marks or designs owned by competitors. The earlier these searches are undertaken, the less costly and time-consuming will be any legal problems which may arise at a later date. Never make assumptions about the rights of third parties. These can be complex agreements between companies to cross-licence each others' patents while European Union laws may impose many rules about what these licences can involve.

In summary, it can be seen that intellectual property protection appropriate to the business venture is important. However, it must match the potential. The complexities of intellectual property can be more easily dealt with if the owner is armed with the right information and the right advisers. The British Patent Office gives considerable assistance to individuals and small business. The relevant Institutes of Patent Agents and Trade Mark Agents provide details of professional help. Patent and trade mark agents are specialists in the area. They have many years of experience and will be qualified by examination in accordance with their institutes. The Chartered Institute of Patent Agents gives free clinics for initial consultations. Most agents will also provide a free initial consultation.

Abacus Polar plc

Newbury, Berkshire

Turnover				
1992	1993	1994	1995	1996
£23M	£31M	£38M	£67M	£98M

Summary: Abacus Polar has grown rapidly in the last few years. A British electronic components distribution business, the company has increased revenues through organic growth of its major account/local office business model and through acquisitions of complementary distribution companies in the UK and Scandinavia. It has also constructed strong relationships with leading international electronics companies. Abacus Polar is focused heavily towards quality and enjoys an enviable reputation for customer service.

The Business

One of the biggest stories in the growth businesses sector in early 1996 was the merger of two electronics components distributors – Abacus and Polar. The rationale of the initiative, debated extensively in the technical press, was to build a bigger, broader-based distribution business. Abacus Polar became at a stroke the sixth largest business in its markets. Abacus, with the larger (£60 million) turnover, led the combination. Polar brought into the unified business Hawke Components, Eiger Technologies and Polar Electronics which turned over £40 million. The new company commands sales of £100 million and it represents a wider platform of services. It offers semiconductors, displays, electro-mechanical and passive products plus a full kitting division, cable harness and electro-mechanical subcontract manufacturing and semiconductor programming.

The story started with Abacus, which began trading in 1972. The present CEO, Brian Murdoch, led an MBO from the founders in 1989 to make Abacus an independent business. Since then he has grown the franchise base, i.e. the suppliers to Abacus, devised a regional company network and kept the company's original sourcing business. This conflicts with some of the franchisee's interests but Murdoch says, 'Where we can supply a franchise's products we obviously do, where we cannot we go outside, and if that helps us keep an order for a whole range of components, including those of a supplier, then everyone, including the customer, is happy.' He has also built the company up through acquisitions leading up to the Polar initiative.

Murdoch's company was hit by the recession in 1990. Abacus slashed and burnt in 1991 to cut stocks and get the business back in step with the market. Since then it has flown. It is run on a very tight financial rein and management has wrung organic growth from the operation and increased its size through acquisitions. Abacus went through a partial flotation in late 1993, when it was characterised as one of the country's fastest-growing component distributors. It then had operating margins of 11.1 per cent, a stock turn of 5.2 and sales per head of £222,000 which were all above average for the sector. The company raised £15 million, some of which was used to pay off debt. Murdoch's company acquired a Nordic regional distributor, Promax A/S, in October 1994. Abacus thus expanded into a fresh geography with a regionally-organised distributor that complemented its own regional culture and added new customers, complementary franchises and an extended outlet for Abacus's existing franchises. Abacus also has a toe dipped in German waters with Abacus GmbH. This is a single office. The company also has a sales office in Singapore which has been added to the original sourcing office there.

Distinctive features

- focus on customer accounts rather than on catalogue business;
- company grown by both acquisition and organic methods;
- extensive pattern of regional offices in mainland Europe and Far East;
- high quality franchises from international electronics manufacturers.

The combined company believes that it forms a stronger platform to take advantage of the vendor reduction trend while still providing good service and staying cost-effective. The company holds ISO 9002 approvals for both distribution and subcontract manufacturing. It also holds high quality franchises such as Toshiba, Phillips Semiconductor, Siemens, Hitachi, and Thomson which complement National Semiconductor, its longest held franchise.

Stratagems

Size and shape

Employees: 460   Locations: 23
Geographical income split: UK 80%, RoW 20%

Like many companies in the general IT sector Abacus Polar has grown through well-driven organic growth and acquisition. This is not surprising as a management-led buyout that succeeds in regenerating its own operation is generally capable of doing the same to other businesses in allied fields and building a bigger and better performing business by so doing. In distribution this logic can be enhanced if the acquired business has new customers and new franchises. The enlarged customer base means a larger buying volume leading to better prices for product which is then sold at greater volume thereby enhancing both sales revenue and margin. By centralising, in so far as possible, administration, sales, buying, marketing and warehousing, internal costs also reduce. In distribution being big in sales and purchase volume is one side of the essential coin, being small in administration, bank charges and virtually everything else internal is the other. It is all about leverage.

Future prospects

- major increase in turnover and pretax profits;
- high growth in customers markets – and therefore increased demand for Abacus products;
- rapid expansion in mainland European and overseas markets.

Components distribution in the UK is divided into off-the-page catalogue business and volume sales. Abacus Polar focuses on volume sales to large accounts looked after by sales reps in local offices. Such reps will handle 20 customers only instead of the more usual 100 or so. This delivers a higher revenue per sales head. The group also tries to satisfy as many requirements as possible in these large accounts by offering cable harnessing and the ability to source non-franchise products. The aim is to grow close to customers, to build a partnering relationship and thus grow with the trend of vendor reduction by customers. They wish to reduce the number of suppliers they do business with and so decrease their costs.

Abacus Polar aims to be a selected supplier and by satisfying a broader range of requirements than their competition, being a high-quality supplier through ISO 9002 accreditation and offering local support they are succeeding in this aim. The company also plans to get franchises for products that meet customer needs in growing markets and so build additional sales volume. Abacus Polar is considering an acquisition in Germany if an opportunity arises. Building up a local office model from the ground up in Germany by using its internal resources will take a long time and much investment. Buying a German equivalent to Promax would short-cut this process. However, acquiring German companies is a difficult business.

Outlook

The group's customers operate in the IT, telecommunications, security products and medical electronics markets. All of these are growth markets. It has a set of high quality franchises and has shown itself capable of strengthening its business through acquisition. Look for the group to increase its coverage of Northern Europe and expand elsewhere overseas where opportunity permits. There is scope for good organic growth through closer integration of the Polar and Promax sides of the business.

Address:

Abacus House, Bone Lane, Newbury, Berkshire RG14 5SF. Tel: 01635 36222. Fax: 01635 38670

Admiral plc

Camberley, Surrey

Turnover				
1993	1994	1995	1996	1997
£37M	£49.5M	£65.5M	£90.8M	£98Me

Summary: Admiral typifies a well-managed business in the computer services sector. It is achieving excellent profitability in a range of sectors. The company designs bespoke software systems and offers both technical consultancy on systems and management services for computer-based projects. It was founded in 1979, gained a full listing in 1987 and is today one of the UK's fastest growing independent IT services enterprises. It has spawned eleven autonomous operating units – six in the UK, two in mainland Europe and others in Eire, Australia, Singapore and Malaysia. In the last year Admiral has benefited from a growing demand for IT services and the deepening of its product and trading base.

The Business

When BT elected to expand the bank of national telephone numbers in 1995, it engaged Admiral to handle the software issues. The telecommunications giant – keen to ensure that the entire project would meet its demanding standards for delivery – brought in an American quality control consultancy. As part of this verification exercise, the US consultancy reviewed Admiral's work. At first, the Americans assumed that their complete control methodology must be flawed since Admiral scored excellently in every area of its operation. The audit team had never seen results like it.

This independent assessment gives vindication of one of the key facets of the Admiral approach – high service quality. The business was founded by current chairman Clay Brendish and MD Dr Ceri James after disillusionment with the short-termism of many software houses of the period. They both believed that the company should be run as a science not an art, and that time must be taken and commitment must be made to quality in order to build client relationships. The founders' first assignment was to train RAF and West German Air Force and Navy on the mainland in avionics software. As a pointer to the future, the duo quickly appointed quality assurance manager Michael Rathbone to write procedures for every business eventuality. 'We believe in structures and procedures. I cannot imagine that there is a business or technical situation which we have not prepared for,' says Dr James.

The early pace of development was slow – intentionally – as the company wanted to create firm foundations. Its name was made in defence circles, providing quality assurance of the software systems produced by larger houses. In the early 1980s, with a moratorium on defence spending, Admiral diversified into financial services. Barclays Bank was an early customer, followed by the development of a gilts office settlement system for the Bank of England and the Stock Exchange. This has blossomed, and, according to broker Greig Middleton, the financial community now accounts for 37 per cent of Admiral's income with commercial and industrial contributing a further 34 per cent.

The business has been cash generative since 1979 and profits have improved year-on-year since the outset. Richard Holway, of the respected industry title *Holway Report*, says that Admiral has succeeded because the company has stuck to what it knows best, benefited from strong leadership and skilful management. 'It avoids mistakes,' he says.

Broker S.G. Warburg comments 'the computer services industry has enjoyed, and is continuing to enjoy, a period of strong growth, boosted by a move to client/server technology where Admiral has particularly extensive expertise. Growth to date has been achieved largely organically but the company has more recently pursued several acquisitions, expanding its skills base in horizontally-related markets and new geographical areas.'

The original monitoring and training has mushroomed into a group of thriving computer services companies. Some provide bespoke services; others deliver off-the-shelf products. These include Admiral Computing (sales £30M), one of the UK's largest dedicated software companies; Admiral Management Services (sales £25M), practical consultancy on IT issues; Admiral Training (sales £6M), bespoke IT training; Admiral Training Centres (sales £5M), face-to-face training; Admiral Software (£3M), principally development and database tools; Admiral Customer Solutions (sales £3M), application packages division formed after the acquisition of the rights to the high ticket Marketing Information Database (MIND); Europe (sales £15M), first mainland foray after purchase of Belgium's Delphy Consultants – similar base to Admiral Computing; and Admiral Asia (sales £5M), similar services to UK parent but with emphasis on quality consultancy and security.

Distinctive features

- broad client base;
- extensive procedures;
- high emphasis on quality;
- sticks to core.

Stratagems

The poor management and service quality of the computer services sector in 1979 prompted Clay Brendish and Ceri James to structure Admiral according to specific commercial disciplines. A sense of order, reliability and high quality are key factors in the enterprise. The originators rely heavily on what they call plain engineering disciplines. This means devising written procedures for every aspect of the business; providing formal training in technology, market sectors and quality assurance; and then ensuring that procedures are carried out. Admiral's management is determined that clients such as the Ministry of Defence, industry and the financial services community are able to depend on the quality of the company's output.

Size and shape

Employees: 1660   Locations: 22
Geographical income split: UK 75%, mainland Europe 20%, RoW 5%

'We spent our first three years investing in and developing our quality principles. This was definitive for the business, but it also meant that during this period we grew rather slowly,' says Dr James. It has provided a model for all the Admiral companies – high early investment for longer, rather than short-term returns. This has become a feature of the strategy for all of its businesses. Dr James comments that the group operates devolved management with each subsidiary responsible for the day-to-day running of its territory. However, strong reporting lines are in place and the core principles of Admiral characterise how subsidiary directors and managers do business. Central to this is a belief that income should be drawn from a range of market sectors. This avoids exposure from concentration on a single sector which could suffer an unexpected downturn. The company also promotes internal synergies, by sharing expertise and client knowledge around the group.

The orientation of subsidiary businesses is defined by the style and disciplines of each market in which they operate. 'Our software distribution company is sales-led and many of the staff work on commission but all our other companies are fee-based. This affects the management style of the companies,' says Dr James. 'We are building subsidiaries which each display a global service capacity.' Unlike other businesses which construct teams around industry groups Admiral recruits people who are capable of working across sectors and who are able to apply their knowledge and expertise in a variety of industrial settings.

Admiral argues that companies have been hypnotised by technology and it seeks to demystify new products and systems. The company is interested in technology only as far as it helps clients to solve particular problems and its specialists are briefed to locate the most appropriate mechanisms for dealing effectively with commercial issues.

Outlook

Future prospects
- growth in all subsidiaries;
- increase market demand;
- further mainland acquisitions;
- Asian expansion.

The engineering-style of the business has served Admiral well during the last 17 years. Its disciplines have been clearly applied to the financial side of the business as well as its client and product faces. And the benefits have been obvious. It has consistently increased profits and added new dimensions to the group – largely organically but also by acquisition. The company is interested in expanding its operation in mainland Europe and Asia. The May 1995 purchase of the Belgian business Delphy and recent acquisition of a similar venture in France indicate that Admiral management is firmly set on an expanded mainland scope for its operation.

Address:

15 Victoria Avenue, Camberley, Surrey GU15 3HP. Tel: 01276 682268. Fax: 01276 671096. E-mail: admiralplc@admiral.co.uk

AES Engineering Ltd

Rotherham, South Yorkshire

Turnover				
1992	1993	1994	1995	1996
£4.4M	£5.8M	£6.7M	£8.3M	£9.7M

Summary: AES Engineering is now Britain's second largest producer and distributor of mechanical seals for engineering, and has also established a strong US presence, despite the previous dominance of a few large, American, companies. An unquoted company, AES is expanding by 25 per cent a year through patient development of its own seal technology and pre-tax profits will exceed the £1m mark this year. It is the only non-US seals manufacturer to have established bases in all 50 US states, and its future looks promising with an extension of both geographical areas and product markets.

The Business

Producing components, which disappear into someone else's product, is a bedrock of UK manufacturing industry. But it is not simply a question of building a better mousetrap. Customers, with their complex patterns of certification and production scheduling/buying policies, can be suspicious of a new design. The 'If it ain't broke, don't fix it' attitude can sometimes outweigh the advantages that a new design can offer. Yet AES Engineering, based in Rotherham, South Yorkshire, has not only overcome such entrenched attitudes, but done so in markets throughout the world – including the ultra-competitive (and, some would say, solidly-entrenched) United States. AES designs, manufactures and distributes mechanical seals – unglamorous pieces of precision engineering which are, nevertheless, essential to rotating equipment to keep liquids and gases in their place. Pumps are a major market for AES; the seals prevent any leakage into the outer mechanism or the atmosphere as a whole.

So the customer base is extensive, ranging across the oil, gas and chemical industries and, with growing world emphasis on environmental controls, into this new and fast growing sector of engineering. In the best tradition of overnight industrial successes, AES Engineering has carved out its place in these world markets only after years of patient work, continuous product development and systematic improvement. Always, the emphasis has been on discovering what customers want, and meeting these needs through design and manufacturing expertise, at a fair market price.

The company began manufacturing mechanical seals in 1981. Today, its range of seals has gradually and successfully evolved to levels comparable with most competitors; patient R&D has always been a prime factor in company operations and budgets. Today, the business's direct workforce is around 250, and the Rotherham-based company is now one of the world's top ten mechanical seal manufacturers. It also operates additional centres in Derby, Belfast, Barrow in Furness, Upminster, Cork, Bradford, Peterborough and Knoxville, USA. From the start, a substantial proportion of profits have been reinvested in additional manufacturing and development capacity, but two Queen's Awards for Export, and a Queen's Award for Technological Achievement – a royal double that is distinctly uncommon – testify to the success of this policy.

Distinctive features

- outstanding growth;
- global reputation;
- design quality;
- earnings potential;
- growth in new markets.

Current year sales are estimated to exceed £13m, and pretax profits, although unpublished, are expected to exceed £1m. The UK accounted for 45 per cent of AES despatches in 1995, the USA about 30 per cent with 20 per cent going to mainland Europe. Chris Rea, the company's managing director, reckons that growth is running at 25 per cent a year – and AES is now thought, by independent sector analysts, to be the second largest company in its sector in the UK.

Stratagems

AES has been managed, and has consequently developed, more like a Silicon Valley electronics business than a metal-cutting engineering company. From the start, the emphasis has been on quality – in design, in manufacture and in customer service and support. A purpose-built employee training centre and testing areas were among the priority developments at the company. Capacity bottlenecks have been avoided, and customer service further improved, by regular establishment of new facilities at home and overseas.

In 1997, a new £2 million factory, already tagged as a global technology centre, will be opened in Rotherham, as part of plans to double the company's size by 2000. Yet in 1981, the business was a small startup with five employees. Two years later, the workforce had doubled – and growth continued unabated. In 1996, output was 90 per cent higher than it was in 1993. According to Rea, this growth has not been simply a case of successful selling or even innovative design. 'It has been achieved only after continued and sustained investment in the best possible manufacturing technology – last year, new CNC lathes and milling machine centres cost the company more than £350,000. The fact that we are an unquoted company and yet still able to underwrite such investments, has been an important factor.'

So have sales operations. Emphasis has been placed on responses in the language of customers, with sales and support staff now comfortable in a total of seven languages. Perhaps not coincidentally, 1995 European sales growth was strongest in countries where two of these languages apply – Italy (27 per cent) and Germany (13 per cent). Language also emerges as a major factor in an initiative where staff both within AES and at established distributors are also encouraged to take correspondence courses – French, German, Spanish and Italian are currently available – to improve their knowledge of the company's products and technology base.

International distribution is chosen to match the market – whether through independent distributor or company presence – but Rea takes some quiet pride in the fact that AES is the only non-USA seal manufacturer to have been able to set up facilities in every one of the 50 states.

Size and shape

Employees: 250   Locations: 9
Geographical income split: UK 45%, US 30%, mainland Europe 20%, RoW 5%

In some countries, AES has helped to establish distribution businesses, taking up to 50 per cent of equity in such deals, but adopting an arm's length position on the operations of such companies – largely ensuring that they major on AES products in the relevant sectors. These too have been a success, and should add over £2m to AES turnover this year. Chairman and managing director Chris Rea strengthened his management team in 1995 with the appointment of Gordon Bridge as CEO and Neville Hodson, a former banker, as non-executive director. But much emphasis has clearly been placed on teamwork at senior and middle management level, each sector or discipline dovetailing into the next. Communication, between employees and, particularly, with customers, always gets unusually high priority.

Outlook

Future prospects

- strong growth in mainland Europe;
- further expansion in the USA;
- consolidation of world class status.

AES Engineering seems to have what most companies dream of: phenomenal growth, indigenous products and an international market place which is itself inexorably expanding as the petrochemicals and environmental engineering industries in emerging economies and new areas establish and develop. That the company has achieved so much without having to resort to a flotation and subsequent market pressures is remarkable. A manageable growth rate of 25 per cent per annum without the financial aid of the Stock Exchange suggests canny hands on the company tiller and products that were good from the drawing board. If Chris Rea and Gordon Bridge can keep the momentum of motivation, while maintaining the quality of product design, manufacturing, the speed and responsiveness of its sales and marketing, then AES should be in a remarkably strong position in the world mechanical seals market in the 21st century. Both, however, are no doubt aware that the climb gets harder and the air more rarefied as you reach the final heights.

Address:

Mangham Road, Barbot Hall Industrial Estate, Rotherham, South Yorkshire S61 4RJ. Tel: 017093 69966. Fax: 01709 720788

Allen plc

Blackrod, Bolton

Turnover				
1992	1993	1994	1995	1996
£59M	£51M	£63M	£107M	£109M

Summary: Allen is now 50 years old and has never made a loss since the company was formed by two brothers after Army demobilisation. They concentrated on flagging, kerbing and the demolition of air raid shelters. Now the organisation is divided into five segments, which, although largely autonomous, are integrated into a single cohesive unit which is seeking further expansion. This diversification, which was in place before the recession, ensured that the decline in house building had no lasting effects on profitability or overall market confidence. Profits dipped for two years but a strong order book and a nationwide chain of tool hire and building plant outlets is reflected in buoyant profits with confident analysts' forecasts for another excellent year ahead. Allen is recognised throughout the sector as one of the best managed companies in the construction industry.

The Business

The recession pulverised the UK building and construction sectors. Few companies escaped undamaged – many went to the wall. Only a handful continued to flourish – and one of those was Allen. This is a business with a distinguished 50 year history but which since the early 1990s has really started to motor. Although profits experienced a downturn as the eighties turned into the nineties, given the calamity facing its sector Allen's achievement in continuing to produce healthy profits at the time was substantial.

Allen was listed on the London Stock Exchange in 1989 and has grown into a highly successful public company. But as chairman Donald Greenhalgh recalls 'the months following our listing were some of the worst of the

35

recession. I think it demonstrates, though, that we can be successful whatever the market conditions.' A regime of tight financial and fiscal control and diversified spread of building and construction sector businesses helped to weather the storm.

The group operates through 24 wholly-owned subsidiaries which cover five key sectors: building contracting, civil engineering contracting, hire services, housebuilding and property develoment and investment. Allen is based in Blackrod, Bolton, once the heart of the Lancashire coalfield, but it is working towards a national presence through its subsidiary businesses. Part of Allen's strength is its growing spread of offices, shops and outlets throughout the United Kingdom. The general building contracting sector works from regional offices in Cheltenham, Derby, Manchester, Sutton Coldfield and Wigan. Civil engineering is located in Devizes and Preston following acquisitions two years ago. Tool hire services are spread throughout around 100 towns in England, Scotland and Wales.

Distinctive features

- geographical/product diversity;
- tight financial controls;
- efficient market forecasting;
- quality performance.

The group's housing division – Allen Homes – operates in seven regions throughout the UK: East, Central, North and West Midlands, North Wales, North West and Yorkshire. In the last three months of 1996 housing reservations rose by 47 per cent. Donald Greenhalgh argues that this is a sure sign of market recovery.

But hire services are the biggest profit maker. In 1991 housebuilding accounted for 41.3 per cent of profits. By 1995, the sector had been overtaken by hire. Housebuilding stood at 34.5 per cent while hire had reached 40.6 per cent. The reason for the rapid growth was the purchase and development of 113 Speedy Hire Centres over several years. The targets are mainly builders and DIY enthusiasts who are keen to hire a concrete mixer, scaffolding and chainsaws and enjoy cost benefits from these centres. Summer fete organisers can even hire candy floss machines! There is also a plant contracting site which concentrates on bigger items like JCBs, lorries, site cabins and other support facilities. Civil engineering, largely abandoned in the days of local authority tendering, now has an increasingly significant role to play after acquisitions since 1993.

Stratagems

The company places great emphasis on its structure and financial controls as key elements in its success. The five-strand business core is designed so that no one single unit is dependent on another. It also means that the company does not experience a high degree of exposure if any one aspect of the group's activities encounter a downturn.

Greenhalgh believes in strong financial controls and he has introduced a simple but effective system which gives the business an opportunity to correct any mistakes before they happen. 'Each business unit reports monthly,' he says. 'And it forecasts for one year ahead on each of the key figures – sales, profits, cashflow.' This gives the management team early warning of potential problems and a chance to take remedial action before a situation warrants a more drastic line. 'It's a simple idea and we set great store by it. If anything is going wrong it is easier to see on a monthly basis rather than once a year. Then it does not prove a great problem to correct any mistakes which are of a minor nature. Some companies set an annual budget which is out of date within three months and find themselves in difficulties. We spend more time looking ahead than most companies.'

Size and shape

Employees: 1500   Locations: 138 (including 113 hire shops)
Geographical income split: UK 100%.

The philosophy of financial planning and accountability spreads to everyone employed by the company. The directors believe in the effectiveness of financial incentive payments to encourage and promote efficiency. This is one of the major reasons why Allen has consistently outperformed many other construction companies over many years. Staff are paid bonuses every quarter. The directors also disclose earnings and shareholdings in the company's annual report – reflecting a policy of openness.

The strategic pattern in the immediate future for Allen is to grow the five core subsidiary businesses. Mr Greenhalgh says that Allen has no plans to open any further divisions but that it will make further acquisitions within these five key areas of the business to broaden the geographical and product spread.

Inside each company, the management enjoys significant latitude to make its own decisions within the framework of achieving centrally-specified targets. The companies also enjoy common cultural approaches which stress high quality output, maximum customer satisfaction and the minimisation of risks in an industry which suffers from peaks and troughs. Allen also believes in quality performance as it will win repeat business.

Outlook

Future prospects

- growth in core businesses;
- benefits from sector integration;
- synergies between group activities;
- rise in demand from DIY buyers.

Allen is looking for further acquisitions to expand its current operation and to become an even bigger name in tool and plant hire. These are areas which the company sees as key growth markets. Greenhalgh speculates about other potential developments for the Allen group but many of these ideas are being researched and so he is unwilling to be drawn. Already apparent is the momentum for further growth in the building, contracting and hire sectors. The string of recession-led failures has encouraged consolidation, and there-fore larger profits for those that remain. In general, each of the business areas looks primed for growth. The housing market is on the upturn and people spend more money on DIY when there is a chance that they can increase the value of their property. In the wider world, he sees interest rates as key to Allen's future strategy. 'But I cannot foresee anything to change an overriding feeling of optimism about the business and our future,' he says.

Address:

Northern House, Chorley Road, Blackrod, Bolton BL6 5JS. Tel: 01204 699277. Fax: 01204 698188

Advanced RISC Machines (ARM)

Cambridge

Turnover			
1993	1994	1995	1996
£2.6M	£7.2M	£10.6M	£16M

Summary: Advanced RISC Machines is a computer industry phenomenon. Started in November 1990 to meet the future microprocessor needs of its twin founders Acorn and Apple, it has long since carved an independent existence. In literal terms, ARM designs, licences and markets the leading microprocessors and peripherals where communications and consumer electronics converge. It is regarded with tremendous respect in the sector, and has formidable influence with a staggering array of blue chip global companies.

The Business

ARM does not physically make anything. Yet this prosperous Cambridge-based enterprise is a dominant force in the global electronics and communications industries. As each year passes its influence steadily grows and more blue chip companies enlist in ARM's family of multinational partnerships. The company designs, licences and markets microprocessors but it does not manufacture. ARM's strategy is to stick to what it knows best. It is a business philosophy which has worked wonders.

CEO Robin Saxby, formerly with Motorola and ES2, explains that Acorn and Apple wanted a research house for new chips and spawned ARM in 1990 to meet that future need. He says that the first thing that Acorn did was to tell him to find new premises, which concentrated his mind. Given that there was no cushion of money to launch the enterprise, after recruiting the handful of individuals who stayed with him throughout the project, he set out to win work. This was a defining moment in the ARM achievement. It has led to an approach which is serious about research but certainly not profligate with funds.

At an early stage, Saxby and his team developed a business model which was created partly out of necessity and partly out of inspiration. It has allowed the ARM architecture to be extended into its markets much more rapidly than many of its competitors. It has led one leading Japanese analyst to say 'ARM really has taken this niche for itself. No other company can touch ARM in terms of innovation, cost-effectiveness and widespread application.' The company itself argues that its latest $20 RISC chip is three times as fast as its competitors and a tenth of the price of Intel's Pentium processor.

The partnering approach centres on joint development of new consumer and telecommunications products with well known multinationals like Digital, GEC Plessey, Alcatel, Samsung and Sharp. 'Products in these markets demand an optimal balance of performance, cost, weight, size and battery life. Companies operating in these sectors want a broad range of application expertise, extensive development support and reliable supply,' says Saxby. This means that rather like some of the better-managed biotechnology companies, ARM has become skilful in managing multi-layered business and research projects. ARM licences its technology to its semiconductor partner companies which will manufacture and market the products which emerge from this process. Strategically, ARM partners with blue chips which will grow the total ARM market and allow ARM to emerge as the global standard.

Distinctive features

- global technology standards;
- dedicated staff;
- compelling business model;
- highly profitable;
- multiple partnerships with blue chip multinationals.

The concept of an ARM family spans the world even though ARM itself has only four locations. In 1996 the company employed around 160 people but more than 1000 people were engaged in ARM projects worldwide. The remainder were client and partner personnel who are dedicated to ARM work.

Stratagems

At the core of the ARM approach is independence. This is a company which will, and does, work with the leading lights in its markets but it enjoys total commercial freedom to choose from a catalogue of potential partners. It has established a global strategy which emphasises its intellectual property and the leverage which springs from its profitable application.

Saxby says 'We draw our income from many sources: licensing; royalties on software; the sale of design tools; consultancy to enable system designs; software and hardware maintenance; and design, engineering, manufacturing, sales and marketing support. Our aim is to build on the relationships we have already created and our reputation for high performance, low cost products.'

ARM has identified key components of the market demand in the future which it is well placed to service. 'Embedded control and digital multimedia are driving computer technology in a new direction. Clients and consumers want high performance, lower price, shorter times to market, a higher degree of functionality in products, access to data, communication and interactivity, lower power consumption and open global standards.' This may appear a tall order but ARM has been meeting such needs since it opened its doors. Its emphasis on high quality and low cost, innovation and applicability has given the company a substantial market advantage.

Size and shape

Employees: 160　　　　　　　　　　　　Locations: 4
Geographical income split: UK 30%. RoW 70%

Saxby defines three golden principles of ARM's success. 'We leverage our global partnerships to set common standards. We increase market awareness of ARM and its architecture. We continuously innovate – we grow our copyright and patent portfolio.' The company works on collaborative projects with companies, university departments and software and tools houses, which spreads acceptance and application of ARM technology. Saxby argues many Fortune 1000 companies – some not immediately obvious – will be using ARM technology in their next generation of products.

As well as 78 per cent compound growth in revenues since the outset, ARM has increased research spending from £500,000 in 1991 to £3.7 million in 1996. Some of the projects are part of wider European Union initiatives such as the ESPIRIT programme or its hotly discussed involvement with Microsoft on chips of the future.

ADVANCED RISC MACHINES (ARM)

Outlook

Future prospects

- more blue chip partners;
- earlier role in product design;
- wider geographical scope;
- enhanced profitability.

It would be hard to believe that ARM's outlook could be anything other than rosy. This is the ultimate focused business. It has established and grown from sets of commanding business relationships with blue chips. It has a purposeful attitude toward innovation which means that although it is constantly in search of the highest quality product, price also plays a key role. ARM has a widely acknowledged capacity to manage multi-layered, multinational research projects and to get the best out of people. But it has also created a developing role for itself as the global standard-setter and this as much as any other aspect of this unique company's approach will be crucial. In 1996 ARM evolved from a chip design facility into a broad-based intellectual property company. This attitudinal shift will characterise the next phase in the ARM career.

Address:

Advanced RISC Machines, 90 Fulborn Road, Cherry Hinton, Cambridge CB1 4JN. Tel: 01223 400400. Fax: 01223 400410. Web site: http//www.arm.co

Ashbourne plc

Glasgow

Turnover		
1994	1995	1996
£23.5M	£26.7M	£32.5M

Summary: Ashbourne plc is a Glasgow-based nursing home operator. The company, which is the UK's fourth largest in its field, has homes with over 2300 beds in Scotland, central England and London. The quoted company has never been a spectacular performer since going to the market in November 1994. It has been hit by over capacity in the sector but is regarded as being well placed to cash in on the much predicted boom in demand. However, medium term, a takeover by American operator Sun Healthcare seems inevitable.

The Business

Ashbourne was founded in February 1993 in a management buy-out from Stakis which divested of its loss-making nursing home division to concentrate on hotels and casinos. The buy-out bid was led by managing director Tom Hamilton. About a year and a half later, in November 1994, the group floated on the Stock Market with shares priced at 150 pence. The general view is that Ashbourne has failed to perform to expectations since the flotation. But the company's belief is that these problems – mostly caused by under-occupancy – are mere hiccups.

Over-capacity has been a problem for the whole nursing home sector, particularly with difficulties arising from the community care programme which is drying up referrals to homes in some geographic areas. But Ashbourne is well placed to ride out this problem with over 40 per cent of its patients paying their own way and another 30 per cent relying on the state only for top-ups. But even that has its problems as patients who pay their own way have been delaying their own admission to nursing homes.

In December last year Ashbourne showed its market leading quality when it became the first UK healthcare company to adopt American methods by selling and leasing back properties to free up cash for its ambitious expansion plans without having to make cash calls on shareholders.

Over the long term Hamilton knows that the demographic trend shows a huge rise in the requirement for elderly people to be cared for. He knows the industry is still very immature and there is strong opportunity for growth. Indeed the group estimates that the market for long-term elderly care services will grow 50 per cent in real terms during the next 25 years.

Distinctive features

- go ahead management;
- not afraid to adapt new methods;
- good mix of private/state patients;
- ambitious expansion programme;
- focused on top end of market.

Stratagems

Managing director Tom Hamilton takes a highly pro-active stance to try and talk up the market at every opportunity. He recently criticised local councils who balk at paying between £350 and £400 pounds a week to keep an elderly patient in a home as having got their sums wrong. He estimates that it can cost twice that much to care for the patient at home.

Ashbourne is focused on the top end of the market, with private fees of around £410 per week. Although this is highly profitable – with gross margins of 35 per cent, among the best in the industry – it means it takes around 18 months for a new home to fill up. Much of the group's recent development has therefore been in the M25 area around London where there are insufficient homes and more people able to pay private fees.

Hamilton and financial director Martin Feeney both see scope for further sale and leaseback agreements in line with the US model but they are disappointed about the dearth of property investment trusts covering the UK nursing homes sector. Ashbourne has already sold five homes to Abbey Life on a sale and leaseback basis, raising nearly £17 million to reduce gearing to nil and creating room for further expansion. But it should not be seen as a sign of any cash crisis. Indeed broker Credit Lyonnaise Laing considers Ashbourne to be the best player in the sector.

The sale and leaseback arrangement has helped the Ashbourne directors stem speculation that the group is looking to raise capital through a rights issue. Hamilton had to issue a statement recently when shares drifted to their year low of 127 pence that the company had 'no plans for a rights issue'.

Size and shape

Employees: 1750   Locations: 29
Geographical income split: UK 100%

Ashbourne has been at the centre of takeover rumours since Sun Healthcare Systems, based in Albuquerque in New Mexico, bought a 15 per cent stake in May 1995 in a bid to move into the UK market. The American company has since increased its stake to 24.6 per cent. Hamilton has made no secret that he believes Sun Healthcare's 'ultimate goal' is a takeover. Indeed the two sides held discussions before Ashbourne decided to float.

Future prospects

- immature industry giving strong growth potential;
- further prospects for innovative sale and leaseback deals;
- demographic trends show huge future demand;
- takeover inevitable but will fuel growth in UK market.

An interesting sideline for Ashbourne has been the establishment of two pharmacy warehouses in Stirling and Manchester in a joint venture with Surgichem, the leading supplier of drug distribution systems for elderly care. Initial results from these two test sites are said to be encouraging, which could pave the way for a chain of pharmacies across the UK serving sheltered housing complexes and private nursing homes.

Outlook

Takeover seems inevitable. Hamilton and his team of directors are relaxed about the prospect of a full scale takeover as long as a 'good price' was paid. Hamilton knows Sun Healthcare have not bought their stake without a reason and that, from a management perspective, expansion into Europe would move forward faster with American rather than European backing. The nursing homes sector is very fragmented at present. Analysts expect it to consolidate like the bus industry, with a small number of leading players buying up smaller operators. With American finance, Ashbourne is set to grow into one of the major operators.

ASHBOURNE PLC

Address:

Ashbourne plc, 58 West Regent Street, Glasgow G2 2QZ. Tel: 0141 331
2222. Fax: 0141 331 2805

Azlan Group plc

COMPUTER INDUSTRY DISTRIBUTOR

Wokingham, Berks

Turnover				
1992	1993	1994	1995	1996
£29M	£41M	£62M	£91M	£196M

Summary: Azlan is the leading value-added distributor of network computer products and services in Europe. Started in 1984, it has expanded rapidly and now services resellers through 11 subsidiaries – one in the UK and the remaining ten scattered throughout mainland Europe. The company recognises that merely shipping product is insufficient for the demands of the modern market and provides detailed technical advice to its customers. Azlan is also highly selective about the range of products which it carries and has developed key relationships with some 25 world class manufacturers.

The Business

Azlan started in 1984 as a PC distributor based in the north of England. 'At an early stage we developed a relationship with Novell which was to be pivotal in the development of the company. Novell was the first company to offer local area network operating software. Azlan – then called ADT – became a distributor for Novell, taking its software to a community of dealers. The Novell relationship became core and the focus of our company became network products distribution,' says CEO Christian Martin. 'We recognised that the market needed knowledge and expertise. The market was new so we did not just let our customers buy a box of network software and get on with it. Our business is about technical expertise and know-how to enable the market to understand and adapt new technologies. The model for the business stems from those early days. The issue is not moving product to market but rather knowledge to market.'

This simple appreciation is the reason why Azlan is so successful. Many distributors are focused on shifting boxes, whereas Azlan works with its customers to understand new developments and the implications for their businesses and those of their clients. The Novell relationship continued to grow but a wider spread of manufacturers introduced products sponsoring an expansion in the scope of networks. Major manufacturers are investing heavily in R&D in order to bring a continuous stream of new products to market. They emphasise the development in product and use distributors, notably Azlan, to explain and move these new devices. The expansion in PC capacities, through networking, means that markets for such products have grown rapidly.

Networking products now outstrip every other area of computing apart from the sales of new PCs. 'We are unquestionably the European market leaders – and probably the world – in our generic model of value-added distribution,' Martin remarks. The philosophy of value-added distribution can be seen in the impact on margins. Most industry distributors achieve between six and seven per cent, whereas Azlan's return is nearer 24 per cent. A key reason for this quality of return is Azlan's deep knowledge of product lifecycles. As the number of manufacturers introducing products expands rapidly, the lifecycle of each new product is becoming progressively shorter. Azlan's management realised at an early stage that it could add value by understanding quickly the impact of an innovation and communicating this to resellers. Clearly, manufacturers appreciate a distributor which can maximise the selling time for their products.

Distinctive features

- European market leadership;
- formidable margins;
- value-added distributor;
- bias towards understanding rather than pure selling;
- massive market potential.

'There are more than 650,000 organisations with more than 30 employees across Europe. Manufacturers have six to nine months to reach these companies. The end-users and the 50,000 dealers cannot absorb the volume of information about new products coming out every day so they turn to Azlan. We train everyone in the chain. First we have to be trained ourselves, then we have to train the dealer and the end-user. Some of it is demand creation and some of it is creation of confidence in the channel. We run seminars on all aspects on networking.'

Discipline is a major facet of Azlan's operation. The company will not take business which looks superficially attractive but which returns low margins. It is entirely focused on those opportunities which can meet its exacting targets on margins. This also applies to its core activity. 'We stick to networking where we can add value. So we do not get confused with hundreds of other products.' Azlan chooses the vendors with the most potential, which tend to be the largest ones.

Stratagems

The awareness that product lifecycles are short has fired Azlan into a strategy of acquisition. 'The bulk of our manufacturers are US-based and they want access to a common European marketplace. We decided in early 1993 that a major European value-added distributor would be crucial to the success of US vendors. Manufacturers could approach a single European market and pan-European customers could source from a single company. We now cover 90 per cent of the European market.' Martin says that Azlan reduced the risk in individual territories by putting all operations on a common IT system, and centralising back office functions, especially purchasing and warehousing, in York. 'Our principal interest in acquiring companies was the quality of their human resource. Since control and logistics would be vested in the centre, we were interested in the extent to which they could provide the value-added aspect of our work.' Azlan pays very little for its purchases but offers targets a chance to benefit from an earn-out from inclusion in a highly successful wider group. A commonality of interest in cutting costs, maximising revenue streams and access to latest products makes the Azlan offer attractive.

Size and shape

Employees: 1100   Locations: 11
Geographical income split: UK 38%, mainland Europe 62%

As well as acquisitional growth, Azlan is achieving outstanding organic expansion. In 1996 Azlan reported sales of £196M – a rise in one year of £105M. 'Ninety per cent of that growth was organic,' says Martin. Azlan has achieved this by a combination of operational and purchasing efficiencies in UK and mainland subsidiaries and it has also benefited from an increasing tendency among vendors to use the company as a distribution channel.

Another significant factor in the growth of the company has been the multiplicity of manufacturers in the networking sector. This means that if an end-user encounters a problem, only a distributor with knowledge of a variety of products can determine a solution. 'The manufacturer cannot provide the same quality of advice because we will have an intimate knowledge of competitor systems which cannot be matched.'

Martin says that this is very much a people-driven business. 'That sounds like jargon but in a business that is growing and developing at this rate, we need to allow people to explore. If an individual comes to me with ideas, I say let's look at it. No-one really knows what the future will be so we need to give people the freedom to seek out new opportunities. In the European context, our operations get all the benefits of being members of the group but also the operational latitude to exploit their local market.'

The company believes that networks will become more complex, so it will invest heavily to ensure that it commands the most extensive knowledge of the discipline. The market will become more fragmented and growth in Europe will come from small to medium sized businesses. Azlan aims to take the world stage. Its customers are operating at a global level and Azlan must match this trend with service provision. In the longer term, Azlan intends to go for the far east, India and the USA.

Outlook

Future prospects

- growth in mainland Europe;
- longterm expansion in far east, India and the USA;
- rapid and wholesale increase in global market for network products

The opportunities for Azlan in mainland Europe are extensive. The company aims to increase its margins through its ten offices on the continent. Its prospects here lie in persuading manufacturers that its approach to distribution – as a common channel for the whole of Europe is the most effective method to reach their customers. Azlan is also certain that the market for network products will expand rapidly and its approach will add significantly to group sales.

Address:

Azlan House, Mulberry Business Park, Fishponds Road, Wokingham RG4 12GY. Tel: 01189 897700. Fax: 01189 770281

AZUR Environmental

Wokingham

Turnover		
1993	1994	1995
$4.75M	$5.2M	$3.9M

Summary: AZUR Environmental, formerly known as Microbics, is an environmental testing company, which produces and markets systems to monitor and improve the quality of life. It uses luminescent micro-organisms as biosensors which respond to samples of materials under test. Its systems vary in design for use on the laboratory bench, on site or for unattended automatic operation. The mainstay is Microtox, a product which has sold over 2000 units to users in 57 countries worldwide. The business was originally spun out of Beckman Instruments in the USA and Microbics (UK) Ltd was set up in 1991 after sales success in British and European markets. A series of factors – including the privatisation of the UK water industry and the opening of new markets in mainland Europe – has encouraged AZUR to place greater emphasis on the UK operation. It has recently established a new European headquarters in Wokingham, Berkshire.

The Business

It is rare that a business created and developed in the United States should enjoy such outstanding success in its British outlet that the company will move its global headquarters to the UK. This is the remarkable achievement of AZUR Environmental. The parent company was spun-off from Beckman Instruments in 1985. At Beckman a research team developed the first commercially sound bioluminescent system for detecting the bioreactivity of wastewater contaminants. A group from Beckman excited by the future potential for the technology acquired the rights and set up Microbics Corporation.

Its product portfolio of test systems measures such diverse elements as toxic contamination of wastewater, surface waters and sediments; genetic damage caused by environmental and industrial samples; the quality of raw materials used in biological production processes; the efficacy of biocides in cooling towers and process streams; and irritation caused by cosmetics. In a world increasingly engaged by environmental issues, AZUR has become world leader in its field.

AZUR claims that its distinctive quality lies in its careful selection, rather than engineering, of organisms. It has particular facility in the selection and preservation of test organisms for specific applications, which enables the provision of a reliable standard measure, responding consistently to the same spectrum of chemicals. The company packages the organisms so they can be transported easily and freeze-stored for up to 18 months. The tests are highly regarded in industry for their speed, practicality and low cost.

It has also tailor-made biosensors designed to meet the specific needs of corporate clients. Test organisms can be chosen for their capacity to respond to either a broad or narrow spectrum of chemicals. AZUR can demonstrate a library of 3000 organisms which it can screen for bespoke customer applications.

Distinctive features

- leadership with established technology;
- strong strategic partnerships;
- excellent patent portfolio;
- alert, flexible management.

Stratagems

'AZUR Environmental plans to be the leading worldwide supplier of rapid biosensor-based measurement systems in the markets which the company has created and currently dominates.' This is how AZUR's president and CEO Dr Anthony Martin sees the role of the business. 'Our strategy is to offer a complete product line of instrumentation, reagents and consumables, strong technical support, and responsive customer services.'

Dr Martin, who is British-born and has outstanding biotech credentials, has recently moved the Carlsbad, California HQ to new premises in the south of England. The move makes sense because the company's short term growth prospects lie in the UK and on mainland Europe. Originally, the UK sales operation was in the hands of a substantial distributor. But in 1991, so positive was the response, Microbics Corporation bought out the British agent and founded Microbics (UK) Ltd. The timing was excellent because the water companies had recently been privatised and the Environment Agency, the sector's regulator, chose AZUR's products to help it fulfil its brief. The EA identified Microtox as the main short-term test to monitor and screen water toxicity. A portable field model of the Microtox – made to EA specifications – is under development and is expected to be launched in late 1997. The US Environmental Protection Agency already uses the benchtop Microtox to check effluents and an additional 500 portable systems are planned to be sold to other regulatory bodies in Europe and North America.

The company is keen to exploit strategic alliances and partnerships as a mechanism to boost awareness of its products and to develop new systems. A worldwide distribution agreement with Siemens UK is among its most impressive. It allows Siemens to be the exclusive manufacturer of Microtox-OS, which is an on-line system for the continuous monitoring of water toxicity. This product was originally developed for Yorkshire Water plc. AZUR will be the exclusive distributor for at least 20 years and it is the exclusive manufacturer of reagents and consumables used in Microtox-OS. The two companies have also formed a strategic alliance to develop future products using AZUR's biosensor and Siemens instrumentation technology.

Size and shape

Employees: 55   Locations: 2 (USA HQ and UK subsidiary)
Income split: US: 37%, Canada: 12%, UK: 19%, mainland Europe: 21%, RoW: 11%

In June 1994, AZUR signed a collaboration with Nalco Chemical Company of Naperville, USA, where AZUR designed and produced a luminescent bacteria biocide test reagent and a dual function portable biocide monitor, known as the Tra-Cide* system, which monitors toxicity and bacterial numbers. Nalco has already begun shipments of this system to the world's biocide market, where it holds a dominant position.

The structure of the business has changed in response to its accelerating growth. The business remains in private hands, with 33 per cent of the equity held by senior management. In total there are 76 shareholders, and directors and employees together account for 40 per cent of the holding. In March 1996 a fund raising brought in $15 million through a private placement with five major UK institutions. Senior management intends to go for a public listing before the end of 1998. The London Stock Exchange is the preferred vehicle but a dual flotation in the UK and on the US NASDAQ market may be considered because 65 per cent of AZUR shares are held in the USA.

Outlook

Dr Martin's vision for the company is straightforward and he is unquenchably upbeat about the company's potential. 'We have a strong patent position and an established technology which our competitors lack.' It can expect to benefit from a growing demand for a range of portable and online systems. 'There are an estimated 223,457 potential sites in North America

Future prospects

- sharp rise in revenues and profits;
- market leadership enhancement;
- broadening of applications to new markets;
- wider strategic alliances.

and Europe for portable and online systems. If AZUR can supply only 1500 on-line and 8000 portable systems within the next six years this will give us a business worth in excess of $100M,' he says. The company also sees great potential in the extension of its strategic partnership approach with key industry leaders in pharmaceuticals, chemicals and cosmetics.

Address:

AZUR Environmental Ltd, 540-545 Eskdale Road, Winnersh Triangle, Wokingham, Berkshire RG41 5TN. Tel: 01189 277000. Fax: 01189 440493

Microtox is a registered trademark of the AZUR Environmental.
*Tra-Cide is a registered trademark of the Nalco Chemical Co.

Biocompatibles International plc   HEALTHCARE

Farnham, Surrey

Turnover			
1993	1994	1995	1996
£86k	£1.5M	£3.8M	£11M

Summary: Biocompatibles International was established in 1984 by Professor Dennis Chapman to exploit the considerable commercial potential of his discoveries in the field of biocompatibility. The company has patented Professor Chapman's core technology of phosphorylcholine (PC) and is developing products and processes with a PC content. The earliest to market are soft contact lenses and cardiovascular devices. The company is working with the Cordis division of Johnson & Johnson (J&J) in order to produce a range of PC coated J&J vascular stents (devices used to keep arteries open). In addition the cardiovascular division of Biocompatibles presently supplies J&J with stent delivery catheters. The company is also investigating opportunities to license its PC technology in orthopaedics, urology, diabetes management and dialysis, as well as a range of other applications, including drug release systems, anti-fouling coatings of the hulls of ships, cosmetics, filtration membranes and packaging.

The Business

Among the many discoveries made by research scientists during the last two decades few have been so universal in their application as the fabrication of phosphorylcholine (PC). This chemical, present in the cell membrane of red blood cells, is the primary natural material which makes substances compatible with the human body. Professor Dennis Chapman, of the Royal Free Hospital School of Medicine, during research into new drug delivery systems, located PC. Independent observers argue that the commercial implications of this find are extensive. In the healthcare field alone a natural

55

substance which harmonises external products with the body will improve their effectiveness and halt the retardation which often afflicts medical devices inserted during surgery. Outside healthcare PC can be used as a stick or non-stick coating which stops erosion, and as such there may be thousands of engineering processes which can benefit from the use of this chemical.

After the discovery of PC in the cell membrane, Prof. Chapman set out to fabricate the chemical and established the company in 1984 to find commercial applications for the substance and its derivatives. These would concentrate on eliminating the deposits which build up on medical devices which are inserted in the body. Bacteria can develop and attract infection. Coating with PC drastically reduces adverse biological responses and allows them to function normally. The first commercial project using PC is a line of contact lenses which it is selling through leading opticians. The introduction of PC lenses will enable the company to make a significant technological leap forward.

Biocompatibles is split into five divisions: eye care, cardiovascular, healthcare, medical and new technologies. In the first two Biocompatibles has developed its own products, in the other three divisions licensing outside organisations to develop applications. J&J, its largest shareholder, is its first multinational partner in cardiovascular devices and potentially other business areas, but Biocompatibles is also talking to leading medical companies about slow release drug delivery systems and even in the non-healthcare field about anti-fouling coatings for ships' hulls. It has licensed the Fiat/Sorin subsidiary Dideco to develop PC coatings for cardiopulmonary devices which are due in the market in the course of 1997. It is discussing applications with cosmetics companies.

PC can be supplied by Biocompatibles in three basic ways: as a coating, as a material from which medical devices can be fabricated, and as a drug delivery system. 'The company has developed Proclear soft contact lenses, which are made from PC,' says CEO Alistair Taylor. 'One of the key attributes of the subtance is its compatibility with body fluids and its retention of water. This makes the Proclear lens very comfortable, especially for people who have compromised tear film. The lenses can be worn comfortably throughout a full day's use because of their increased comfort due to reduced dehydration, improved oxygen transfer to the cornea, and reduced protein and lipid spoilation. The company has signed a letter of intent with Chiron in the USA in the area of permanent ocular implants. It is also investigating drug delivery to the eye using a "bandage" contact lens.' The cardiovascular division is primarily focused on developing PC coated products in coronary angioplasty. This is a medical procedure enjoying increased popularity with cardiologists. According to broker Merrill Lynch this involves 'the introduction of a small guidewire and catheter tube in

Distinctive features

- owns new technology with manifold applications;
- working with blue chips in eye-care, healthcare, cosmetics and pharmaceuticals;
- copious non-healthcare applications;
- massive long-term earnings.

the femoral artery in the leg, through the blood vessels to the point of a blockage and then inflating a small balloon at the site, thus reopening the vessel.' Angioplasty suffers a high failure rate, so stainless steel stents – or small scaffolding – devices are introduced at the site. These are potentially thrombotic. PC-coated stents have worked well in clinical trials and should improve the long-term success of the angioplasty procedure. Merrill Lynch says that J&J commands 70 per cent of the market for stents. By the year 2000 this market will be worth $2.2 billion. The introduction of PC-coated stents would, says the broker, substantially increase the value of the world market and further increase J&J's share.

Size and shape

Employees: 440   Locations: 4
Geographical income split: Japan 5%, UK/mainland Europe 30%, North America 65%

Stratagems

The universal applicability of PC in medical, healthcare, industrial and commercial processes means that Biocompatibles has taken a strategic decision to be highly focused about which products it intends to develop itself and those which it will license. Taylor says that it will manufacture and sell contact lenses and cardiovascular products and potentially license all other applications. Jeremy Curnock Cook, chairman, says 'We will commit significant resources only where we believe the application of the company's technology will contribute to a significant competitive advantage in a major market. We have brought PC-coated eye care and cardiovascular products to market and our healthcare division has jointly developed PC coatings for cardiopulmonary products. We are actively engaged in further R&D programmes in each of these areas, including non-vascular stenting, urology, diabetes and wound management.

The eye care division has acquired a soft contact lens manufacturing operation in Norfolk, Virginia and in 1996 also acquired Atlantis Catheter, which makes products for the balloon angioplasty market. This latter $17.5 million purchase gave Biocompatibles production facilities in complementary markets based in Ireland and California. Proclear is being distributed in North America, Europe and more recently, under an agreement with Nippon Oils and Fats, in the far east. Biocompatibles has also signed a potentially highly lucrative deal with the pharmaceutical company Novo Nordisk. This partner is a major supplier of insulin and insulin delivery systems. The deal outlines a joint research programme into PC-coated insulin vials and delivery systems.

Outlook

Future prospects

- early significant profitability;
- further exciting new projects in the pipeline;
- more blue chip partnerships;
- wider spread of applications.

Biocompatibles has patented one of the most exciting technologies to be discovered in decades and it has developed a detailed plan for its exploitation. The company has astutely taken the view that it must concentrate on a core group of products which it can manufacture and sell itself. There is still massive potential in licensing other businesses to develop its core technology for other applications. Its recently launched contact lenses are starting to make an impact in a market worth $1.9 billion worldwide. Biocompatibles is also developing a solution to make existing lenses more lubricious – this global market is estimated at $1.6 billion. This company is going to be a major player in years to come. Income from its activities and licensing agreements will make the shareholders in this business very happy indeed.

Address:

Frensham House, Farnham Business Park, Weydon Lane, Farnham, Surrey GU9 8QL. Tel: 01252 732732. Fax: 01252 732777

Bluebird Toys plc

Swindon, Wilts

Turnover				
1992	1993	1994	1995	1996
£46M	£68.9M	£99.4M	£87.3M	£67.7M

Summary: Bluebird Toys is the world leader in the design and manufacture of minature toys. It makes a comprehensive range of products based on internationally famous characters such as Batman or the Disney series and also creates its own brands including the highly successful Polly Pocket and Lucy Locket. The company has dominated the UK domestic market since the mid 1980s and enjoys a formidable international reputation. Its success derives from innovative design, rapid concept to delivery performance, attractive licensing arrangements, low cost manufacture and strong financial controls in the business.

The Business

Europe was once the toy workshop of the world. The vibrancy and variety of the industry here has, however, long been superseded by competitors in North America and the far east. In a way it is hardly surprising since many of the children's characters on which toys are inevitably based stem from the global television and film industries. But one company has proved that Europe and especially the UK can be at the forefront of the industry. Swindon's Bluebird Toys is a global market leader in minature collectables – a highly profitable and deeply popular facet of the toys market. Throughout the worldwide toy industry, in its own field, there is no company to touch Bluebird.

It was opened in 1980 by Torquil Norman, an established inventor of children's products. His first success as an independent was a big yellow teapot, which is now a familiar feature of many toy cupboards. In the early part of the 1980s, Bluebird developed a justified reputation as an innovative and skilled toy producer and it produced impressive financial results.

Business slowed in the second half of the decade but the quality of ideas did not dim. Within a few years, the company achieved UK market leadership. All its efforts were focused on the domestic market. It designed and manufactured purely for the UK.

As the 1980s gave way to the 1990s a new set of priorities emerged. Bluebird management studied the opportunities, both for the future of the industry and for the company. They realised the only way forward lay in the capacity of companies to compete in an international environment. Toys, once largely domestic products, now spanned the world. Bluebird began to move its emphasis to the worldwide sale of its own toys and those it produced under licensing agreements with the owners of international characters. Bluebird's core expertise is the design and production of miniature toys. The first of its own brands to achieve global status was Polly Pocket. This bright and colourful brand offers younger girls the opportunity to collect miniature dolls houses at an affordable price.

Polly's debut in 1990 was an outstanding success. Each year new variations on the Polly Pocket theme were introduced, taking themes such as the wedding day, birthday party and pony show. These packages and the tiny plastic personalities which go with them are enthusiastically received by little girls because they replicate a full doll's house and should any part be lost they are inexpensive to replace. A boys edition, Mighty Max, reached the shops in 1993 and although it did not have the same impact as Polly, it is still a strong revenue earner for the company. In a move which would fundamentally alter its entire commercial approach, Bluebird also moved into the production of licensed toys for the international market. A keynote deal with Disney for toys in the *Pocahontas* and *Lion King* series led to substantial sellers. It was a forerunner of many similar agreements and gives considerable depth to Bluebird's international image. The company is proud of its capacity to generate fresh toy ideas for the licensed markets, and its capacity to deliver quickly has impressed licensors and major international toy distributors alike.

Distinctive features

- world leader in miniature collectables;
- leading design team;
- portfolio of stable brands;
- strict cost control;
- intimacy of decision-making.

CEO Chris Burgin says 'We are the only toymaker in the UK or mainland

Europe which produces substantially for the international market. There are other companies here in Britain and on the mainland but none of them compete for global markets. Our competitors are the major players among the US and Japanese companies.'

Stratagems

When Bluebird embarked on its adventure to woo overseas markets in 1990, its management knew that they could rely on several notable corporate strengths which distinguished Bluebird from many of the top US and far eastern businesses in the industry. Bluebird is an unchallenged innovator in design. Its small company flexibility gives the business a capacity to respond quickly and directly to new inspiration while retaining the quality of management which insists on tight control of the purse strings and multinational perspective. The company draws its ideas from many sources: independent toy inventors, feedback from retailers, dialogue with distributors and licensors. A team of 12–15 people – some external but mostly internal – meets

---

Size and shape

Employees: 120   Locations: 2
Geo. income split: UK/Eire 49%, North America 23%, mainland Europe 17%, RoW 11%

---

to take ideas from concept stage to production. This group will examine every aspect of a proposal and test its suitability to address potential demand. 'Everyone from the most senior to the most junior has a voice,' says Burgin. This is a rigorous process as the investment in new concepts is high and the future profitability of the company rests on its ability to create products which can capture the imagination of each new generation.

Manufacturing is done by several plants part owned by government or government agencies in China where costs are appreciably lower than in Europe. 'We could not afford to make Polly Pocket, with the intricacy of design, in the UK,' he says. The biggest cost is tooling – moulding the steel which will make the toys. 'We aim to recover the cost of manufacture and design in the first year. Some toy companies will spread development costs, especially the larger packages, over three years. But the brand life of modern toy characters can be as short as one to three years. So if a profit is to be made, discipline is needed.' This is a key factor in the Bluebird Toys success – its capacity to develop its new products quickly, to recover costs early in their life-cycles.

The business floated on the Unlisted Securities Market in 1985 and achieved elevation to the full market in 1994. The City warmed to Bluebird since the growth of its global income, which has given the company a 20 per cent turn on sales. Analysts say they appreciate its cost disciplines and the tight control on production, distribution and marketing costs. It is among the most professionally managed toy businesses in the world and observers say that its flexibility and short reporting lines give it an edge over many of the larger US and Japanese corporations.

Few brands in the sector enjoy longevity. The market leaders like Batman, Disney and Polly Pocket are the exception. Burgin says that his aim is to broaden the proportion of revenue which comes from these stable brands. One of his greatest hopes is that the company could produce a boys' brand with a similar profile and long-term earning potential to Polly Pocket.

Outlook

Future prospects

- consolidation of UK toy industry dominance;
- more new global licensing deals;
- refinement of design leadership.

Bluebird has been on a rapid growth curve since the early 1990s. Its global profile through innovative toys from its own stable and for industry giants is now very solid. Using this status as a platform, it intends to compete more directly and intensively for world markets. All of this growth will be organic because the company has no plans to make acquisitions and can see no point in rescuing ailing UK toymakers. Its high level of investment in research will continue and it also anticipates that it will increase the number of distribution deals it operates with industry leaders.

Address:

The Mulberrys, Kembrey Park, Swindon SN2 6YP. Tel: 01793 437777. Fax: 01793 437788

Bookham Technology Ltd   HIGH TECHNOLOGY

Rutherford Appleton Laboratory, Chilton, Oxon

Turnover			
1994	1995	1996	1997
£77,000	£300,000	£3Me	£13Me

Summary: Bookham Technology has developed a unique low-cost process for manufacturing integrated optical circuits in silicon. This process, called ASOC ™ (Active Silicon Integrated Optical Circuits), is likely to have the same impact in the field of multimedia technology as silicon integrated circuits previously had in computers. The potential demand for ASOC™ optical chips – initially in the telecomms and datacoms markets, but with a host of other applications already identified – is immense. The company believes that it has a three-year development lead-time over its competitors and has established a series of alliances with key blue-chip customers and collaborators to ensure that future demand is based on identified customer prospects.

The Business

Dr Andrew Rickman has created a core technology of the near future. Few people will ever know what his product is, how it works and how it will transform their lives. But revolutionise them it will. His fibre optic chip will act as a gateway to interactive and multimedia facilities in both the home and business of the early 21st century. His ASOC™ chip broadens the range and capacity of cable and telephone connections. It makes possible television with hundreds of channels, instant selection of video and film from central databanks and interactive connection with home shopping and live programmes.

Rickman founded Bookham in 1989 to exploit his central idea. He located the company at the Rutherford Appleton Laboratory in Oxford, where it continues to have access to the government site's modern clean-room facilities. His principal concept was to use silicon as a base for fibre optic technology which he evolved when studying for his PhD in Integrated Optics at the University of Surrey. Until that time, optical chips were made from lithium niobate, which was expensive and required high precision engineering.

ASOC™ technology is based on the same processing techniques as those used in the production of silicon electronic chips. Bookham has combined these standard methods with silicon micromachining and innovative integrated optical designs to eliminate inefficient manufacturing steps and to improve device performance. By so doing, it is able to make optical chips at one-tenth of the cost of traditional methods. It has a multitude of applications across a spread of industrial sectors. One of its most prominent uses would be in the field of cable TV and home information services. It will permit cost effective manufacture of set-top boxes, capable of receiving data directly from fibre optic cables. Running fibre optic cables, rather than coaxial copper cables, into the home will allow the transmission of hundreds of channels of interactive audio and video and will grant public access to the information superhighway at higher speeds.

In 1995 the market potential for ASOC™ was estimated at $1.65bn (£1.1bn) which was forecast to rise to $15bn (£9.7bn) by 1997. The company's sales figures, as yet, hardly reflect Bookham's potential to capitalise on its remarkable technological asset. But the Bookham's management team has taken the view that first it must create an unbeatable product, second research alliances with blue chip companies and third, when all else is locked in, secure major sales. It has, nevertheless, set itself a demanding sales target for the next three years. Figures for 1995 showed turnover of £300,000. By 1997 Rickman wants to generate £13 million.

Distinctive features

- unique technology;
- developed R&D network;
- strong customer base;
- relevant to range of large and growing markets.

Stratagems

Rickman had earlier been a venture capitalist and he was determined that Bookham should not repeat the mistakes he commonly saw in start-up companies. For this reason, he obtained an MBA from Cranfield and at the same time gained his PhD. His overriding philosophy was that the company should be based on a single enabling technology which was suitable for a wide range of expanding markets. Another central tenet of Bookham's strategy states that potential customers should be brought in as part of the product development phase. This is essential if Bookham is to understand how its markets are likely to develop. Rickman is critical of the traditional approach of his competitors who conduct research in a vacuum and then adapt it to the nearest suitable market. By working closely with the customer base, Bookham can be sure that once a product has passed the prototype stage, a ready market for it will exist based on identified customer needs without further adaptations to the product being necessary.

Bookham also aims to work with the market leaders in each of its chosen market sectors. Partners to date include Honeywell, Newbridge Networks, E G & G and Ford Motor Company. It is also involved in a DTI sponsored joint development with Ford Motors. 'We have a technological lead, we are addressing all of the major industrial markets and we have the right partners,' says Rickman. The involvement of the DTI highlights another of Bookham's objectives. To date, it has been extremely successful in obtaining state and European funding of research projects.

Size and shape

Employees: 70   Locations: 3
Geographical earnings split: UK 50%, North America 50%

Bookham's overall market consists of three application market segments: optical fibre switching, optical fibre transceivers and optical sensors. The company's goal is to develop chips itself for niche markets, but licence the technology for large-volume application. Its primary high growth markets will be accessed in three ways:

- OEM (original equipment manufacturers) customers in each market segment;
- technology licensing to, and joint ventures with, major Japanese and US firms;
- direct sales and distribution of Bookham developed products.

The immediate marketing focus is in the telecomms sectors, where the market for multimedia services, such as the Internet, is driving demand for optical fibre communications. Bookham uses available production capacity in silicon foundries which are operating in the microelectronics industry. This allows expansion of production capacity and avoids the need for major investment in silicon fabrication facilities. The initial emphasis will be on the domestic and business application of ASOC™ in multimedia technology but the potential uses of the chip are vast. The company already sees markets in telecom and datacom components, industrial distance measurement and control, environmental control, high performance computing and medical diagnostics. Bookham believes that its investment in R&D has paid off and that it is at least three years ahead of any competitor. To protect its position the company has applied for worldwide patents and developed an unrivalled R&D network and is also seeking ISO 9000 accreditation.

FD Neil Lethby is preparing the company for a flotation in 1998 – either in London or on NASDAQ in New York. In 1995 Bookham raised more than £3 million in sponsorship from a range of funders to support its ongoing investment programme. One particularly significant backer is Terry Matthews, founder and CEO of Newbridge Networks. This is a groundbreaking Canadian data-networking systems supplier. Matthews would not be interested unless there was some direct benefit for him.

Outlook

Future prospects

- growth of UK market share;
- broadening of applications for the technology;
- long term penetration of mainland European and US markets;
- enhancement of competitive edge.

Bookham finds itself at the leading edge of an industry which is forecast to grow substantially over the next 20 years. It has developed a unique technology which has an enormous range of applications and which is three years ahead of the competition. Rickman himself puts it 'The potential, if not limitless, is certainly vast.' Industry analysts comment that of all the new and emerging businesses in this division of the high technology sector Bookham Technology is among the strongest placed to make a substantial contribution to the future.

Address:

Bookham Technology Ltd, Rutherford Appleton Laboratory, Chilton, Oxfordshire OX11 0QX. Tel: 01235 445377. Fax: 01235 446854. E-mail: marketing@bookham.co.uk

Brann Limited

Cirencester, Gloucestershire; Bristol; and London

Turnover				
1992	1993	1994	1995	1996
£19.6M	£20.7M	£29.5M	£39.6M	£41M

Summary: Brann is a direct communications business which helps companies to enhance their contact with their customers. Increasingly, Brann is concentrating on high level consultancy and planning, assisting its clients with initial conceptual planning as well as implemention of specific campaigns. Its strengths lie in understanding the dialogue between companies and their customers and demonstrating to clients how they can improve their customer service. Brann is progressively broadening the scope of its work for its key revenue earners, a philosophy which has already contributed to a 90 per cent compound growth in sales since 1994.

The Business

Direct marketing found its feet in the 1990s. After several years at the periphery of the marketing plans of many mainstream companies, business managers realised that customers and potential customers could be reached more effectively through professionally produced and targeted direct marketing initiatives. Credit for the success of the discipline is due in large measure to companies like Brann which have represented the top end of the industry. They have shown that broad brush techniques such as television advertising can be less effective in generating new and continuing the business than tightly targeted direct marketing.

Brann has experienced several incarnations. The company which is a market leader today – Brann Limited – was the product of a management buyout in January 1994. It is a business based on three sites – Cirencester, Bristol and London – which employs 677 people, with the majority roughly equally divided between Cirencester and Bristol, with 20 based in the new London office. It was originally launched as Christian Brann by the

67

eponymous founder who was a marketing guru in the sixties. Current chairman Alan Bigg explains that the founder sold out in two stages to BIS in the late 1970s and early 1980s. In 1986 the US telephony and cable television giant Nynex bought BIS but found that the commercial dynamics of the sector were at odds with its normal pattern of business. Nynex sold BIS to ACT in 1993, which soon made its focus on pure computing clear – and so the opportunity for independence arose. In autumn 1993 four long-standing Brann managers, including Alan Bigg and the present CEO Chris Gater, assembled an MBO proposal which was successful within a few months.

At the outset of the present company, Brann was structured in three major divisions which embraced systems (mainly database construction and management), telemarketing and marketing communications. 'We spend a considerable amount of time talking to and listening to our clients and we decided to reshape the business based on what they were telling us. We are now a single company on two sites offering five key products: planning and consultancy, creative, contact (telephone such as customer care lines), systems and printed products,' says Chris Gater. This greater coherence and integration has already paid dividends. Joe Hansel, managing director, explains that sales have grown 90 per cent compound in the two years since the MBO. 'Although we have several principal competitors in each of our product areas, we have no direct rival which has replicated our move to integrate our services in one structure. We have already achieved significant results as a direct consequence of the move to our new format.'

Distinctive features

- deep understanding of the customer relationship;
- strong people management;
- emphasis on consultative role;
- integrated service portfolio.

Stratagems

One of the central elements of the Brann strategy is its people management. Chris Gater quotes the director of General Electric in the USA who said 'We take care of our people, who take care of our clients who take care of our bottom line'. It is a refreshing approach in an industry with high staff attrition rates and heavy – almost exclusive – concentration on financial returns. 'Whereas some MDs or CEOs would emphasise return on sales or capital employed, I am concerned about staff utilisation. And I take the view that employees cannot be effective unless they are stimulated in their work.'

His argument is endorsed by one of the company's seven client principals, Lynn Ashman, who comments that her time is evenly divided between contact with clients and managing her people. 'I take the recruitment process very seriously. We devote considerable resources to training, formal review and evaluation and listening to personal career objectives.' The company has recently initiated its Brann Diploma set of courses which give staff in-depth insight into the management of the business and the role of other product disciplines within the company. 'With clients, my job involves building multi-disciplinary teams to service specific needs. Our junior staff get as much experience as possible in different areas of the business to give them the opportunity to build on their strengths. As they become more senior, that experience becomes focused on key clients and sectors.'

The emergence of a people culture within Brann – which has always been a good employer – reflects a key trend in client business. Brann's motto used to be 'Creating loyal customers', it has now moved on, says Gater, to helping customers to create loyal brands. It is part of his four phase analysis which summarises the company's appreciation of where the industry is going.

Size and shape

Employees: 677   Locations: 3 (Cirencester, Bristol and London)
Geographical income split: UK 95%, mainland Europe 5%

'We tell clients that we are in the age of the individual, where consumers' experience will determine brand perception. Marketeers have to transform the buying process by helping customers to create loyal brands.' This key market reading shows that customers – not companies – control the process and that the role of businesses is to illuminate factors which assist consumer choices. The value of Brann's input is to influence the basis – both theoretical and practical – of the key decisions made by senior corporate marketing directors in approaching their markets. Brann works with respected organisations (e.g. The Henley Centre) to identify trends in market development.

The progressively earlier involvement of Brann personnel in market planning activity means that the company is broadening the base of its relationship with its major clients. 'Our top 20 revenue earners now account for 70 per cent of our income and our top 30 some 80 per cent,' says Gater. 'This is a development which we are working to enhance.' As the business grows its management focus will concentrate on elevating its relationships with clients still further and to draw higher percentages of revenue from consultancy rather than volume products such as telemarketing, customer care lines, database construction and printed mailings. In fact, some of the volume work is now contracted out to agencies which supply Brann. This more strategic role is seen in the work which the company has done for direct general insurers Touchline and Zurich Municipal where Brann has played a central role in defining the product. For Peugeot Brann has created market analysis tools which help to locate individuals most likely to buy the motor company's cars and then go back to Peugeot for future purchases. Carrier DHL has asked Brann to create a sophisticated computer disc package for customers. This award winning project gives its full worldwide tariff guide together with a screensaver and a series of games which require codes from DHL invoices to be able to play.

Brann's specialists appreciate the full catalogue of relationships inherent in the buying process probably better than any other agency. Gater believes that the company is, therefore, in an excellent position to contribute to customer choice. Whether this comes from reading potential and identified consumer demand, enabling distributors to improve the quality of their information to customers or influencing the initial marketing decisions at the client, Brann is at the edge of industry thinking.

Outlook

Future prospects

- stronger client consultative role;
- broader base to client relationships;
- high turnover and profit growth;
- sector and geographical expansion.

Brann is building on a strong base. It has enjoyed a high reputation since its inception in the 1960s. The MBO, though, has had a cathartic effect on the business. The management team has capitalised on its strengths and integrated the core components into a coherent whole. They have also elevated its relationship with clients. Brann possesses the vision to grow into the foremost direct marketing enterprise in the UK and perhaps also in Europe.

Address:

Brann Limited, Phoenix Way, Cirencester, Gloucestershire GL7 1RY. Tel: 01285 644744. Fax: 01285 654952. E-mail: marketing@Brann.co.uk

British Biotech plc   PHARMACEUTICALS/BIOTECHNOLOGY

Oxford

Turnover				
1991	1992	1993	1994	1995
£2.9M	£1.2M	£2.5M	£2.3M	£3.2M

Summary: British Biotech is the largest and most respected company operating in the UK biotechnology sector, but its scope is wider than pure biotechnology and it is more correctly viewed as a pharmaceuticals business. Founded by the former directors of a US multinational's UK research arm, British Biotech has several products in clinical trials covering potential therapies for cancer. The earnings potential for the company has attracted widespread interest and the share price rocketed to £30 in mid 1996. The company has patented its products and retained all the rights. In certain areas it intends to market its own products but in others, especially GP products, it will link up with a blue chip partner.

The Business

Ask any analyst which is the leading biotech company in the UK and most will answer, without hesitation, British Biotech. But it won't be long before a caveat is added. 'Of course, British Biotech is not really a biotechnology business but a pharmaceutical company.' Despite its outstandingly high rating – its shares reached £30 each in mid year 1996 – British Biotech is not well understood. It is a development stage pharmaceutical company which uses whichever technology is most appropriate to develop valuable products. This means that the company exploits both biotechnology and traditional chemical methodologies for its current programme of projects.

Research and development director Peter Lewis says 'It is the products not the technologies which excite us. British Biotech was set up by two former executives of a major US pharmaceutical multinational and they have always believed in focusing the company on product development. Biotechnology is one of our approaches and it is extremely valuable to us. But we are excited by the potential of products. The technology is only a means to an end.'

The two founding directors, Brian Richards and current CEO Keith McCullagh, ran G. D. Searle's impressive research facility at High Wycombe. When Monsanto captured G. D. Searle in 1985, the new owner decided that the UK R&D centre should be shut. McCullagh was given nine months to close the facility down. One day after closure, he and Richards started British Biotech. The founding directors were keen to exploit the opportunities which biotechnology offered but they started out as a development phase pharmaceuticals company. The aim was to be empowered by technology not limited by definitions.

Acutely aware of the need for financing without any promise of early return, Richards and McCullagh went to four venture capital funds, three of which had industry credentials and raised £2.5 million. At G. D. Searle, McCullagh and Richards had been aware of a series of potential therapeutic concepts which had never been exploited by the US company. When they opened British Biotech, they decided to follow their instincts but they had no idea then that it would lead to a series of prospective treatments which may take therapeutics several steps forward.

There are two platforms for drugs – oral or intravenous. The real profits come from those which can be taken orally. In the main, biotech preparations are administered by injection while traditional chemical compounds can be used by mouth. So British Biotech wants to produce drugs which can generate high revenues as well as those which will be steady but smaller earners. A broad pipeline of products has been developed. 'We intend to concentrate primarily on cancer and acute care products – Marimastat, an oral cancer drug is in large scale patient trials, and BB-10010 in clinical trials. Zaantex is awaiting European registration to treat patients with acute pancreatitis. At an earlier stage we have anti-arthritic, anti-thrombotic and multiple sclerosis preparations.'

Distinctive features

- two drugs in Phase III clinical trials and/or registration;
- top quality management;
- product orientation;
- massive earnings potential.

Stratagems

Lewis explains that the intention now, as at the outset, is to produce a broad portfolio of drugs by whatever technology seems suitable. The priorities of a pharmaceuticals company rather than a biotech business were not lost on the founders and continue to characterise the operational strategy of the enterprise. The aim is to produce exciting new drugs which will prove key revenue earners. The drugs which will be sold to hospitals will be marketed by British Biotech, those which have more widespread application to general practitioners will be marketed by a blue chip partner. For example, on oral BB-2983 to treat arthritis, British Biotech has linked up with Glaxo Wellcome. Unlike the majority of biotech companies, British Biotechnology intends to sell and market some of its own products. It does not plan to manufacture, as there is ample spare capacity in the market to make the investment in plant unrealistic. However, the company can manufacture sufficient quantities for clinical trials.

Size and shape

Employees: 400   Locations: 3 (2 in Oxford, 1 in the USA)
Geographical income split: too early to tell

The wisdom and patience of the early investors and those who bought equity at the company's 1992 London and NASDAQ float is creditworthy but they are still a long way from seeing the company make money. The initial investors had to wait six years before the option of an exit route became available. Since listing the share price has achieved stratospheric proportions and the opportunity has existed for profit taking. The turnover figures for the company merely show the tranches of cash made by partners as milestone payments. In 1996 British Biotech reported a £25 million loss. It will not start to make money until its pipeline products come out, successfully, of clinical trials and go into production. Keith McCullagh will not fix a date for a move into profits but analysts confidently expect that it will be in the early years of the next decade.

When British Biotech goes into the black, it should immediately report millions of pounds of profit because its products are major market drugs each with the capacity to take specialist therapeutics a major leap forward. The company believes that at least one of its pipeline drugs is a blockbuster. Estimates are conservative but this could be one of the most profitable pharmaceutical companies in the world.

BRITISH BIOTECH PLC

Outlook

> **Future prospects**
> - high earnings;
> - more new drugs in the pipeline;
> - further partnerships.

British Biotech is a shrewdly managed company which is business rather than technology led. Its pipeline of important new drugs is among the most impressive in the sector. Its cancer, multiple sclerosis, arthritis, and pancreatitis drugs all represent steps forward. The mixture of scientific ability, innovative management, retention of rights and good luck has placed British Biotech in the vanguard of its sector. It looks destined to capitalise on outstanding returns in the early part of the 21st century but its researchers are already planning the next batch of targets. Management is highly focused and although scientists are given maximum freedom to innovate, they do so within a delineated plan.

Address:

Watlington Road, Oxford OX4 5LY. Tel: 01865 748747. Fax: 01865 781047

British Technology Group plc TECHNOLOGY TRANSFER

Elephant & Castle, London

Turnover		
1993	1994	1995
£26.8M	£29.02M	£23.41M

Summary: British Technology Group (BTG) is the leading technology transfer company in the UK. It owes this status to its worldwide ability to capture and license intellectual property value through patents. Privatised in 1993, it gained a stock market listing in 1995 at 225p a share and its cash-generating potential has driven the price to more than £12.50. In early 1996 it passed through an earnings dip caused by the ending of revenues from its lucrative Pyrethrin insecticide. But the company is making outstanding progress in building new revenue streams by diversifying its licensing and invention sourcing activities. BTG is a well rounded enterprise which is skilled in searching out new technologies, bringing together ideas from diverse sources and locating prime new markets.

The Business

One of the key rationales for success in business is to prosecute a unique commercial formula. BTG's achievement has been to create a platform where many groups and individuals can exploit current trends and the latest demands. 'This is a unique company,' says Merrill Lynch analyst Keith Woolcock. 'No other technology transfer business possesses expertise in such a broad range of disciplines. Take its patenting and legal functions. These are more like a department in a major City law firm than a commercial company.' Managers at BTG certainly require an unusual set of skills. This company is part detective, part scientist, part negotiator, part integrator. It is

75

one of the world's leading technology transfer enterprises with a remarkable facility for locating new technologies, fusing them, providing them with a correct legal structure and selling them hard. BTG is distinguished by its abilities in all of these areas. This is not solely a clearing house with a great enthusiasm for locating bright new ideas. One of the key reasons why BTG has risen to its position at the top table of global technology transfer companies is its ability to translate those innovative concepts into definitive commercial successes. It has a staggering capacity to read and interpret future market demand and dig out ideas which will address such needs. Nor is it a venture capital agency. Chief executive Ian Harvey says 'We don't act as an investment house. The patent is what we sell. It's absolutely critical.'

BTG assesses the potential commercial value in an invention or technology, protects that value behind a patent wall, licenses it and ensures licensees pay the royalties which are due. The company is expert in patent law and employs 15 lawyers who are specialists in every aspect of technology transfer. 'We're proud of our patenting skills. Our team is as good as the best and better than most by world standards.'

The group's history began with the National Research and Development Council, set up in 1948 to commercialise publicly-funded research. The NRDC and the National Enterprise Board – formed in 1975 to invest public funds in private companies – became the British Technology Group in 1981. This was privatised in a management buy-out in 1992 and achieved a full listing on the London Stock Exchange in July 1995. The extent of market confidence in BTG is demonstrated by the growth in its share price. At listing BTG shares sold at 225p each – by March 1996 they had risen to £12.50, which is a rise of 550 per cent in eight months.

BTG is run by Ian Harvey, who came to the company via the World Bank and Harvard Business School. He has been CEO for nine years and has organised BTG into four divisions: pharmaceutical and agricultural chemicals, electronics and telecommunications, engineering and Torotrak, which concentrates on the development and licensing of an infinitely variable vehicle transmission. Boundaries between these divisions are fluid. The company has grain stripper patents which apply to agricultural machinery and engineering patents which concern syringes used in medicine.

Distinctive features

- capacity to bring together several innovative ideas in one patent;
- wide knowledge of commercial and academic inventive sources;
- outstanding in patenting and legal skills;
- large portfolio of patents in diverse market sectors.

Stratagems

At the core of the BTG strategy is the location of greater numbers of high value patents. Two factors are at work here. One is the location of new patents, but secondly the fact that these patents generate high net worth. In early 1996, BTG had more than 9000 patents – each one grants its owner a 20 year monopoly from the date of filing. Keith Woolcock says that BTG has been pruning its portfolio of patents to shed the poor earners and concentrate on the ones with greatest potential. Some 50 per cent of all BTG patents are sourced from UK academic departments. This is a reliance on UK academic talents which the company aims to scale down and it is opening up other sources of new inventions, both from the commercial rather than academic world and from external markets such as mainland Europe, South Africa and the USA. BTG argues that in transfer technology terms these markets are relatively immature.

Size and shape

Employees: 170   Locations: London, Philadelphia, Tokyo, Bombay
Geo. income split: US 32.8%, EU (excl UK) 26.7%, UK 19.7%, Japan 17.8%, RoW 3%

Barry Cartwright, marketing director, says that the company's emphasis has now moved to supplying market demand rather than developing ideas for their own intrinsic merits and then looking for sales opportunities. This policy has led to a steady reduction in the number of new inventions accepted in the last three years. In 1993 the company took 197 new ideas, whereas in 1995 this was down to 150. Inventions in portfolio, licences signed and licences in portfolio have reduced similarly as BTG moves towards higher value patents.

Revenue streams can start years after filing, so BTG's task is to maximise earnings from individual patents. Part of its skills has been to prolong streams by developing the intellectual property. An example of this approach is its continuing work with a team from Nottingham University developing magnetic resonance imaging and filing new patents as the technology develops. Licence revenues are split 50:50 with the inventive sources after deducting BTG's costs. This means significant rewards for the inventive source, such as the university research departments which are keen to work with BTG to realise early commercial gains for their ideas. Revenues can fall if products using BTG technology suffer price cuts in a recession. So the company plans and executes a portfolio of patents spread across market sectors and geographical regions. Each one is valued on a risk-adjusted net present value basis. This process helps to define how much money the company will spend on a specific invention. The bulk of costs are enshrined in patent development and filing. A patent filing exercise may cost as much as £250,000.

Outlook

> **Future prospects**
>
> - rapid rise in revenue and profits;
> - well placed to exploit social trends;
> - higher return from patents;
> - enhanced competitive advantage.

Financially the company expected revenues and profits to decline in 1996 but then enjoy a sudden and sustained upswing as patents in the pipeline start to generate revenues. BTG's market position is remarkably secure and appears certain to remain so. Few technology transfer businesses can match BTG's distinctive combination of high quality skills in its core disciplines. The company's prospects are also assisted by the barrier to entry for potential competitors provided by the long lead time between patent filing and licence revenue. BTG is well placed to exploit macro social trends such as the growing proportion of elderly people in the population and wider concern for the environment. Increased demand for precision and control in all kinds of delivery and transmission systems, such as logistics, telecommunications bandwidth, drugs and fluid flow, favours the company. Its wealth of academic contacts and inventive sources in business, capacity for negotiation and patenting, combines with its existing portfolio of licences to offer an exciting future.

Address:

101 Newington Crescent, London SE1 6BU. Tel: 0171 403 6666. Fax: 0171 403 7586

The Brockbank Group plc

Central London

Turnover				
1992	1993	1994	1995	1996
£4.7M	£5.9M	£6.1M	£7M	£26.1M

Summary: The Brockbank Group is one of the leading Lloyd's managing agencies. By virtue of its outstanding underwriting record it has remained consistently profitable throughout the worst years of the market's crisis. It operates three underwriting syndicates, one of which includes Admiral, the only UK direct motor insurer within Lloyd's. Mid Ocean, the Bermudan reinsurance giant, has acquired a 51 per cent interest in Brockbank Group's business in exchange for a £50M injection of underwriting capital and should significantly enhance its business development.

The Business

The Brockbank Group was formed in 1984 and, having enjoyed virtually uninterrupted growth since that time, is now one of the leading managing agencies at Lloyd's. It is dedicated to the underwriting of a wide range of insurance risks and operates three syndicates – two composites and one concentrating on motor business. In 1996, the group planned to write more than £450M of premium income through its managed syndicates.

Brockbank's largest syndicate in capacity terms is 861. This is a composite syndicate which underwrites a balanced portfolio of risks across 14 separate classes of business. It began life as a pure marine syndicate and still insures a majority of the world's fleets. However, expansion in capacity enabled a range of further classes to be added. It now insures 80 per cent of the world's airlines against war and political risks, and also covers professional indemnity, US and international property, accident and health and engineering classes.

Syndicate 588 is another large composite syndicate and predominately concentrates on six major accounts – space, excess of loss, marine hull, energy, liabilities and war. Space is the largest single class and the syndicate has developed a pre-eminent role in this specialist market, continuing to produce excellent results even during years in which the global space market has produced losses. The syndicate also writes a significant excess of loss account providing reinsurance protection for direct insurers.

Brockbank's third syndicate, 253, is a long established private motor account which was restructured during 1993 and is now in receipt of two sources of revenue. The first of these relates to Admiral, Brockbank's direct response insurer. Admiral is Lloyd's only UK direct motor insurer and, in only three years, it has become one of the best known such insurers in the UK. As a direct insurer, Admiral is able to monitor responses to rate changes on a daily basis and can respond to market requirements very rapidly. It concentrates on higher value private cars and on drivers in the 20–40 age group, mainly offering comprehensive cover. It also offers a range of ancillary products.

Distinctive features

- consistently profitable underwriting skills;
- syndicate leadership capabilities;
- heavy IT and management investment;
- access to dedicated corporate capital.

Syndicate 253's other source of income is Zenith, Brockbank's traditional private motor account operated through a panel of more than 1000 high street brokers. Zenith concentrates on the lower risk sectors of the market and in recent years has expanded to include specialised areas such as motorcycles, agricultural vehicles and small fleets.

The most significant development for Brockbank over the last 12 months has been the investment by Mid Ocean, a highly respected Bermudan reinsurance company. Under this agreement, Brockbank has contributed all its underwriting businesses, and Mid Ocean two corporate vehicles capitalised with £50 million in cash, to an enlarged entity in which Brockbank has an effective 49 per cent stake. This association represents a major advance for Brockbank, giving it an interest in a company which acts as a principal in its own underwriting business and allowing it access to dedicated corporate capital to support its underwriting activities.

Stratagems

Brockbank's stated objective is 'to be pre-eminent in its market by achieving consistently superior returns through high quality underwriting supported by rigorous management controls'. Accordingly, the company places great emphasis on combining highly skilled underwriters with its experienced and professional management team.

> ### Size and shape
>
> Employees: 950+   Locations: 3
> Geo. premium income split: UK 41%, N. America 30%, mainland Europe 15%, RoW 14%

The quality of the company's underwriting skills are widely acknowledged and are best evidenced by the fact that the two composite syndicates have remained consistently profitable throughout what have been extremely difficult years in Lloyd's recent history. The company's underwriting philosophy is to balance the portfolio by avoiding any undue aggregation of risk in a particular class or event, while switching capacity between classes in order to maximise opportunities across the market. By developing large syndicates, Brockbank also ensures that any class of business in which it participates is generally written by a specialist in that particular field. Large syndicates also offer significant economies of scale in terms of cost and management. Standard & Poor's now ranks all Lloyd's syndicates – 861 and 588 are two of only 28, out of a total of around 150 syndicates, to have been awarded the top ranking of five crowns.

> ### Future prospects
>
> - substantial growth from profitably managed syndicates;
> - major increases from motor insurance business;
> - enhanced work from the link with Mid Ocean.

It is not only in its underwriting activities, however, that the company strives for excellence. Brockbank has established in-house expertise across all its support functions. A central part of this strategy is the recruitment of staff from outside Lloyd's and the insurance sector generally. The company feels that a diversity of experience gives it a wider breadth of vision in order to manage the business successfully through times of considerable change in the industry. Brockbank invests heavily in IT systems. The company believes it can derive a competitive advantage by computerising as much of its administration and paper flow as possible, and it is significantly ahead of its competitors in this area. Sophisticated systems are particularly important in the motor insurance business; Admiral, for example, writes more than 150,000 new policies annually. It is also introducing an EDI (Electronic Data Interchange) system at Zenith.

Finally, the Mid Ocean transaction is a key strategic development. The alignment of a Lloyd's managing agent with a major world reinsurer should significantly enhance Brockbank's prospects. It provides additional capital to support its underwriting activities, while adding to its overall financial strength and stability. It also effectively allows Brockbank to participate in its own underwriting success as a principal.

Outlook

With Lloyd's problems now seemingly behind it, and the commitment of substantial corporate capital from Mid Ocean, Brockbank seems destined to go from strength to strength. Its composite syndicates should continue to enjoy a strong underwriting performance based on good quality business, while Admiral should thrive in the fastest growing sector of the motor insurance market. Furthermore, the investment which Brockbank has made in its technical and management infrastructure should allow it to manage this growth successfully.

Address:

Fitzwilliam House, 10 St Mary Axe, London EC3A 8BS. Tel: 0171 648 1000. Fax: 0171 648 1002

Bruntcliffe Aggregates plc

Bromsgrove, Worcestershire

Turnover		
1994	1995	1996
£21M	£24M	£27.9M

Summary: Bruntcliffe owns and operates a collection of quarries in the UK and the USA. This is a small but rapidly growing business run by highly experienced sector managers. Although the company has faced specific and industry problems which are not of its making, it is overcoming these distractions and moving steadfastly forward. After its initial series of acquisitions, it is achieving its current growth through quality management of its portfolio and able stewardship. The company has achieved impressive growth in its operating businesses through tighter financial and operational controls, attention to product and service issues, rapid decision-making and responsiveness to its customers.

The Business

In 1992 Mike Wallis was managing director of Tarmac USA when the parent conducted a merger with which he profoundly disagreed. He could have continued in post but decided that he would leave to form his own business. As a senior director of one of the leaders in the aggregate industry, he knew that the majors were shedding non-core assets at a realistic price rather than an inflated multiple of earnings. In particular, Tarmac's central management wanted to remove a group of non-core businesses at that point and Wallis decided to bid for an integrated group of five quarries in the north of Scotland. Thistle Aggregates produced sand and gravel from the quarries

83

based in an area bounded by Dundee, Aberdeen, Ullapool and Blairatholl. He lined up capital from the City and made his move. But Wallis, now CEO of Bruntcliffe, says that Tarmac dragged its feet. There were other potential offers and he suspects that the local Thistle management did not want to sell.

In early 1993, at the same time as the Thistle negotiations were in progress, he was approached by a small company called Bruntcliffe Investments. Originally active in the textile industry, the company had three assets: a quarry at Church Lawford near Rugby, and two sites at Pittsburgh in the USA. One of these was a coal mine and held much promise as a generator of cash. Bruntcliffe's owners wanted Wallis to take over as CEO. His backers in the institutions were unhappy about funding the purchase of Thistle, if Wallis were chief executive of another company. 'In the end we bought Thistle as part of Bruntcliffe,' he recalls.

The business adopted plc status with Thistle, Rugby (Ideal Aggregates) and the US holdings. Shortly, afterwards Bruntcliffe bought a small profitable limestone quarry in the USA and in May 1994 secured a sand, gravel and ready mix operation in Virginia which has been profitable from day one. In practice, the Lorasen Coal – the putative generator of profits – was beset by problems and never realised its potential. Wallis is blunt about the business. 'It was a dog. In the end we sold it.'

Bruntcliffe's Scottish, English and other US holdings however showed an early and sustained return. In a matter of months the company's management team working with local personnel introduced changes into the operational structure of these businesses to capitalise on their potential. A key facet of the changes implemented was the introduction of basic financial reporting and controls. This is a conservatively and thoroughly managed enterprise with a tiny central establishment. There is nothing revolutionary about its approach. It has merely applied sound business principles to operations which lacked focus, direction and proper planning and forecasting mechanisms. In addition, the value of the sites is maximised by improving the product mix, quality and service while reducing costs and making selected capital investments to enhance productivity. The largest part of the company is the Scottish holding, which turns over between £12 million and £14 million a year, generating profits of £1.5 million. Wallis applied basic reporting disciplines to Thistle and immediately improved performance. The business has a flat management structure which facilitates quick decision-making and improved customer service. The operation at Rugby, which is directly managed by Wallis personally, is highly profitable. Leigh Interests holds a contract for landfill and landscaping. Bruntcliffe pays a small royalty to Leigh. The mining business has improved extraction to 250,000 tonnes a year for which it achieves £1 a tonne.

Distinctive features

- highly profitable quarries, both in the UK and in America;
- top quality management with years of experience in the extractive sector;
- room for substantial organic growth;
- flat management structure, allowing flexibility and customer responsiveness.

It was not all bad news in the USA. In the first two months of operation, the sand and gravel operation in Pittsburgh enjoyed record results and now it produces 450,000 tonnes a year, earning $450,000. Wallis says there is still a strong potential organic growth in each of its sites. It plans to acquire more pits but does not want to increase its gearing beyond 55 per cent. In the UK, demand has been influenced by a reduction in road building in England. This does not affect Bruntcliffe directly but it does alter City perceptions of the industry. At present 80 per cent of the industry is held by five big players, including Tarmac, ARC and Redland. But the opportunities for companies such as Bruntcliffe are good because the majors are constrained by long reporting lines and slow decision-making.

Size and shape

Employees: 300   Locations: 19
Geographical income split: UK 55%, US 45%

Stratagems

The Bruntcliffe approach to managing its quarries is straightforward. Its objective is to improve shareholder value, which means it is creating a well-managed business which seeks to enhance the quality and performance of its operations. The experience of the directors in the aggregates sector is a major advantage in assessing the potential for growth. Wallis and team cut through unnecessary costs and secure improvements in operating efficiency. They analyse the potential for products in local markets. 'The extent of a market for an individual quarry is no more than a 30-mile radius of the site, so we must have a clear appreciation of the needs of local customers. We can then adapt our product mix to suit these requirements.'

Future prospects

- long term acquisition strategy in the UK and the USA;
- higher margins through improved reporting and attention to the product mix;
- appropriate and selective capital investment in certain operations.

The industry is unfamiliar with proper financial controls and with detailed management reporting. Bruntcliffe insists on daily information on the cash position and weekly reports on sales. Wallis says that with these and other essential figures, accurate forecasting of demand can take place. Capital investment is made on a selective basis. All remedial expenditure has been made and since the end of 1995 all new investment will be made to further enhance returns or for new projects.

Outlook

The sector has been depressed by reductions in road building but the Scottish programme is progressing, which is good for business at Thistle. A legal dispute involving two former US directors and a former business associate has involved Bruntcliffe by extension but has little bearing on the daily operation of the business. Wallis says that there is a series of promising projects in Virginia and in the longer term the company will look to make further purchases.

Address:

6 Edgar St, Worcester WR1 2LR Tel: 01905 617106. Fax: 01905 61705

Cairn Energy plc

Edinburgh

Turnover				
1992	1993	1994	1995	1996
£13M	£18M	£16M	£22M	£37M

Summary: During the last financial year, Cairn Energy has transformed the scale, spread and quality of its business in a period of intense activity. In March 1996, Cairn discovered the Sangu gas field offshore Bangladesh. By the end of the year, it had entered into a ground-breaking alliance agreement with the giant American contractor Halliburton for the fast-track development of the field, signed a long-term drilling contract and completed a gas purchase and sale agreement with the Bangladeshi authorities. In the same period, Cairn acquired Command Petroleum of Australia. Command's principal asset was a 22.5 per cent operated interest in the Ravva oilfield, offshore eastern India. This acquisition gives Cairn direct control of additional assets and cashflows from which to grow and consolidate its presence in southern Asia.

The Business

Cairn Energy's current market capitalisation stands at more than £1 billion – less than five years ago it was only £6 million. And in the same period the share price has risen more than twentyfold. The growth has been achieved by careful adherence to a clearly defined strategy for development and growth. Cairn, which has been operating in its present form since 1989, plans to pursue growth through a combination of acquisitions, active asset management and exploration. The core theme of this philosophy is the careful assessment of the balance of exploration risk to reward. The main illustration of this theme is the Sangu gas field strike.

Chief executive Bill Gammell, a former Scotland rugby international, worked on the north sea rigs as a roustabout during university vacations on the way to qualifying in accountancy and economics. His father was an oilman too. He set up his own management company in 1978 and eight years later was awarded the management contract for Caledonian Offshore Oil. Three years later he headed a successful buy out and changed the name to Cairn – as a statement of what was to be achieved. He sums it up: 'a cairn is a pile of stones at the top of a mountain and the vision of the company when we set out was to try and build a company that was built on solid foundations but had the ability to attain a pinnacle.' To that end he insists on control of when and where to drill wells, relying on the best expert seismological advice available. It is about having the right structure and the right people in the right place at the right time.

The drilling off Bangladesh – and the projected rewards are more than substantial because of rising demand in India – came because of technical indications and Bill Gammell's gut instinct which convinced him of success. It typified his assessment of risk and the pros and cons of ugly versus beautiful. In other words to identify something that might be perceived by others to be almost worthless and undertake a metamorphic transformation.

The plan, which involved carefully calculated risks, worked for the Sangu strike. In Gammell's words: 'the ugly duckling became a swan and then turned into a goose which will lay more than a clutch of golden eggs.' It represents what Gammell describes as an 'unbelievable' return on investment.

Distinctive features

- concentration on adding and realising value;
- seeking maximisation of commercial and technical expertise;
- exploitation of competitive edge in all aspects of the business;
- apply 'go or grow' philosophy.

Stratagems

Increase in shareholder value can be achieved from an increase in oil or gas prices, imaginative acquisitions and exploration success. The company realises it has little influence in this first category and consequently directs its efforts towards strategic acquisitions and organic growth from exploration. But central to the theme is a ruthless determination on 'go or grow'. To this end any section of the business which is perceived to be incapable of contributing more than ten per cent towards asset value is axed.

Motivation is a vitally important factor in taking the company forward and the staff are instilled with self belief and willingness to succeed. They are encouraged to play devil's advocate by expressing contradictory views in an overall strategy framework. Says Gammell: 'The most important aspect of the job is to balance risk against reward. If you happen to be right, make sure you are very right.'

To this end there are well defined basic rules: a careful consideration of whether or not to double the risk and halve the reward, but, as corporate risk assessment insists, don't bet the farm – keep a grubstake, and if all the eggs are in one basket, watch that basket carefully. Goals are set, focused and the aim is high. Strategy in action meant the acquisition of Holland Sea Search for £17.9 million in 1994 to give Cairn 100 per cent of two block exploration off Bangladesh. Then it purchased Clyde Petroleum (North Sea) Ltd for £338.8 million to take a ten per cent interest in the Gryphon field. Assets in Spain and the USA were sold under the philosophy of go or grow.

Size and shape:

Employees: 200   Locations: 8
Geographical income split: India 50% UK 35% mainland Europe 15%

In 1995, Cairn acquired Command Petroleum Limited for £186 million in a strategic move which delivered producing assets, exploration upside, and a major presence in India. With the real possibility of gas export from Bangladesh to fuel-starved India, Cairn is ideally placed to take advantage of the enormous growth potential offered by both countries. Cairn has also signed up three blocks of offshore southern China, a country which it considers to have considerable growth potential. The company has recently acquired a block in northern Thailand.

Outlook

Future prospects

- exploiting the full potential of the Bangladeshi acreage;
- gas export to India;
- exploration in India, China and Thailand;
- alliances with third parties which add value.

The first gas from Sangu is due in April 1998. A second bidding round for the remaining acreage in Bangladesh has recently been announced by its government. Cairn has indicated that it will participate in bidding for new blocks and has announced that it is in discussions with Shell on a joint venture there. While Bangladesh will undoubtedly continue to be a key area of focus, Cairn's view is that substantial growth opportunities are also available in South Asia and the far east. The company continues to develop relationships or alliances with third parties where complementary skills can add value.

Address:

Cairn Energy plc, Cairn House, 61 Dublin Street, Edinburgh EH3 6NL. Tel: 0131 557 2299. Fax: 0131 557 2220/0577

Cambridge Antibody Technology BIOTECHNOLOGY

Melbourn Science Park, Cambridgeshire

Turnover				
1992	1993	1994	1995	1996
£337,000	£981,000	£2.1M	£2.9M	£2.1M

Summary: Cambridge Antibody Technology (CAT) is the world leader in human antibodies for therapeutic and diagnostic purposes. This conservatively managed business is a genuine biotechnology company. It deals with the selections, isolation and development of monoclonal antibodies. CAT's technology has applications both in the development of antibody-based therapeutic products and as a drug discovery tool. Previous antibodies have been based on mouse proteins which can be *humanised* to make them 90 per cent human. CAT makes completely human monoclonal antibodies from its libraries of more than 10 billion human antibody genes, which represents a giant step forward.

The Business

The 1984 Nobel prize-winning discovery of monoclonal antibodies by Milstein and Kohler, working at the Medical Research Council's laboratories in Cambridge, heralded a new era for diagnostics and therapeutics. Following the initial publication of the discovery in 1975, laboratory diagnostics were revolutionised by this work. However the harnessing of the potential of monoclonal antibodies as therapeutic products proved much more difficult. The major drawback lay in the fact that the antibodies were derived from immunising mouse or other non-human species and that following injection into man they were rejected by the body. Scientists around the world – especially at the Medical Research Council's laboratories attempted to minimise the mouse content – and improve the human element – in these antibodies by molecular engineering, so-called *humanisation*. By the late 1980s one of the MRC's star scientists, Greg Winter, believed that he could produce entirely human antibodies *de novo* without the need for immunisation. With the active co-operation of the MRC, Winter and David Chiswell (now CAT's chief executive), and with other scientist colleagues, incorporated CAT in 1989 and began operations in January 1990 to produce wholly human antibodies for the commercial market. Peptech, an Australian biotech company, provided £750,000 initial funding.

CAT seized the initiative and began the process which would result in this company beating the world to the production of wholly human antibodies. The implications for the global pharmaceuticals industry could be revolutionary. A whole new generation of products based on CAT's human antibodies can be envisaged.

'The first four years were spent quietly perfecting the technology,' says Dr David Glover, vice-president of medical development. CAT first developed the Phage-Antibody System. This enables CAT to display human antibody fragments on the surface of a bacteriophage, a harmless virus which infects bacteria. These fragments function as an antibody by recognising an antigen and binding it. The virus particle contains the human antibody genes which encode for that specific antibody. Using recombinant DNA techniques huge libraries or repertoires of antibodies have been created with enormous diversity of specificities for different antigens. CAT's libraries contain more than 10 billion different antibodies and are so powerful that, to date, the company has never failed to isolate antibodies to a chosen antigen, regardless of whether the antigen is a human or foreign protein, enzyme, small molecule or hapten. In practical terms this means that the company can use bacterial viruses to isolate human proteins for potential therapeutic benefit. If clinical tests bear out the company's argument, this could be one of the biggest advances in the recent history of therapeutic medicine.

Distinctive features

- world class technology;
- high demand;
- blue chip alliances;
- superb calibre personnel.

CAT is markedly different from its competitors. While the rejection factor with CAT antibodies is expected to be reduced, it is its speed of operation which is crucial; its technology allows CAT to identify candidate antibodies within days rather than months with other processes and also avoids the need for immunisation. Another key difference is that candidates can be further engineered for therapy using the Phage-Antibody System and other techniques, taking them beyond what is possible by immunisation.

'We aim to have a number of human antibodies in clinical trials in the next two years for treatment of fibrotic diseases, inflammation and cancer,' says Dr Glover. The company, realising the huge commercial value of its technology, has patented in Europe – and filed in the USA – for the creation of libraries of antibody genes and other related discoveries. CAT has been pursuing a series of active partnerships with leading blue chip pharmaceuticals companies, among them Pfizer, Mitsubishi, BASF/Knoll, Genetics Institute, Eli Lilly and Genentech. Work with some of these leading companies has provided capital for the business prior to the company going ahead with its own clinical trials.

Stratagems

CAT's financial strategy is characteristic of a business which has been conservatively managed. Dr Glover cautions that CAT has not yet begun clinical trials and so the weight of the cost burden has yet to be imposed on the company. Nevertheless from an impressive roster of agreements with leading businesses, CAT has managed to generate operational capital. These agreements have another major advantage – they have started a series of relationships which will be key to the company as it moves into the broader span of its work.

Size and shape

Employees: 67   Locations: 1
Geographical income split: diverse

CAT has actively collaborated with Winter's group at the MRC since 1990. MRC took 10 per cent of the equity. Peptech took another 40 per cent. In 1993 a share placement raised more capital and broadened the shareholder base to fund CAT's further development. Chief executive David Chiswell told the *Wall Street Journal* in March 1995 'We think the evolution of the technology has ended. Our library is now pretty much equivalent to the human body's potential for making antibodies.'

Among the exciting potential applications for CAT's antibodies are autoimmune diseases such as rheumatoid arthritis and major killers such as cancer. 'Since this is a completely natural product, intrinsic toxicity is virtually non-existent,' Dr Chiswell told told the *WSJ*. In product terms,

CAT's management wants to further refine the usability of its technology. Public listing was completed in March 1997 with the aim that the income from the listing will help the business to carry through the financially onerous period of clinical trials and offer improved visibility for the company and its technology. Finance is vital for research companies. Although income has been generated from agreements, the new finance will be used to expand the base of its product potential. In the last few years, the company has taken on nearly 30 PhDs, mainly molecular biologists, to work in its laboratories to enhance the scientific base.

Outlook

Future prospects

- potentially huge returns;
- clinical trials of human antibodies for cancer, fibrosis prevention, arthritis and inflammatory diseases;
- raise capital through public listing;
- further blue chip alliances.

When clinical trials are completed CAT will really know if its repertories of antibodies are the financial and therapeutic goldmine which they now appear to be. CAT has been extremely thorough in locating and developing the scientific base for its business. And along the way it has managed to convince leading blue chips that the technology is valid and can make a considerable impact on the pharma industry in the next few years. The potential in its concept is extensive and CAT should see powerful rewards.

Address:

The Science Park, Melbourn, Royston, Cambridgeshire SG8 6JJ. Tel: 01763 263233. Fax: 01763 263413

Capita Group plc

London

Turnover				
1992	1993	1994	1995	1996
£33.1M	£50.2M	£73.8M	£87M	£112M

Summary: Capita Group is a leading outsourcer and professional support services provider. It has consistently achieved high growth in sales, profits and since listing in earnings per share. The industry's *Holway Report* named Capita as the best compound growth company in the IT services sector over ten years. Outsourcing accounts for 69 per cent of profits and will probably expand, as a proportion of PBT, to perhaps 80 per cent in five years. Many of Capita's clients lie in the public sector, engaging the company in long-term contracts. In the commercial sector its portfolio embraces TSB, Westland Helicopters and Yorkshire Water.

The Business

Capita's field of operations is expanding rapidly. The business, whose heartland lies in public sector IT and financial services, is spreading its portfolio of customers and products. Despite being avowedly risk averse – cautious may be a more representative designation – the company is in the middle of wholesale expansion. This is one of the emerging businesses which will be one of the bedrock stocks of the next decade.

It was created in 1984 as a commercial subsidiary of the Chartered Institute of Public Finance and Accountancy (Cipfa), the professional body for public sector accountants. Rod Aldridge, now chairman and CEO, says that Cipfa Computer Services was opened to offer IT consultancy to government institutions. 'It was doing rather well but after three years, we – the management team – wanted to go out on our own,' he remembers. In 1987, an MBO was proposed but Cipfa was reluctant. It represented an excellent source of funds for the body but the management team felt that its development was being constricted. Eventually, the 30-strong unit concluded the MBO, funded by 3I, which put in £600,000. Two years later, Capita floated on the Unlisted Securities Market, valued at £8 million.

Initially, it operated as a niche management consultancy, providing advice on the growing area of compulsory competitive tendering. But in 1989 the shape of the business began to change with the first of its ongoing series of acquisitions, Penn Communications. 'By 1990 we had recognised that management philosophy had started its process of change towards outsourcing. We realised that this was a service which we could offer very effectively and we began the movement which would make us predominantly an organisation providing outsourced services to mainly public sector clients.'

This was strategically astute. Outsourcing now accounts for around 80 per cent of the business. Sales have grown from £8.7 million in 1989 to £112 million in 1996. Pretax profits have seen a similar expansion from £1.5 million to £12.3 million over the same period. Staff numbers have risen from 30 people in one office to 4200 in 56 locations. In all senses Capita has been a rapid success. It has developed into a broad-based group, grown by organic means and acquisition, with businesses in outsourcing, and property services. The biggest subsidiary is Capita Managed Services, enjoying the lion's share of the work and employees. It provides a range of business and IT services to a range of mainly public sector clients across the country. Its four principal divisions are: customer services (e.g. telephone call centres for customers of clients), back-office support services (payroll, pensions and revenue services), IT support and site services, provision of the infrastructure on which CMSL's services are based.

Distinctive features

- market leader in UK public sector outsourcing;
- rapid sales and pretax profits growth;
- wide range of financial, IT, back office and property skills;
- high degrees of innovation and flexibility in service.

Aldridge says one of the key factors in the continuity of success in the business is the negotiation of long-term service contracts, paid in advance. Traditionally, service contracts were one year in length; many of Capita's are five years or more. Another major development has been the transfer of employees from client to Capita. The CEO comments that in 1994 the London Borough of Bromley started the trend with the transfer of 170 of its 190 finance staff to Capita employment. So Capita runs the contract but also absorbs the personnel. This is potentially highly positive for the employees because the opportunities for career development are much greater than they were in a single authority. The catalogue of public sector organisations for which Capita provides services is immense – from Bromley, Hounslow, Bexley, Westminster, Kensington & Chelsea, Kent County Council and Mendip District Council through to the Driving Standards Agency, the Teachers' Pensions Agency and the administration of the pre-school nursery vouchers scheme for the Department of Education and Employment.

Stratagems

Capita stands on the verge of a major breakthrough. Its pre-eminence in public work, commanding longer contract periods and ever more demanding assignments, means that the company is respected and trusted in government purchasing circles. As yet only a small proportion of all potential outsourcing in the public sector has been commissioned. This means that Capita can

Size and shape

Employees: 4200   Locations: 56
Geographical income split: UK 99%, RoW 1%

anticipate higher shares of work from existing clients, which have outsourced perhaps only 20 per cent of the services which could be put out to contract. Equally, there are some agencies which have yet to do much outsourcing and Capita, with its wealth of experience and proven appreciation of the market, would be in a leading position to secure whatever assignments they will offer in the future. Aldridge says that the market perceives the company to have grown largely by acquisition but this is untrue since the biggest driver to expansion has been organic development, which has accounted for 70 per cent of the group's growth. It has consistently won lucrative new business and expanded the range of assignments from existing clients.

Future prospects

- growth in outsourcing;
- higher contribution from the private sector;
- further service refinements.

Aldridge says that the appetite for outsourcing in the public sector is growing. The pressures on budgets are greater than ever, and outsourcing presents an opportunity to cut costs, improve efficiencies and concentrate on core activities. In mid-1996 Capita operated 80 contracts, it collected £6 billion on behalf of its clients, dealt with four million taxpayers, processed seven million forms and provided software, through its SIMS and Academy subsidiaries, to 20,000 schools and 300 local authorities. The CEO comments that in local government only 10 per cent of the market has been outsourced. The potential contract value of revenue services is £800 million a year and IT of £600 million a year. In central government only four white collar contracts have been let, and given 500,000 civil servants and an annual spend of £30 billion there are ample opportunities for expansion. Aldridge says that the political and economic climate must force more contracts into the market.

On the positive side, these contracts often last five or more years and agencies pay some of the costs upfront. On the downside, it can take six to nine months to win a contract. But this means that the barriers to entry are high. Capita has worked diligently to ensure that its relationships with agencies are strong and the quality of the service provision is excellent. 'We aim to differentiate ourselves further from our competitors by the diversity of work which we are handling and level of trust we have achieved with our clients. We intend to address both the public and private sectors and we wish to build a business which is drawn 40 per cent from local government, 30 per cent from central government and 30 per cent from the private sector.'

Outlook

Capita is a substantial business with major potential for growth. The market for outsourcing will grow rapidly in the coming decade and Capita anticipates that it will secure a large slice of that new business. In the next few years, it will expand the contribution from the private sector as well as from government and public agencies.

Address:

61–71 Victoria Street, London SW1H 0XA. Tel: 0171 799 1525. Fax: 0171 799 1526

Card Clear plc

Woking, Surrey

Turnover		
1994	1995	1996
£118k	£4.4M	£5.8M

Summary: Card Clear is a child of the modern age. It has captured an expanding and profitable niche of the IT sector to provide card payment and fraud prevention services to the retail sector. The company has a close relationship with the banking industry and its integrated product range fully supports the bankers' preferred methods for approving card transactions. It provides retailers with a single system for processing all types of plastic card transactions. In its short life Card Clear has enlisted an outstanding variety of blue chip names as customers. These include Barclays, NatWest, Lloyds, Midland, American Express, Diners Club, Royal Bank of Scotland, Texaco, Mobil, Argos and Burmah.

The Business

One of the major problems which has dogged operators and users of credit and debit cards is the incidence of theft and fraud associated with them. Credit Clear was created in 1991 to address this compelling need. Its founders realised that if a single system could be found to check plastic cards simply and effectively then retailers and bankers would be queueing up to take part. This vision has been converted into an expanding reality.

Card Clear's management told City analysts in presentations during February 1997, at the time of the company's preliminary results, that the company's technology now operates in 7500 retail outlets across the UK, it is now the preferred system at all major petrol retailers and that Tesco, Sainsbury, Asda and Argos have signed up for Card Clear terminals. A deal with Jet, announced in January 1997, will install Card Clear's Hot Card Broadcasting (HCB) product at more than 220 sites across the country.

As well as Card Clear's deep penetration of the UK market, it has begun trials in mainland Europe for its HCB services in six locations in north eastern France and it has been assisting Credit Mutuel to stop stolen UK cards in French motorway toll booths. During the same presentation, it announced that it had entered into an agreement with Masterchange, the foreign exchange card provider, to assist expansion into mainland Europe. Card Clear has secured an option to acquire a significant interest in the business.

Card Clear launched its first full service in early 1994 and quickly established itself as the market leader in card fraud. More than 3,000 sites were signed up in the first two years. The banking industry's strategy over the next few years is to increase the volume of electronic rather than paper transactions. It wants to increase the volume of card transactions authorised at time of purchase to 50 per cent to protect higher value, high risk transactions. These objectives complement Card Clear's strategy, which is greatly to extend the number of outlets using its systems.

Card Clear's HCB system is now used by all the leading UK banks and card issuers. A hot card warning system is installed at the retailer's point of sale to prevent fraud. Lost or stolen card information is continuously updated by data broadcasting on the ITV network. Since its inception, HCB has been chosen by more major UK retailers than any competitive system. It is capable of holding details of more than four million missing cards.

Distinctive features

- UK market leader;
- rapid take-up of hot card broadcasting system;
- conforms with rigorous European security standards;
- close relationships with customers.

Stratagems

At the core of Card Clear's strategy are three basic principles: leading edge technology, close relationships with customers and suppliers, and high quality and articulate employees. This approach has really paid dividends because in the 1996 financial results pretax profits were up 338 per cent to £1.6 million. This period included the successful merger and integration with competitor Cardcast. The takeover, which needed Office of Fair Trading clearance, was aimed to cut duplication of resources and effort, to sharpen sales and marketing initiatives, cut the sales cycle and speed up growth, to

improve technical systems and to add to international expansion and profitability.

The process was a true merger and both the chairman and managing
director of Cardcast joined the main board of the merged company as
chairman and operations director respectively.

Size and shape:

Employees: 27   Locations: 1
Geographical income split: UK 100%

The merger has already given impetus to two new services which are being
developed by Card Clear — an online service called Card*Express* and a
security service for Internet users called Inter Clear. Card*Express* involves
joint ventures with Paknet (Vodafone) and AT&T. It takes the product
forward to the next generation of card payments protection to outside
payment terminals such as petrol stations and online debit cards – Electron,
Maestro and Solo. The launch of Inter Clear reflects the fact that electronic
commerce is the fastest growing area of Internet use, where security is seen
as the biggest barrier to expansion. Visa and MasterCard which set the
standards insist on digital certificates which the financial community is
promoting. By 2005 the industry estimates that 50 per cent of all plastic card
transactions will take place on the Internet and at present Card Clear is the
only UK company offering this service. Public trials will take place during
1997 and it is scheduled to go live in early 1998.

In March 1997 Card Clear announced that it had made its first step into the
USA with an acquisition of Transaction Billing Resources. This private
company provides credit card fraud detection services to the telecommunications industry.

Outlook

Future prospects

- expansion to online and Internet services;
- outside as well as inside point sale positions;
- mainland European expansion.

Card Clear is the UK market leader and it is viewed by the banking sector as the operator with the most relevant technology to meet its needs. The company is already ahead of the pack in terms of technological innovation and simplicity of use. It aims to grow its digital and Internet services to meet the expanding and changing nature of the market.

Address:

Card Clear plc, Card Clear House, 30 St Johns Road, Woking, Surrey GU21 1SA. Tel: 07000 777000. Fax: 07000 777999

The Carphone Warehouse

London

Turnover				
1992	1993	1994	1995	1996
£5M	£7M	£20M	£70M	£120M

Summary: The Carphone Warehouse is one of the great retailing success stories of the 1990s. Born in 1989, it identified a growing market trend and determined to be the best operator in the retail market for mobile phones. Its financial performance is spectacular and it brands itself as one of the fastest growing private companies in Britain. The sales expansion of the company is a strong enough pointer to the impact that the business has had in a comparatively short time.

The Business

The *Independent on Sunday* newspaper publishes annual league tables of the most impressive small businesses. The *Independent 100* measures success by growth in turnover. In the 1996 listing the Carphone Warehouse came top. One year later the 1997 survey showed that the company had repeated the feat by coming fourth with a 95 per cent growth in sales. The sales figures for the last five years, as shown above, tell a similar story. This is a company which has selected its marketplace, laid out its stall and provided service levels which are designed to set the standard for the industry.

Charles Dunstone, founder and managing director, explains 'Our philosophy is to ensure that shopping with us is an enjoyable experience and to achieve this, we must maintain courtesy, excellent knowledge of our products and services, and above all give honest advice.' The company has recognised many of the key issues which define customer service and put them into play inside the business.

Carphone Warehouse takes the view that the customer should be empowered to make the most appropriate decision for his or her personal needs. 'As a company we do not promote any particular tariff, network or product. We seek only to provide our customers with honest impartial advice,' says Dunstone. The company's over-riding commercial objective is that when potential customers think of buying a mobile phone they should automatically go to a branch of the Carphone Warehouse. The company's outlets should be the first point of call for anyone interested in selecting from a wide range of networks, tariffs or handsets.

Customers can select from products which embrace all six networks and more than 20 types of tariff. This has led to the company being able to claim 11 per cent of all new connections, 47 per cent of all high street sales by connection and 49 per cent of all high street sales by value.

The pattern of expansion in the enterprise is striking. At Christmas 1989, Carphone Warehouse began its first advertising campaign on London's largest commercial radio station, Capital Radio. Within a year it had opened its first shop in Marylebone, followed swiftly in the next year with three more outlets. By Christmas 1992 there were six Carphone Warehouse shops. In the period to Christmas 1994 the business boosted its network of shops to 23, launched its first product catalogue, introduced a repair centre and opened a concession in Harrods. In September 1994 the Japanese telecomms giant NTT visited Carphone Warehouse to learn its retail philosophy to apply to the cellular division NTT DoCoMo.

Further highlights in the apparently whirlwind progression of the company included: April 1995 industry awards where Carphone Warehouse won most innovative product or service and best large dealer, in the autumn of the same year its first television campaign, and at Christmas 1995 the opening of the 50th store. In spring 1996 the company collected three industry accolades: best large dealer (again), industry personality of the year for MD Dunstone and the editor's award for services to the mobile phone industry. In December the store tally reached 80 and in March 1997, it claimed the title of best large dealer for the third year running.

Distinctive features

- rapid and sustained financial growth;
- continuing store opening programme;
- tight focus on customer service;
- independent, high quality advice;
- wide range of products and services;
- addresses key issues of customer concern.

Stratagems

At the heart of The Carphone Warehouse is a clear understanding of its markets, the profile of its customers and its commitment to independent, impartial advice. A key insight into how it has built business is its extensive use of commercial radio as a marketing tool. It launched itself with Capital Radio at Christmas 1989 and has been an extensive user of the medium ever since. This shows that Carphone Warehouse knows who its principal customer is: someone younger rather than older, on the move, active and discriminating.

It charts its retail philosophy under two sub-headings: the rational proposition and the emotional proposition. These twin elements combine to create a total impression for the customer. On the rational side it is associated with impartiality, range, choice, knowledge, meaningful guarantees, integrity and a reliable brand name. On the more emotional side the company is young, enthusiastic, unconventional, fast growing, friendly, customer-focused and innovative. Through this combination of qualities, the company aims to make itself the champion of the customer in mobile phones.

Size and shape

Employees: 650   Locations: 90+
Geographical income split: UK 100%

The retail philosophy underpins the business and has served to create The Carphone Warehouse culture. It is an environment where young or independently minded people feel comfortable. They believe that they are getting the best advice and not being sold a pup – so that the salesman can record more commission. As a central plank of its retail approach it has deliberately set out to understand which issues buyers of mobile phones feel most strongly about – and to react to that knowledge.

Central to this is customer concern about the right to exchange a phone or not to be locked into a binding agreement with specific networks on onerous tariffs. Its 14-day exchange plan allows customers time to decide if they have chosen the right network and tariff. In addition its total freedom guarantee allows customers to return their handset within 12 months and receive up to 50 per cent of the handset price and terminate their airtime contract with no penalty.

Another defining principle of The Carphone Warehouse is that the range of products, networks and tariffs should be as wide as possible. To ensure independent impartial advice, sales staff are not incentivised to sell one product, network or tariff over another. In particular, the company has invested heavily in staff training in order that it can genuinely offer impartial and well qualified advice.

Future prospects

- further expansion of store network;
- higher market share;
- greater investment in training;
- bigger profit margins.

Outlook

The Carphone Warehouse looks set to become a fixture on the high street. Its speedy exploitation of the market through expert knowledge and impartiality plus an enduring vision of the customer has made this company the market leader. Analysts say that the company has plenty of room for further dramatic expansion.

Address:

North Acton Business Park, Wales Farm Road, London W3 6RS. Tel: 0181 896 5000. Fax: 0181 896 5055

Cedardata plc

New Malden, Surrey

Turnover				
1992	1993	1994	1995	1996
£4.3M	£5.2M	£6.1M	£8.9M	£12.1M

Summary: Cedardata is one of the UK's leading suppliers of financial management and procurement software. Its Oracle-based *cfacs* financial accounting system has now been installed in more than 270 customer sites and the company is winning a significant number of major contracts in both the public and private sectors. Cedardata's sales and PBT growth has been outstanding. Since its flotation two years ago, Cedardata has substantially strengthened its internal infrastructure in preparation for future growth. The proven functionality of *cfacs*, together with the increasing range of ancillary services which the company provides, position it ideally for continued expansion.

The Business

Cedardata was established in 1983 by Leon Fattal, its current managing director, and a group of other individuals as a computer services bureau. Based on their experiences in industry, the team had identified a market need for a financial management system to deal with increasingly complex and constantly changing user requirements.

Today, the company's principal product is *cfacs*. This is a financial accounting system which consists of a suite of totally integrated modules covering most aspects of financial management, including the core ledgers, order processing, commitment accounting, budgeting, time recording, project and activity-based costing and spreadsheet integration. *cfacs* has been developed entirely in Oracle, the world's leading relational database management system, thereby creating a system which is powerful, flexible and simple to use. Oracle's advanced architecture also allows the user to distribute data and applications across multiple sites and facilitates multi-user transactions.

Cedardata was the first company in the UK to take advantage of the advanced Oracle technology for a fully integrated financial system. It has proved an ideal environment for the development of a truly 'open' solution, combining flexibility and accuracy with a well proven and mature system which meets the demands of today's rapidly changing business organisations.

Cedardata has already established a highly impressive client list and *cfacs* has now been installed in more than 270 sites in the UK and a further 25 overseas. Much of the company's growth in recent years has been the result of its expansion into the public sector. Here demand has increased sharply following government reforms and the shift to accruals-based accounting. In 1995 Cedardata won a major contract as part of a consortium supplying software and services to the Foreign and Commonwealth Office. In the field of healthcare, the company has announced major deals with a number of NHS Trust hospitals (including the world-famous Papworth Hospital and St Mary's Paddington) and health authorities. Cedardata has also had great success in the area of education, with *cfacs* being installed in a number of universities and further education colleges, and with other public sector bodies like the Scottish Office and Serious Fraud Office.

Distinctive features

- key relationship with Oracle;
- strong financial stability;
- high employee involvement;
- high quality product.

In the private sector, Cedardata has developed a particular expertise with energy companies where it already has a relationship with Gulf Oil and BP Chemicals. Other major clients include Cellnet, Group 4, Hays Business Services and Thames Power. Over the last year, the company has expanded its sales and marketing team to capitalise on the increased awareness of its products and tap the considerable potential which it believes exists in the private sector.

There has also been a substantial increase in revenues from Cedardata's non-*cfacs* products. In large part, this is due to the preference of many of its customers for 'one-stop' shopping, allowing Cedardata to act also as a supplier of related products such as bank payment integration software and database interrogation tools. The company is also offering an increasing range of project management, consultancy and training services. Finally, Cedardata still provides its original function – bureau services. Although these have now declined in importance, they continue to be a useful source of cashflow.

Stratagems

Cedardata has recognised that effective financial management is vital in the current business environment and there will be a steadily growing demand for flexible systems which can provide accurate and up-to-date information. The company's strategy is to become a leading supplier of such systems in the UK and abroad.

One of the key factors in its success is undoubtedly the quality of its product. This has been achieved through continual investment in new product development to enhance the system's capability. Over the last 12 months a graphical user interface and extended client/server technology has been introduced into *cfacs*. Similarly, Cedardata's business partners – particularly Oracle, but also Digital, Bull and ICL – are some of the most respected companies in the field of IT.

Size and shape

Employees: 130   Locations: 1
Geographical income split: UK 100%.

Companies which have recommended *cfacs* include Price Waterhouse and KPMG Peat Marwick as well as a number of leading systems integrators. The company is also deeply committed to the principle of customer service. Cedardata's philosophy is to focus on the customer's needs so as to deliver a total business solution. This will include the provision of comprehensive user documentation, full training facilities (on-site if required) and on-going support. All customers will also be invited to join the *cfacs* User Group – an independent and self-financing forum within which users can discuss any issue concerning *cfacs*. Cedardata prides itself on its relationship with its customers and has established a reputation for delivering the product on time and within budget.

Future prospects

- major growth potential in private sector;
- steady expansion in the public sector;
- long-term overseas growth prospects.

Cedardata places great emphasis on the attitude of its employees. Each individual is recognised as playing a vital role in the company's success and this is reflected in a long-term history of very low staff turnover and high morale. Many of its staff are specialist financial and IT professionals with extensive experience in the computer services market. Another of the company's main strengths is its ability to work effectively with third parties. This leads to frequent invitations to participate in major systems conversion projects which the company is currently too small to manage in its own right. Cedardata has established strong relationships with accountancy firms and other industry participants, which can provide a regular source of referred work. This is enhanced by the company's 'can-do' approach to doing business.

Conscious of the experience of some of its predecessors in the computing industry, the company has deliberately adopted a policy of somewhat cautious expansion and this explains the action it has taken over the last two years to ensure that its internal systems and management structure is properly in place to underpin future growth.

Outlook

While Cedardata's approach may not be the most dynamic, it has achieved consistently impressive results over the last ten years. The company has developed an excellent product, and its standing is enhanced considerably through its relationship with Oracle. Demand for its products from the public sector will continue to grow steadily, while the potential in the private sector is considerable. In addition, the company should enjoy an increasing contribution from non-*cfacs* products. In the longer term, expansion overseas – particularly in the USA, given its link with Oracle – seems inevitable but at the moment Cedardata remains confident there is still plenty to go for in the UK.

Address:

Oriel House, 52 Coombe Road, New Malden, Surrey KT3 4QH. Tel: 0181 949 7057. Fax: 0181 949 8723.

Celsis International plc

Cambridge

Turnover				
1993	1994	1995	1996	1997
£0.15M	£0.3M	£1.7M	£5.2M	£12Me

Summary: Celsis was set up in 1992 and in the short time since formation has significantly increased its turnover in the field of product testing for harmful microbiological organisms in products ranging from food to toiletries and cosmetics. Forecasters estimate that a revolution in this particularly critical and cost-conscious field will increase the company's turnover to £40 million with current losses being turned into substantial pro-rata profits in 1998. Celsis insists it has brought modern day technological expertise to a basic process in which the essential science has remained unchanged for 100 years. Celsis has been widely praised in the scientific and commercial communities for the quality of its work.

The Business

In the last few years public concerns of the quality and efficacy of food and other products which come into contact with the body have grown rapidly. Consumers are no longer uncritical buyers of what producers are prepared to generate. Many people now scrutinise the contents of foodstuffs when they take them down from the supermarket shelves. The customer is highly attuned to the principal issues governing food safety and quality. For manufacturers across every industry, from food to pharmaceuticals, this means increasingly rigorous quality assurance testing requirements.

Celsis has capitalised on this growing demand for quality assurance testing based on its procedures for speedy and accurate results. A series of widespread alarms has put the general public on its mettle about food processing and ingredients. Two nationwide *cause celebres* of the late 1980s brought the issues into sharp focus: salmonella in eggs and listeria in cheese. These two instances led to intensive consumer demand for the highest standards of all available products and quality assurance departments (QA) needed to rethink their methodologies. This process was an immensely important step forward for Celsis. The resultant demand from manufacturers for improved but cost-effective quality testing greatly favoured the company. Throughout the world, QA facilities were comparatively immune to pressures on cost containment and speed of testing but were under increasing pressure from company finance departments to cut costs and reduce delays in result release. Other significant pressure came from technical departments to meet increasingly stringent regulations and from product distributors for speedier response times.

The company has built on the pressure which it feels is justified because microbiological QA has failed to modernise in line with other departments. Many current methods rely on incubating samples over anything from a week to up to three weeks from start to finish to detect, count and identify specific microbes. The new age techniques used by Celsis reduce this time-span to days, and in many situations, only hours. Says chief executive Arthur Holden, 'It is unsurprising that industry is keen to apply our methods.'

The basic testing principles set up by the company, floated in 1993, are speed, sensitivity, and reliability across a range of applications. Celsis' research and development department claims to have trailblazed the most sensitive reagents available and the most reliable systems. Customers are using its reagents in preference to those previously purchased with rival systems. The company's energies are focused on finding solutions that are user friendly for the microbiologists.

Celsis maintains that simple tests in novel packaging formats will extend a pioneering position in serving the QA market. One of Celsis' significant technologies is its *Digital* system, a one stop operation for QA, combining a previous time-consuming, three-stage process into a single operation of speed and efficiency. This, in turn, is expected to provide the platform for a wide range of industry specific applications.

Distinctive features

- operates in markets with potential major demand;
- multiplicity of applications;
- dedicated research and development facilities;
- capacity for marketing and distribution around the world;
- proprietary technologies.

CELSIS INTERNATIONAL PLC

Stratagems

Finance director Mark Clement describes the QA market as appearing fairly unremarkable. But behind that disarming appraisal lies a clinically structured campaign to become world leader in an area of significantly growing demand. A total of four billion tests are carried out world wide every year and the growing market is dominated by a technology which has basically remained unchanged since the days of Pasteur and Lister. Celsis is innovative – in terms of products, services and marketing. And the company is setting its sights on top targets with the multinationals as first priority.

But it is building from a sure foundation: value added services, training, support, pre-validation – and the pro-active management of big companies. The strategy has directly targeted big names. Colgate Palmolive, Procter and Gamble, Unilever, Glaxo Wellcome and Body Shop are already collaborating. This leads to spin off acceptability from smaller companies. Clement says Celsis has cherry-picked a strong marketing team with a pedigree of managing change. Prospective clients are asked to satisfy themselves that Celsis products, when tested against traditional tests or competitive approaches, at the very least achieve the same standard and usually are more efficient.

Size and shape

Employees: 130   Locations: 4
Geographical income split: Europe 60%, US 37%, RoW 3%

Clement, a former banker who went to Celsis after recognising its true potential, says 'At various stages we are sequentially selling to customers and binding them into our timetable. At the end we present a financial analysis on how much money we can save them by significantly reducing testing times.' A pitch to Colgate in Manhattan put Celsis into eight of the major's 80 plants scattered throughout the world. They will be in 16 by the end of the year.

Future prospects

- establishment of key accounts in major market sectors;
- product flow to position Celsis as a supplier of choice;
- concentration on maximising company's distribution channels;
- tight targeting of new business;
- aim to become world leader in market worth £6.2bn by 2000.

Simple scientific hygiene testing at home is another market which Celsis is actively researching and investigating to capitalise on the growing awareness of people to domestic germ dangers, particularly affecting the old and young. They are thinking of something as easy to use as a home pregnancy testing kit, but in swipe card form – with the object of bringing what is today a complicated scientific process simply and cost effectively to the masses. This is seen as a huge market and if exploited correctly will put Celsis in an extremely strong commercial position.

Outlook

Celsis is buoyant, and more than ready to capitalise on the knowledge and fact that testing for bugs costs industry and commerce billions of dollars a year in terms of claims, lost brand awareness, products having to be jetisoned because they are faulty, product recall and tied up working capital. Testing is here to stay with projected legislation to make it both more frequent and more stringent. There is what Clement describes as 'unprecedented interest in the products at the moment because of the pressure for more testing and the emergence of Celsis as a brand leader'. This should give Celsis a three-year head start on any collective opposition which is seeking to exploit growing demand.

Address:

Cambridge Science Park, Milton Road, Cambridge CB4 4FX. Tel: 01223 426008. Fax: 01223 426003

Checkout Computer Systems

Dunstable, Bedfordshire

Turnover			
1994	1995	1996	1997
£8M	£12.4M	£19M	£22Me

Summary: Checkout Computer Systems has revolutionised electronic point-of-sale systems in restaurants and pubs by providing touch screen technology that copes with the large food and drink choices found today, provides fast response, is easy to use, enhances staff control and productivity, and can withstand the food and drink spillage characteristic of catering environments. Checkout has installed 90 per cent of touch screens in the UK hospitality sector. It is expanding into Europe and has introduced mobile systems to further increase serving staff sales productivity. The company forecasts a doubling of sales and pretax profits from 1994 to 1997.

The Business

Many sectors in the UK economy have experienced wholesale change in the last decade. None more so than the hospitality area – principally pubs and restaurants. In other reports in this book we have shown how pubs have been refocused away from beer selling towards higher margin retail management. An essential tool in this realignment has been technology. Out went manual tills; in came electronic point of sale (EPoS) systems which gave owners and managers the capacity to achieve greater efficiencies in their businesses and broader understanding of the dynamics of the entirety of their outlets. EPoS supplies valuable information on customer preferences and strongly performing lines. It also presents detailed centralised statistical information which provides operational management, accurate data on which to base their strategy plans.

At the heart of the EPoS revolution in the hospitality sector is Checkout

Computer Systems. This is the dominant – and specialist – supplier in the market. The novel touch screen technology, which is the most visible aspect of Checkout's product, was introduced in 1989. Since then Checkout has installed more than 14,000 units – 90 per cent of all EPoS systems in the sector. The company designs, manufactures and sells its own products using standard components. It has become a classic niche success by successfully overcoming problems, such as the harsh environment of spilled drink and food and the very wide range of item choices which make keyboard-based systems difficult, slow and unreliable to use. This new technology and a disciplined focus on solving hospitality business problems has enabled it to leapfrog its competitors.

Managing director Ed Dayan started Checkout in 1982. Early venture capital has crystallised into a long term investment but Checkout has remained a private company whose business is the supplying of EPoS systems to the hospitality market – pubs, restaurants and hotels. It has no immediately obvious reason for seeking a stock market listing. The twin reasons for floating – visibility and capital – are currently not a problem for Dayan. With 90 per cent penetration, its reputation in its chosen niche market is formidable. Also its financial prospects have never been better, despite an uneven financial performance earlier in the 1990s.

Checkout has won major orders since early in its development. These large contracts can distort revenues and cause the results to appear unrepresentative when the rollout completes. The 1994 results show the impact of a large rollout. Checkout's response is to broaden its customer base so as to even out such influences. The overall product range is modular, includes back office management systems, is easily upgradable and highly reliable. It is backed up with training and a good support service in operation 365 days a year, 15.5 hours a day – catering hours. The business has grown steadily and sales outside the UK started in late 1994. There are distributors across Europe, in the middle and far East and South Africa. More than 130 dealers applied for rights to sell Checkout solutions in mainland Europe in March 1996.

Checkout's competitors are responding with touch screen products of their own but they are not focused exclusively on the hospitality market, being generalists, whereas Checkout is firmly wedded to its core hospitality specialism. Innovative applications of technology are a key strength for the company and Checkout provides the standard against which the generalists are judged. For example, serving staff can now use mobile touch screen terminals to transmit orders direct from table. In one instance this increased a hotel's banqueting takings by £500 a night. Proximity buttons worn by serving staff to identify them to a terminal are ready and colour screen technology is waiting in the wings.

Distinctive features

- dominant force in its market sector;
- expanding overseas orders;
- rapidly growing revenues;
- technological excellence.

Value is also constantly being added with the software and the facility to support customer loyalty schemes is indicative of this. The technology enables menu choices to be seen on-screen and prompts serving staff to cross-sell and respond quickly to customer orders. Pilferage and wastage is sharply reduced and stock becomes much more manageable. Orders can go straight to kitchens with table waiting warnings to avoid serving delays. Checkout systems also support interactive drink dispensing which means that the bar problem of 'lost drinks' goes away.

Stratagems

The keystone of Checkout's success is that it understands that the technology is a means to an end. Sales and marketing director John Bowen says, 'We make our products, write our software, to be a profit generating tool for our customers.' The focus is on the hospitality market exclusively and understanding its customers and their problems. This is how the company has competed against major retail EPoS competitors like ICL and NCR, and won sales and how Checkout intends to continue growing its business.

Size and shape

Employees: 250   Locations: 1
Geographical income split: UK 95%, RoW 5%

Controlled growth is a second plank of the strategy and orders are being reined back as Checkout keeps manufacturing capabilities in synchrony with sales to avoid overheating. Component lead times can be up to six months and Checkout does not want to see customers having to wait too long for products. Bowen says the company recognises that it will need to increase manufacturing capability if growth continues at its present pace.

The company plans to expand its overseas activities. In non-English speaking countries Checkout terminals are sold attached to distributors' back office systems. In English-speaking countries, Checkout also sells its own back office systems. Since Checkout terminals have been so successful in the UK market there is every reason to expect that success to be replicated overseas.

Future prospects

- strong growth in mainland Europe;
- technological expansion in hardware and software;
- further concentration on customer solutions.

In general, Checkout aims to work with established partners abroad rather than start up distributors. Denmark has been especially successful as a territory because of this approach. Management is looking at the potential for its products in the USA but has no definite plans to enter it yet. Exports now represent five per cent of overall turnover with 10 per cent forecast for 1996. Bowen expects this export percentage to rise steadily, within the framework of controlled expansion.

Outlook

Checkout's commanding share of the UK market provides a convincing platform from which it can expand. The options for corporate growth include: further assignments for existing clients, adding new UK customers and broadening its reach to overseas markets. Its capacity to secure new business will be strengthened by its investment in new hardware and software, and its deep understanding of its sector which means that it can provide thoughtful solutions to customer problems. Its competitors are generalists while Checkout's specialist knowledge will count greatly in its drive for enhanced profitability.

Address:

The Checkout Centre, Townsend Farm Road, Townsend Industrial Estate, Houghton Regis, Dunstable LU5 5BA. Tel: 01582 471112. Fax: 01582 471118

Chernikeeff Group

South West London

Turnover				
1992	1993	1994	1995	1996
£9.3M	£15.5M	£19.5M	£21.3M	£28M

Summary: The Chernikeeff Group is composed of a computer internetworking business and a telecommunications company. The driving force in the group is the rapidly expanding networks activity. The company is a UK market leader in products which network and integrate diverse computer systems. The current UK market for network products is estimated to be in excess of £380 million and is expected to grow substantially over the next four years and despite increasing competition Chernikeeff will continue to be a leading player in the UK. Its relationship with Cisco Systems, the US manufacturer of network products, plays a key part in its market profile.

The Business

Few companies can command such romantic origins as the Chernikeeff Group. In the early 1920s, Captain Chernikeeff, who had served in the Imperial Russian Navy, and some White Russian friends created the standard-bearing marine log systems business. In the mid 1970s the company was reborn under the leadership of its present chairman and managing director Peter Harrison who gave the business a new direction first in telex message switching products and then in local area network (LAN) and wide area network (WAN) network integration.

The captain's company enjoyed a formidable reputation for several decades but by 1976 was barely breaking even. It was then absorbed by Crest Nicholson, an industrial conglomerate. CN's manager responsible for acquisition integration was Harrison – a chartered accountant who was determined to make his own money and took a personal stake in the business. Within three years, he and his colleagues had tripled turnover and brought the company into a healthy profit.

Harrison, after a year in practice as an accountant, had joined Ford's forward planning unit in Dagenham in 1961. Six years later he became an acquisitions and integration manager for the conglomerate Firth Cleveland, and then he joined Crest Nicholson where he ran several of its subsidiaries. The challenge presented by Chernikeeff intrigued him and in 1979 he bought the business outright. 'For the first couple of years we sold Aquoprobe products but the opportunities for the naval market were limited. In 1979, we diversified into telecommunications by developing and manufacturing message switching systems based on telex and these took a couple of years to establish themselves. Our first big contract was the Shell Centre where another contractor was unable to fulfil its obligation. We suggested that Shell rent our system until the other company was able to meet its commitment. In the end Shell was convinced that our system was more efficient and cost-effective. The next step forward came when we won a major tender for the Home Office for the emergency communications networks. These two assignments established Chernikeeff Telecommunications as a major operator in the market.'

Harrison's background in forward planning encouraged him to look ahead for the next trend. In 1987 he knew that fax would replace telex and that computer networks would be big business. The company searched for new products to meet the potential demand and through an initiative by the commercial division of the US embassy he came into contact with the nascent Cisco Systems. Cisco had developed a network router product for the Stanford University network, in California, which linked several thousand host computers manufactured by 18 different suppliers, over a single unified network. This tiny company, a Silicon Valley start-up, had produced a high speed, multi-protocol router, which for many years was the only device in the market which could transport data between multiple host computer systems using the unified network, as a common highway.

Distinctive features

- UK market leader in network integration;
- close relationship with Cisco Systems;
- market growing to £1 billion plus in four years;
- major earnings potential.

Chernikeeff had a stand at the 1987 Brighton telecommunications exhibition and invited Cisco to bring as many of its routers as the founders could carry.

The initial reaction was slow and Harrison says that they had to sell the concept before they sold the product. But quickly major corporations linked into the fact that the Cisco router had several advantages which saved costs on tariffs and eliminated unnecessary transmission of broadcast data packets. In 1988 Chernikeeff signed an exclusive two-year distribution and installation contract with Cisco which is still paying dividends in 1997. Chernikeeff has long been synonymous in the minds of customers with Cisco products. Even though Cisco opened in the UK in 1991 and created other distribution channels, Chernikeeff remains one of the largest integrators of Cisco products. Harrison maintains that the relationships with customers are so strong that whenever a new Cisco product is launched, clients turn to Chernikeeff for advice on their applicability.

Stratagems

One of the key lessons which Harrison has learned from the Cisco experience is that Chernikeeff can benefit enormously from identifying young technology companies and establishing relationships with them. He has sourced mainly from US emergent businesses new products which Chernikeeff can distribute and integrate. Among the new companies with which Chernikeeff has established relationships are: Ascend, for corporate remote access and Internet service providers (ISPs); FORE Systems for Powerhubs and ATM switches; Xyplex for hubs and routers; and Network Appliance for NFS fileservers.

Size and shape

Employees: 127   Locations: 3
Geographical income split: UK 92%, RoW 8%

Chernikeeff's added value is that it understands network design and its clients' network systems intimately. Its expertise lies in the design and integration of systems and products from a range of manufacturers and providing maintenance and support for the resultant network. Harrison argues that Chernikeeff is better placed than any single manufacturer to advise on the most appropriate devices for client-specific systems.

The relationship with Cisco remains critical however and its best service organisation award from Cisco's Europe, Middle East and Africa division in April 1996 is among Harrison's greatest achievements. It is the latest in a stream of awards from Cisco stretching back to the onset of the relationship between the companies. Chernikeeff is gold partner to Cisco and was also the first CIP-IBM certificated company for the integration of IBM products outside the USA, which is a key factor in their dialogue. More than 1000 corporates, 80 universities for whom Chernikeeff built the SuperJANET academic network, government departments, and many UK-based multinationals, use Chernikeeff for network integration solutions because of its deep appreciation of the latest portfolio of products, applications, network management and support.

The vast majority of Chernikeeff's work is based in the UK, although it does some work overseas for UK customers. Given the huge potential in British markets, Chernikeeff has concentrated its efforts in the UK. It has also developed reciprocal relationships with companies of a similar size and approach in key European and far eastern territories. These companies act as a global alliance sharing and referring work to each other.

Outlook

Future prospects

- improving market size and revenue despite greater competition;
- further expansion of client base;
- strengthening of product supplier relationships.

The potential for Chernikeeff in network integration remains massive. During the next four years the value of the UK network integration market should exceed £1 billion – and, providing Chernikeeff can maintain its market share, it aims to increase substantially its annual revenue by the year 2000. As established market leader, the company will benefit from its experience and strong relationships with clients and manufacturers. Looking further forward, Chernikeeff will add sales from the growing corporate interest in the Internet and its dialogue with Cisco and other new product originators. Harrison has created a business which has a tough persona and commanding knowledge base. It has an established reputation for designing and supporting its clients' networks to high quality standards of performance and reliability.

Address:

Windmill Court, Brooklands Close, Sunbury-on-Thames, Middx TW16 7DX. Tel: 01932 814800. Fax: 01932 814808. E-mail: info@Chernikeeff.co.uk

Chiroscience Group plc

Turnover		
1994	1995	1996
£2M	£1.7M	£5M

Summary: Chiroscience is an innovative and emerging pharmaceutical company based around the exploitation of diverse technologies. It has expanded beyond the core chiral technology since the acquisition of Darwin – a US gene-based biotech company. As a result Chiroscience is now a company with the biology as well as the chemistry for innovative drug discovery. Chiroscience has developed a sophisticated 'toolbox' of development techniques which it is using both to improve existing drugs and in new drug discovery programmes. It has concentrated its activities on drug candidates which it believes offer substantial commercial potential, by targeting unmet medical needs, seeking significant therapeutic benefits or reduced side effects as compared with existing products. Chiroscience has entered into a series of collaborative arrangements with many of the world's top 20 drug companies to exploit its market-leading research. It floated in early 1994 in London, raising £36 million, and in June 1996 collected a further £40.3 million from a placing and open offer.

The Business

Chiroscience was founded in November 1993, from a previous vehicle called Chiros, in order to capitalise on its founders' expertise in chiral technologies and the anticipated growth in chiral drugs. Chirality is a property of molecules, known as racemates, which have identical chemical formulae but different physical structures (called isomers) in that one form is a mirror image of the other. This is important in drug design because biological systems are structurally specific and only interact with one partner of the chiral pair. The other partner may be inactive, or it may interact elsewhere in the body causing side effects. In addition, regulatory bodies are demanding more information on the different isomers in a drug, so there is a trend towards single isomer drugs based on safety and economic arguments.

The company's ChiroTech division provides consultancy and advice for leading pharmaceutical companies on their chiral technology issues. It is currently working with pharmaceutical partners on eight development programmes, two of which are in Phase III of clinical trials. Phase III compounds have a 60 per cent chance of reaching the market. The company also supplies specialist chiral intermediates and generic actives such as (S)-Naproxen, the widely-used non-steroidal anti-inflammatory drug. It has recently entered into manufacturing and marketing agreements for this drug around the world. One of the principal attractions of ChiroTech is that it is revenue-earning in the short term, considerably easing the cashflow constraints that typically characterise a biotech business in its early stages.

The second leg of Chiroscience's business is its work in improving existing racemate drugs. A number of currently marketed drugs are known to have sub-optimal efficacy or produce unpleasant or dangerous side effects. By developing them into 'single isomer' products, they can have a longer commercial life and a greater range of therapeutic uses. Prominent among Chiroscience's pipeline of single isomer drugs are dexketoprofen and levo-bupivacaine. Dexketoprofen is an anti-inflammatory drug developed in collaboration with Menarini, which has launched the drug under the brand name Enantyum in Spain in June 1996. Levobupivacaine is a long-acting local anaesthetic which has a significantly reduced effect on the cardiac function and the central nervous system compared to existing drugs. Chiro-science has recently withdrawn from a collaborative agreement with Pharmacia & Upjohn and chosen instead to invest £12 million in taking the compound through the clinic in the UK and the USA. The company will reconsider marketing partners nearer launch. European registration will occur in December 1997 and US registration in April 1998.

Chiroscience is also working on single isomer developments for attention deficit disorder, breast and other cancers, and cardiovascular disease.

Distinctive features

- enormous market potential;
- alliances with global top 20 pharmaceutical companies;
- broad-based discovery programmes;
- world class technology.

However, it is Chiroscience's novel drug discovery programme which is the most exciting of its activities and will provide the vast majority of its revenue in the long term. From its inception in 1993, this has focused on the disease processes involved in inflammation and cancer and, in particular, on the role of Matrix Metalloproteinase (MMP) inhibitors in these diseases. D5410, which is designed to treat rheumatoid and osteo arthritis, is Chiroscience's first novel drug to enter development but the company is also researching compounds for cancer, inflammatory and skin disorders and heart disease. Any of these drugs, if successful, would have blockbuster potential.

Stratagems

Chiroscience's strategy is to build up its research and development pipeline through the exploitation of its core technology and, by so doing, design and develop improved drugs to meet areas of unmet clinical need. The areas of cancer, pain and inflammation are those of substantial, unfilled medical need with no truly effective or disease-modifying therapies. Furthermore with a global market for drug therapies of more than $10bn, they offer great commercial potential.

Nevertheless, the company recognises that drug development is inherently an uncertain business and has adopted a number of strategies intended to minimise risk. Its approach to single isomer developments is commercially led, with the objective of maximising short and medium term revenue streams from these development programmes. The company avoids drug candidates in which the therapeutic benefit or potential market return is open to question and concentrates on those with the greatest therapeutic advantage and the largest accessible markets.

Size and shape

Employees: 300   Locations: 4
Geographical income split: UK 14%, US 47%, mainland Europe 29%, RoW 10%

The company has also identified the increasing trend towards the out-sourcing of R&D by the major pharmaceutical firms. Drug development can be an extremely costly process – for a successful product, worth $600 million a year in the marketplace, each additional day that the drug spends in development adds $2 million to the development costs in lost revenue time – and many firms no longer have the expertise to develop compounds in-house within an acceptable time-scale. The growing need for cost-effective R&D programmes presents a major opportunity for a company such as Chiroscience. The company is recognised as the leading provider of chiral solutions to complex drug development problems and is working with many of the leading pharmaceutical companies to provide processes for key intermediates and drug actives.

In its novel drug discovery programme, Chiroscience's unique *Chiral Template* approach uses blueprints to create rapid access to new enzyme inhibitors. This results in improved access to a range of therapeutic endpoints hence allowing a series of commercial returns. This gives the company a considerable competitive advantage, allowing the research teams to discover lead compounds more rapidly and progress the programmes efficiently, while working at the forefront of scientific knowledge.

Future prospects

- pipeline of high potential compounds;
- further alliances with blue chip pharma companies;
- early and strong returns.

To maintain its technological lead, Chiroscience aims to recruit the most talented people in the industry. In addition, its current staff of highly-trained and experienced chemists, biologists and analytical scientists is supported through collaborations with worldwide centres of scientific, academic and medical excellence. For example, it has recently licensed the rights to an asymmetric chemical catalyst technology from DuPont and acquired a licence for similar applications from Stanford University. Further similar arrangements are expected in the next two years to broaden the base of Chiroscience's activities.

Outlook

Pharmaceutical companies and regulatory authorities are increasingly recognising the importance of chirality in drug design. The proportion of marketed drugs which are chiral is predicted to increase to around 80 per cent by the year 2000. As a world leader in chiral technologies, Chiroscience is able to exploit the considerable commercial opportunities afforded by the discovery and development of new chiral pharmaceutical products. Following a recent share placing, the company now has sufficient funds to finance its development to a time when revenue from its drug development programme will start to come on stream.

CHIROSCIENCE GROUP PLC

Address:

Cambridge Science Park, Milton Road, Cambridge CB4 4WE. Tel: 01223 420430. Fax: 01223 420440

Close Brothers Group plc

City of London

Pretax profits				
1992	1993	1994	1995	1996
£13M	£18M	£33M	£34M	£45M

Summary: Close Brothers is a group of specialist and separate, rather than integrated, financial businesses. It is the only merchant bank in the UK to have achieved a management buy-out and it has consistently improved profits year-on-year since the mid 1970s. It has emphatically chosen not to compete with the large integrated City houses, believing that there is room in the UK for at least one well-managed, medium-sized merchant bank. It is led by principles of high quality service, integrity, uncompromising professionalism, effective use of capital, extensive operational freedom for subsidiaries and narrowly targeted markets. Around one half of its income comes from traditional banking activities, with the balance from fee-based services and marketmaking. In the next few years Close Brothers particularly hopes to grow its specialist fee-earning businesses.

The Business

Close Brothers opened its doors in 1878. The present top management team, who arrived in the mid-1970s, bought the bank 101 years later from its then owner Consolidated GoldFields. 'The MBO, one of the first documented, occurred in the aftermath of the secondary banking crisis when smaller banks were *persona non grata* in the City,' says finance director Peter Winkworth, a former KPMG accountant. The original trio – managing director Rod Kent (MBA INSEAD), previously with Schroders, former Slaughter & May solicitor Peter Stone, and Winkworth – took out double or triple mortgages to invest in the MBO when in their early thirties.

At the outset the bank had capital of some £1 million, employed six people and enjoyed profits of around £100,000. As a result of the efforts of the core team the group now employs shareholders' funds of around £190 million, has approaching 650 people on the payroll and in 1997 analysts predict pretax profit of around £54 million. Profits have grown every year since the mid-1970s and Close Brothers has reported a compound growth in earnings per share of 18.5 per cent per annum. The bank's cost-to-income ratio is significantly lower than other City merchant banks and its opportunity for organic growth is regarded, by knowledgeable observers, as high.

Key to understanding Close Brothers is an appreciation of the MBO founders' conviction that a smaller bank could be highly profitable if it were well managed. Close is managed as a business with sound commercial principles on the use of capital and the exploitation of markets. This is a bank which operates like a company rather than a traditional City institution. Close Brothers is not given to ostentation, but, like a well-run engineering enterprise, it pays great attention to precision, performance and results. Close Brothers is made up of a small central unit in Appold Street in the City and some 14 separate businesses within three divisions – some based in London and others based around the UK. The specialist divisions embrace: City merchant banking (including corporate finance, treasury, commercial loans, insurance premium finance (PROMPT), investment management, debt factoring and agency debt collection), asset financing, and market-making.

Close has created its network of activities through a mixed process of in-house organic development, rolling start-ups and acquisition. Among its key reasons for choosing target markets is the bank's capacity to make an impact and turn a profit. Close Brothers is remarkably light on its feet and low on costs.

Distinctive factors

- highly specialist;
- low cost/income ratio;
- high EPS growth;
- unbroken profits growth;
- capacity to pick winners.

Stratagems

The strategic direction of the Close Brothers is an expression of the way it conducts business. The cultural values of the bank underpin the key factors of its commercial strategy and policy. For example, the company chose at the outset to be specialist in each of its various businesses. In the case of lending activities, the strategy is for loans to be spread across sectors and to be secured on specific assets with good second-hand values. In other words, asset-based rather than covenant-based. Furthermore, the funding strategy is to utilise committed term facilities – rather than deposits – of duration longer than the loan book. At July 1996 more than 50 per cent of the loan book of some £570 million was repayable within 12 months.

> **Size and shape**
>
> Employees: 650. Key locations: City of London, Doncaster, Newbury, Sheffield, Kingston upon Thames.
> Geo. income split: essentially wholly UK

One of the lessons of the early period was, when the directors' personal livelihoods were on the line, that capital is a scarce resource to be deployed sparingly. Close Brothers therefore seeks activities where turnover is relatively low and margins relatively high. 'This sense of making capital work most efficiently and effectively – and never wasting resources – is still with us,' says Rod Kent. Such activities can be in small sub-markets in which Close Brothers may be dominant or a key player (e.g. PROMPT, light aircraft and Heidelberg printing equipment finance, development capital) and which are not of obvious interest to larger banks. Alternatively, Close Brothers can take a focused approach in larger sectors, for example used cars, in the northern part of the country (where bad debts are low); new cars, to British Armed Forces in Germany; debt factoring, targeted at the smaller company; agency debt collection, targeted at the larger company but not the customer.

Close has also opened some innovative new businesses of its own. Peter Stone came up with the idea for PROMPT. This is a method of financing all the insurance premiums of a business through a monthly payment at a competitive cost to the borrower. This is a high repeat business which is marketed for Close Brothers by more than 3500 UK insurance brokers, who are then relieved of the credit control function with their clients.

These activities involve the bank in businesses where the income is generally reliable and predictable. So the decision, in 1993, to buy Winterflood Securities, a marketmaking business, seems a little out of character. But again all is not what it seems at first glance. Winterflood was a prize in its own right. It has steadily improved its profit performance, even through the recession, which impressed the Close management team.

When Winterflood was originally set up with Union Discount, Close Brothers advised on the structure of the relationship. This was based on

CLOSE BROTHERS GROUP PLC

Close's own approach with its subsidiaries and can be summed up as: great operational freedom, incentivised management with a stake in the business, subsidiary management set annual financial targets and absolute and total honesty about problems. 'The centre is here to help, The greatest sin in Close Brothers is to sit on a problem. We have resources and expertise to assist the managers of subsidiary companies,' says Peter Winkworth.

Outlook

Future prospects

- growing fund management arm;
- investment or rights;
- issue money;
- enhance profitability;
- further expansion of specialist businesses.

Close Brothers is special. Not only is it well managed and highly profitable, but it is practically unique in the current City as a successful and independent merchant bank. Opportunities for Close Brothers to selectively apply its approach to markets – where the bigger boys would find turning a respectable profit onerous – continue to exist. The group is still sitting on much of £53 million rights issue cash from September 1995. This will be deployed into activities only as quality opportunities permit. The top management team which clearly works together very effectively is still relatively young and keen to seek new opportunities. Rod Kent comments that during the last two decades the group has found 12 specialist markets in which to lend money in the crowded banking sector, and he hopes that in the coming years this strategy can be deployed in the crowded fund management sector.

Address:

12 Appold Street, London EC2A 2AA. Tel: 0171 426 4000. Fax: 0171 426 4044

CMG plc

Central London

Turnover				
1992	1993	1994	1995	1996
£108M	£129M	£146M	£197M	£245M

Summary: CMG is a leading European IT services company, providing business information solutions through consultancy, systems and services. It was started in 1964 and now draws the bulk of its revenues from assignments in the UK, the Netherlands and Germany. Its principal markets are financial services, public sector, telecommunications trade and industry, and processing and facilities management. The company is listed in London and Amsterdam, and has a significant employee shareholding.

The Business

CMG began life as a data processing company in London in 1964 selling a time measurement product for lawyers, accountants, architects and other professionals who billed by the hour. Called ACT, it recorded the time spent on client assignments and provided automatic invoicing. Software developers, needed by CMG but under-utilised, were sold by the hour to other companies. This gave birth to CMG as a software house. In 1968, a London client needed help with its Dutch sister operation, which led to the creation of CMG in the Netherlands. The client portfolio and service provision of the UK and Dutch operations prospered, and it became an Anglo-Dutch enterprise in the tradition of Shell and Unilever.

Current chairman Cor Stutterheim suggests that the British and the Dutch share similar cultural values. 'The only occasion when we have been at war was over trade.' CMG moved into Germany in 1974 and it has grown to 56 operating divisions in these three countries at the end of 1996. It has customers in more than 30 countries around the world; some are serviced nationally and others internationally. 'We are exceptionally customer-driven and more than 80 per cent of our business comes from the same clients,' he remarks. Some 35 per cent of sales comes from CMG's top 15 clients. Its largest customer is ABN-AMRO, which accounts for 5.1 per cent of total turnover. Around 85 per cent of revenue is drawn from three areas: consultancy, software development and systems integration, and 15 per cent from data processing.

The business majors on systems development. Another 20 per cent – an area of the business which is expanding rapidly – is the connection of a variety of commercial and industrial machines to computers. An example is an assignment to provide the software to control the Rotterdam flood barrier.

A key distinctive factor of CMG is the extent of the employee involvement in the business. From the outset, the company has encouraged all employees to be shareholders in the company and it is a prerequisite for managers to take a stake in the business. The level of the manager holdings is set at a minimum of half a year's gross pay. 'The combination of career development and high income earning together with wealth creation is one which works exceptionally well. It has made us a very profit and service-alert business.'

CMG's rationale and enthusiasm for business is driven by one factor, and one alone. Both the technology and its distinctive commercial approach serve this core goal. 'We exist to make a profit. That's it,' says Stutterheim. This overriding principle governs everything. There is no deflection and none is tolerated. 'It means that we work very hard to ensure that the quality of our service to our clients is total. Our image is good and expensive.' It also colours the nature of its relationship with the customer. CMG does not conceive of clients as institutions or as companies. 'The National Westminster Bank is a client. We tell the company that we are people and the people at the Nat West are our clients, not the bank. We try to build personal relationships and make the people at the bank more successful. What we are trying to achieve is that the individual as the client believes that working with CMG will make him or her more successful.'

Distinctive features

- high quality approach;
- solid, reliable income stream;
- growing world markets;
- extensive employee ownership;
- selective approach to client building.

CMG runs an account management system. Managing and divisional directors focus solely on one market sector or even one customer. Their product or staff responsibilities are subsidiary to the fulfilment of relationship building. The aim is to become a preferred supplier to companies like Esso, ING, Shell, Telecom Italia, Kleinwort Benson and Deutsche Bank. The trend among large multinationals to pare their supplier lists down to a tight core group favours CMG, due to its outstanding reputation. CMG's relationship with customers extends as far as formal management consultancy on IT and software implementation issues. Financial services businesses now account for 31 per cent of turnover, trade and industry 23 per cent, public sector 19 per cent, telecommunications 12 per cent and 15 per cent processing and facilities management.

Stratagems

CMG is highly selective about the work which it handles. 'We have three requirements which characterise the prospects which we seek. We summarise these as change, volume and money. Any organisation which we serve must experience continuous change. Volume means complexity. If companies have simple IT problems, we are not the right people to contact; we deliver solutions to complex problems. Money is the capacity of companies to pay our fees. This envitably leads to us working mainly for the largest organisations.'

Size and shape

Employees: 3512   Locations: 20
Geographical income split: UK 22%, mainland Europe 78%

All the major oil companies and many of the leading banks in Europe are clients. In the telecommunications sector, many of the fastest growing service providers use CMG. The Dutch, Swiss and the Scandinavian PTTs have come together and CMG provides IT services for the group. Given the massive demand in the telecommunications sector, CMG expects to see double-digit growth in this area. The company's client base is blue chip in the extreme.

CMG's market features a high degree of competition where demonstration of distinctive qualities is crucial. CMG concentrates on a core group of industrial, commercial and public sector disciplines. Its managers are specialists first in the market, then in the technology. 'Our secret is the way we use our people. The better we can utilise them, the more money we make. Extra productivity makes a marked difference to our profitability. We have computerised every productive person, so we can assess the productivity of each individual.'

The high emphasis on people is reflected in CMG's open culture. Information on every aspect of the running of the business – especially salaries, targets and returns – is shared by everyone. Every director must explain to his or her team on a monthly basis the key issues which influence their department. CMG looks for people who are talented, involved and ambitious.

The company has grown organically in the main but occasionally it will make strategic acquisitions to add value or critical mass. CMG's purchase of PECOM in Germany is a typical example. 'We could have grown organically in Germany but it would have taken us rather longer than we wished. So we bought PECOM. We have traditionally bought small companies – relative to our size – which are easy to integrate. Generally we think organic growth is more successful,' says finance director Chris Banks. 'We intend to grow from our existing bases. If our clients need us to be based in other locations, we will examine the opportunities as they arise.'

Outlook

Future prospects

- expansion of margins;
- growth in business for British, Dutch and German operations;
- introduction of new niche products for niche markets;
- further enhancement of customer relationships.

CMG is set for further expansion. Several of its industry divisions operate in sectors which predict substantial growth. Competition is very tight but CMG has a unique combination of factors. It is highly selective about its clients, it focuses very closely on key markets and it enjoys a highly committed workforce. CMG is driven by its customers and their requirements. The pattern of development of these major players in the world economy will fashion the future for this highly able business.

Address:

Telford House, Tothill Street, London SW1H 9NB. Tel: 0171 233 0288. Fax: 0171 799 3435

CODA Group plc

COMPUTER SOFTWARE

Harrogate, Yorkshire

Turnover				
1992	1993	1994	1995	1996
£18M	£23M	£23M	£33M	£34M

Summary: CODA produces accountancy/financial reporting software. The company can stake a claim to be world leader in flexible accountancy packages. Its software has been bought by businesses in more than 50 countries worldwide. CODA has, not without pain, overcome a mid-life product crisis and has laid the groundwork for later generations of an evolving package as well as attempting to get an early lead in tomorrow's computer technology.

The Business

Every large company operates a computerised accountancy system but today this is no longer simply a question of automated bookkeeping. Now, it must also be usable as a fast and responsive database providing immediate answers to an often bewildering variety of requests for financial information. Companies spend considerable sums of money on computer hardware, however much the costs of better technology might appear to be reducing; it is the software that makes such an investment show a realistic return. CODA devised and developed its financial software for an earlier generation of operating systems on mini-computers, the final descendants of the type operated by highly paid IT specialists, dressed in white coats occupying 'no entry' sanctums. Then the computer world changed. Rapidly.

Suddenly, computerised data became the lifeblood of every organisation. PCs were stationed on every desk. Prevailing management philosophy shifted to decentralisation and accountability. Increasing numbers of people needed access to fast and flexible software applications, especially in the financial sphere. These programs needed to process vast amounts of management information to refine management decision-making. CODA was, briefly, in some danger of slowly becoming promoters of yesterday's package as consumer attitudes and computer systems changed.

The key to understanding why CODA is such an impressive business is the speed and innovation with which it responded to the challenge of change. At the heart of the move was a structural reorientation which facilitated the company's capacity to deliver new methodologies and products. After a bruising 1994, when the company was faced with an 'out with the old and in with the new' balancing act, sales of an improved client/server package accelerated in 1995. The company quickly returned to profitability. Sales continue to climb and CODA now has more than 1300 users worldwide. Continuing development is one of the strengths of the package, especially its growing internationalisation.

Today, CODA can supply its software tailored to suit seven European languages, with two more imminent. Work is already under way on the difficult, but not impossible, transition into Japanese, and a simplified Chinese version has also emerged. Software licence revenue rose by almost 60 per cent in 1995 to over £16M on the back of a 23 per cent increase in open client/server demand. Obviously, the cost of such evolution has been high. Not only have sizeable structural change costs, especially in the USA, had to be met, but R&D expenditure was more than £6 million in 1995. This kept pretax profit to £1 million, against a £3.1 million loss the previous year. No dividend was paid. Chairman Rodney Potts has emphasised that the company has chosen to limit short term profitability, but, with analysts suggesting that 1996 pretax will double, he appears confident of improved returns in 1997.

Distinctive features

- respected international product;
- capacity for change;
- sales in 50 countries;
- high R&D spend.

Stratagems

The CODA strategy is simple and direct. It believes in sticking to what it knows best. CEO Robert Brown and his team are working on constant refinements to the package. CODA is now selling what Brown says is Mark 4 of its financial software and is convinced that the shelf life of the product is still unlimited. The mushrooming market for financial software would suggest that he is right.

As markets are becoming more global, businesses are forced to become increasingly more competitive. Management demands tighter financial controls and software must respond to these challenges. Investment at CODA is concentrated at developing its core package. It draws heavily on the comments of customers to provide modifications which will increase the effectiveness of the program. But, inevitably, something new is hovering on the horizon: open architecture technology, using computer software components. This would allow companies to choose whichever financial package, CAD/CAM program, manufacturing control system they wish and put them all together in one tailor-made highly integrated electronic parcel.

This package would be available for all systems down to the office micro running Windows 95.

Size and shape

Employees: 470   Locations: 25
Geographical income split: Europe 60%, RoW 40%

In theory, the ultimate objective is nirvana – or at least the business equivalent of it: a total business software solution from the shop floor to the chief executive's desk, a system which can do anything that is needed, give what information is required by anyone authorised to obtain it. CODA has become an early advocate of, and investor in, open architecture and one of nine members (total turnover more than $2.4 billion) of the Open Application Group (OAG), developing industry standards for easy integration of applications from multiple vendors.

This commitment is already paying off. Already, a major chemical company has become its first customer for such software. Another company using CODA's latest software has cut the time it takes to perform its monthly closing from eight hours to eight minutes.

Future prospects

- international growth;
- high R&D investment in open architecture;
- growing demand for its software.

Brown says that CODA has the best broad-based package available. The company has introduced new functions in the management of fixed assets, order processing and credit management. These adaptations will further enhance the process of management decision-making and contribute substantially to competitive advantage.

CODA's customers are only too aware of the benefits of such a software system and they are prepared to pay for it where they would probably jib at the cost of purpose written software, as well as the time involved in shaking it down. As one customer observed: 'We wanted state of the art systems but off the shelf state of the art systems.'

CODA has no interest in sideways expansion. 'We are very focused,' he says, 'we want to be the best in what we do.' This is why there is constant emphasis on broadening and adding depth to the existing software, and expanding its use within a company.

Outlook

CODA is set for substantial growth. Open architecture will be the key to business computing before the end of this century. Providing the software to operate entirely in the language of a customer, and incorporating individual national requirements gives CODA obvious strength. It will further enhance its products to give businesses the tools for instant financial information, which will contribute greatly to CODA's prospects. Management, sales and R&D will be further strengthened to exploit the software's international appeal.

Address:

Cardale Park, Beckwith Head Road, Harrogate HG3 1RY. Tel: 01423 509999 Fax: 01423 530527

Colleagues Group

Bath

Turnover				
1991	1992	1993	1994	1995
£10M	£18M	£27M	£36M	£45M

Summary: Described by a leading journalist as the blueprint for agencies of the 1990s, Colleagues is one of the UK's leading providers of consumer direct marketing services. Effectively a super project manager, Colleagues adopts a controlled approach to handling the enormous logistical and production exercises inherent in direct marketing campaigns. Not only is this the part that clients are happy to outsource, Colleagues' emphasis on systems, technology and heavyweight buying power generates measurable cost savings for its clients in an industry that is already growing significantly.

The Business

Colleagues fits in somewhere between an agency and a provider of services. This is its strength. While Colleagues' habitat is in a marketing environment, the company's roots are in logistics, systems and production. It views direct marketing as an enormous control exercise and has a firm grasp of what it takes to make this activity more profitable. Colleagues treats its clients as outright marketing professionals, as business partners, and a virtually seamless join with its clients makes for a compelling package. Its successes to date, whether measured by profitability or client loyalty, more than hint at a successful philosophy.

Direct marketing, in its many forms, is certainly a growth business. All the indicators point to a continued acceleration in the marketing spend devoted to direct techniques, as advertisers migrate from high level, above the line brand support to more targeted, direct marketing of key brands in an increasingly fragmented, sophisticated market place. The direct marketing industry was estimated by the Henley Centre, in a study for the Direct Marketing Association, to be worth around £4.5 billion in 1995, and growing rapidly. Although only around £300m of this total is currently spent through agencies, the trend to outsource is increasing. Colleagues is the UK's largest independent direct marketing agency and, more importantly, one of the fastest growing.

Colleagues was formed in 1987 by James Robson, chairman and previously marketing director of the Damart Group, and was joined soon after by Andrew Bennett, managing director, who was also with Damart. The business has grown rapidly since its formation. It has added £10M to turnover in each of the last three years, to stand at £36M in 1994. Gross margins are of the order of 18 per cent. If higher margins can be found elsewhere, that is because Colleagues concentrates on logistics, not consultancy, and buys in an enormous amount of costs. But it generates these margins on very high turnover. Profit before tax of over £3M, which has also risen by around £1M per annum, equates to net profit margins of around eight per cent.

Remarkably, these levels of profitability are achieved with only 80 people, ranking Colleagues first in profitability per employee in direct marketing (*Marketing Magazine*, March 1994). This merits further consideration. James Robson says 'Our customers are principally high volume, experienced advertisers operating with large budgets and a strong commitment to the benefits that can be achieved through direct marketing. We provide a comprehensive range of services to these blue chip clients, but it is perhaps our emphasis on logistics and systems that distinguishes Colleagues from the competition, and the effective use of technology has become a core ingredient in our success. By approaching direct marketing as a rigorous control exercise, even the most complex programmes can be handled.'

This demands high levels of investment, and the company spends millions of pounds on information technology. Some 55 of its 80 staff are actively and exclusively involved in controlling direct marketing programmes. Colleagues is effectively the orchestrator, buying-in and controlling an array of inputs and services to the production process. The use of on-line systems linking both customers and suppliers is a key feature of Colleagues' style of working.

Colleagues provides a comprehensive range of services and offers a 'complete solution' to clients. Its strengths are in the print, production and design of marketing material; media inserts and media programme management; and lists, databases and fulfilment.

Print, production and design

This is the most significant activity, accounting for around 57 per cent of gross profits. The company was responsible for the production and despatch of over 30 million direct mail items in 1994, and with print production representing the major campaign expense for many customers, the operation lies at the heart of Colleagues' business. All creative services are driven by cost-effectiveness, making clients' marketing budgets work as hard as possible.

Media inserts and programme management

Colleagues is the UK market leader in media inserts and media programme management, and is on target to place over one billion inserts in 1995. Working with five out of the top ten users brings exceptional buying power and priority access to key media. Such economies of scale will only increase with the number of inserts Colleagues places and as the range of potential carriers is expanded.

Lists and database management

Lists and database management might not sound a glamorous aspect of marketing, but it is one of the fastest-growing. Colleagues derives 15 per cent of its profits from these activities, but this figure reflects more on the scale of its print production and media insert operations, rather than a lower emphasis on lists and databases.

Distinctive features

- comprehensive range of services;
- high investment in the business;
- deep knowledge of customers and markets;
- close relationship with clients.

There are commonalities across all of these activities. One of Colleagues' key strengths is a proven ability to deliver material cost savings and enhanced response rates from customers' direct marketing programmes. This in turn rests on extensive and effective use of interactive technology and advanced proprietary software. Colleagues emphasis on excellent logistics and systems distinguishes it from many of its competitors, who typically are part of large creative or marketing service groups.

The 'competition' actually comes from the in-house marketing departments of potential clients as much as other agencies. In persuading these departments to outsource, Colleagues has to demonstrate clearly that it does not form an on-cost, instead adding real value to a project by improving response rates and reducing costs. Some of its successes are spectacular, reflecting either the skill and expertise of its project managers, or simply by combining the requirements of several clients to drive costs downwards.

To describe Colleagues' customers as important is a massive understatement. For all intents and purposes, the two are the same – or at least the link between client and agency is quite transparent. Through on-line facilities, clients can monitor a project easily and precisely, and control Colleagues' staff as if they were their own. This special relationship is at the heart of Colleagues' success and provides a clue to the origin of the agency's name.

Colleagues remains a very ambitious company despite its low profile and has already demonstrated its ability to grow sales and profits consistently during a recessionary period. The company is now in the enviable position of being able to exploit its strong market position without any need to change a successful formula. Clearly the company is very comfortable in handling high volume direct marketing campaigns and should attract new business from companies switching budgets into this form of marketing communications as well as expanding services to existing clients.

Colleagues' client base is based exclusively in the UK and the agency has no declared ambitions at this stage to be particularly active in Europe. The UK lags well behind Europe and the USA in terms of using direct marketing techniques, but appears to be ready and willing to catch up. That should keep Colleagues busy enough and the company is confident that it will secure an increasing share of this prospective new business.

However, Europe is certainly not out of bounds for suppliers. In searching for the best and lowest cost suppliers of the many print and media services it buys for its clients, Colleagues scours the continent, indeed the world. Part of Colleagues' strategy is to build strong structural relationships with its suppliers, even to the extent of installing compatible systems. This cements confidence and tightens the vital degree of control that sharpens Colleagues' competitive edge.

Colleagues' strategy to maintain its leading position is to prescribe 'more of the same'. That means extending its strategic services, identifying and securing large, experienced or inexperienced clients with big marketing budgets. There is also scope to expand into adjacent areas of direct marketing, such as fulfilment, telemarketing and door-to-door distribution.

Colleagues floated 31 per cent of its shares (directors and employees still retain 54.7 per cent) on the London Stock Exchange in March 1995. In its flotation prospectus, the company suggested that future expansion could come through organic growth, acquisition or joint venture. Growth to date has been achieved exclusively by organic means, and the directors will almost certainly need to be convinced of a very compelling case in order to move down the acquisition trail. Colleagues is certainly not a marketing agency driven by large egos and is unlikely to make the same mistakes as some agencies in the late 1980s who believed big was beautiful.

At first, Colleagues appears to be very non-agency-like in terms of culture and this is perhaps one reason why it has enjoyed considerable success and endearment to its clients. Systems and technology are more prominent than creative juices. The senior management is a tightly-knit team, comprising chairman, chief executive, and finance director, supported by two non-executive directors. This lean structure permeates throughout the company. When 80 people are handling an annual turnover of £36 million, there is neither time nor room for baggage. The agency does not have any client account directors – just hands-on specialists in their respective disciplines. Many come from a client background and probably hardly notice the difference in their work.

Future prospects

- expansion of client base;
- broadening of product/service portfolio;
- greater exploitation of proprietary techniques.

To motivate further a high calibre staff, the founders of the business generously gave away equity to them. Employee shareholders are good allies of ambition and success, and creating them was a prominent reason behind the company's decision to list its shares. Despite heavy investment in technology, Colleagues did not really need the money – the company is cash positive and also cash generative. No acquisitions were planned. Instead, it provided a real market for Colleagues' shares and enhanced the company's important share ownership culture.

Outlook

Colleagues has restructured the nature of the relationship between the client and the agency. It has achieved a dominant position in the market by substantially winning the client service battle. Through strong operational performance and innovative approach to service delivery, it is poised to build on its pattern of remarkable growth. It has achieved its remarkable results by improving response times to mailings, cutting costs for all clients by buying media collectively and effective use of interactive technology.

A disciplined, controlled approach, and serious investment in technology, enables Colleagues to handle very large projects with small numbers of specialist staff. It can easily leverage this dynamic and expand business without copying agencies who pursued growth in size and scope that was unsustainable and uncontrollable. Colleagues is unlikely to make similar mistakes or hasty decisions.

The company has re-defined the agency:client relationship. By concentrating on logistics, project management and cost-effectiveness, it appears as an extension of a company's direct marketing operation. The value it adds is real and has made outsourcing profitable for both parties. It all sounds so simple but that is its beauty, and perhaps provides a clue to its description as the blueprint for agencies of the 1990s.

Address:

Colleagues Group plc, Colleagues House, 122 Wells Road, Bath BA2 3AH. Tel: 01225 447003. Fax: 01225 469988

Compel Group plc

Welwyn Garden City, Hertfordshire

Turnover				
1994	1995	1996	1997	1998
£54.5M	£70M	£85M	£110Me	£160Me

Summary: Compel is one of the UK's leading providers of computer services to large corporations. It focuses in particular on the client/server, and networked PC and workstation market. It has established a reputation for designing, supplying and supporting innovative and high quality computer solutions. The company also prides itself on forming strong, long-term relationships with its blue chip customer base. Its competitive advantages should ensure that the company takes a greater share of a market which is itself growing substantially, as corporate customers increasingly look to a single external source to provide sophisticated computer services.

The Business

Compel provides a full range of integrated computer systems and services to major end-users throughout the UK. IT has increasingly become important to large organisations and this is reflected in ever higher levels of expenditure, with client/server technology, workstations and PCs taking a growing proportion of this spend. As technology is used in more widespread and demanding applications, large companies are seeking closer and more comprehensive relationships with IT providers.

Compel offers a simple one-stop shop approach to integrated solutions. As a computer reseller, it supplies customers with hardware and software from all leading manufacturers. Although it has strong relationships with each of these companies Compel has deliberately pursued a policy of independence. This allows the business to provide clients with impartial advice on the most appropriate systems, while still achieving the best price. Since most IT requirements are best met by a tailored combination of products from

147

different makers, multi-supplier purchasing is vital for most large users. Compel has attained the highest level of appropriate reseller authorisation and technical accreditation with all major manufacturers.

In addition to systems expertise, the company also offers an increasing number of ancilliary services. These typically include consultancy and design, project management, cabling and installation, while its SystemCare provides comprehensive systems support for all leading PC and Unix-based environments. Compel has also developed a training programme which can be tailored to each customer's specific requirements. With outsourcing becoming an increasingly popular option for many companies, Compel has taken a modular approach enabling clients to bring together whichever elements are suitable for their needs. Provision of services accounts for only 15 per cent of the Compel turnover at present, but this is expected to grow significantly in the near future.

Distinctive features

- defined long-term strategy;
- reputation for quality and delivery;
- blue chip clients;
- nationwide infrastructure.

Compel focuses exclusively on large corporate customers. Over the years, it has gathered an impressive client base and recent major customers include BNFL, Glaxo, the Post Office, SmithKline Beecham and the Woolwich Building Society. By concentrating on customers with broadly similar computing needs, Compel has acquired an unrivalled level of knowledge about the problems most likely to arise. Within this framework, it is then able to provide a personalised service which can be adapted to specific requirements. This style of customer-cultivation appears to work because this company has an excellent record of retaining clients and increasing the range of services it provides to those customers. Also, its eight sites across the UK offer the opportunity for a full nationwide service.

The company has yet to establish a presence overseas. This is primarily because its commitment to quality determines that it must be as good as the best of the local operators and Compel wants to be absolutely certain that it is delivering best value for money for its customers. At present, where companies want overseas work done, it locates the best local partner.

Stratagems

The key to the company's success is that it is extremely well-focused on the markets and customers it wishes to serve. As a result, it now occupies a pre-eminent position in what is a fast growing niche of the IT market. In concentrating on the client/server market and networked PC and work-station market, Compel has established itself in a sector which is expected to grow strongly (both in absolute terms and as a proportion of the total UK IT market) during the next few years. As the technological capacities of servers, workstations and networks increase, they will be used in more complex and wide-ranging applications, often replacing mini-computers and mainframes. There will also be a greater demand for open systems in which client/servers and networked PCs and workstations will play a major role.

Compel is committed to providing a quality service for all its customers. It is extremely customer-focused and it works in close partnership with them to ensure that their requirements are met in full. More than ten per cent of staff work permanently on customer sites. Compel was the first systems integrator in the UK to achieve quality standard BS5750 and is rigorous in measuring its performance against agreed targets. It has also set out to engender a quality culture inside the organisation, reinforced by a spread of ongoing pro-grammes and initiatives.

Size and shape

Employees: 525   Locations: 10
Geographical income split: UK 100%

Price is not the sole issue for many of Compel's clients. Instead these blue chip businesses demand systems which are both flexible and responsive to change. Increasingly they also want their IT provider to come up with solutions to their computer problems. Compel's long standing expertise gives the company significant competitive advantage in these core areas for the business. Compel also places considerable importance on the calibre of its new recruits. It invests heavily in training and sets out to ensure that all of its employees understand where they fit into the organisation. As a result of its efforts to bind employees into the daily running of the enterprise, Compel enjoys one of the most highly qualified, most loyal and best regarded workforces in the industry.

To foster the key client relationships which are at the core of the business's success, Compel has developed a professionally managed and structured sales approach. All customers are assigned an account manager, responsible for developing the depth and breadth of each relationship. Contact is then built up at director, operational, adminstrative, technical and financial levels. Furthermore, Compel's sales staff are incentivised and their performance is monitored by measures based on gross profit rather than turnover. Compel does not believe in market share for its own sake, merely as an expression of the quality and performance of the business.

It has set itself the target of becoming the best computer services company in the UK – the one that clients and prospective clients turn to automatically. It believes that its expertise, commitment to quality services and its capacity to understand its customers intimately will be key factors in winning this accolade.

Outlook

Future prospects

- continued growth of IT market;
- expansion of Compel's coverage;
- larger client base;
- more work for existing clients.

Rather astutely, Compel has established itself as market leader in a sector of the IT industry which is forecast to grow rapidly in the next century. The company can claim with some force that it commands significant competitive advantage in critical mass, reputation for quality, integrity, national coverage and long-term track record of delivering results for clients. The expansion of the client/service and networked PC markets can only benefit a business which is so well-entrenched with its clients and so expert in these disciplines. Compel is indeed in the right place at the right time to claim a major share of the earnings from these markets in the next decade.

Address:

Millenium Place, 2 Swiftfields, Welwyn Garden City, Herts AL7 1HP. Tel: 01707 288000. Fax: 01707 288001

The Corporate Services Group plc

London

Turnover				
1993	1994	1995	1996	1997
£42M	£83M	£133M	£255M	£300Me

Summary: The Corporate Services Group, formed as recently as 1987, is, by far, the UK's largest dedicated supplier of contract labour. It has thousands of people on assignment with a range of businesses – many of them blue chips – at any one time. The company supplies every type of skilled personnel from scientists and doctors to lower skilled labour. The business has grown both through astute acquisition and outstanding organic performance. As yet contract labour accounts for a relatively small percentage of the workforce but, as a proportion, it will rise rapidly and Corporate Services Group is poised to exploit the opportunities created by this trend.

The Business

Contract labour, as a percentage of the UK workforce, is tiny, perhaps around two per cent. Yet in France this highly cost effective and efficient way of staffing businesses accounts for as much as 20 per cent of all employees. The same story can be told of Germany (18 per cent) and the USA (15 per cent). Corporate Services Group, which has concentrated on this market since 1990, is the UK sector leader and strongest advocate of the benefits of contract labour. Founding chairman Jeffrey Fowler argues that the demand for contract labour will grow rapidly as companies recognise that it offers them greater employment flexibility and substantial cost savings.

He explains that the advantages of contract labour are widespread. 'There are some businesses which it does not suit but those that it does, benefit handsomely,' he says. Typical examples are those companies which encounter seasonal variation in demand for their products. In some food sectors, for

151

example, demand peaks before Easter and again before Christmas. Corporate Services Group through one of its divisions will guarantee to supply skilled labour for, say, three months up to Christmas and three months up to Easter. The employer then has no worries about finding the necessary numbers of capable people to reach targets. The CSG takes care of the payroll details while the employer pays a fee to CSG. 'We can supply as little or as much of the people requirement as necessary. Some clients source all their workers from us. Others have only a handful.' Fowler adds that government agencies and scientific establishments with limited budgets use CSG regularly. 'A company may need a group of research chemists for a fixed term – a three-year research contract, for example. We will find the most appropriate people with precisely the right scientific background.'

CSG operates across the industrial landscape. It sources doctors worldwide and places them in hospitals. In the UK, through its network of 210 locations, CSG is active in catering, healthcare, telecommunications, manufacturing, railways, aeronautics, distribution and retail. The company says that 60 per cent of its income comes from the industrial sector, 20 per cent from technical, 15 per cent from healthcare and five per cent from commercial. The recent acquisition of the Blue Arrow business will shift these figures and introduce catering as key element.

Distinctive features

- market leader in contract labour;
- top two in almost every sector;
- high margin, strong profits;
- accelerating demand.

Blue Arrow is the latest and most important in a series of purchases made by CSG to strengthen its base in contract labour, provide access to a wider range of core clients and talented personnel. It also allowed CSG to enter two new disciplines – white collar staff and catering. Broker Henderson Crosthwaite commented 'The rationale of the deal lies not in the economies of scale but opportunities to convert a significiant proportion of Blue Arrow's existing business into contract labour. It is higher margin, higher growth and less susceptible to an economic downturn than temporary labour which currently makes up more than 95 per cent of Blue Arrow's non-permanent placings. After the acquisition, contract labour will fall from 50 per cent to 30 per cent of group sales. We estimate that this will return to 60 per cent within three years.

'The logic of acquiring Blue Arrow was: the quality of its customer base, which includes more than 30 per cent of the FTSE 250; minimal client overlap with CSG; BA operates in sectors with a growing demand for contract labour; and Blue Arrow will strengthen the group's national coverage in its largest sectors – industrial and commercial, CSG will be market leader in the catering sector.'

Stratagems

The market opportunity for CSG is highly promising. The low level of contract labour in the UK employment sector, as compared to other European majors, points to the marked likelihood that it will increase substantially. Commercial logic suggests that it might rise to as much as six to eight per cent in the next five years. As the chief British protagonist for contract labour – and its most articulate advocate – Corporate Services Group can justifiably expect to be the most notable beneficiary from such growth. The integration of Blue Arrow will give the group a major platform from which to encourage the expansion in the market. The corporate appetite for contract labour is almost certain to expand, which means that CSG must advance. One of its key targets is to convert many of Blue Arrow's blue chip clients to the concept. Also its leadership position in catering – and the cost savings which can be made there from clients adopting a contract rather than temporary labour policy – should make a key contribution to CSG growth.

Size and shape

Employees: 2000 (50,000 on assignment) Locations: 210
Geographical income split: UK 90% RoW 10%

Corporate Services Group has gained a strong reputation for making sensible acquisitions and turning them to great advantage. Some brokers argue that CSG's success has largely been acquisition-driven. This is only partly the case and the business has achieved powerful organic growth alongside the derived benefit from its purchases. Fowler says that in 1994 turnover growth, exclusive of acqusitions, achieved 28 per cent. In 1995, again without the benefit of businesses brought into the group, sales grew organically by 35 per cent.

He puts this down to effective management of the group at the centre, and the motivation of high quality personnel in its divisions. The quality of customer service is a central plank of the strategy. 'Our objective is to achieve close working partnerships with our clients to discover their employment needs and to deliver the most appropriate solutions to meet their demand.'

The financial management of the group is one of the best analysed for this project. It is comparable to many of the leading blue chip companies which CSG aims to serve. But Fowler is adamant that its success does not derive from emulation of industrial majors. 'We must never forget that we are a small and growing business. If we do we are lost,' he remarks. He aims to retain the flexibility, flair, tight cost control and innovation of the best of the UK's cadre of growth companies.

Outlook

Future prospects

- dominant position in contract labour;
- strong organic growth in key divisions;
- enhanced client base.

CSG has moved deftly and strategically to capture the best businesses in its sector. Its stability has been enhanced by the growing proportion of its fixed contract work with leading UK industrials. Its healthcare, catering, training and industrial divisions, especially, will enjoy the strongest improvements. CSG's skill in managing its acquisitions and enhancing organic growth are both expected to contribute strongly to its projected improvement in its overall performance.

Address:

Glaston Park, Spring Lane, Glaston, Leicestershire LE15 9BX. Tel: 01572 822931. Fax: 01572 823616. Internet: http://www.corpserv.co.uk

Cortecs International

Isleworth, Middlesex

Turnover			
1993	1994	1995	1996
£5M	£5M	7.5M	£10M

Summary: Cortecs International is among the world's most advanced biopharmaceuticals companies, and has developed two highly innovative enabling technologies – oral drug delivery systems and rapid point of care diagnostics. It is now applying these technologies to a range of disease states; in particular, osteoporosis, *H. pylori* infection and diabetes. The company combines relatively low technical and clinical risks with significant market potential and has also entered into a number of important collaborations covering R&D syndication, co-development and distribution agreements.

The Business

Cortecs was created in 1986 following the takeover of a UK contract research organisation by an Australian healthcare investment company. Having divested its clinical research business, the company then acquired rights to a range of technologies and is now developing a portfolio of products principally including rapid point-of-care diagnostics and orally delivered drugs.

In the short-term, Cortecs' principal product will be Helisal, its *H. pylori* diagnostic test. *H. pylori*, a bacterium which lives in the stomach, is thought to be one of the most common human pathogens and has been linked to ulcers and gastric cancer. The Helisal test unit allows a GP to test for the bacterium in five minutes; previously this would have involved laboratory tests and complex hospital procedures. The company has also entered into a R&D syndicate to develop an oral therapeutic vaccine against the *H. pylori* infection.

Of greater medium-term significance is Cortecs' work on the diagnosis and treatment of osteoporosis (a condition of reduced bone density that leads to

155

reduced bone strength). Calcitonin is currently recognised as the most effective treatment for osteoporosis since it has minimal side effects, and Cortecs is developing an oral formulation of this drug. Phase II results were announced earlier this year and were extremely positive, showing a 50 per cent reduction in the rate of bone breakdown. If further trials are successful, the company envisages submitting a product licence application to the European Medicines Evaluation Agency by the end of the year. Cortecs has also produced a working prototype of a rapid blood test for osteoporosis, using the unique Cross-Laps technology of the Danish company Osteometer. Again, the ability to carry out a test in a doctor's office in only five minutes is a significant advancement over current methods of diagnosis.

The third leg of Cortecs' disease management strategy is diabetes. The most common treatment for the disease is insulin, which until recently could only be reliably delivered by injection. Cortecs has been working for a number of years to develop an oral formulation of insulin with animal studies being performed and preliminary human studies planned for 1996. In collaboration with Exocell, the company will also be launching a prototype of a diagnostic test later this year.

Distinctive features

- world leading drug delivery technology;
- considerable market potential;
- strong academic research base;
- low technical and clinical risk.

Longer-term, the company's oral drug delivery technology will be applied to other disease states. Its cystic fibrosis, chronic bronchitis and flu vaccines are now in clinical trials. Other areas of research include the HALO system which is being used to create an oral testosterone form for male hormone replacement.

Unusually for a biotech company, Cortecs also sells a range of prescription drugs and a number of OTC sports health products. While the company acknowledges that this is not a core competence, it gives Cortecs important experience in sales and distribution, as well as providing cashflow to the group in its early stages of development.

Stratagems

Cortecs' strategy has been to focus on two core technologies – oral drug delivery systems and rapid point of care diagnostics – in which it has a market-leading position and which offer significant patient benefit. Theoretically, it can then apply these technologies to a range of disease states, although to date it has focused largely on three – osteoporosis, *H. pylori* and diabetes.

The rapid point-of-care diagnostics market is forecast to grow substantially in the near future. There is a growing demand for inexpensive and effective tests for diseases and infections which can be performed rapidly by the physician or even the patient. The alternative of taking samples and sending them to laboratories is both time-consuming and expensive. Similarly, oral drugs offer greater convenience and safety for the patient, while Cortecs' new technology allows consistent and accurate drug levels to be delivered.

Size and shape

Employees: 230   Locations: 6
Geographical income split: Europe 85%, Australia 15%

Each of the three disease states which Cortecs has selected is characterised by enormous market potential. *H. pylori* has recently been classified as a Grade 1 carcinogen by the WHO's international agency for cancer research and it is estimated that 50 per cent of the population of industrialised countries over the age of 50 and up to 100 per cent of the population in less developed countries are infected. Osteoporosis is currently a disease that is both poorly treated and diagnosed. By 2000, healthcare costs relating to the disease will reach $30bn. Finally, diabetes is a serious and rising global epidemic, being the third leading cause of death by disease in the USA. The WHO has estimated that, in 1993, more than 100 million people worldwide were suffering from the disease.

Future prospects

- enormous market potential for its products;
- further blue chip alliances in the near future;
- early and strong financial returns.

The company has a pragmatic attitude to fundamental research and places teams within academic institutions where they are in touch with the latest science trends and able to maximise creativity. This gives Cortecs access to additional technologies and expertise, while saving on overhead costs. It is working with five leading universities in the UK, Singapore and Australia. It also has a series of collaborations with pharma majors for drug and diagnostic distribution. In late 1995, it signed an exclusive 15 year deal with Towa Pharmaceutical to distribute oral calcitronin in Japan. This grants significant milestone payments to Cortecs, underwriting its research costs. Also through an exclusive distribution arrangement, Boehringer Mannheim will market Helisal throughout Europe. Cortecs is also using the European sales force of Astra to educate physicians regarding *H. pylori*.

Finally, Cortecs is acknowledged to have an experienced senior management team. Both founders remain; Glen Travers, its chairman, has a background in investment banking and is responsible for the firm's investments in the pharmaceutical industry, while Dr Michael Flynn (president) oversees its research activities. They are supported by a small team with strong technical and financial skills.

Outlook

The outlook for Cortecs is extremely promising. It has developed two technologies, both of which are set to grow significantly in popularity and importance, and is focusing on three disease states which offer enormous commercial potential. Its range of drug developments make the company low-risk in technical and commercial terms, while many of research costs are underwritten by third parties. Following a recent share placing, the company now has sufficient cash to fund its long-term aspirations and ultimately the group's technology will be applied to a new range of disease states.

Address:

The Old Blue School, Lower Square, Isleworth, Middlesex. Tel: 0181 568 7071. Fax: 0181 569 7592

Cranswick plc

Driffield, Yorkshire

Turnover				
1992	1993	1994	1995	1996
£93M	£109M	£106M	£115M	£141M

Summary: Cranswick began life as a modest local joint venture in the mid-70s, when local farmers in the Driffield region of the East Riding of Yorkshire decided, with bank help, to launch their own animal feed manufacturing business. From then expansion was measured and logical into grain trading, pigs, pork products, pet foods and finally tropical fish. The company is now a major player in each of these markets, with pretax profits rising in five years, from £1.3M in 1991 to £3.1M in 1996. The company provides a textbook example of an ideal combination of organic and acquisitive expansion, which, even when undertaken on a cautious scale, can result in rich, sustained growth.

The Business

There is a local tradition of sturdy independence in the quiet, rolling wolds of East Yorkshire, especially among the agricultural community. This is some of the best farming country in the north, where values of local sufficiency, and determination still predominate. So a long-considered decision of pig farmers in Driffield, in the mid-1970s, to establish their own feed plant seemed a logical move. Given the feisty independence of the region, the founders regarded their initiative as a purely East Riding concern. That commitment launched a company which now sells more than £100 million worth of products. There were 23 original investors in the mill, who along with local banks, provided the finance, so it was not a co-operative in the accepted sense of the word. It was more a private company manufacturing pig feed from local cereals to meet the specific requirements of those 23 farmers. But its modern equipment, and ready local access to the high quality cereals, soon saw it selling pig feed to other farmers in East Yorkshire.

The logical progression of Cranswick is deeply in keeping with the temperament of the founders: a steady and sustained rise in sales and profits built on a firm foundation. There was a virtuous product circle obvious even at the outset; a local farmer with 300 acres of cereals probably had a sizeable pig business too. Cranswick, with its capacity to do business on a more advantageous basis for them in cereals and feed, could also sell the pigs for the farmers. It could and it did – and throughout Britain. And as the mill itself was successful, a greater volume and variety of grains were being offered. So Cranswick almost naturally expanded into the grain trading business, serving such customers as flour millers.

To smooth out the supply/demand cycle for pigs, it seemed natural to rear them, thus hedging against the volatility of the pig demand cycle. By 1985, the company had 58 shareholders, and was highly profitable. Given this success, an unofficial market was developing in its shares; going public provided both a formal market, and the financial resources needed to expand the original processing mill.

Cranswick was, and still is, a relatively cautious company. It took another three years before it made another related advance – into food manufacturing. The pig meat market was a logical move to add value to existing raw materials which were volatile – in recent years, pig prices have swung between 80p per kilo and 180p per kilo. Cranswick's management believed it could successfully smooth out another cycle. New legislation on food safety offered an opportunity for Cranswick to supply food supported by all the assurances a retailer could require, given that the business controlled virtually every part of the chain, from processing grain to packaging the pork – in an acquired butchery plant in Hull.

Distinctive features

- strong identification with its regional markets;
- control over raw materials;
- accelerating demand – both in the UK and overseas;
- logical sequence of product development and introduction.

The most recent move was into another added value sector, pet foods, which would add value to materials being handled as part of the grain marketing business. Bird food was an obvious possibility after a customer sought a supply for its own business. In 1993 that customer was soon partially, then wholly, acquired by Cranswick, which proceeded to expand into other pet food areas where it had a knowledge of the raw materials needed. The pet food activities were developed further in 1995 and 1996 with the acquisition of a second bird food business and the purchase of an acquatics company involved in the supply of tropical fish, fish food and related products. But the company steered carefully clear of the cat and dog food trench warfare, with its multi-million pounds marketing offensives. Today, Cranswick is an example of a small local business made good, a company which has, after patient forethought, successfully expanded; one which prefers to fully digest each new venture before continuing. In 1996– 97 turnover was up 23 per cent with pretax profits rising to £3.1 million. Exports are growing and are comprised of both pig feed and acquatic products.

Stratagems

The business has, from the start, used its specialist expertise and, always, in-company resources to dictate its own expansion. This has allowed Cranswick to minimise risk and maximise opportunities, an organisational philosophy that also brings substantial trading between the various arms of the business. So the twenty year progression from a modest joint venture designed to produce better pig feed for local farmers to a multi-role agribusiness of the late 1990s, has always been logical and enabled the company to buffer itself against several notoriously volatile market areas. In less than ten years, Cranswick, bolstered by a close and growing relationship with J. Sainsbury, has won a place on the strength of the quality of its products as one of Britain's top five pork product manufacturers. All the pigs it takes in come from approved farms, and can thus be fully documented; given recent scares in the food industry, such meticulous quality control will become of even greater importance in coming years. The company buys in more than 1,000,000 pigs a year and its own specialist abattoir in Hull can process more than 500,000 pigs a year. Chief executive Martin Davey points to parallel planning and experience before the company's latest venture, into the pet food market.

Size and shape

Employees: 500 Locations: 9
Geographical income split: UK 90%, RoW 10%

Future prospects

- increased links with UK supermarket chains;
- growing spread of interlinked businesses;
- attractive products for mainland European markets.

'The pet sector will, according to most forecasts, increase at a rate greater than that achieved by the UK economy as a whole. This, then, can only happen by a greater proportion of disposable income being spent on pets. We have also seen changes in the retail format, such as larger retailers and cash and carry wholesalers. We also sense a subtle change under way, away from those pets requiring greater care and attention. Birds and fish require less attention; 3.5M households keep fish and 1.6M keep birds, apart from people who feed wild birds.' The most recent acquisition was a tropical marine fish supplier, yet Davey still sees a direct and usable link with the original grain processing business that launched Cranswick as a company.

Cranswick has significant plans for expansion within each of its three main product groups: food processing, agri-business and pet foods. It again plans to combine organic growth with appropriate acquisitions. But the key criteria will be the acquisition of businesses – not necessarily large businesses – which are: successful, have good management teams and can be developed further. In this way, the company fosters both the business and the management team.

Outlook

After each quantum move comes a period of consolidation and integration before new advances are made at Cranswick. Few of those shrewd farmers, seeking a better deal on their pig feed more than twenty years ago, could have foreseen the extent of Cranswick's success and growth. Or did they ? A large proportion of the shares in the company issued at the launch of the business are still in the hands of the original families. Given the nature of market change, with more consumers turning to white meats such as pork and chicken, Cranswick will continue to benefit.

Address:

Cranswick, Driffield, Yorkshire YO25 9PF. Tel: 01377 270649. Fax: 01377 270994

Critchley Group plc

Cirencester, Gloucestershire

Turnover				
1992	1993	1994	1995	1996
£19M	£24M	£29M	£36M	£43M

Summary: Critchley Group is a network of autonomous companies supplying products to the electronic and electrical industries. It is world leader in cable identification, where demand has grown due to increasing complexity of systems. Critchley is also a major supplier to the growing telecommunications industry with a series of wound magnetic components. Some 56 per cent of sales are derived in global markets, achieved through quality of its output and a series of strategic acquisitions. It is a key policy objective to open new manufacturing facilities in new markets overseas.

The Business

The Critchley Group has certainly come a long way since its inception as a Quaker company in 1883. Originally, it was a business making metal needles and pins for the textile industry which moved into production in plastics after the Second World War. In 1950 it diversified into producing small cable accessories. This development was initially a tiny aspect of the company's activities but its decision engineered a key turning point in the growth of the enterprise. Today it is one of the world's leaders in cable accessory products. It makes thousands of tags, labels and guides to identify and manage industrial cables. 'Our products could be characterised as haberdashery for cables,' says group finance director Christopher Humphrey.

Another major development in the progress of the company was a management buy-out (MBO) in 1984 which valued the business at £4.5 million. Critchley grew mainly by organic techniques but also by acquisition prior to its London flotation in 1992 – at which stage it was worth £25 million. An open offer in 1994 brought in £10 million to buy a German company and

163

in mid-year 1996 a rights issue added a further £11.4 million net. In May 1996 Critchley's market capitalisation had reached £130 million.

There are two main areas of business: 70 per cent of which is cable accessories and the other 30 per cent is electronic component transformers that service the telecommunications industry. 'There is far more complexity in the electrical industry today. There are many more computers, sensors and controllers in industrial processes. Inevitably this means more wires. It is no longer a case of colour coding these wires – it is too difficult for that – engineers need techniques for identifying cables so that they can be terminated, fitted and maintained correctly. So we are selling into a wide range of industries – industrial control, process and information. Critchley also sells to the utilities – water, oil and gas, and to the rail, aerospace and defence sectors. Each of our customers in these markets exhibits similar characteristics: complexity of wiring but also a heavy use of sub-contractors unfamiliar with the idiosyncrasies of client systems.' In addition, many companies operate demanding quality standards which require that wiring should be efficiently and safely maintained.

Critchley has been steadily growing its earnings during the last half decade. Humphrey says that it has experienced a compound growth of around 20 per cent a year. Three quarters of this is organic, supplemented by acquisitions to add critical mass in territories and products. Customers are steady and stable. They are not fast moving consumer goods companies but industrial concerns which are long-term reliable businesses in the electrical sector. They are cautious and safety-conscious. Products have a lifespan of more than 20 years with significant amounts of repeat business supplied to specific customer requirements.

Distinctive features

- world leader in cable identification;
- major slice of international markets;
- heavy emphasis on reliable client base and continuing sales;
- excellence in a unique technology.

At the time of the MBO around 90 per cent of sales were UK-based; now more than half of the group's turnover is derived outside the UK. In 1984 Critchley started its overseas expansion with the purchase of a distributor in Australia but the real movement came in the late 1980s with the development of a product called heat shrinkage identification (HSI). HSI allows the client company to print out all its wiring configurations on separate, distinctive labels which are then fixed around the appropriate cable. This technology became the springboard for Critchley's development outside the UK. There are similar products to the HSI technology but none is capable of transferring the data to the label in the same way. Critchley opened green-field sales sites in the USA and France and entered these markets through some of the top aerospace and defence companies in those markets. The spread of offices in the USA accelerated as demand quickened. 'We have grown our American business by about 20 per cent a year over the last five years.'

Stratagems

Strategy at Critchley is governed by three principles: strongly managed autonomous companies, acquisition of businesses with complementary products, and the development of overseas markets. Central controls are strategic – agreement of targets, appointment of senior management, promotion of potential synergies and the establishment of reporting structures.

Size and shape

Employees: 633   Locations: 17
Geo. income split: UK 44%, mainland Europe 29%, North America 16%, RoW 11%

The acquisitional path has been followed to expand geographical and product range. The purchase of the German business, Idento, is a typical example. Critchley had monitored this company for eight years and made three approaches before the acquisition was agreed. Humphrey says that Idento was a third to a quarter of the size of the UK business but the German market is four to five times larger than the British. It has a complementary list of products to Critchley but had no equivalent of the HSI system. Therefore the market potential for Idento, already a highly profitable business with clients such as ABB, Siemens and Deutsche Telekom, is massive. The group has provided tighter control and sharper appreciation of strategic possibilities.

Future prospects

- powerful and sustained growth in all of its core markets;
- further acquisitions to add critical territorial and product mass;
- extension of HSI technology to new markets;
- high emphasis on development of external opportunities.

New businesses are monitored on a daily basis, which has become easier with the development of information technologies. Humphrey says the daily focus is relaxed to weekly reporting for the more established and mature subsidiaries. All the businesses provide detailed monthly accounts. 'The market is highly fragmented with lots of family-owned operations and divisions of much larger enterprises. Few can match our focused knowledge and experience of this market. If a client is serious about solving its cable identification problems then it will come to us. We are talking to a number of competitors as potential purchases. This is a very long process and there is no guarantee of success.' Some of the best opportunities lie with the family-owned companies where there is no obvious succession management. Further growth will come from expanding the reach of existing subsidiaries. The group encourages its subsidiaries to export beyond its immediate regional focus. The Hong Kong businesses will eventually sell into China and even the US labelling company sends 50 per cent of its sales overseas.

Outlook

Critchley Group intends to continue its distinctive approach to markets where it is already a significant international player. It forecasts a range of opportunities in new territories, with fresh clients and with additions to the product range. The business is on the edge of extensive expansion.

Address:

Monmouth House, 26–28 Thomas Street, Cirencester, Gloucestershire GL7 2BD. Tel: 01285 641 187. Fax: 01285 641 213

Dagenham Motors Group plc

Dagenham, Essex

Turnover				
1992	1993	1994	1995	1996
£156M	£187M	£228M	£268M	£291.9M

Summary: Dagenham Motors is one of the largest and best-known Ford dealers in the UK. Since its flotation in 1988, the company has expanded considerably and it now operates 15 main dealerships in the M25 area. It has remained consistently profitable in the face of difficult trading conditions by adopting a strategy of customer focus and strong financial control. Ford's relaxation of its policy on adjacent dealerships should enable Dagenham Motors to establish larger, more profitable outlets in future, and the company is also examining ways of growing its higher-margin used car business.

The Business

Dagenham Motors was founded in 1981 by its current managing director, David Philip, in what was the first management buy-out of a motor dealership. The company was floated seven years later and a £10M rights issue in 1994 secured for the company access to the long-term finance necessary for it to expand successfully. Dagenham Motors deals in both new and used cars, as well as providing a range of ancillary services such as vehicle servicing and accident repair, and currently operates 16 main dealerships located around the M25.

In terms of turnover and profitability, the company's single most important activity is the sale of new cars. In 1995, sales increased by 19 per cent to reach a record 11,248 units – a performance which is all the more impressive when compared to a mere 1.8 per cent increase in the UK market nationally. Much of this growth came from Dagenham Motors' retail customer base and was generated by a strong line-up of new Ford products. In particular, the

167

Galaxy, which was launched in June, soon advanced to the number one position in its class and by the end of the year was outselling its nearest rival by a factor of three to one. The new Fiesta, launched five months later, has also proved extremely popular. Margins, however, while increasing slightly in 1995, continue to remain tight in what is a highly competitive market-place.

The company's second largest activity is the sale of used cars. Dagenham's used car sales, which includes non-Ford makes, rose by 10 per cent (to 8448 units) in 1995, again against a background of difficult trading conditions caused by a nation-wide surplus of used cars. Nonetheless, the company believes there is tremendous future potential in its used car business and is actively seeking additional retailing sites.

Distinctive features

- strong relationship with Ford;
- experienced and motivated management team;
- reputation for quality service;
- expanding range of dealerships.

Dagenham Motors is also heavily involved in the commercial vehicle sector. Its new commercial vehicle sales of Ford and Iveco Ford products have shown substantial growth in recent years, with increases particularly marked at the light (i.e. below 3.5 tonnes) and heavy duty (i.e. above 17 tonnes) ends of the market. The company has enjoyed similar success in the used commercial vehicle market, and the company intends to expand this activity further in the near future.

In addition to its retail functions, Dagenham Motors has moved into the provision of ancillary services. For example, it has a highly professional finance and insurance sales operation, and this is likely to become an increasingly important source of revenue. It also undertakes extensive vehicle servicing activities, and in this context has successfully targeted the owners of older vehicles.

In 1995, the company opened an accident repair factory at its Enfield site. In contrast to its smaller, Ford-oriented repair bodyshops, the Enfield factory caters for all makes and is already winning significant levels of business. The performance of the firm's parts operation has also improved as a result of introducing greater efficiencies in distribution and increasing margins. Finally, Dagenham Motors' Browning Electric subsidiary provides a range of electrical and mechanical motors repairs.

Stratagems

Dagenham Motors operates in a highly competitive market which has historically been characterised by low operating margins. The company has chosen to differentiate itself, and counter the traditional antipathy felt by many towards the motor trade, by exploiting its relationship with Ford and providing a high level of customer service.

Ford continues to dominate the new car sales tables. It has a market leadership of six per cent ahead of its nearest rival and, for the second year in succession, all top three places in the national vehicle registration table were held by the Escort, Fiesta and Mondeo. The manufacturer's strong line-up is completed by the Probe, Maverick and Scorpio models, as well as the highly successful Galaxy.

Size and shape

Employees: 1300   Locations: 16
Geographical income split: UK 100%

Dagenham Motors' Woking dealership has emerged as the top-selling dealer of this new model. The strength of Dagenham Motors' relationship with Ford should be more apparent as Ford relaxes its policy on adjacent dealerships. In the past, Ford has refused to allow the same company to run dealerships in adjacent territories. In order to build larger, more profitable dealerships, this policy has now been relaxed. Dagenham Motors is expected to be one of the principal beneficiaries of this change, allowing the company access to a number of locations in the M25 area from which it was previously excluded. This will enhance the company's already aggressive dealership expansion programme. Dagenham Motors has acquired four dealerships – Strood, Woking, Weybridge and Tottenham – in the last 18 months and will be opening another, in Kingston, later this year. It is the company's long-term intention to build a global ring of dealerships around the M25 serving the whole of London. Until this is achieved, and there are presently still a number of gaps in the network, it will not expand outside the south-east.

Future prospects

- wider economies of scale;
- better used car market profitability;
- greater value-added services.

169

The company has adopted a strategy of focusing on the more profitable retail end of the market. Accordingly, it believes that placing great emphasis on customer service can give it a significant competitive advantage. This approach is especially true in today's competitive environment. Attention to the customer is manifested in all aspects of the company's operations. For example, in its vehicle servicing activities, its *Motor-Tech Direct* reception process enables service customers to enjoy personal attention coupled with professional care. The company has also launched a Lifetime Care Service Plan. Dagenham Motors is one of the motor dealerships to have received an ISO 9000 accreditation. The business is tightly controlled by strong central management. Some of its senior management have been with the firm since its inception and are tied into it through share options.

Outlook

Over the last ten years, Dagenham Motors has demonstrated that, even in an adverse trading environment, it can consistently operate profitably. To date it has pursued an extremely successful acquisition policy, and this is expected to continue, especially given Ford's change in stance. Furthermore, as the company grows, it is able to exploit a wider range of economies of scale in administration, purchasing and distribution. Its strategy of customer care, an increasing focus on the more profitable used car market and a greater provision of added-value services all point to a future of steady and sustained growth for the company.

Address:

Ford House, New Road, Dagenham, Essex RM9 6EX. Tel: 0181 592 6655. Fax: 0181 526 3110

Datrontech Group plc

COMPUTER PRODUCTS DISTRIBUTION

Aldershot, Hants

Turnover				
1992	1993	1994	1995	1996
£25M	£46M	£86M	£130M	207M

Summary: Datrontech distributes personal memory products to trade customers. It has grown from a one man operation to a £130 million turnover on the back of a sustained boom in demand and a once-in-a-decade deal with an American supplier. The cash generated by this deal and its 1995 flotation is funding expansion into mainland Europe and expansion of the product range upwards into higher margin computer products and services. Pretax profits have risen steeply from £1.7 million in 1991 to £8.1 million in 1996. Sales in 1996 were £207 million, producing a PBT of £9.5 million. The business has majored on quality systems and JIT methodology to enhance customer service.

The Business

Business is a combination of inspiration, hard work and luck. Some entrepreneurs say that they make their own luck but whatever factor was uppermost in 1989 when Datrontech encountered the US supplier Kingston has proved an unmitigated success for both companies. Datrontech was a small but fast growing distributor which wanted to increase its product range. Kingston was a $40 million provider of memory upgrades for personal computers (PCs). Datrontech's managing director Steve King and marketing director Ian Boyle became agents for Kingston in the UK with exclusive rights to the product range and price protection. It was the catalyst which would lift Datrontech into a major player in its sector, not least because the timing was so opportune. Graphical user interfaces were added to PC software and needed additional memory. The 1980s recession meant people kept their

171

PCs longer and upgraded rather than replaced them. Kingston became a $1 billion company and Datrontech grew its revenues sixteenfold.

The arrangement brought a degree of professionalism into what was decidedly a niche market and transformed its dynamics into the mainstream, with Datrontech becoming Kingston's largest international distributor. The Kingston deal had prompted Datrontech to re-examine its relationship with its customers and focus on how it could be distinctive. The company's management concluded that resellers needed to satisfy their customers and ensure that its performance outstripped its competition.

Datrontech grew fast and floated in 1995 with a valuation of £43.7 million. The founders already had their eyes on product and geographic expansion and started buying companies in February 1995 with Partronics, a Kingston distributor in Belgium. After flotation two more smallish distributors were bought, one in Switzerland, another in Germany. This series of acquisitions was paralleled at home. Datrontech bought a portable computer peripherals company, a storage distributor, and another components distributor in the UK plus a small Eastern European distributor. This brought the total to eight acquisitions since the float. It recently moved into the service sector and acquired two companies in this market.

In the British business, King and Boyle sharpened the effectiveness of the management controls in the company. The group has recently appointed Mark Mulford as MD. Datrontech applied for BS 5750 accreditation and succeeded. It adopted just-in-time methodology across the operation and slashed cash collection times from the industry average of 60 days to 48 days. Much of the improvement in performance came from polishing customer service and installing effective financial and quality control procedures. Datrontech did the simple wholesale things very well with a qualified enthusiastic team of customer-facing people supported by a very lean logistics machine and efficient money management. King ensures that his people are well-motivated, passionate and knowledgeable about the business and enjoy their work. Mulford intends to sharpen up the infrastructure of the business.

Distinctive features

- multilevel marketing campaigns;
- less than 0.01% returns;
- strong quality orientation;
- excellent cash collection.

The first year's results after flotation showed its acquisitions performing well.

Datrontech's capacity to manage and maximise returns from its purchases were endorsed. But in April 1996 it faced a problem which could have posed a serious threat to the domestic business. Kingston decided to open up a direct operation in the UK and take away Datrontech's UK exclusivity. After successful negotiations Kingston got Datrontech staff to set up its UK operation plus Datrontech's seven largest UK customers – about £10 million of business annually. In return Datrontech got the right to sell Kingston products anywhere in Europe and retained some measure of price protection. This is very valuable as memory prices can drop deeply and suddenly with catastrophic effects on profitability.

The impact of these changes to the group promised strong results in 1996 and brokers appear to agree. To build on its existing strengths, it has also opened up a server division selling higher margin goods and is executing a well developed strategy aimed at growing the business.

Stratagems

Steven King has developed a three point strategic plan for the immediate progression of the company. He sees growth coming from a wider and higher margin product range, and expanded geographic coverage in mainland Europe and the USA. Growth will also come, if the opportunity arises, through fresh acquisitions of complementary and high margin product distributors.

Size and shape

Employees: 540   Locations: 15
Geographical income split: UK 80%, mainland Europe 10%, US 3%, RoW 7%

The product range will broaden to include networking and client/server products. These are higher margin and enable Datrontech to offer a more complete product range to its customers.

Datrontech is determined that its mainland European presence will be expanded. This is a two phased plan. Initially the entrepreneurial spirit of the memory-focused subsidiaries will be fostered and, 'tied around a good logistics machine'. Subsequently a wider product range in the UK will be, 'taken into mainland Europe using these existing bases without losing focus on the memory business', says King. He does not foresee problems in taking the Datrontech culture across the channel, 'It is all about small sales, and success through focus, and understanding the customer's needs and delivering them'. This is not unique to the UK.

A third strategic objective with a three-year timescale is to expand the US business and grow into the far east, where a Hong Kong office was opened in 1996. All these strategies depend upon Datrontech keeping its people entrepreneurial and focused on the customer, continuing to centralise logistics and enjoy cost savings, and building a good management information system.

Future prospects

- strong growth in mainland Europe;
- move into services;
- improvements in returns;
- enhancement of quality systems.

King has got Datrontech motoring effectively. He has a good base to build on in mainland Europe with a range of successful distribution products in the UK ready to roll out across Europe. Demand for computer peripherals remains high and Datrontech has a proven ability to attract and satisfy trade customers. If the company can translate its UK success into mainland Europe then further success is there for the taking.

Outlook

Datrontech's expansion plans with increased presence in mainland Europe and a move to distribute higher-margin products and services should increase revenues. The demand for personal computer, workstation and server computer products remains high and Datrontech should be able to grow much faster than the market. The returns on its expansion programme look promising. In June 1996 Datrontech added to its range by buying Connectivity Group for £6.4 million. This gives the business a foothold in the growing networks market. In less than a decade the company will have grown from £300,000 to £300 million. The return in this sector is traditionally not high in relation to turnover but observers confidently expect Datrontech to report above average pretax profits.

Address:

42–44 Birchett Road, Aldershot, Hants GU11 1LU. Tel: 01252 303 3333. Fax: 01252 303444

DBS Management plc

FINANCIAL SERVICES

Huddersfield, West Yorkshire

Turnover				
1992	1993	1994	1995	1996
£26M	£38M	£51M	£56M	£77M

Summary: The core business of the DBS Group is a network of more than 2600 independent financial advisers (IFAs) throughout the UK, to whom it provides comprehensive support, advisory and training facilities. It also places all business from them with product providers, receiving a percentage of their commission. DBS lays down supervisory and compliance conditions of its own and has demonstrated its willingness to expel members who fail to meet these standards. Pretax profits have ranged between £1M in 1991 and £3.3M in 1996.

The Business

Many highly successful businesses are built on a spark of inspiration which encourages the founders to follow their instincts rather than conduct meticulous market research and weigh the possibilities. Ken Davy was once a small, independent financial adviser who was convinced the idea which ultimately translated into DBS needed expression. Davy's idea centred on new legislation in his industry which would bring the need for collective central support and security. He not only backed his concept, but kept his nerve – and this must have been tested – and is now head of a business that has a commanding presence in this sector of the financial services industry.

He devised the DBS concept after sensing that, by 1970s standards, draconian legislation would result from government concern about some excesses in the financial services industry. Although these issues were usually connected with secondary banking and somewhat less with the retailing of financial services, the weight of such legislation would fall equally on the small independent practitioner, selling insurance, investments and pensions

175

often to long standing customers. Indeed, IFAs could become a thing of the past if it were uneconomical for them to meet the sort of regulatory requirements that, he believed, could emerge.

The real success of DBS has been its capacity to grow the business against a background of an increasingly stringent regulatory climate in financial services. The company has majored on its ability to efficiently handle all core services for small IFA businesses – one to four people – thus freeing them to devote more time to selling whichever financial products are relevant to their customers. It has not all been a picture of undisturbed expansion. In 1994, pre-tax profits sagged to £447,000 when DBS was affected – along with a number of building societies and other organisations – by problems with a product which attempted to solve the problem for the elderly of being house rich and cash poor.

Since the start of operations a decade ago, DBS has always placed considerable emphasis on the quality and efficiency of its support services, and the benefit to members of its increasingly powerful buying strength with financial product providers. There were only 20 members in 1983, and when legislation became imminent, Ken Davy and his colleagues knew they needed 100 members to survive. They had 60 by November 1987 and 120 a year later.

Growth proved even stronger as DBS services expanded, and word of mouth reflection of success created interest throughout what is still a close-knit industry. Today, DBS has about 2600 members, serviced from a beautifully restored brownstone complex on the outskirts of Huddersfield in Yorkshire. Currently quoted on the AIM market in London, a full stock exchange listing now appears inevitable.

Distinctive features

- established market leadership;
- strong cashflows;
- growing network of IFAs;
- tight membership selection.

Stratagems

'I was a small practitioner myself, I considered I was doing a very good job for my clients and for the community. It was not a service that could be provided satisfactorily by banks or building societies; I was often advising the children and the grandchildren of original clients.' Davy came up with the tailored network concept which he describes as 'like minded people coming together so that they can continue to work as independents applying their skills in the market place without being overwhelmed by the administrative burdens placed on them.'

Size and shape

Employees: 200   Locations: 1700 (advisers 2600)
Geographical income split: UK 100%

A core tenet of the DBS strategy is that replication is pointless and wasteful. When new rules or rule changes are introduced, DBS deals will all the implications centrally on behalf of all members of the network. Davy admits that had a decent network existed then, he would have joined and not started one of his own. His network concept still operates through three basic elements. DBS acts as a mini regulator overseeing all the business that members transact. Members continue to trade as fully independent advisors but the business they obtain is placed through DBS. So, members advise and arrange and DBS effects the transaction on their behalf.

All commissions from the product providers are paid first to DBS which then distributes the commissions to members, less a small percentage of each transaction. It is a system that he likens to a wheel. DBS is the hub, the members are the spokes, and compliance and supervision make up the rim. It has worked well and the appointment of Godfrey Gillings, ex-FIMBRA CEO, as a non-executive deputy chairman strengthens the standing of DBS in a sector often riven with feuds and mutual suspicion.

Outlook

Future prospects

- IFA network growth;
- improved buying power of financial products;
- better margins.

DBS has built an apparently unassailable position in an important segment of the financial services market. By channelling the business of so many members through its central controls, DBS has secured real buying power with the pension, insurance and investment industries. DBS has retained the independance of the participants by resisting any temptation to put together own brand financial products. This policy will continue so that the network can enjoy the benefits of economies of scale at the same time as allowing members continued operational freedom.

DBS spends time and money developing its skills base. It shows: DBS has around 10 per cent of the IFA sector. So in real terms, this amounts to a 2.5 per cent share of the financial services markets. Davy wants 3000 advisers by 1998–99. If his target is achieved, and the company can take a listing in its stride, then the influence of DBS in an often fragmented, ill-disciplined market sector will be significant.

Address:

Independence House, Holly Bank Road, Huddersfield HD3 3HW. Tel: 01484 422224. Fax: 01484 426180

DCS Group plc

Leamington Spa, Warwickshire

Turnover				
1993	1994	1995	1996	1997
£5.5M	£6.4M	£8.7M	£30.5M	£35Me

Summary: DCS is a highly respected software company which operates on a worldwide basis, supplying products and services to the automotive and distributive trades. The company characterises its work as 'wheels software'. It started in Coventry, a city synonymous with the motor trade, and moved to the more picturesque and attractive town of Leamington Spa as the business began to expand. After a series of strategic acquisitions in the UK and keynote equity stakes in mainland European distributors, the company is well positioned to enjoy rapid growth. Analysts say that the most valuable purchase was the Leeds-based CSI (Computing Services for Industry) which has a broader industry client list and complements the DCS importer and dealership systems. Together they will lift estimated group sales to £35 million in 1997.

The Business

The West Midlands, and especially Coventry, resonates to the rhythm of the motor business. At its peak in the 1960s the city's economy was based wholly on the industry and hundreds of small businesses were fashioned to service the sector giants. The founders of DCS were steeped in the business. Sean Convey and a group of his colleagues engaged in data processing departments in major car companies flew solo to create software products for dealership management and warehousing. In 1988 the company was acquired by Robin Lodge's Nesco Investments plc whose main business at the time was the Nigerian Electrical Supply Company. He bought the business with the express intention of creating an entirely new operation in

179

distribution software. In a few short months in 1993, Nesco divested the business in Africa, as planned, and concentrated wholly on wheels software. The company was renamed the DCS Group plc.

Current international director Nick Ellis says that the company absorbed two smaller companies in dealer management systems, principally to gain access to their databases and client relationships. Then came the big one – CSI. 'The fit has been remarkably successful. After the merger the employees of both companies met and after quarter of an hour it was clear that we spoke the same language, had the same goals and worked in the same way. It was as if we had been in business together for years.' The CSI merger lifted the potential earnings from the combined group substantially. The commonality of approach was evident in many areas. Historically the founders had worked alongside each other, the majority of their operating systems were shared – both used the IBM A/S 400 series platform, both were industry specialists and, crucially, their attitude to customer service was more or less identical. DCS and CSI, independently of each other, had achieved accreditation under the quality standard ISO 9001 and all procedures are fully documented. The businesses are run separately but within the structure of the DCS Group so that far-reaching mutual benefits can be exploited. In strictly financial terms, DCS is generally a first half performer while CSI's returns are usually strongest in the second. The strength and continuity which this gives DCS Group is axiomatic. A significant percentage of turnover comes from an inherently loyal customer base which adds further consistency to the group.

Distinctive features

- No.1 IBM (UK) business associate;
- IBM business partner worldwide;
- world leader in automotive systems;
- outstanding industry knowledge;
- major earnings potential;
- strong international orientation.

The new plc structure and the merger with CSI gave an opportunity to give extra clarity to the group. The group now operates in three distinct areas: automotive industry, supply chain management and outsourcing and technical services. The first area is handled by DCS and the second two by CSI. Broker Greig Middleton commented 'The acquisition of CSI has resulted in a group with a balanced operating base with considerably less dependence on customers in the automotive sector. The combination will be a major player in the provision of software (both off-the-shelf and bespoke packages) and services into industry in the UK.'

DCS is world market leader in the provision of software systems for importers and among the top three in the UK for dealership management systems. CSI concentrates on vertical markets in manufacturing, distribution and logistics. Clients for the group include Inchcape, Ford Japan, Toyota, Hyundai, Renault, Komatsu, AudiVW and Fiat-Hitachi (DCS) and ICI, Boots, Bass, Smith & Nephew, Ciba Geigy and Northern Foods (CSI). CSI, in particular, works very closely with IBM and DCS Group has recently established a relationship with Hewlett Packard.

Stratagems

The group is now in an excellent position to exploit the opportunities available in the marketplace. It has sharpened its focus and identified the direction which it intends to pursue. Nick Ellis says the group has a clear strategy for products and distribution channels. In DCS, the company is working directly with motor dealers, vehicle importers and industrial and agricultural dealers. Its principal software products are industry standard and run on most leading hardware platforms. 'We are not bewitched by technology. We are interested in the best system to meet the needs of our customers.' Some 71 per cent of staff are active in customer service because the group's management is acutely aware of the critical role of service to building stable business relationships. Excellent customer service leads directly to repeat and expanded business from core clients. A further 11 per cent of employees work on research and development because DCS Group needs to be ahead of the market in terms of understanding the commercial needs of clients and to anticipate suitable solutions. In CSI this includes further extending its world class services in warehouse management, logistics, client/server applications, manufacturing systems and IT outsourcing operations. This last discipline is projected to be a rich field and CSI is well suited to make substantial gains.

Size and shape

Employees: 700   Locations: 14 (+ 16 agents around the world)
Geographical income split: UK 70%, RoW 30%

DCS is alert to pan-European prospects and has adopted a unique approach to building business in selected mainland European companies. In France and Spain, DCS has identified the best distributors for its products and taken an equity stake in each company. During 1997–98, it aims to do the same in Portugal, Italy, Germany, Benelux and Scandinavia. DCS MD Chris Merriman sits on the board of each of these companies. Merriman's appointment was a major coup for the company – he had been number two in UK market leader in dealership management systems Kalamazoo.

Future prospects

- rapidly rising profits;
- growth in market share in DMS and outsourcing;
- consolidation of world leadership in importer systems;
- broader European coverage.

Both DCS and CSI stay at the leading edge of technology. As one of IBM's leading business associates, CSI advises the computer giant on applications for a wide range of industrial and commercial situations.

CSI took a strategic decision in 1994 to put investment into its client/server applications and PC-based solutions. The company is active in systems integration, outsourcing, customer service products, external logistics, management consultancy, facilities management, technical support and applications management.

Outlook

The DCS Group, now led by group CEO Bob Williams, is on course for substantial success. The selection of CSI as a merger partner could not have been better. The compatibility of CSI with the rest of DCS is striking. Sales in 1995, pre intregration of CSI, was £8.7M while analysts' projections indicate that the new group will report £35M in 1997. Its global leadership in importer systems is likely to be consolidated further. And in the European dealership systems market DCS could confidently anticipate growth in share since it operates industry standard technologies, its levels of customer satisfaction are very high and its approach to growing key mainland markets is innovative. CSI, a profitmaker since the start, will continue to expand its services to a broad catalogue of blue chip clients and expand its business outside the UK.

Address:

Clarendon House, Clarendon Square, Leamington Spa, Warwickshire CV32 5QJ Tel: 01926 831401. Fax: 01926 452032

Demon Internet Limited

Finchley, North London

Turnover				
1993	1994	1995	1996	1997
£0.2M	£0.8M	£2.7M	£9Me	£19.6Me

Summary: Demon Internet is a company which supplies access to the Internet for £10 a month. It is the UK market leader in these services and plans to expand its operations to mainland Europe. Its vision is to be the largest Internet access provider in Europe. Started as recently as 1992, Demon now commands a membership list of more than 95,000 UK subscribers. It is structured to supply its services to a quarter of a million users. Its commitment to constantly pioneering new ways to service the customer is exemplified by its £15 million investment in a high quality DS3 line to the USA and its annual R&D expenditure which accounts for around 55 per cent of turnover.

The Business

Many companies start with a pioneering spirit. They achieve success through the vitality of their ideas or the persistence and enthusiasm of the founder. Demon Internet is one of the few businesses which is as passionate about innovation today as it was when it opened. A burning conviction in new ideas and novel ways to service its clients is the hallmark of its achievment. The astonishing growth in Demon's membership (buyers of its services) pays testament to its sharp appreciation of the potential demand for low cost, instant access to cyberspace. In 1992 when the company opened it aimed to bring together 200 people who would pay £10 each a month for access to the Internet. By May 1996 it had recruited 65,000 members and had replaced its original cramped quarters for offices in London, Dorking and Amsterdam. The burgeoning company has created sufficient infrastructure to support 250,000 members, which it confidently anticipates it will enlist by the end of 1997.

Demon was started by accountant Clifford Stanford in July 1992. 'Access to the Internet was very expensive then. It cost around £24,000 a year. I thought that if I could get 200 people to pay £10 a month, then together we could share the access. The idea was immensely popular and by the end of the first year I had secured 1400 members. This was much greater than I had ever anticipated and it showed me that potentially there was a huge market of people wanting Internet access. The £10 monthly charge was fixed because people tend not to miss it. It is a discretionary spend and if they use the access, £10 is a small sum for the value they get for their membership.'

Demand for the Demon service continued to outstrip Stanford's optimistic forecasts. In the second year membership grew to 7000 and by a factor of five in the third year to 35,000. Many of his customers were not only users in growing businesses like his own but also departments in larger companies which also found the temptation of £10 a month access too attractive to refuse. Stanford's key challenge in this period was – as it is today – recruiting and training people of sufficient calibre to supply high quality support to the customer. Staff attrition rates are low in the company but given that it was growing at 15 per cent a month at one time, even the most adept blue chips would have found staffing at that speed daunting. The rate of growth has slowed to a more managable, and welcome, eight per cent and planning can be undertaken in a calmer atmosphere. Eight per cent a month is still 96 per cent a year, which in many companies would be considered breathtaking.

Distinctive features

- remarkable growth in customers;
- pioneering approach;
- heavy investment in development;
- UK market leadership.

Stratagems

If any company was in the right place at the right time it was Demon. The potential for a business which provides low cost Internet access is considerable. It is a first principle at Demon that it remains true to its original offer. This is the key reason why Demon has been so successful. It supplies a gateway to the most exciting new development in modern computing. Most of the major hardware and software multinationals argue that the Internet is their primary focus for the next decade. Demon judged correctly in 1992 that a £10 a month access fee would be unmissable. Initially the company did not fully appreciate the enormity of the potential demand but within a few months of launch it was apparent that there were thousands of people interested in Internet access who were attracted to the Demon offer.

Managing the growth is now a core discipline at Demon. At 15 per cent a month, planning was an issue of instant logistics. But by mid 1996, a monthly increase in subscriptions of eight per cent proved less cathartic and allowed senior management time to consider how to meet future customer demand. Stanford has also strengthened the senior management team.

He says that his customers expect Demon to implement new services ahead of the market and so, combined with the innovative ethos of the company, commitment to high spending on technological and service implementation, is a cornerstone of its approach. In 1996, when turnover stood at £9 million, Stanford took the decision to invest £5 million a year, for three years, in a leading edge DS3 line to the United States. DS3 offers much greater bandwidth, allowing 900,000 users to access the Internet. Previously Demon had two DS1 lines, each offering 30,000 connections. This is a high risk, high cost strategy, says Stanford. Other innovations which will become standard at Demon are: private space on the Internet and live audio files for free.

Size and shape

Employees: 350   Locations: 5
Geographical income split: UK 100%

Competitors are not geared up to meeting Demon on the battleground of technological innovation. The company delights in pushing back the boundaries of what is possible and how that can be passed on to subscribers. Demon aims to add more and more standard features for £10 a month members. 'Subscribers demand increasingly higher performance from the company and it is our task to supply services ahead of the customer's anticipation of a service requirement.' Rivals will catch up but not before Demon has made the next jump forward.

Future prospects

- major mainland European opportunities;
- further technological and services advances;
- rapid expansion of UK customer base;
- concerted marketing.

In geographical terms, all of the company's income comes from the UK, but during 1996 this should change. A new office has been opened in Amsterdam to service the huge potential demand in the Netherlands. This is the first stage in a plan to become the largest European access provider. Further excursions into the mainland are planned but their fulfilment will be influenced by the success of the Dutch operation. Stanford is certain that the market opportunties are immense but he also wants to be clear how the business will enter the principal markets. Each territory will be taken on its merits but the company sees clear market potential in enough countries to make its ultimate objective achievable.

Outlook

The potential for Demon Internet is immense. UK business is virtually certain to reach Demon's targets, if only because interest in the Internet is large and growing. The company is continuing its major investment in service provision, but in addition it is planning to market its services in a more concerted fashion and to foster alliances with leading complementary businesses in the sector. It aims to introduce Internet access for mobile PCs during 1996. The mainland European business also offers major possibilities. The quality of current provision is not high quality and Demon could make significant inroads. It is taking a toe-in-the-water approach at least initially to excursions across the Channel. The combination of rapidly rising UK business and promising new markets in mainland Europe presents Demon with a golden opportunity for the future.

Address:

Gateway House, 322 Regent's Park Road, London N3 2QQ. Tel: 0181 371 1000. Fax: 0181 371 1150. Internet: internet@demon.net. Web reference: http://www.demon.net/

Domnick Hunter Group plc

Birtley, Co. Durham

Turnover				
1992	1993	1994	1995	1996
£27.3M	£30.6M	£36.7M	£44.2M	£50.7M

Summary: Domnick Hunter Group is one of the world's leading makers of high efficiency filtration and purification equipment. The group is composed of three divisions: industrial, gas generation and process, and it operates in more than 50 countries throughout the world. Its products are available in 80 countries worldwide. The group has a lively and direct approach to management which has an unbroken growth record. It has won three Queen's awards for export and two for technology.

The Business

Domnick Hunter Group is one of the most exciting growth companies in the North East. It is a coherently managed enterprise which holds world leadership positions in many of its products. The company makes high efficiency filters and dryers for compressed air and gases. It also has a significant presence in the global market for air sterilisation filters and, increasingly, liquid filters. Based on its core group of products, it has developed associated lines such as respiratory and environmental protection equipment and units for nitrogen gas generation.

The company is based on three activities: industrial, process and gas generation. Industrial makes compressed air filters and dryers. Process comprises air sterilisation and liquid filters; and gas generation produces nitrogen gas generators. The company is based on Tyneside and it has an additional site in Essen, Germany plus a series of sales offices worldwide.

Domnick Hunter enjoys an enviable reputation for innovation and creativity which has been recognised by numerous industry awards. In June 1996 management turned its attention internally with the objective of enhancing the business to compete in global markets. A strategy called Focus 2000 was announced. This is the group's medium term core strategy designed to guarantee the organisation strong and profitable growth into the next century. The five elements of this approach are: developing the structure and management of the company, expanding the group's markets internationally, the formation of strategic alliances to broaden the group's technological and market bases, reducing the time to market, and promoting human resource development.

There is a heavy accent on innovation in the group to keep it at the forefront of new technology and to anticipate market demand. In 1996 the company invested £2.4 million in new facilities to meet volume demand. In its industrial division, for example, the company opened a new Alocrom plant for the treatment of aluminium castings and extrusions while the process division upgraded and expanded its clean room areas. Expenditure on tooling for new products for enhanced value from existing products was a major priority. Research and development is one of the cornerstones of the business and a custom built dryer test rig was installed with the capacity to simulate operating conditions in any part of the world. It has also brought on line a rapid cycle dryer test station that will put several dryers throughout their paces simultaneously to speed up production.

Distinctive features

- high investment in research and development;
- strong profitability;
- international reputation and distribution network;
- highly focused strategic direction.

The company has been working to reduce the lead time on new products to reduce their time to market. It has made extensive use of 3D computer modelling techniques, especially in the area of finite element analysis. This optimises product strength for the minimum use of construction materials. Domnick Hunter has gained 70 per cent savings in materials cost from using this system.

Its electronic design data is used to prototype a model of the product under development before the data is transferred to a toolmaker or machinist without the need to produce physical drawings. The databases are common throughout the group so information is shared and no drawings are needed anywhere in the company.

DOMNICK HUNTER GROUP PLC

Stratagems

The group's commercial strategy which has won it widespread respect around the world is to concentrate on high quality and innovative design in its core markets. This has necessitated significant levels of investment in R&D. The company argues that this is crucial for the business to maintain its status as a world leader.

In corporate terms, the company has established its medium term strategic goals to be able to compete more effectively in the global market. Under the banner of Focus 2000, it aims to streamline the group's effort to be more competitive and effective. New CEO Colin Billiet has also identified three areas of immediate strategic importance.

Size and shape

Employees: 847   Locations: 15
Income: UK 31.3%, Europe 33.8%, N. America 15.6%, far east 14.6%, RoW 4.7%

Domnick Hunter has invested heavily in information technology since its flotation. Billiet says 'The benefits to the operational efficiency of the businesses are now being felt, enabling the group to provide better customer service, to eliminate waste and generally to make our employees more productive, thus generating a competitive advantage in the market.'

The company's drive on improved human resources planning is continuing. 'Human resource development is vital to our present and future. Employees at all levels are the group's greatest asset and investment here is vital.' The third area of current strategic initiative is to address the cost and supply of materials. 'A major review of the group's policies and practices in this area was carried out through 1996.' The company has found ways to make further cost savings, not least restructuring its purchasing organisation.

Distinctive features

- accelerating growth in all divisions;
- further external expansion;
- achieving strategic targets.

Although the group has created a third – gas generation – division, its revenues to date have arisen from its industrial and process activities. Industrial is the larger of the two, accounting for around three quarters of all income. It services clients in a wide range of market sectors, including semiconductor businesses, automotive manufacturers, TV makers, oil companies and even aquatic parks. Process, although somewhat smaller, has an equally diverse group of customers. Many are in the leisure and entertainment fields including winemakers, video cassette manufacturers and opthalmic lens producers. But it is also active in medical and environmental markets. The new gas generation division provides on-site gas generation equipment, particularly for the production of low cost nitrogen gas in food, beverage, chemical and electronics industries.

Outlook

Domnick Hunter is one of the fastest growing companies in the North East. It has deliberately focused on three key divisions where it can achieve or challenge world leadership positions. Its investment in people and innovation, the company believes, combined with its highly targeted medium term corporate goals will enable the business to build on its existing profitable activities.

Address:

Domnick Hunter Group plc, Durham Road, Birtley, Co Durham. Tel: 0191 410 5121. Fax: 0191 410 8452

Dorling Kindersley plc

Covent Garden, London

Turnover				
1992	1993	1994	1995	1996
£71M	£87M	£107M	£139M	£174M

Summary: Dorling Kindersley is a distinctive non-fiction publisher which has shown remarkable growth, especially since the late 1980s. Its success has focused on its highly individual Eyewitness style for its books and latterly its videos and CD-ROMs, the international orientation of its products and therefore sales and marketing, the application of its innovative design to adult non-fiction titles and its high level of in-house research into future publishing opportunities. DK enjoys excellent return on sales for its products, and an outstanding number of published titles still in print.

The Business

DK started in Peter Kindersley's back room in 1974. The plan to launch a new publishing company was not based on a revolutionary concept but a belief that the founders could make a living from publishing illustrated books. The company easily found a market niche and progressed to creditable performance but the real step forward came in the late 1980s when the business developed its Eyewitness design approach. 'There was no one single publication which was the standard bearer for the design,' says current MD Rod Hare. 'But rather a process evolved by several designers working over a period. In the end we created a distinctive format which we were able to apply to all of our titles.'

The intrinsic message of the DK design approach is to make the words more accessible and to slow down the pictures. 'Our products are designed for people who grew up in the television age. They are used to fast imagery and to taking information in bitesize chunks. Our readers like the information delivered in this way; it requires less attention span. We start with the creative use of white pages, placing the images on the page in a way which is attractive and captures the imagination. The text is wrapped around the picture. Initially we applied this approach to children's factual books such as encyclopaedias, animal books or crafts but very quickly we saw that the format would work with our adult titles as well. Our travel books, especially the city guides, gardening, cookery and sport.'

Hare says that the bright visual concept immediately appealed to its audience and DK rapidly became the brand leader in the UK. But he and his colleagues were after the international market. 'Our products are designed with international sales in mind. We produce our titles with English-language sales in view but our target is more ambitious. We seek to translate the text into a variety of worldwide languages. Our initial print run in English is 150,000 – we do not consider titles which sell less than this worth doing. From the outset – and this is where we differ markedly from other publishers – we have chosen books because of their international sales potential and often they are translated into 40 languages and sell to more than 80 countries.'

Sales are made through bookshops around the world but DK also markets its books through direct mail and also through its network of local distribution agents. Hare places great emphasis on the value of the agents in building the brand. 'These people hold local parties – rather like Tupperware, Avon Cosmetics or even Ann Summers – and most people who see our books this way can't wait to buy them.'

The company is acutely aware of the extent of the contribution of home distribution agents in the UK and is doing the same in the USA – and now Australia and Russia. Hare says that brand has been built so strongly here that people now go into bookshops and ask specifically for a DK book on a selected subject. He is attempting to secure the same degree of market awareness and loyalty in the USA where DK is making strong inroads into the stranglehold of traditionally domestic publishers.

Distinctive features

- market-leading brand;
- major profits growth;
- distinctive design format;
- strong inhouse research.

Stratagems

At a time when many publishers are slimming their establishments and outsourcing many of their functions, DK is placing increasing reliance on its inhouse research and design departments. Rod Hare explains that instead of waiting for authors or agents to present ideas for new projects, DK places heavy emphasis on staff reading the marketplace and deciding what will be needed in the next batch of publications. Well known writers are regularly commissioned, but often DK's internal teams prepare the text.

Hare comments that when the research teams have developed the concept for a new book, it will go into the design department to produce a cover, some specimen layouts and a contents list. These packages are then taken to various bookfairs, such as Frankfurt, where they are presold and those which achieve their targets are then put into production. The company is then also able to assess the potential demand for language versions of each new title. 'We invest heavily in putative projects and we are able to read very accurately what our core markets will produce.'

The biggest expansion in the company's portfolio during the last few years has been DK Multimedia. This covers the creation of CD-ROMs for multimedia computer systems. Dorling Kindersley moved into multimedia in autumn 1994. In Spring 1995, DK had nine titles in the market with the first four foreign language sets including French and Spanish, with German, Finnish, Italian, Japanese, Korean, Norwegian and Portuguese in the pipeline. In 1996 the company aimed to relase a further eight titles including *Anne Hooper's Ultimate Sex Guide*, *Eyewitness Virtual Reality Bird*, *Eyewitness Virtual Reality Cat* and *The American Medical Association Family Medical Guide*. In addition it wants to boost the number of titles available for Mac users to 13.

Size and shape

Employees: 880   Locations: 5
Geographical income split: UK 23%, US 34%, RoW 43%

DK is now working on a combined CD-ROM/online format which would put its images on CD-ROM while the latest text would be available down the line. 'Pictures are still very slow on online, ' says Hare. 'So for the time being we would keep them on CD-ROM but give access to the latest, up-to-the-minute text online,' he says. Clearly this is an incomplete solution and DK is looking forward to the day when it can provide a range of online services.

The business also has an extremely successful video production arm – DK Vision. *Eyewitness*, its natural history co-operation with the BBC, has chalked up 80 licence deals in more than 50 countries and its second series is in production. *Eyewitness* in the USA and *Dig and Dug* and *Hullabaloo* in the UK have been broadcast by network television. DK is regularly on the

Public Broadcast System network in the USA and its *Animated Horror Stories* are expected to be transmitted by PBS and Carlton in Britain. Various agencies have discussed the idea of a children's educational channel with the company but, as Rod Hare points out, material of DK's quality is expensive to produce and television eats material. He is concerned that DK's reputation could be injured by a channel which is not properly funded or managed. The company is casting its net wider and it has experienced notable growth in the USA and its latest success story, remarkably enough, is Moscow, where its books are shifting at a premium to the market.

Outlook

Future prospects

- new geographical markets;
- burgeoning multimedia opportunities;
- online and television projects.

DK is the brokers' favourite. Few other publishers give the financial community such a consistent source of joy. Unlike other businesses in the sector, it set out to be a publisher of international and distinctive titles. Out of the 1400 titles it has issued since starting 22 years ago, some 1200 remain in print. Many have found new language versions. DK's investment in new projects is directly comparably with high R&D spend in some IT businesses. And indeed the multimedia division is clearly going to provide high profitability for many years to come. Its originality and innovation are much in demand and open the paths to as yet uncharted opportunities.

Address:

9 Henrietta Street, Covent Garden, London WC2E 8PS. Tel: 0171 836 5411. Fax: 0171 836 7570

Eldridge Pope

Dorchester

Pretax profit				
1992	1993	1994	1995	1996
£0.9M	£1.8M	£2.6M	£3.5M	£4.2Me

Summary: The brewing industry has been galvanised by change during the last six years. A rapid decline in beer sales has proved the catalyst to wide-ranging movements in the structure of the industry. Eldridge Pope was in the vanguard of the regional brewers which saw the writing on the wall. Opened in 1833, the company has passed through four generations of the Pope family and is a West Country institution. In the early 1990s it refocused its business towards retail pub management, where the majority of the profits now derive. The Eldridge Pope management has embraced change and through effective use of assets, market leading training policies, structural reorganisation, and appropriate investment, the business is on a progressive path.

The Business

The catharsis came in 1991. Eldridge Pope had attempted two significant diversifications but neither worked as expected. Out of the crisis which ensued, however, came opportunity and the EP board saw that the business needed wholesale change. Managing director Jeremy Pope explains that the industry faced rapid and significant reorganisation but in the early 1990s few practitioners realised the extent and ramifications of this movement. 'Our vale of tears prompted us to look again at our company and the major shifts which were at work in the industry as a whole.'

Paradoxically, EP's crisis was a major blessing. Only a handful of regional brewers had developed the insight to see that the rationale of making profits from selling beers through tied houses was approaching its end. Profits in future would come from managing outlets to achieve a higher return on assets. Brewing beer would no longer be an inviolate central thrust of the activity of businesses such as EP. The accent in the future would be on raising the quality of outlets in the estate to attract a higher return from customers. 'Our estate of pubs – around 200 – included many which were on council estates and some were in a poorer condition than would be acceptable to us today. They were run primarily for the sale of beer. We took a highly critical look at the estate and revamped it completely. We sold some of the sites, invested heavily in our buildings and relocated others. We also acquired pubs in locations where we could add value.'

Another key factor in the elevation of standards within EP's portfolio is the company's commitment to training. Chairman Christopher Pope comments 'We changed 50 per cent of the management of our pubs – and around 100 per cent of the staff – in a two-year period. We invested very heavily in training at all levels to give our managers and staff appropriate skills and the very best opportunity to please the customer.'

The structure of the business now embraces pub management, brewing, distribution, packaging and the wine business. Retail director Mike Collins has been charged with revitalising the pub estate. 'This is one discipline at which we are now highly skilled,' he says. 'We are able to identify the potential that we can get out of a pub and which markets it should address. Our recruitment process is now finely tuned and our training has also reached and exceeded industry standard. EP company is installing a computer information system (EPoS) which will rival that of the majors.'

In half a decade the business has moved from a beer-sales orientation with a high percentage of fairly basic pubs to an upmarket operation using highly skilled and talented employees, the latest management information skills and higher than average return on assets. The pubs are graded. Quality traditional pubs and the broad-based local pubs account for the bulk of the estate. These are the outlets which are clean, bright and attract families, where people with higher spending power gravitate. Foods now account for an aggregate 22 per cent of revenue in these pubs.

The original heartland of Eldridge Pope was from Dorchester eastwards to Portsmouth and north to Winchester. Today with instant communication potentially anywhere in the UK could be included in the estate: the company is aggresively pressing up to the M4, into London initially and hopes to expand further. The traditional wines business, started by Sarah Eldridge in 1833, continues to flourish, although that too is in the process of re-evaluation.

Distinctive features

- managed houses orientation;
- commitment to quality;
- enthusiasm for change;
- high growth in earnings.

Stratagems

In the early part of this decade, after its diversification troubles, the company conducted a thorough analysis of its business and its direction. An idea of co-operation with other regional brewers was dismissed in favour of relationships with larger operators. The outcome was a deal with Carlsberg-Tetley where EP sold most of its beer wholesaling activities for £5.8 million. C-T wholesales EP cask ales in Wessex and EP retails C-T lagers, bought at a heavy discount.

'The benefits of the deal were an injection of cash which we badly needed and the time to simplify and re-focus the business. We were able to adapt to change, and manage our cost reduction programme. It also gave us space to allow our market to mature,' says Jeremy Pope.

Size and shape

Employees: 1200 　　　　　　　　　　Locations: 200+
Geographical income split: UK 98%, RoW 2%

Finance director John Harper says 'As a result of the strategic changes we have made, each area of the business now has to justify itself. We do not want cross-subsidy to exist. The pubs can take beers from our brewery at cost but they are free to buy elsewhere if the terms are right and their clientele prefer other brews. We have seen substantial growth in the business as a whole in the last two to three years. Turnover in 1995 was £55m million – a rise of 30 per cent on 1994. Pretax profits climbed 34 per cent over the same period and we expect to see an on-going average of 20 per cent in sales, PBT and earnings per share for the next few years.'

Unlike some other companies in the sector, EP has not shut or sold off its brewery. Instead it is keeping a watching brief on the brewing side. In mid 1996 the company, now renamed the Thomas Hardy Brewery after the most famous son of Wessex, is enjoying full capacity through a series of major orders. The packaging and distribution businesses are intimately linked into the fortunes of the brewery.

The directors of the business are confident that as long as they remain committed to excellent service to the customers, improve the quality and performance of the assets, train and motivate their staff, and stick to what they are good at delivering they will continue to be successful. 'There is permanent change in our industry. We cannot afford to be complacent,' says Jeremy Pope.

Outlook

Future prospects
- further growth;
- wider estate with higher asset value;
- further improvements in individual businesses.

Eldridge Pope is a family business but as chairman Christopher Pope comments 'There are no sacred cows'. At present the extended family remain key players in the ownership of the business but the chairman says that could and should change if the best interests of the business are served by new leadership and ownership. But the family and its key colleagues appear to be pursuing a strong path to prosperity. The quality and value of the business has improved substantially since 1990 and is certain to accrue greater worth. This is a powerfully managed enterprise with perceptive leaders who understand the forces at work in the industry. Independent observers anticipate even stronger performance in the years to come.

Address:

Weymouth Avenue, Dorchester, Dorset DT1 1QT. Tel: 01305 251251. Fax: 01305 258300

Epitaxial Products International Limited

St Mellons, Cardiff

Sales				
1992	1993	1994	1995	1996
£3.2M	£3.6M	£4.9M	£5.9M	£7M

Summary: Epitaxial Products International (EPI) is a world leader in its sector. It provides compound semiconductor epitaxial wafers for use in the global electronics and telecommunications industries. These wafers are used by component manufacturers to supply products as diverse as laser heads in CDs and ultra high brightness light emitting diodes (LEDs). EPI's wafers are so much in demand by blue chip multinationals that 96 per cent of its output is exported. North America and the Far East account for 80 per cent of all sales. EPI takes around 70 per cent of the global market in optical epitaxy and a growing share of the world's electronic epitaxy sector.

The Business

In the mid 1980s multinational companies started to talk core. They aimed to strip away their non-essential services and stick to what they knew best. Some operations, previously regarded as key, would be contracted out, or outsourced, to expert suppliers. The benefits to the multinationals would be extensive: huge chunks of cost would be taken out of corporate budgets, while the burden of investment would be passed on to others. Expert suppliers would compete to provide a service which at the same time would be cost-effective, and leading edge. Some in-house departments were demerged and in others personnel in non-core areas left to establish expert supplier businesses. EPI is one of these. Drew Nelson, now EPI's managing director, was a manager at BT's research centre at Martlesham. Along with

200

a colleague at Plessey – Mike Scott – he realised that the process known as epitaxy, although essential for the development of any mainstream electronics and telecommunications products, is costly and time-consuming for in-house departments. Nelson and Scott suggest that it can be provided more effectively by a dedicated supplier business rather than a multinational.

Epitaxy is the first stage process in the creation of many of today's leading electronics products. It provides the semiconductor material structures from which component manufacturers supply the lasers for CDs and high brightness LEDs. EPI makes semiconductor wafers – either two, three or four inches in diameter – from a complex combination of base elements, some highly toxic. The wafer discs are made by bringing together these diverse elements, often in minute quantities and baking them in a reactor at more than 800 degrees centigrade. This is a bespoke service. So each order is made to the customer's precise specifications.

The word epitaxy is derived from ancient Greek and refers to the precise arrangement of one atomic structure upon another. Very few companies worldwide make epitaxial wafers and EPI has carved out an impressive market niche in a comparatively short time. EPI now works for seven out of the top 10 Japanese electronics companies and most of the world's top 20 electronics businesses. It also supplies many of the top components suppliers across the globe. Each of these customers wants a piece of customised precision atomic engineering directly applicable to their products or processes. EPI's management determined that the base for their wafers would be gallium arsenide or indium phosphide which were more effective in new applications than traditional silicon-based chips. The epitaxial wafers are then made from elements in groups III and V of the periodic table.

The company opened in July 1988 but for the better part of the first year it established its operating facility and spoke to potential clients about its projected service. Locating the funding required was onerous, since the initial capital investment in state of the art technology was high. Eventually Shell Ventures took an 88 per cent stake in EPI, but in May 1996 EPI's management led an MBO which put the company firmly back in the ownership of its operational team.

Distinctive factors

- customised services;
- leading edge technology;
- world class customer base;
- high R&D investment;
- 96% of products exported.

EPITAXIAL PRODUCTS INTERNATIONAL LIMITED

Stratagems

EPI is founded on defined strategic principles. Its existence is the product of a strategic decision by manufacturers to move out of the expensive business of producing semiconductor material in-house. The founders realised that blue chip companies could better address their development budgets to component and device production. Epitaxy is a drain on resources when conducted internally. This appreciation gives EPI its first strategic principle. This is to persuade top 20 electronics companies that its process should be done by EPI rather than the client company. And EPI seems to have been remarkably succcessful in this first approach.

The second part of its strategy was to supply components manufacturers, many of whom are world class small businesses. 'We could have taken a decision to compete directly with the components manufacturers but these are our customers so we concluded at an early stage that we would stick to our core product and process,' says Dr Nelson. This gives EPI a balance of customers between huge multinational corporations and smaller highly energetic enterprises. By supplying both EPI can foresee that demand for its products will mushroom.

A key part of the EPI approach is to provide a customised service for all its clients. Each of the blue chips and their components suppliers require wafers which are produced in precise values according to the specific need. Servicing the particular requirements of individual clients gives the company a distinctive edge over its competitors. The product portfolio includes semiconductor wafers made to specific bespoke requirements for component and device manufacture but also test wafers for research purposes.

Size and shape

Employees: 85   Locations: 4
Income split: N. America 55%, far east 25%, rest 20%

EPI now operates in epitaxy for two distinct applications – optical and electronic. In the optical epitaxy market, it is world leader, taking around 70 per cent of all sales. In the electronic epitaxy sector, EPI faces greater competition and comes home with around 10 per cent. Drs Nelson and Scott and their colleagues want to build on their strengths in the optical market as first priority but in addition they believe that they can carve out a bigger share of the electronic epitaxy business. EPI has also broadened out of its original base among electronics companies in providing materials for the telecoms industry. Since electronics and telecommunications will be among the largest growth industries in the next decade, EPI is well placed to take advantage of prevailing trends.

The company has the highest expenditure of any business in this area on research and development. EPI's directors believe that this gives them an appreciable commercial advantage over rivals, and has led to substantial refinements in production capacity. At the outset EPI was able to manufacture one two-inch wafer every five hours; now it is capable of providing three an hour, a productivity increase of fifteenfold. Although this capacity is yet to be fully utilised, EPI is profitable and as capacity is taken up, profitability is set to rise sharply.

Another key aspect of the company's approach is to maintain total client confidentiality. This has been an important contributor to building the business. EPI's wafers are key elements in creating the new products of the future and clients want their competitive advantage protected. Many are based in Japan and the USA and development will be focused there. Eventually, Cardiff will feed Europe, while a second facility will cover North America and the Pacific Rim.

Outlook

Future prospects

- high increase in sales/profitability;
- expansion of telecommunications sector work;
- joint venture manufacturing in the USA or Far East;
- growth in its electronic epitaxy activities;
- further technological advancement.

EPI is on the verge of rapid expansion. Its wafers remain in growing demand among industry blue chips. The company has shown the savings which clients can make by putting epitaxy out to EPI. Many new electronics and telecommunications products require EPI's wafers at the first stage of component delivery and given the widening scope of products and processes using these wafers, business cannot do otherwise than to grow. With 96 per cent of its output exported, EPI plans to open a new plant in North America or the Far East where it does most of its business.

Address:

Pascal Close, Cypress Drive, St Mellons, Cardiff CF3 0EG. Tel: 01222 794422. Fax: 01222 779929

European Telecom plc

Slough, Berks

Turnover				
1992	1993	1994	1995	1996
£9.8M	£21.3M	£39.1M	£78.4M	£142M

Summary: European Telecom is a worldwide distributor of mobile telephones, accessories and associated data products. It is the largest company in its sector in Europe and among the top three globally. ET has one of the fastest growth rates of any telecoms company in the UK. During the last four years it has experienced a compound growth of 114 per cent. Around two-thirds of the products which it handles are exported to more than 60 countries around the globe. It is currently in the process of establishing a series of regional offices to further enhance its customer service.

The Business

The growth rate of European Telecom has been extraordinary. It has racked up 114 per cent compound growth in sales in only four years. In June 1996 ET was listed on the main market of the London Stock Exchange. In the few months which followed its share price has doubled, valuing the business at £71.4 million. The company started with one man, Warren Hardy, an office, a telephone and an urgent desire to make a living. 'I had seven years of successful selling in the cellular phones industry and I knew there was demand out there so I started building accounts.' During November 1990, as Margaret Thatcher was shunted out of No. 10 Downing Street, Warren Hardy made his first sales for the nascent business. By 1997 it was turning over £142 million and employing 92 people.

This is a hard driving enterprise and people are expected to achieve demanding daily targets, but the results, especially the margins, are outstanding. The company is a primary supplier to dealers, retailers, others distributors, service providers and network operators. ET operates as a primary and secondary supplier to markets where businesses are looking for reliable sources of supply. Its first big international contract came from Hong Kong in 1991. 'There was a shortage of Motorola analogue phones. We agreed to source them for Hong Kong Telecom – one of the colony's network operators, which is part of Cable & Wireless. The order was worth £250,000 and as an extra blessing we were paid through C&W UK.'

Hardy says 'We had never exported before but within a few months we had developed a client list of more than 30 companies in Hong Kong. The colony shares common serial numbers with the UK so I was able to source telephones in the UK and ship them to Hong Kong. We quickly developed a reputation for speed of delivery and efficiency.' ET then turned its attention to other companies with common serial numbers – Kuwait and United Arab Emirates. All three countries were wealthy, enjoyed a fondness for the latest technology and responded with enthusiasm to ET's approach. Both Kuwait and the UAE were adapting to the new digital markets and so were at an ideal stage of development for ET's sales people to exploit the opportunties of the market. Some of ET's HK customers were also buying for China, which was expanding its markets at a phenomenal rate.

At the same time as European Telecom was expanding its international sales, its UK business was rapidly moving into the status of national market leader. In 1992 Cellnet and Vodafone, the UK's two major network operators, slashed their tariffs which led, as intended, to explosion of demand in the consumer market. The UK model for the development of national cellular markets will be replicated throughout the world, the company suggests.

Distinctive features

- highest growth in the sector;
- demanding financial targets;
- servicing world markets;
- speed and reliability of delivery;
- understanding of customers and markets.

The strength of the business is built on its drive, its reliability, its understanding of its markets and its willingness to meet customer demand. 'We are also able to take calculated risks on buying stock in a volatile market because we have an extensive global customer base which all require the same products,' says Hardy. As the organisation grows larger, it can command significant economies of scale and extend even further already high margins.

EUROPEAN TELECOM PLC

European Telecom moves rapidly and deftly and deals with some of the largest companies in the world. Its bad debts are tiny – only £40,000.

Stratagems

The growth in cellular phone subscribers is expected to more than triple by the year 2001. In 1992 the number of subscribers stood at 23.5 million. By 1996 this had leapt to 116.8 million; within five years the total will have topped 370 million, according to Dataquest Europe. In the UK alone European Telecom expects subscribers to rise from its current figure of seven million to 16.3 million in 2001. These statistics hold two messages for the business: even if it just keeps pace with the current trends – and it expects to outstrip them – its UK turnover will double and its global income will increase by a factor of three. In the last five years the number of countries with commercial networks has grown from eight to more than 100.

Hardy says that his company must benefit from the overall expansion in users and in networks. It is a leading distributor of cellular telephones and related products, respected for its speed of delivery and reliability, which gives it a strong commercial advantage over existing or putative competitors. The company's plans to grow the business outside the UK and the rate of increase in the domestic market puts European Telecom in the forefront of industry expansion.

Size and shape

Employees: 92   Locations: 4
Inc. split: UK 32%, mainland Europe 39% Asia/Pacific 23%, Middle East & Africa 6%

Hardy expects to see the widespread introduction of competition in cellular networks, following the British experience of high access through low cost. This means that the demand throughout the world for cellular telephones will expand exponentially. ET, predicted this development, and laid plans at an early stage to meet the challenge of heavily increased requests from existing customers and the introduction of high volume.

Certainly the City was impressed with the company when it went to market in June 1996. One of the key factors which impressed the financial community was its level of understanding of its suppliers and its customers. Also the company has invested heavily in its own technology, especially its system for developing prospects. Research is a major facet in ET's success.

Poor forecasting has previously blighted the industry but European Telecom has distinguished itself with the quality of its understanding of the dynamics of the market, new products and potential customers.

This appreciation has led ET to initiate a programme of opening regional offices. Since the entire stock turn was a remarkable 36 times a year, or once every ten days, with the new regional offices, this can be expected to reduce further, perhaps to once a week. Other offices will add to the geographical symmetry and orders potential of the business. While ET's growth is organic and generally not led by a buying strategy, the company is now looking at possible acquisitions and investments which will complement its core activity. ET is now the leading telecoms distributor outside the USA and without too much effort could be the world's second largest. Its ultimate target is to be number one.

Outlook

Future prospects

- rapid expansion of domestic and international markets;
- worldwide industry growth;
- new product ranges;
- expansion of service provision.

ET intends to be a major world player in the distribution of cellular telephones, accessories and value added products. Demand will rocket in the next decade, outstripping previous volumes by hundreds of percentage points, says the company. ET believes that it has formidable competitive advantage which it should translate into major financial gains. It plans to open further regional offices to supplement its coverage. ET has achieved its reputation on the basis of sweat, astute perception of opportunity, the quality of its relationships with suppliers and customers and determination. It promises more of the same.

Address:

European Telecom plc, Heathrow Office, Slough, Berks. Tel: 01753 764100. Fax: 01753 764200

FI Group plc

Hemel Hempstead

Turnover				
1992	1993	1994	1995	1996
£24.9M	£27.8M	£41.6M	£61.7M	£78.8M

Summary: FI Group is a UK market leader in applications management – the outsourcing of IT software to a third party contractor. Floated in April 1996, FI Group concentrates on blue chip companies where it can provide all or part of the applications management service. The company is a remarkable success story, demonstrating growth in sales, PBT and, crucially, length of service contracts. Typically the sector operates on one-year terms; FI Group has many contracts of three and five years' duration. Some 70 per cent of its revenue is drawn from its top 20 clients. The company won the New Company of the Year title in the PLC Awards in 1996.

The Business

Applications management is a relatively recent phenomenon in industry. It is the outsourcing to third party contractors of part or the entirety of a company's IT applications software function. As early as 1987 the new CEO of FI Group, Hilary Cropper, saw which way the wind was blowing and refocused the company towards applications management. FI Group had been started in 1962 by Steve Shirley as one of the earliest companies specialising in bespoke software for businesses. By the mid 1980s companies were moving towards the concept of sticking to core and outsourcing of non-core activities was emerging as an effective way of ensuring that provision could meet a high and improving standard, costs are saved, and investment in changing technology is carried by suppliers.

In 1985 FI Group reported sales of £7 million. By 1996 its turnover had climbed to £78.8 million and its role as a UK market leader in applications management was confirmed. The real growth in the company has come since it changed direction and focused on providing blue chip companies with outsourced applications management. *The Holway Report*, a highly respected industry annual, reports that the market for applications management is expected to more than double between 1995 and 1999 – from £315 million to £730 million. Broker UBS says that in 1995 some 80 per cent of large organisations were involved in some kind of outsourcing and that 40 per cent of IT budgets were contracted out. In only two years, the IT figure had leapt from 20 per cent. This suggests that cost control, a desire to eliminate risks and the drive to be more competitive, are encouraging blue chips to put further, larger tranches of their IT spends out to contractors.

The group offers a range of professional IT services including: applications management (70 per cent), training and personnel placement (17 per cent) and consultancy and other services (13 per cent).

Distinctive features

- UK market leadership;
- substantial blue chip client base;
- longterm contracts with clients;
- rapidly growing sector;
- skilful financial management.

Typical of these services is a seven year outsourcing contract with The Co-operative Bank, a five year insourcing arrangement with Thames Water and a Software Factory relationship with Tesco which has been running on a rolling contract basis with Tesco for ten years. FI Group supports the software needs for Barclaycard card processing and has done so for three years. Training also scored a major coup recently when it won a £500,000 deal with TNT to develop and deliver training courses and materials to support the worldwide rollout of its business applications, and recently launched Maxim, a complementary business process implementation service.

Stratagems

FI Group's strategy is governed by several factors: the increasing sophistication of its markets, the larger role which it and its competitors are now playing in supplying these needs, the drive for quality services to clients, the expansion of the markets and the culture and composition of the company itself. In 1991 a workforce buy-in resulted in them gaining effective control of the company. And even today as much as half of the business is owned by its employees. This is a key asset for the company because employee motivation levels and staff retentions are extremely high. Finance director David Best explains that employee attrition rates are low compared with the industry. He says that staff motivation is encouraged by the open, participative management style of the business and the profit sharing and share option schemes which are available to employees, in addition to flexible employment contracts.

When the company considered flotation, 95 per cent of the workforce took part in a vote to determine whether it should go ahead and 99.4 per cent were in favour. Cropper explains that more than 50 per cent of the people working for the business are salaried employees, another 15–20 per cent are full time associates, a smaller group are part time associates and around 250 are contractors brought in at market rates to fulfil specific tasks. 'Our aim is to increase the proportion of our workforce who are salaried employees. This is the least expensive part of our staff costs.' The increase in longer term contracts means that the business will experience greater stability and therefore be able to plan more effectively. More salaried employees means reduced costs. It also means more managed career development and skills enhancement.

Size and shape

Workforce: 1900 Locations: 7
Geographical income split: UK 100%

The industry, Cropper comments, characterises orders for future work in terms of what is called the order bank. These are the contracts which are guaranteed income for the future. At the time of the employee buy-out in 1991, virtually all of the orders in the bank were of one year duration. In 1995–96 12 per cent were for less than one year, 54 per cent for between two to five years and 34 per cent for more than five years. This is a formidable leap forward and pays testimony both to the precision of Cropper's vision for FI Group and the quality of the work done by its people.

The aim is to provide excellent quality service to its clients, with which FI builds relationships of increasing longevity. By understanding its clients better, it is able to improve the value-added element of its work and to anticipate future need. Cropper explains that its top 20 clients are drawn from three market sectors: finance (Barclays, TSB, Royal Bank of Scotland, The Co-operative Bank, Eagle Star, Royal Insurance), services (BT, Dun & Bradstreet, ITSA, London Electricity, Hyder, Thames Water) and retail/

leisure (B&Q, Granada UK Rental, Sainsbury, Tesco, Whitbread). Finance sector companies accounted for 36 per cent of 1996 turnover, services 38 per cent and retail/leisure 26 per cent. She says that FI Group focuses on supplying industries which have a high reliance on IT, and aims to keep these three sectors in rough balance to avoid exposure to downturns in any one. In some cases the group absorbs the client's IT people. A good example is The Co-operative Bank where 128 personnel transferred to FI Group. It is an increasing trend.

Outlook

Future prospects

- potential offshore base;
- growth in outsourcing assignments;
- absorbing more client personnel.

FI Group looks ready to continue its record of substantial growth. Its policy of focusing on blue chips has paid dividends in terms of expansion of assignments for key customers. Given the growth in outsourcing in major companies, it can expect to pick up a sizeable chunk of new business. The company is actively considering setting up offshore – perhaps in Asia or the Far East – to source services from markets where labour is cheaper for its domestic clients. If this option is chosen, then ultimately it may sell in those markets. But overseas sales are some way off. Hilary Cropper is keen to build on the impressive success of the business to date and to consolidate FI's market leadership. The industry is engaged in wholesale change and so the group's principal efforts will be concentrated on building its share of a growing market.

Address:

Campus 300, Maylands Avenue, Hemel Hempstead, Herts HP2 7TQ. Tel: 01442 233339. Fax: 01442 238400

Filtronic Comtek plc

Shipley, Yorkshire

Turnover				
1992	1993	1994	1995	1996
£1M	£3M	£10	£25M	£33.4M

Summary: Filtronic Comtek has, within four years, established a place as a major world supplier of filters and allied equipment for the base stations which are an essential part of the operation of analogue and digital cellular telephone systems. In 1994 there were approximately 50 million cellular phone users; by 2000, even conservative estimates suggest this number could have risen to 400 million. The company uses advanced engineering at various worldwide locations to provide the necessary filter components for these base stations.

The Business

With more than 1000 papers and books to his name and a sheaf of international awards recognising his research work in circuit theory and microwave engineering, a move from academia into manufacturing was inevitable for Professor David Rhodes of Leeds University. His private company Filtronic rapidly established itself in military electronics. The expanding use of cellular telephones was, by 1989, providing a fertile area within the company's technological orbit. However, civilian engineering sat uneasily with military disciplines so Filtronic Comtek was demerged and then floated in 1994 to raise around £15M for the company.

This allowed and helped underwrite a rapid expansion of the company's manufacturing base. Filtronic Comtek now operates with more than 300 employees at two factories in the UK, two in the USA and a Pacific Rim base in Australia. Investment in research and development is high. In 1995, it stood at £1.1 million, representing 32 per cent of profits, but the majority of this work is determined by the requests, of specific customers. The company's main UK and US facilities are ISO 9001 accredited, which means that all of its quality processes are documented for every stage of product development.

The components supplied for base station use are highly complex technically, but can be tailored for all the major world cellular systems. Each base station services up to 2000 subscribers and is capable of handling up to 100 simultaneous calls. Given the estimate of 400 million cellular phone users within five years, the demand for high quality, proven base station components is obvious. Professor Rhodes is executive chairman, with Dr Stephan Matykiewicz, who played a major role in the company's early business development, as marketing director. Dr Christopher Mobbs, also from Leeds University, is engineering director. He has been responsible for many of the subsystems products currently used.

Distinctive features

- no alternative to its technology;
- high R&D spend;
- applicable to both main cellular systems;
- rapid expansion.

To provide customers with the most cost effective solution to their needs, the company harnesses design and manufacture at the earliest possible stage. These parallel processes are embodied in proprietary software to ensure the complete integrity of the design-to-manufacture route. This is paralleled by modern purchasing and inventory management to maintain total support throughout the length of each customer programme. Filtronic Comtek is able to dovetail its products into whatever cellular system is proposed, while meeting industry demand for diminishing components which still provide equivalent or enhanced performance. The combination of these skills has allowed the company to achieve its world leadership in technology and also in manufacturing production.

Stratagems

For Filtronic Comtek, managing quite astonishing company growth while maintaining the technical excellence which has propelled it into a worldwide market will be the challenge of the late 1990s. 'In the next five years we can see at least a tenfold increase in cellular telephone growth so we must increase output at least tenfold to even hold the same market share,' maintains Professor Rhodes.

No alternative – or smaller, smarter – technology is beckoning, due, he says, to the fundamental laws of physics. Even the extent to which a base station's size can be further reduced and optimum performance maintained, is now limited. A similar position exists with the portable phones. After all, the fixed distance between mouth and ear sets its own criteria, and if it fits the pocket, it is, manufacturers now feel, small enough.

Size and shape

Employees: 300   Locations: 5
Geographical income split: n\a

Almost half the shares in Filtronic Comtek are currently held by institutions but Dr Rhodes rebuffs any suggestion of pressure from them for immediate results. 'Our investors are interested in what we are trying to achieve in the medium and long term. I believe there is a myth about short-termism in the City today. Obviously, certain adverse financial results can have a short term effect on the share price, that is the nature of our society, but I think major investors ignore that and look for the longer term growth. Ours do.'

The public will feel the impact of this growth in cellular communications too. Competition among operators will increase, perhaps more through the quality of service offered than price, as a mobile phone becomes a fact of everyday life. 'I can see some mobile phones having dual mode capability, so when you are in your home or your office, the phone clicks over to a different system and you pay only normal rates. Once we have that facility, and a personal number, then there may be no point in having a fixed telephone.

'A few weeks ago I was 400 miles north of Helsinki, more or less on the Arctic Circle, yet people could, and did, get through to me on my mobile phone. They didn't know where I was. It didn't matter. We could speak to each other: communicate.'

Future prospects

- dramatic rise in demand;
- technological advances;
- growth in manufacturing;
- strengthening of management.

Outlook

The sector anticipates exceptional growth in the next decade. Demand for the technology will increase pressure on manufacturers to perform to increasingly high standards. Development will be characterised by nimble and effective R&D programmes, as well as the enforcement of quality disciplines at each of the manufacturing plants. As microwave systems themselves grow, Filtronic Comtek's customers will expect substantial component suppliers, capable of providing global support. The company is in a strong position to exploit the demand for its components. Its 1995 sales increase of 152 per cent will be a yardstick for coming years. Its new manufacturing sites will have an increasing impact on efficiency within the business and overall performance. This is a business with the potential to be a major player in one of the fastest growing markets in the world.

Address:

The Waterfront, Salts Mill Lane, Shipley, West Yorkshire BD18 3TT. Tel: 01274 530622. Fax: 01274 531561

Finelist Group plc

Stratford-upon-Avon, Warwickshire

Turnover				
1993	1994	1995	1996	1997
£16.1M	£24.1M	£98M	£105M	£200Me

Summary: Finelist Group is the UK's largest network of motor vehicle parts suppliers. It has grown rapidly by organic means and by acquisition. In 1995 sales alone rose by 307 per cent and pretax profits climbed 197 per cent. Although its roots can be traced back to the turn of the century the rapid growth in Finelist has come in the 1990s. After a year of consolidation its core motor factor division during the financial year which ended in March 1996, Finelist grew its business substantially in 1997. Motor factor division has grown to 208 sites. Motor World Group plc was acquired for £48 million in August 1996. Ferraris Piston Service was bought in February 1997 for £52 million after a rights issue, and packager and warehouse distributor of car parts First Line was also secured at the same time.

The Business

The early history of the Finelist Group began with the Autela Components company. Started at the turn of the century, AC was acquired by Lockheed in 1971. Its manufacturing division, making brake linings and exhausts, was absorbed into Lockheed's manufacturing locations and the Autela brand remained distinct only as a distributor. In 1986 BBA bought Autela but in 1991 decided that vehicle parts distribution was not core and sold out to the management. The MBO team comprised the managing director, the finance director, the marketing director and the operations director Chris Swan. 'Over the following 15 months I bought out my partners and with some venture capital from 3i and Nat West Markets I launched the business. My equity vehicle was an off-the-shelf company called Finelist. It was nothing more than that but the name seems to have stuck.'

He recalls that Autela had a network of 30 branches and was turning over £12–13 million. Profits were not outstanding at £250,000. 'But we had a good team and this has carried us through.' In February 1994 the company was reporting £2.45 million in pretax profits and went for a London Stock Market listing. 'I could not have launched the group without the support my venture capital backers had provided but I wanted to take advantage of the equity markets. They were better suited to a more flexible regime of rapid expansion.' On the strength of a successful float he bought Edmunds Walker, a business with sales of £60 million but losses of two and a half million pounds. Among its greater attractions was a network of 90 branches which immediately lifted Finelist to a substantial operation. 'Edmunds Walker was three times as big as us but we managed the transformation because we planned at an early stage precisely what we were going to do with the company once we took control and we had made similar improvements in the Autela branches.'

Distinctive features

- commanding position in UK markets;
- superbly run in a poorly managed sector;
- obsessional about quality;
- great flair for marketing;
- huge market potential.

The branches now stock more than 2500 individual parts. They sell directly to small garages which repair cars of all makes. These businesses do not keep a wide range of parts in stock and need to be able to access a variety of spares very quickly. Garages within a nine mile radius of a Finelist branch receive parts within one hour of an order. Customers inside a 50-mile radius are included in deliveries which occur twice daily. A glance at the Finelist map of branches reveals that very few customers are more than 50 miles away from an outlet. The group has cut out wasteful practices and procedures, and installed an integrated computer system. Its recent IT development is Concept 2000 which it installs at customers' locations to help them provide better service to their customers. This is a computer system which, with five keystrokes, allows the garage to quote on a particular job, including the margin which they earn on the spares. The system also helps with bookkeeping and the sales ledger. As soon as a job is booked the order for parts its electronically communicated to the local group location. It also tells the garage how long the task should take.

In August 1996 Finelist bought Motor World Group. This has formed the

217

basis of the group's retail division. Motor World and Charlie Brown's are leading operators in the retail field with 340 sites in total. In February 1997 Finelist acquired Ferraris Piston Services, which is a warehouse distributor in the automotive aftermarket. It operates from 17 sites around the UK with a head office in North London. The company now forms the warehouse distribution division of Finelist. February was a busy month for Swan. He also bought First Line which, with Autogem, now forms the manufacturing and packaging division.

Stratagems

The composition of the marketplace has a direct bearing on why Finelist has been so remarkably successful. There are three large vehicle parts distributors of which Finelist is one. The rest of this £1 billion sector is populated with around 1900 smaller operators with one or two sites. Swan says that they do much the same job as Finelist but they do not offer the same speed and quality of service, the staff are not as well trained, they do not enjoy the same economies of scale and they are generally poorly managed. Swan saw that the market was contracting and realised that many of the smaller distributors would be pleased to leave the field. 'Our aim is to build a network of 400–500 branches in three to five years. The short term target, which was set in mid year 1995, is to reach 250.'

Size and shape

Employees: 1700   Locations: 201
Geographical income split: UK 100%

These new acquisitions will be high quality businesses. 'I bought a business in Bolton on Friday night. It turns over about £750,000 a year, makes a profit of £30,000 a year and has net assets of £250,000. We paid a small premium over net assets. We apply our purchasing terms and it makes a fundamental difference. We apply our philosophy on customer service and it makes a big difference. Our core margin in Autela is north of ten per cent return on sales. That's the figure that we have to achieve. We've got Edmunds Walker up to about eight per cent but when we took it over only two years ago it was making a major annual loss. We improve margins by a number of methods: we will remove unprofitable business, expand the customer and product mix and remove unnecessary administration by feeding it into the centre.The growth contributed by the acquisitions – in terms of the core margin – is exponential because I have an overhead base in place, a regional management and administration structure capable of absorbing 250 branches comfortably. I always try to build the management at least a year ahead.'

Finelist plans – from both a customer and a financial perspective – well in advance and it is obsessive about doing what it says it will do. 'The drive, the passion, the achievement are very important to us.' The company has a flat structure and it is highly decentralised. Control on systems, finance and purchasing is vested in the centre but everything else is driven locally. A high degree of emphasis is placed on people management. Finelist operates some of the most advanced training courses in the motor industry and its career progression paths are well laid out. 'We bring people in at 16 and help them develop. In the last quarter we have needed 16 new managers and 12 came from inside the business.' Quality is key in Finelist; IS 9002 is in place at all branches.

Future prospects

- growth to 500 sites in retail;
- all Finelist divisions to reach a 10% return;
- further advanced marketing campaigns;
- closer customer integration.

Growth by organic means is as important as acquisition. 'We can do a lot better on market penetration. We aim to improve share on existing customers by management motivation and advanced marketing. We are giving our customers an early service, a quality product and a competitive price. The image of many independent garages is bad, so we introduced Concept 2000. In August 1996 we intend to open a franchise operation called Nationwide Auto Service. This will improve the image, branding and reputation of independents as part of our national network. Our pilot garages showed a 25 per cent rise in their sales. Around 400 or 500 garages will be tied into us subtly through parts procurement.'

Outlook

Chris Swan is an astute manager who realised the fragmentation of the industry could not continue, that consolidation would gather pace and that rich pickings were available for anyone who had the vision and skill to transform a poorly managed set of businesses. If this company has not yet become the UK market leader, then there is no doubt that it will be. His computerisation of his branches and his customers, the advanced marketing which he employs, the high degree of loyalty and motivation of his staff, the tight control on central functions and the vision will continue to carry the Finelist Group to greater achievement. Above all it succeeds because Swan knows this business intimately and he loves every minute of being its boss.

Address:

Regal House, Birmingham Road, Stratford-upon-Avon, Warwickshire CV37 0BN Tel: 01789 414545. Fax: 01789 414580

Flying Flowers Ltd

MAIL ORDER/HORTICULTURE

St Lawrence, Jersey

Turnover				
1992	1993	1994	1995	1996
£5.3M	£7M	£14.7M	£26.1M	£35.3M

Summary: One of the Channel Islands' notable commercial success stories, Flying Flowers is an outstandingly successful mail order and horticultural group. It traces its modern history back to 1984 when current managing director Tim Dunningham formed a 50:50 partnership with the principal of a family-owned tomato and carnation growing enterprise called Trident. In 1993 Flying Flowers floated in London following the arrival of former Black & Decker senior manager Walter Goldsmith as chairman. Since then, the company has added to the core business by acquisition.

The Business

Flying Flowers started business as a carnation nursery in 1984. Its present MD Tim Dunningham created a partnership with the founding family and grew the operation on a modest basis until Walter Goldsmith arrived as chairman from Black & Decker. At the time of its flotation in 1993, it was a single product mail order company but the joint leadership of Goldsmith and Dunningham forged the company into a broadly-based horticultural enterprise. The initial development of the business was hindered by a policy of the Jersey government to take the steam out of an overheating local economy by instituting a zero jobs growth initiative. This meant that Dunningham needed to be even more resourceful than most British business managers in building business. He was partly assisted by the closure of a local Allied Lyons tea factory, which permitted Flying Flowers to absorb six of the redundant employees.

The recession nullified the need for the government's restrictions and Flying Flowers was able to take on more personnel. Its planned flotation

221

went ahead in July 1993 and the company began to thrive. 'Coming to the market provided the necessary equity to develop the business further,' says Dunningham. Today the group has four main mail order brands. Flying Flowers is the core brand, which continues to grow at a steady rate. Gardening Direct, a division which sells bedding plants was created by the first acquisition – DPA Direct. 'We have taken the company's successful bedding plants products and enhanced its profitability by building a nursery to grow a substantial number of them ourselves and by advertising to build up our own database,' he explains.

Distinctive features

- broad-based mail order business;
- niche market leadership in a series of related sectors;
- core activities in the horticulture sector;
- high turnover, high margin operations;
- major recent acquisitional strategy.

Blooms of Bressingham, part of a £5.2 million triple acquisition deal made in May 1996 is the group's third mail order business. This horticultural company specialises in outdoor plants and is a market leader. The fourth arm in this division is Benham – also part of the May 1996 shopping spree – which produces first day covers. This is a specialist mail order business for which stamps are the raw material. The cover designs are produced by Benham in-house. Taken as one entity, the group's mail order division now has an annual turnover in excess of 20 million, making it one of the largest niche mail order businesses in the country, trailing only the large catalogue shopping companies and the newspaper insert publication *Innovations*.

'It is a high turnover, high margin business,' says Dunningham. 'And we are able to use the same expertise in all brands. Our strategy is to go into the more specialised product knowledge businesses. Most operators in the mail order field all source their products from the same suppliers and what differentiates them is the manner in which they promote themselves. Our products, by and large, are not sold by anyone else. Our philosophy is to ally product knowledge with marketing expertise.'

Stratagems

A key reason for the success of the Flying Flowers operation is the philosophy of building interlocking businesses. Dunningham has seen the potential synergies between a series of core activities in the mail order sector. Its separate divisions knit together to form a largely self-sufficient group and exploit the knowledge and expertise in common. Since the 1993 flotation the business has expanded by both organic and acquisitional means. The listing has provided capital to fund its energetic buying campaign. The logic of this strategy was that it quickly created a major group in the mail order and horticultural sectors. It has also provided the foundation for further expansion.

The most graphic example of the strategy occurred in May 1996 with the simultaneous purchase of three companies – Bloom's of Bressingham, Benham and Clarke & Spears. The third leg of the purchase is an indoor plants specialist. The linkage between the companies has created a platform for new markets. For example, cut flowers from the Flying Flowers business, indoor pot plants from Clarke & Spears and outdoor plants from Bloom's unite to provide material for retail on garage forecourts in the UK.

Size and shape

Employees: 3800   Locations: 18
Geo. income split: UK 59%, mainland Europe 18.1%, North America 15.6%, RoW 7.3%

Future prospects

- extensive expansion programme to boost series of profitable market niche;
- higher emphasis on retailing through Bloom's of Bressingham plant centres;
- ongoing programme of acquisitions – three in May 1996;
- identification of mainland Europe as key market development objective.

Retailing has become a major strategic thrust for the group. Dunningham's objective is now to expand the retailing side through Bloom's of Bressingham's plant centres. 'The concept is to recreate what a garden centre was 25 years ago,' he says. 'We are employing staff with a good knowledge of the products they are selling and we intend to aim the centres at the keen gardener. We believe that we can expand our other horticultural selling areas and create new ones to enable us to sell in greater quantities by using more innovative routes to market.'

FLYING FLOWERS LTD

Outlook

The entirety of the Flying Flowers business has been conducted in the UK. This will change in the next few years as the company develops a larger International operation with major businesses on the mainland and expansion into other areas of operations.

Address:

Flying Flowers, St Lawrence, Jersey. Tel: 01534 865665. Fax: 01534 865666

Forward Group plc   PRINTED CIRCUITBOARD MAKER

Tamworth, Staffordshire

Turnover				
1993	1994	1995	1996	1997
£12.5M	£20.7M	£23.8M	£66.8M	£105M

Summary: Forward is a group of companies which designs and manufactures a wide range of printed circuit boards for blue chip companies in electronics, telecoms, aerospace, military, medical and other applications. It has five operating companies: Forward Circuits (International), Forward Circuits, Exacta Circuits, Manchester Circuits and Technograph Microcircuits. Turnover rose 181 per cent, and pretax profits by 103 per cent, in 1996. This was achieved by a combination of acquisitions and outstanding organic growth. The group's objective is to be the number one circuit board maker in Europe, supplying a complete range of interconnect solutions.

The Business

Ray Chamberlain is an entrepreneur to his fingertips. After launching two highly successful businesses, one in central heating systems, he saw an opportunity in printed circuit boards (PCBs). In 1979 Chamberlain opened Forward Circuits in a small facility in Dosthill, Tamworth where he rigorously applied his conviction that customer service must be excellent. Many PCB makers took up to six weeks to supply their customers; Forward took three to five days. 'Ray concentrated on high quality boards, made to order in low volumes for a wide spread of customers,' says finance director Martin Glanfield. 'He is one of those few people in business who chase a long-term goal. He took very little out in terms of a salary or director's fees. Instead he ploughed money back into the business to develop its long-term potential.'

Now Forward is among the top four PCB makers in Europe, currently running at an annual turnover of £100 million. Its target is to be the most respected and profitable PCB manufacturer in Europe. It achieved its early status by building on the Chamberlain philosophy and adding low performing acquisitions, some of which were in receivership. The first significant purchase came in 1986 with Arnold Electronics in Rugby. The following year it acquired Technograph Microcircuits of Portsmouth, which makes hybrid PCBs, a specialist business which now accounts for 10 per cent of group sales. In 1989 the group absorbed Powertracks, which designs boards, and in 1993 it bought Central Circuits in Telford, again from the receiver. During the last recession Forward was the only quoted specialist PCB company which stayed in profit, according to Glanfield.

Derrick Bumpsteed, current CEO, takes up the story. 'The big year for acquisitions was 1995. We bought Ferranti Special Products in Oldham, Ferranti Hybrids in Bracknell which we took into Technograph and Exacta Circuits in Scotland. On the back of these three purchases we left the USM and moved to the Official List of the London Stock Exchange.' The Exacta purchase was key to Forward's one-stop shop strategy. This is a PCB manufacturer with a high quotient of international sales. Both Forward and Exacta were brand market leaders in their own sub-sectors of the PCB market. Forward was high margin, low volume and Exacta was high margin, high volume. Both had good people, strong markets and excellent technology but their approaches were different. Exacta focused on a narrower band of customers – around 80 – all blue chips. The coming together of Forward and Exacta has created a really powerful company. At the time 90 per cent of Forward's sales were in the UK but 60 per cent of Exacta's were overseas. So a group with both strong UK and extensive European markets was created instantly. The two customer bases did not overlap, which created impressive cross-selling opportunities.

In 1996 Forward Group bought another hybrid facility, this time from GEC-Marconi, which means that Technograph is now probably the UK's premier hybrid company. At the same time Forward acquired Manchester Circuits, which is a special products company making PCBs using non-standard materials. The group now has five divisions, which gives the business a total product range. There are only three executive directors, three non-executive directors and a total of five personnel in the head office.

Distinctive features

- PCB one-stop shop facility;
- brand leadership;
- pre-eminent customer service;
- high quality products;
- speed of delivery;
- high margins.

In late 1993, Forward Circuits International (FCI), a sales orientated company, was established. 'We source boards from selected vendors overseas and we have relationships with such companies in Korea, Taiwan and South Africa.' These are all ISO 9000 manufacturers. Blue chip companies ask Forward to manage their total PCB requirements. They are not bothered where the boards come from, provided they meet predetermined price and quality standards and hit their lines without causing any problems. 'Many new customers do not have a background in PCBs; they are customer-focused concentrating on the end product. Forward always had a large customer base but when it was asked to do the large volumes it did not have the capacity. They do larger volumes than Exacta and in different technologies. They are rather like another manufacturing facility. We take responsibility for the quality.' This relatively new international company already accounts for five per cent of turnover.

Stratagems

Glanfield says the move to one-stop shopping stemmed from a change in management philosophy among clients in the late 1980s. 'Major clients came to us and said that they were reducing their number of preferred suppliers and they wanted us to be among the small group which continued to supply PCB products. But they could not use Forward as long as we specialised solely in prototypes. They wanted us to be able to offer both high and low volumes as well as quality. An example was Siemens-Plessey, a long standing client, which aimed to strip its PCB supplier list from 20 to three and Forward would be among them. Ray Chamberlain decided to establish FCI so we could supply volume requirements to high degrees of complexity. The FCI vendors are very good at high volume, price sensitive work.' The rest of the group concentrates on high quality engineering for which it can charge a premium.

Size and shape		
Employees: 1900		Locations: 9
Geographical income split: UK 61%, mainland Europe 37%, RoW 2%		

The more recent acquisitions have brought extra skills into the group so the base of PCB services which it can supply to an increasingly large client base is much broader. 'There is no other PCB company in Europe which can match the range of services which Forward Group can deliver. Its market capitalisation is greater than twice the sum of all the other UK quoted PCB manufacturers. The market now recognises our strategy and we have helped re-establish the reputation of PCB companies within the City.'

The market for PCBs in the next few years will grow rapidly with original equipment manufacturers depending increasingly on fewer suppliers which work intimately with their clients. Broker Williams de Broe says 'The results should be enhanced margins and longer term contracts for those players remaining in the game. Customers will become more reliant on Forward rather than vice versa, a significant structural change in the PCB market. There will be a shake-out of the smaller companies in a market which is estimated to be growing considerably faster than the economy in general.' By enhancing its relationships with existing clients, including Alcatel, British Aerospace, Digital, Ericsson, GEC, Hewlett Packard, Lucas, Motorola and Rank Xerox, and broadening its range, Forward is on target to be European leader in PCBs.

Outlook

Future prospects

- European market leader in printed circuit boards;
- further acquisitions in the UK and overseas;
- continued investment in research and development.

Forward has read the market astutely. It has constructed the group into a brand leader in the European market. The spread of its operations, coupled with its superb production quality, has guaranteed its status of preferred supplier to blue chip companies in the fastest growing sectors of the world economy. Forward Group has carved out an enviable position as a respected supplier of high margin products but can also provide low margin, high volume boards. Clients can rely on Forward to meet high customer specification as well as speed of delivery. Brokers are enthusiastic about the group, especially as analysts suggest that sales and pretax profits will double to £131 million and £15 million in 1998.

Address:

Hedging Lane, Dosthill, Tamworth, Staffordshire B77 5HH. Tel: 01827 263200. Fax: 01827 263210

GWR Group plc

Swindon, Wilts

Turnover				
1993	1994	1995	1996	1997
£9.8M	£21.7M	£26.5M	£39.1M	£63.8M

Summary: GWR Group plc is one of the fastest growing commercial radio groups in the UK. It has expanded from two licences in Swindon to 32, including Bristol, Nottingham, Derby, Norwich, Ipswich, Cambridge, Peterborough, Luton, Bedford, Coventry and Bournemouth. It also has strategic stakes in two stations in London, Plymouth Sound, Stray FM and Minster Sound. The company is active in Eastern Europe and recently bought – and sold – Prospect, the largest and most successful independent radio group in New Zealand. At the end of summer 1996 it announced that it would be buying Classic FM, which will mean a series of changes to its current portfolio of licences and a complete reorganisation of the group.

The Business

Commercial radio is the rapid growth sector of the media industry. In 1993 radio stations collectively took 1.8 per cent of all advertising budgets. Three years later it reached 4.3 per cent. Since running costs of individual outlets have hardly grown, the net result is transferred to the bottom line. At least, for the better managed stations and groups, improved profitability is a happy outcome of decades battling against restrictive industry regulation. GWR is one of the largest groups, starting in the West Country and energetically expanding to include the East Midlands, East Anglia, Wolverhampton, Coventry, and the Thames Valley. In 1996 it bought the national classical music station Classic FM which has refocused its interests. It also acquired from Reuter, in partnership with ITN, the new London frequencies. GWR undertook to manage the AM frequency which it rechristened LBC – a powerful brand name in London radio. Outside the capital, as the upper limitations on numbers of licences have been raised, GWR has acquired contiguous areas – groups of stations which enjoy a geographical symmetry. One of the toughest fights was its hostile takeover of the Chiltern Group which lasted far longer than GWR would have liked. It also acquired the strategically valuable Mid-Anglia Group, which embraced Peterborough, Cambridge and Kings Lynn and which led to the 1996 purchase of East Anglian Radio.

GWR is now a major force in the industry. Its domain stretches from Bristol to the Wash and up to the Yorkshire borders. 'Developments in commercial radio are currently like a game of Monopoly,' says GWR CEO Ralph Bernard. 'Groups are acquiring properties which they may then merge into their own structure or sell on.' There are around 200 radio licences in the UK and three dominant groups – Capital Radio, GWR and EMAP. Other groups such as CLT, Virgin and Chrysalis are also trying to form bridgeheads in the sector. The latest set of regulations in the Broadcasting Act removed the restrictions on numbers of licences held, providing that total holdings do not comprise more than 15 per cent of the industry. A points system prevails with small stations accounting for fractions of one point and major market licences such as London rating as much as 25 points. This means that in potential purchases, as well as all the other considerations, radio group managers need to consider whether they would overshoot points allocation. This phase in the development of industry will see substantial buying and selling to solidify groups and secure the most valuable licences.

Distinctive features

- management and strategic coherence and vision;
- market dominance in each of its key markets;
- exceptional financial returns;
- expanding overseas interests.

The group's overseas holdings have worked well. Its involvement in Eastern Europe has proceeded successfully. Radio FM Plus in Sofia, a rock station, is a market leader and has bought a coastal station at Varna. Inforadio in Poland, a joint venture with the BBC and other partners, looks set to gain a licence for Warsaw. In 1996 it bid for the privatised Radio New Zealand but was pipped at the post. Instead it acquired Prospect, the largest independent commercial group, but this holding has since been shed.

GWR has achieved its notable success by detailed market research and understanding the requirements of particular audiences. Cambridge is a recent example of the change in fortunes which GWR had managed to achieve. CN-FM was a poor performer when GWR took it over. Within months, GWR had relaunched the station as Q103 and turned it into the market leader, generating £250,000 annual profit. The achievement can be attributed to careful targeting, improved local content, trained presenters and market research.

Stratagems

Ralph Bernard is clear that the room for expansion in the group's UK radio interests is limited. 'We will see a period of buying and selling as the groups settle down but we are close to our limit in both points and licences. There will be more growth in numbers of licences and we will bid for the last London FM franchise to provide a sports and business station.' But the same opportunity for growth as existed in the first half of the decade will not be replicated.

Size and shape

Employees: 900   Locations: 29 (27 UK, 2 Bulgaria)
Geographical income split: UK 95%, RoW 5%

However GWR will expand through the rise in advertising revenue which goes to radio stations. The group, along with Capital Radio, has been a chief protagonist for selling radio as a generic concept through the Radio Advertising Bureau. The industry has also benefited from the awareness among companies and advertising agencies of the sector as a commercial medium by the opening of national radio stations. GWR has also achieved considerable organic growth in its stations. Trent FM is now producing a return on sales of nearly 30 per cent. Bernard says that he expects stations in the group to turn in at least a 20 per cent return on sales.

A key development in the last two years has been the deepening of quality of management in the group. The core management team has been supplemented by the addition of Patrick Taylor, finance director of Capital Radio, who planned to join GWR in September 1996. Programming and sales departments are regarded by observers as the strongest in the industry. Bernard is keen to produce levels of teamworking between programmes and sales which have not previously been achieved in the sector. He attributes the success of the relaunch of Chiltern to this policy.

Given the restrictions on growth in the UK, GWR is spreading its wings overseas. It has already taken sizeable interests in a couple of eastern European ventures and is cautiously examining others. 'We also looked at every significant commercial radio market to see where we would be able to enter. Our success in the UK has shown us that we really need to dominate a market if we are going to achieve our commercial objectives. We researched the USA, Canada, Caribbean, mainland European countries, India and South Africa.' Many of these territories had barrriers to entry. 'We concluded that the Pacific Basin offered the best opportunities. But finding the most attractive base was the most difficult problem. The tender for Radio New Zealand led us to find Prospect. There are openings in Singapore, Malaysia, Philippines and China. We will also look at Australia but that of course is a highly developed radio market and requires great study.'

Outlook

Future prospects

- growing overseas radio presence;
- higher returns from existing radio franchises;
- further strategic minority stakes in UK radio.

GWR has set itself the target to be the leading radio company in the UK. Given that Capital runs London, Birmingham and the south, it seems unlikely that GWR will overtake the market leader. But there is plenty of room for growth – further improvements in the UK radio network and singularly exciting opportunities overseas. Until recently GWR was solely a radio business, but the management team is now open to expansion in other forms of media.

Address:

3B2, Westlea, Swindon, Wiltshire SN5 7HF. Tel: 0118 928 4313. Fax: 01793 422771

Havelock Europa plc

Dalgety Bay, Fife

Turnover				
1992	1993	1994	1995	1996
£33M	£35M	£40M	£56M	£67.7M

Summary: Havelock Europa is Britain's leading storefitting company, specialising in large scale work at the upper end of the market both at home and overseas. Company restructuring has slimmed down its labour force and placed more reliance on modern technology. This innovative approach, coupled with in-house design facilities, has enabled Havelock Europa to lead the way in refurbishing a wide range of financial institutions to make them more user friendly. Activities also extend to offices, hospitals, travel centres and hotels. The recession hit the company by cutting profits. But it is now poised for more extensive growth by organic expansion and, if necessary, by acquisition.

The Business

The face of shopping has changed out of all proportion in the last 20 years. Retailers slowly realised that they could no longer rely on mediocre service, poor stock and unattractive surroundings. Customers became discriminating and demanded ease of access and value for money. The most impressive impact of this trend has been on the high street where traditional shop-keeping values have been turned on their heads. Supermarkets, chain stores and financial institutions have radically shifted their perceptions of service. In the banks, for example, 70 per cent of floorspace in outlets used to be devoted to back office processing with barely 30 per cent used by the customers. In 1996 those percentages have been reversed. In supermarkets and chain stores, customer facilities are lighter, brighter and easier to use. Retailers have relied increasingly on shopfitting companies to undertake the redesign and presentation of their branches to the consumer.

Havelock Europa is in the vanguard of those companies refitting high street outlets, banks and building societies. The company has also broadened

233

its range in recent years to cover commercial premises and offices. Given the gentle resurgence of the UK and mainland European economies, Havelock is well-placed to benefit from new orders and expanded business from its rich repertoire of existing clients. The list is impressive in all sections of the business: Boots, Woolworths, House of Fraser, Debenhams, Asda, Marks & Spencer, Safeway, Tesco, Harrods, Burtons, Dixons, Currys. And chief executive Hew Balfour has not been slow to see the potential of the National Lottery. He secured a Camelot contract to build in excess of 10,000 play stations where customers fill in their entries.

The recession was not kind to Havelock Europa as many of the company's best customers cut back on orders. Turnover decreased and jobs disappeared. But a strengthened management team headed by CEO Hew Balfour, who joined the group in 1989, restricted operations and sought new markets to effect a remarkable recovery. An immediate priority was to transform productivity at the group's factories in Dalgety Bay, Nottingham and Letchworth. And it set great store by inhouse design and innovative products. Such was the effect of the recession that when Balfour joined there were five similar quoted companies. Now there are only two. The others either went under or were swallowed up.

Havelock's survival and consequent prosperity owes much to the shrewdness and perception of Balfour and his team. Management saw that manufacturing times had to be cut significantly to offer customers the kind of service they needed. And they went all out to capture the lion's share of the financial services market – a tactic which has succeeded to no mean effect. But first the business needed to reshape its technology and design facilities by upgrading its computer operations. Manufacturing time was cut from nine weeks to three weeks and the company is now a year into a two and a half year technology update which will further reduce lead times from three weeks to five days. It has also spent heavily on business process re-engineering to shorten process times, improve quality, drive down unit production costs and increase productivity. The key long-term objective of the group is to increase the proportion of its own manufactured goods and improve specialist capacity in metal manufacturing operations, which are still limited.

Distinctive features

- speed of operation;
- superb inhouse design facility;
- unique products;
- high customer satisfaction;
- coherent management.

But its sea change came four years ago when the company saw the opportunity for growth in the financial services market. Then it accounted for 12 per cent of business. The figure in 1995 was 44 per cent and rising. A total of 56 Bank of Scotland branches were refurbished in 1995 with a further 41 achieved in 1996. The TSB is also a customer. Balfour is now seeking to extend the company's expertise to building societies and more banks.

'Bank branches were not really user friendly. They were like fortresses with long queues and a lack of space which meant customer irritation and a low return on valuable square footage. We designed a modular system which is quickly installed, in weeks rather than months, and which makes much better use of the space available. It is transportable and reusable so that when requirements change the whole layout can be altered. The parts are standard but each branch is unique and individual.' And the Havelock-ocktagon panelling system has made the refitting of banks a much quicker process. The company is investing in further developing the unique system.

Design innovation has also been the key to sustaining relationships with major retail groups. A Havelock designed merchandising system is now standard in all Marks & Spencer UK outlets.

Size and shape

Employees: 1000   Locations: 4
Geographical income split: UK 91%, mainland Europe 7%, RoW 1%

M&S is now able to use one type of equipment to satisfy all types of merchandise, as well as retaining the flexibility to change a product range overnight within or between departments, without the introduction of new equipment or outside staff.

Stratagems

The company's future is geared to finding new markets, reducing manufacturing unit costs, adding to design resources and, where necessary, forming strategic alliances with other companies. Havelock Europa will continue to grow its non-food retailing work but the biggest expansion will be seen in an increasing diversification to financial services outlets and food retailers. The recession which reduced the number of rival companies means that Havelock is often the only organisation with the resources to handle a number of big projects simultaneously.

Future prospects

- strong growth in Asia and USA;
- financial services to take 50% of sales;
- improved profitability from more efficiency.

An undoubted strength is a determination to make operations more efficient than the already current high level of effectiveness. Most of the components used in contracts are factory produced, ending the need for expensive on-site joinery. Now there is a fast track assembly of pre-made components. The January 1995 acquisition of Showcard Group in a £12.8 million deal gave additional expertise in acrylics and graphics. It meant an added attraction to potential customers who can do a one-stop shop with Havelock Europa. Further expansion in the PoS market took place in February 1996 with the acquisition of Bristol-based Hartcliffe, a major graphics printing company.

Outlook

The potential for increased penetration of the financial services market is immense. And HE is in a strong position as a major UK shopfitting company to take advantage of its leading position. But that expansion will not come at the expense of food and non-food operations. Most retail companies want or need to refurbish approximately every five years. Balfour has turned his gaze towards six new out of town shopping centres which are either under construction or to be built at Manchester, Glasgow, Leeds, Dartford, Bristol and Southampton by 1999. It means an extra five million square feet over the next two years. He says 'We have not seen an explosion like that since the late 80s. Even if we only get a proportionate share of the business there are big targets to aim for. But if we can get a bigger share, it presents a considerable opportunity for us.'

Address:

Mossway, Hillend, Dalgety Bay, Fife KY11 5JS Tel: 01383 820044 626224. Fax: 01383 820064

Headlam Group plc

Northampton

Turnover				
1992	1993	1994	1995	1996
£58.8M	£107M	£134.3M	£146.9M	£186.4M

Summary: The story of the Headlam Group is sustained, consistent and outstanding success. Primarily engaged in carpet distribution to independent retailers – although the company has recently moved into soft furnishings – Headlam Group has made a rapid and significant impact in a market which was formerly characterised by inconsistent and inefficient service. In five short years, through acquisition, capable management, high quality service and effective use of technology, it has become the market leading distributor of floor coverings in the UK. As its onward march continues domestically, it has spread its wings into mainland Europe and into the USA primarily through its soft furnishings activities.

The Business

In 1991, Graham Waldron and Ian Kirkham effectively reversed into a shell company called Headlam Group with the intention of creating an efficiently managed and service-orientated wholesale carpet distribution business. Every year since the company has increased sales, pretax profit, earnings per share and dividends per share. In 1991 the company's market capitalisation was assessed at £4 million, but by March 1997 this had risen to £200 million. Although organic growth played a major part in the company's definitive rise, an acquisitions strategy was central to the growth of the group.

Every year the group has made several acquisitions, culminating in its purchase in December 1996 of the Gradus Group plc for £32.9 million. Gradus had two divisions – flooring accessories in Macclesfield and its carpets operation based in Poynton. The reason for the takeover was to extend Headlam into the area of project and specification contract carpets which is forecast to enjoy rapid growth.

Floor coverings accounts for 67 per cent of Headlam's operating profits and soft furnishing fabrics 33 per cent. The company's carpets division covers the UK from eight depots and in February 1996 bought Lethem-Vergeer in the Netherlands as the first step in an expansion programme in mainland Europe. Headlam entered the highly fragmented soft furnishings market with the acquisition of Claremont Fabrics in June 1993. The subsequent purchase of other business in this sector has continued to add to the group's bottom line. Notably, Lethem-Vergeer's fabric business and the subsequent takeover of another Dutch business, Interplan, have built Headlam's presence on the mainland. In January 1997, Headlam signed a distribution agreement with Covington Industries, one of the USA's largest fabric coverters. While Headlam has no sales in the USA as yet, the agreement will allow the designs produced by its subsidiaries Claremont, Gordon John, Edinburgh Weavers and Sundour access to the largest soft furnishing market in the world.

Distinctive features

- top two carpet distributor in the UK;
- rapid growth by acquisition and organically;
- expansion in mainland Europe and the USA;
- high quality service to independent retailers.

Stratagems

When Headlam entered the carpet distribution sector, it was fragmented and poorly managed. Service was at best inconsistent for the independent high street retailer and the two senior directors realised that by setting new standards for service they could gain a major share of the market.

The strategy has relied on three basic principles: growth by acquisition, innovative (for the sector) use of technology and reliable service. One analyst comments 'The independent carpet retailers were coming under pressure from the major out-of-town players. Their sites were too small to hold large volumes of carpet and so they could not offer the service which the big players could supply. Headlam immediately changed the situation by offering these businesses reliable next day delivery. Their customers could visit the high street shop, choose a carpet and take delivery within a day. Headlam's depots are placed so that it can gain effective penetration of the country and its customers are close enough for speedy delivery.'

The combination of acquisition of significant local players and enhanced service to the retailer has made a major impact on Headlam's profitability.

The application of technology centrally and the depots means that the group is ahead of any of its competitors in meeting the needs of the high street carpet store.

> **Size and shape**
>
> Employees: 1400   Locations: 16
> Geographical income split: UK 90%, mainland Europe 10%

As the company has reached a major position in the UK floor covering distribution market it has chosen two avenues in which to diversify – geographical expansion into mainland Europe and product development into soft furnishing fabrics. One commentator on the sector says 'The floor coverings market in mainland Europe is immense. As a first step the company has bought two Dutch companies on the basis that the customer in the Netherlands is very similar in approach and culture to the UK.

'Headlam plans to buy other businesses in mainland Europe as opportunities arise. Its expansion into the USA in the soft furnishing fabrics sector is an attempt to enter the largest market worldwide for these goods.'

> **Future prospects**
>
> • extending UK market leadership;
> • further European/US growth;
> • more acquisitions.

Outlook

Headlam aims to grow in every area of its business. Its objective in the UK is to be the most efficient, cost effective and profitable distributor of floor coverings. Outside the British Isles it plans a long-term expansion into mainland Europe and to test the water in North America. The company believes that it can still further improve the efficiencies of its core business and add to their strength and range. The substantial growth in its share price would suggest that investors share its vision.

Address:

Headlam Group plc, Riverside Way, Bedford Road, Northampton NN1 5NH. Tel: 01604 234121. Fax: 01504 27105

Howell, Henry, Chaldecott, Lury and Partners

London

Turnover				
1992	1993	1994	1995	1996
£3.9M	£4.5M	£7.7M	£10M	£13M

Summary: The formation of Howell, Henry, Chaldecott, Lury and Partners in 1987 was the first time in the history of the UK advertising sector where a founding partner came with impeccable business credentials from outside the industry. This key decision shaped the nature of the business – HHCL would be run on strictly commercial lines. But it is also one of the most creative agencies in Britain, winning award after award and pitch after pitch. The company has succeeded because it understands its clients' businesses intimately and offers a holistic approach to their communications.

The Business

The Automobile Association (AA) represents a good example of how HHCL works with its clients. 'The previous agency had done a very popular job with its campaign "A very nice man", but the patrolmen were tired of the campaign and it had done nothing to increase membership or improve retention. We talked to many AA people throughout the UK and tried to find out what was special about the organisation. We dreamed up "The fourth emergency service", which restored the patrolmen's pride and increased both new membership and retention rates. As a result we were subsequently involved in the redesign of the uniform and the whole pattern of the way in which the AA communicates.'

The speaker is Rupert Howell, first name on the plate of the groundbreaking advertising agency HHCL and Partners. This award-winning former head of new business development at Young and Rubicam brought together the team which would form the nucleus of HHCL and fashion a generation

240

of ads, including the Harry Enfield campaign for Mercury, a series defining Tango as a keynote soft drinks brand, and a rather eliptical approach to telephone banker First Direct.

Howell wanted to run his own agency. His first, and defining, recruit as unnamed founding partner was Robin Price. 'I had known Robin for years and we assumed that one day we would go into business together. His involvement was key because no other agency had ever launched with a non-industry individual as a partner. I wanted us to have a clearer vision of the business priorities of our clients than any of our rivals. This is one of our strengths. We spend time and effort appreciating what makes our clients tick and what they are trying to achieve from their communications.

'Next I met Steve Henry. He and his partner Axel Chaldecott had done some excellent work at GGT and WCRS. Henry was the copywriter and Chaldecott the art director. Their partnership was inspired. But they were keen to try something new. Our final choice was Adam Lury, a frustrated planner at BMP. He had presented a paper on how to revolutionise planning and they weren't interested. Once we brought the team together, we deliberately spent six months getting to know each other before we announced our decision to form the agency.' Previous launches had been undermined by people who had not planned sufficiently well. 'Then we started three weeks before Black Monday. People said it was a terrible time to open an agency. I rather took the opposite view. We were a lean operation. We did not have to fire anyone and incur ill will. Accounts were changing hands and clients were looking for a different perspective.'

Distinctive features

- holistic client approach;
- top UK creative team;
- businessman as founding partner;
- highly profitable.

Stratagems

'Robin Price has drummed into me a key lesson about profitability. It is not just about maximising revenue and minimising costs; it is about maximising revenue and maximising the efficient use of resources. We do this in several ways. The first is by honing our negotiating skills. All of our management, all of our account directors and all of our TV and print producers have been on negotiation skills courses. We negotiate professionally with our clients and also on behalf of them. Another problem the industry has is chasing unprofitable business. In order to stop ourselves doing this we have always set a mimimum fee level and stuck to it. It has meant that we have had to pass up some potentially sexy accounts. I believe loss leaders are a terminally bad idea in our business.

'We do not work on commission; I am not an estate agent! I want to be free to advise clients to spend less on advertising where appropriate and I want to service their needs without worrying about whether we are going to make a profit. We much prefer the fee system. Our method is resource allocation and workload based. We are totally transparent and it's great to have no skeletons in the cupboard. But the real reason we are able to do this is because our clients pay us properly in the first place.'

Size and shape

Employees: 160   Locations: 1
Geographical income split: UK 90%, mainland Europe 7%. RoW 3%

Another key strength for the business is its creative approach to income streams. 'Our core agency offers a service which we call 3D Marketing Communications which combines the strategic skills of advertising, direct marketing and sales promotion in a seamless structure under one contract with a client. The extent to which we get involved in the execution of direct marketing and sales promotion varies but we always execute the advertising. We also earn income from creative development research and from directing our own commercials.' The business also set up three separate divisions: Lury Price Associates, a planning consultancy; Environment Marketing, PR and product placement; and Project Management Services. 'We have also established the HHCL Brasserie. The analogy is taken from classy restaurants in London, where they have a main restaurant and a brasserie. The HHCL Brasserie works on a project basis for clients who might be with other agencies but want something special outside the remit of their mainstream relationship.' In addition HHCL has a joint venture media strategy company and a business called 'In Real Life' which covers so-called face-to-face communications – conferences, exhibitions, roadshows, internal communications and even designing theme parks.

Another important business approach at HHCL is chasing debts. 'Historically there is a belief if you sue clients or ex-clients you will get a reputation for being litigious and scare future clients. This is nonsense. We want to be taken seriously as a business and so we stand up for our rights.' HHCL is a great believer in actively learning from mistakes. 'Everyone makes mistakes. What sets apart both businesses and individuals is the degree to which they learn from them.' The business specifies six classifications of where it has been 'stitched up like a kipper' and has vowed never to make the same mistake again. These include accepting verbal promises of profit-related bonuses and a lower initial fee; jam tomorrow – accepting a lower fee this year in favour of continued work and a higher rate next year; delayed negotiations, where the client has not yet signed the contract but you have a great creative idea that you wish to push through; always covering in the contract what is not included in the fee as well as what is; new business bullying, similar to delayed negotiations, where the prospective client says there is another agency and will you cut your fee?; and one called 'higher authority' where a trusted client genuinely has no more money to spend and HHCL now says 'which service do you wish to cut?' rather than just cutting the fee.

Outlook

Future prospects

- business growth from 3D approach;
- rapid expansion of subsidiaries;
- further organic growth;
- greater international work.

HHCL is convinced that the old concept of an advertising agency just informing customers about new products has gone. 'The unique selling proposition (USP) which inspired the industry for decades is finished. We need a radically new approach and one which incorporates the customer into the process. The perspective will always be holistic and the emphasis will be on integrated thinking.' HHCL is well placed to benefit from the changing pattern of marketing. It is highly reputed, creatively and as a business. Its knowledge and understanding of clients is outstanding. HHCL is a standard bearer in the sector.

Address:

Howell, Henry, Chaldecott, Lury and Partners, Market Place, Kent House, 14–17 Great Titchfield Street, London W1N 7AJ. Tel: 0171 436 3333. Fax: 0171 436 2677

Hozelock Ltd

Aylesbury, Bucks

Turnover				
1992	1993	1994	1995	1996
£27M	£32M	£38M	£52M	£51M

Summary: Hozelock dominates the UK gardening equipment sector. It manufactures watering, spraying, pond and foundation, and outdoor clothes-drying products. Given the increasing domestic interest in gardening, UK demand for its products is expected to grow at a rapid rate. The company is expanding the portfolio of its products available for the local gardening community and is making substantial inroads into equally promising mainland European markets. Hozelock invests heavily in capital projects to boost its capacity for future profitable expansion.

The Business

The British passion for gardening achieved new heights in the last decade. Garden centres flourished; mass-market magazines about the pastime and inch-thin books on every variety and species of plant sold in record volumes. Suburban plots radiated with every colour and shade, and gave a home to infinite varieties of new and traditional flowers, shrubs, bushes and trees. The subtext over wider public concern about the quality of food fostered a lively interest in the arts of fruit and vegetable cultivation. This was excellent news for the gardening equipment manufacturer Hozelock, which has reported substantial increases in the growth of its sales and pretax profits and was honoured in 1995 with the top prize in Britain's most prestigious small business competition – the PLC Awards.

Its recent – and most relevant – history began in 1990 when its owner, the shipping, property and engineering conglomerate Ropner plc, sold its then gardening equipment arm to management and City investors for £24 million. In five years its market capitalisation had risen by a factor of five to £120 million. In the interim, mid-year 1993, it floated on the London Stock

Exchange. The company operates in four key product areas and draws three-fifths of its revenues from garden watering. Its two premier product areas are described by the company as garden watering equipment and sprayers. Gardening watering makes 25 million miles of hose pipe every year – enough to stretch three quarters of the way around the world. Sprayers produces 2.9 million units a year for applications as diverse as spraying water during ironing and applying suntan oil, as well as the more conventional garden sprinklers.

Its other divisions embrace gardens aquatics and outdoor drying equipment. Aquatics features ponds, pumps, pond linings, fountains and lighting. These two divisions each account for between ten and 14 per cent of turnover. Three quarters of its production is bought by UK customers, through garden centres and high street stockists, which makes the Hozelock brand a formidable force in the industry. Mainland European sales account for the vast bulk of the remainder with the focus on Scandinavia, the Benelux countries and France. A subsidiary company in France was established before the buyout in 1990 to bring sales and marketing closer to the major retailers to manage a small stock. Hozelock also bought out its Dutch and Swedish distributors in October 1994 and March 1995 respectively, leading to a fresh spurt of sales in these markets. To sustain its rapid growth the company is feeding some £14 million a year into capital investment. It has built a new assembly plant in Birmingham and is investing £8 million in an on-site warehouse which started operations in the autumn of 1996.

Distinctive features

- commanding leads in UK gardening watering markets;
- heavy emphasis on sticking to its core markets;
- rapid growth in domestic gardening sectors;
- strong capital investment programme;
- developing mainland European business.

Stratagems

Hozelock's dominant share in the UK market – it now accounts for around 70 per cent of all watering equipment sold in Britain – means that the company has chosen to direct its attention overseas to maintain its superb growth record. Across mainland Europe its share of markets falls to as little as ten per cent. Therefore, Hozelock's management reckons that its brightest hopes lie in carving out a larger chunk of garden spending on the continent.

It faces only one substantial competitor on mainland Europe, which is the German company Gardena. This business is extremely strong on its home turf but Hozelock's market research shows that the best opportunities for confronting its German rival are in Scandinavia, the Benelux countries and France. As a result, it has initiated an active campaign to target these territories.

The virgin gardens of Eastern Europe offer immense potential. Remarkably, Gardena does not have a presence in the east and so Hozelock encounters no entrenched opposition.

Size and shape

Employees: 661   Locations: 3
Geographical income split: UK 69%, mainland Europe 26%, RoW 5%

The company is even planning to extend the scope of its influence to the southern hemisphere. Beyond the obvious sales and marketing advantages, this strategy has the added benefit of soaking up spare capacity in the bitter English winter. Hozelock's management team has also decided to build the aquatics side of the business, believing that there is still plenty of sales mileage in ponds and fountains, and that the company could become the first pan-European aquatics business.

Future prospects

- expansion in selected mainland European markets;
- new assembly and warehousing complex in Birmingham to come on-line;
- intention to build the first pan-European garden aquatics company.

Besides its overseas adventures, Hozelock's management is conscious of the need to stay ahead in its heartland. In 1995 the company offered 277 Hozelock-branded products in the UK market. Around ten per cent of these were completely new. It is this degree of innovation which the business needs to retain and grow in share and it spends around £1.2 million a year in new product tooling alone. A key strategic objective is to be the lowest cost manufacturer in its sector. When Hozelock products are designed, this intention is a major factor in the planning. The experience of the managers at its plastics injection moulding installation in Buckinghamshire are a major asset in this process.

Heavy investment in capacity should enable the company to ensure that there is no over-dependence on costly sub-contracting in the peak season. Flexible recruitment practices are central to cost control. A high proportion of the workforce is made up of temporary staff who are employed for only the spring and summer. In Birmingham, many alternate their Hozelock employment with autumn and winter work in the jewellery quarter. Increasing volumes are also making the implementation of automation on the line highly cost-effective.

Outlook

Hozelock is popular with City analysts, who see the company as proficiently-managed with a glowing future. Particularly impressive is the quality of operating margins which often achieve around 18 per cent. Both the company and its admirers in the financial community see further large scale potential in the UK gardens sectors, especially in sales of automatic sprinklers. It has many cost advantages over its principal mainland competitor which will assist its further penetration on the continent.

Address:

Haddenham, Aylesbury, Buckinghamshire HP17 8JD. Tel: 01844 291881. Fax: 01844 290344

Huntleigh Technology plc

Luton, Beds

Turnover				
1992	1993	1994	1995	1996
£28M	£36M	£70M	£92M	£93M

Summary: Huntleigh Technology supplies bed, mattress, hoist and diagnostic systems to support the care of patients in hospitals, nursing homes and private residencies. It is the largest European manufacturer of advanced mattresses and hand-held Doppler products and has won four Queen's Awards for exporting and technical achievement. The group is becoming worldwide in its orientation and aims to derive benefits from synergies between its manufacturing operations and technologies. The long-term trend in society towards ageing and the increasing prevalence of community care operate strongly in Huntleigh's favour. The structure of multiple divisions, each with P&L responsibility, should encourage its vigorous growth.

The Business

Many family-owned businesses prosper but few achieve the status of world class companies with outstanding international reputations for their technical integrity and quality of management. Huntleigh Technology is one of the latter group, widely acknowledged as a producer of quality products for global healthcare markets. Rolf Schild and other senior executives have grown the group from a rump engineering businesses. Healthcare became the focus of Huntleigh's core activities in 1980. It now has three principal areas of expertise: pressure-reducing mattresses, ultrasonics and load cells for weighing. Although it has 16 main subsidiaries and two joint ventures, Huntleigh's central strategy for growth has been organic. Sales have escalated from £21 million in 1991 to a market estimate of £101 million in 1997. Pretax profits have shown a similar rate of rise from £1.62 million to a projected £14.6 million in 1997. Return on sales now stands at 14 per cent. The group's operations spread from the UK where it has six locations to mainland Europe, Australia and the USA.

Huntleigh's two core producers are mattresses and Doppler scanners. The mattresses reduce the incidence of pressure sores among patients and involve plastics and pumping technologies. The original advance was to produce lower-cost mattresses with the performance of more expensive ones through better engineering. They are sold directly, by distributors or supplied through rental operations. In 1994 Huntleigh bought Nesbit Evans, an established hospital bedmaker, and now produces the beds which support Huntleigh's mattresses as well as a range of examination couches. The Nesbit Evans purchase has been so successful that after the first full year sales have climbed by 97 per cent and pretax profit by 42 per cent. The bed range being energetically developed using newer materials and designs will increase levels of nursing staff productivity.

Its ultrasonic division is experiencing rapid sales growth. The Cardiff manufacturing base has been developed into a global centre of excellence, where its Doppler products provide foetal heartbeat and blood vessel monitoring technology. Finance director and deputy chairman Julian Schild argues that much of Huntleigh's market advantage in this sector derives from its skills in electronics and software engineering. Schild maintains that Oxford Instruments was formerly the market leader but Huntleigh has now taken over the top spot due to its stronger and sharper focus. The company is also active in the market for remote diagnostics products. 'We have seen the trend to move diagnostics responsibilities out of hospitals. Our products will capitalise on the ensuing demand for diagnostics kits in GP surgeries and for home use.'

Distinctive features

- rapid sales and PBT growth;
- international reputation;
- high market potential;
- engineering value-added;
- export orientation.

Huntleigh also produces hoisting equipment for disabled and elderly patients. Nesbit Evans brought in a hospital furniture business so the group can offer a package of beds, mattresses, and furniture. Such collections appeal directly to community care centres and the group is growing Huntleigh National Care and Huntleigh Community Care to exploit this trend. It also has a catalogue operation selling a whole range of healthcare products, operates rental centres and has a physiotherapy product unit called Huntleigh Akron.

The load cell technology resides in a joint venture, Tedea-Huntleigh, which Schild characterises as a 'sleeping partner'. It provided an £800,000 contribution to profits in 1995 and there are opportunities to exploit its technology in future beds which weigh patients. 'We believe that we should add weights to beds and harnesses. These products are currently in development.' The US rental business is a joint venture called SpectraCair and the group considers further joint venture arrangements will be welcome. Schild points out 'One hundred per cent ownership of any venture is unnecessary for it to be a success.'

Stratagems

At the heart of the Huntleigh Technology strategy is export. Schild argues that the group needs its contribution from sales overseas to build critical mass. It faces a series of short term impedances in the UK but the domestic market is a long term prospect for strong growth. He suggests the strength of its short term British order book is hindered by delays caused by both the insistence of UK buyers on budgeting and the slow development of the community care initiative. Despite these hurdles, Huntleigh's impressive growth is testimony to the group's intrinsic strength and its positive outlook.

Size and shape

Employees: 1279   Locations: 11
Geographical income split: UK 44%, USA 27%, mainland Europe 20%, RoW 9%

A major potential opportunity for the company is the developing countries, where there are openings for beds, mattresses and Doppler scanners.

Future prospects

- major opportunities for export;
- series of product development;
- significant sales growth;
- substantial long-term UK business.

Huntleigh invests heavily in product development. Healthcare is a demanding marketplace where standards are consistently pushed higher and higher. Schild says that the company can add value to beds through improved electronics. As a management philosophy, Schild believes that the group should control the technologies which are at the core of its products. This is so its R&D people can fully exploit all the synergies available from complementary companies working in the same broad industrial sector. For example, the motors and controllers used in its hoists are also applied to its construction of beds.

Part of the company's expansion will be generated from the creation of new niche markets which Huntleigh can dominate. Beds are a core part of the group's turnover and it is currently developing a range of day beds for patients who enter hospital for outpatient surgery or investigation of symptoms.

Outlook

Huntleigh Healthcare is a company with a long-term future. It is running an energetic export campaign operation in mainland Europe, the USA and Australia. In mid-year 1996 export accounts for 56 per cent of all sales. In the years to come, turnover generated overseas will far outstrip sales in the UK. Healthcare markets are growing worldwide. Huntleigh is market leader in many of its disciplines and territories and this should give the company a head start when it comes to winning over. Also the group is focusing on synergies from its divisions and is providing greater value-added in its range.

Address:

310–312 Dallow Road, Luton, Bedfordshire LU1 1TD. Tel: 01582 459000. Fax: 01582 402589

Ideal Hardware plc ELECTRONICS/DISTRIBUTION

New Malden, Surrey

Turnover				
1992	1993	1994	1995	1996
£30M	£45M	£72M	£102M	£138M

Summary: Ideal Hardware is the largest and most respected data storage peripherals distributor in the UK. It enjoys a commanding lead on its rivals in terms of relationships with blue chip manufacturers and quality of service to its customers. Ideal's facility with its markets is demonstrated by its outstanding sales and pretax profits growth during the last five years. Averaged annualised growth in profits is 56 per cent and in sales 89 per cent. One of the company's key strengths is its capacity to understand, translate and communicate simply the ever-increasing technical complexity and range of products.

The Business

The business concept which brought Ideal Hardware into being remains, in a developed form, at the heart of the enterprise today. In 1987 managing director James Wickes identified an accelerating trend in the computer industry: products, especially in his field of data storage, would become more complex and their shelf life would scale down dramatically. The distributor would therefore need to become an expert discriminator between these systems and occupy a unique, almost consultative, position in the chain between manufacturers and end-users. Wilkes argued that providing clear information which was easily understood by the resellers created significant added value – and therefore commercial success for distributors. Ideal Hardware believes inherently in its role of information provider as essential precursor to continuing sales.

In examining this company it is hard to underplay the benefits which its facility as a communicator has brought. Ideal has grown from two floors of a

Queen Anne house in Mayfair, through a site at Tolworth Tower near Kingston in Surrey, to its own development at nearby New Malden. In seven years the business expanded from three individuals to a fully listed company on the London Stock Exchange employing 220 people at two sites. Since 1990 sales have risen from £11 million to £138 million and pretax profits have climbed from £816,000 to £7.8 million. MD Wickes says that his target by the end of 1997 is turnover of £250 million.

The core of the business is data storage products which it sells to more than 4500 resellers across the UK. To classify Ideal's position in the market is difficult but in summary among all distributors of computer products – around 60 – it is number five. But among distributors of data storage products it is national leader, occupying around 15 per cent of market – estimated by Dataquest to be worth approaching US$700 million. Some 95 per cent of Ideal's income is derived from the UK with an additional five per cent source from mainland Europe.

It hasn't all been plain sailing though. In 1991, according to operations director Simon Barker, Ideal brought in management consultants to help them plan their strategy. 'Apart from telling us the usual stuff about maximising returns and slashing costs, they conducted the first survey of our customers. This proved a revelation. Customers thought we were the best of a bad bunch.' MD Wickes continues 'Since I had always intended that this would be a highly respected business, ultimately regarded with as much esteem as Marks & Spencer, for example, I was shocked. We listened very carefully to what the resellers were saying.' One immediate result of the survey was the decision to base delivery in-house. Until then, like all other distributors, Ideal had used national carriers to deliver their products. The outcome had been disenchanted customers left holding damaged and dented goods. Ideal's management immediately recruited and trained 30 staff drivers and commissioned liveried vehicles.

Distinctive features

- capacity to communicate;
- closeness with makers;
- understanding of customers;
- extensive product range.

Stratagems

The business is guided by simple strategic principles: strong liaison with all major manufacturers, tight control on costs, broad range of products, deep understanding of product development and market shifts, constant dialogue with customers, achieving strong discounts for customers by virtue of buying power, a core belief in its role as an information provider, and a commitment to its own brand. This last point is telling. Almost all the other distributors in this sector emphasise the brands of their products rather their own identity. 'We have done this to show that we are not tied to any one range of products or single supplier. We distribute products from all major manufacturers. Ideal has built a close rapport with companies as diverse as IBM, Digital, Panasonic and Siemens Nixdorf plus many of the more specialist manufacturers,' says Wickes.

Decisions are taken by three executives working as a team – MD Wickes, operations director Barker and sales director Kevin Harper. 'There are really three MDs. We each have our strengths and those are respected. I deal with strategy, Kevin is Mr Gross Profit and Simon is Mr Net Profit. There are no challenges to our individual areas of expertise and we make decisions collectively,' says Wickes. Heavy emphasis is placed on the position of cash in the financial management of the business and borrowing – a key factor in the 1980s – has been stripped out. Barker again. 'We keep daily track of our key financial measures, which are stock turn, daily turnover, gross profit and debtor days. Every morning the management team reviews our performance in each of these areas and looks for targets for improvement.' Efficient day to day management of working capital is seen as a core principle, supported, as one might expect from a computer industry business, by the latest real-time technology. The decision to go for a listing in London allowed Ideal to raise £5 million to invest in its new site at New Malden.

Size and shape

Employees: 300   Locations: 2 (head office and second warehouse)
Geographical income split: UK 95%, mainland Europe 5%

Part of this investment has gone into a panoply of communications and television products. A weekly Channel Vision television programme was the foundation stone for a complete IT product information network wholly-owned by Ideal, which now broadcasts by satellite to distributors three times a day. Profile, an online product information database, lists all products currently available at Ideal, with a full spec sheet and photograph of each one but with the added advantage of a short video clip giving an abbreviated pitch for each product. A bi-monthly magazine called *Change*, the *Vogue* of the Ideal collection, deals in full colour with key industry issues and major product developments. The company has also launched what it calls Cyber

Seminars to provide interactive training for distributors. Ideal's approach has certainly won friends in the City. Ian Forsyth, analyst with jobbers Winterflood Securities, says 'I am surprised that none of the other distributors have tried to emulate Ideal's approach. The problem for competitors is that they would need to invest so heavily to attempt to match Ideal that this is an effective bar to entry. The company could confidently expect to increase its share of the UK market to around 40 per cent in the next few years.'

In addition it is building a new £9 million warehouse at Tolworth which will greatly expand its capacity. As might be expected from a company which is driven by leading edge methodology, Ideal's new complex will incorporate the latest systems for meeting exacting customer service deadlines.

Future prospects

- growth of UK market share to 40 per cent;
- enhancement of manufacturer and reseller relationships;
- long-term penetration of mainland European market;
- broadening its distribution base.

Outlook

The potential for expansion of its market share, overall sales and profitability remain high. Ideal has chosen to differentiate itself from its rivals by heavy investment in information provision and quality of customer service. It now enjoys excellent relationships with the manufacturers and with many of its customers. In fact Ideal has become invaluable to the makers because it provides an independent expert channel to the resellers. The company has also taken great pains through enhanced customer service teams and its catalogue of information services to ensure that the resellers are fully informed. Balanced by tough financial management, this should allow the business to achieve its sales and profitability targets. MD Wickes says that after the company has reached a quarter of a billion turnover in late 1997, it may start building its business in mainland Europe. But given the scope for growing market share here the company may be fully tied up for at least the next five years.

Address:

265 Burlington Road, New Malden, Surrey KT3 4NE. Tel: 0181 286 5000. Fax: 0181 286 5056. Web address: http://www.ideal.co.uk

IES Group

West Malling, Kent

Turnover		
1994	1995	1996
£3M	£4.4M	£6M

Summary: The IES Group supplies leading edge technology and services to the booming UK security market which is expected to be valued – in all its aspects – at £6.3 billion by 1998. Launched only three and a half years ago through IES Ltd, the group operates in three divisions which develop, assemble and market electronic security and information technology equipment, and provide management and administrative services to the commercial and industrial sectors. It leads the market in software solutions for security problems such as the fraudulent withdrawal from cash machines. Centred on digital image capture, storage and transmission, the technology provides a picture of the perpetrator which can be enhanced and then transmitted anywhere. The group has floated on the Alternative Investment Market.

The Business

The future growth and success of the IES Group is founded largely on the fact that it has invented something for the future, taking the security businesses from the hidebound world of the status quo to the exciting new horizons of technology which will virtually guarantee greater success in the fight against industrial and commercial crime.

Its landmark invention is a high-tech security system, based on digital technology, which will record and store pictures of every person that moves within range of its cameras. Seeing is believing – that hoary old adage – lies at the heart of this revolutionary advance in the detection of fraud, vandalism, and the failure of technologies considered failsafe.

It heralds a new era of unmanned petrol station forecourts and bank and building society cash machines where anything untoward is captured automatically on digital images.

The technology itself provides an instant retrieval or an image selected by time and location. This digital image will not degrade and can be enhanced before transmitting it down a telephone line, providing remote and visual verification. It operates simply with television cameras trained on petrol pumps and the credit card machines used by customers to pay for the fuel. The technology records digitally compressed moving images on to a computer hard disk. When it runs out of capacity, the images are downloaded on to a digital tape recorder.

Distinctive features

- highly innovative technology;
- widespread application in diverse industrial and commercial settings;
- revolutionary impact on security industry.

Both storage devices can be accessed through modems which allow remote security guards to monitor premises 24 hours a day. The system has the widest applications for a broad range of customers in a variety of commercial and industrial settings. Kuwait Petroleum is testing it in an unmanned forecourt in Ely, Cambridge. Abbey National is also trying the technology and was updating its automatic telling machines with the technology during 1996 with the IES system. 'If someone abuses an unmanned petrol outlet, there will be a record of the face and a car number plate,' says Roy Ricks, chairman and managing director of the IES group.

British Airways signed a contract with IES to provide its technology for a digital security system that should allow for 100 per cent proof surveillance of its cargo areas around the world. 'If British Airways gets something stolen, there will be a record of it,' says Ricks. 'And through the system, BA technicians in New York can dial into a cargo area in Heathrow or any other airport where it operates.'

There are also important applications in the fuel and energy industries. The video motion detection software module can be used to detect, from long distance, smoke emanating from machinery, enabling rapid shutdown of equipment to prevent extensive damage. IES has conducted successful trials on this equipment with Nuclear Electric.

Stratagems

The genesis of IES Group came from IES Limited in late 1992. Roy Ricks, its founder, developed a loop alarm system that allowed retailers to protect goods on open display. It secured Dixons as a major customer and began to broaden its product range and enhance its design expertise.

The group was formed in December 1993 and rapidly began a series of acquisitions. The first, in March 1994, was the purchase of ICM Security Products which had been created in 1991 to specify, design and manufacture a series of niche hardware-based electronic security products. IES Group increased its product range with two additional acquisitions – Paramount Security Services in October 1994 and Audio and Visual Verification in March 1995. To develop its visual verification system, IES added Hawkeye Visual Systems and Digital Direct to the group.

Ricks says the reason for the purchases was strategic not financial. 'We bought people and technology. People who had ideas but who could not exploit them commercially.' IES now boasts a customer list which includes Dixons Stores, House of Fraser, Chubb Alarms, Thorn Security, Boots, Comet, Texas Homecare, Somerfield, Homebase, Abbey National, Alliance and Leicester, Tesco, Asda, Texaco, Kuwait Oil and British Airways.

From the outset the group's strategy has been based on three tenets: to provide total commitment to the primacy of client and client need; to target niche markets neglected by the industry; and to give funding priority to research and development.

Future prospects

- growth in retail sector;
- further acquisitions to add to technological expertise;
- greater R&D spend.

The extraordinary growth of IES and the inroads it has made into the traditional security services market, looks set to continue. The group has deliberately chosen a strategy which makes it innovation-focused and customer-led. In a sector which has been dilatory about attending to the needs of its customers, IES aims for market leadership.

Address:

IES Group, West Malling, Kent. Tel: 01732 879300. Fax: 01732 872431

Innovative Technologies Group plc HEALTHCARE

Winsford, Cheshire

Turnover			
1994	1995	1996	1997
£30k	£0.7M	£5.5M	£15Me

Summary: Innovative Technologies designs, develops and manufactures between 20 and 30 medical devices fabricated from specially designed, functional polymers using novel processing technology. Its mission is to be the world market leader in the invention of disposable devices for healthcare, effectively a one-stop shop for biomaterials and medical fabrication technology. Its customers are leading international distributors and suppliers of medical devices in Europe, North America and the Pacific. Since its launch in 1991, IT has grown its staff to 130 and its sales to in excess of £5 million. It originally listed in December 1994 on the USM and moved to a full listing in early 1996. Its market capitalisation in mid-year 1996 was £61 million.

The Business

IT was created in November 1991. Husband and wife team Dr Keith Gilding, a polymer chemist, and Dr Diane Mitchell, an internationally respected geneticist, and four associates staked £80,000 to create a new generation of biomaterials for the medical devices market. The initial base was primitive – a ten feet by six feet potting shed in the garden of the couple's home in Wettenhall, near Winsford. The experience and expertise of this multi-disciplinary team spanned the spectrum of synthetic to natural polymers and its members had a track record of significant roles in the medical disposable, pharmaceutical and textile sectors.

Financial backing came from South African entrepreneur Clifford Gundle. He was inspired by the opportunity after watching Gilding discuss wound care products with Prince Charles on BBC TV's *Tomorrow's World*.

In 1994, IT raised £8 million from a rights issue and a float on the USM. During 1995, new personnel were recruited to form its custom conversion group, along with a technical director, wound care product manager and a director of regulatory affairs.

The principal activities of the group centre on the design, development and supply of medical products based on novel high performance natural and synthetic polymers. IT has focused its core technology initially on a vertically integrated manufacturing facility for alginate and film wound dressings. The polyurethanes developed for wound care have also been exploited for catheters, gloves and textiles. IT has embarked on a simple strategy in a complex field: to become a one-stop shop for biomaterials, primarily for healthcare, but also with myriad applications in niche industrial markets. The science of IT's processes can be characterised as molecular engineering. The company replicates the positive values of well observed biological processes with the controlled creation of synthetic polymers and the modification of natural biopolymer composites.

'The study and development of biopolymers, using derivatives of seaweed and other natural resources, leads to particularly exciting possibilities. New products that have greater compatibility with human tissue will bring cost-reducing advantages to nursing care and post-operative procedures. IT is already at the forefront of wet spinning non-woven alginates for medical and allied products for the healthcare market,' says Gilding. Production is precise and controlled. Each batch is pre-tested and profiled to ensure that established interactions create the specific properties desired. In the medical field this is particularly important. IT's leadership in the market has facilitated the purchase of a reactor capacity geared to manufacturing to a range of high performance polymers with the flexibility to meet many different criteria.

Distinctive features

- unique technology and products;
- worldwide distribution to blue chips;
- initial target of annual sales of £100 million;
- vertical integration of manufacture.

Through intensive research and development, much has already been achieved. A host of advanced products and formulations, exclusive to the company, help the body heal more quickly and more comfortably; protect against secondary infections, irritation and physical damage; and bring many benefits beyond the core applications in healthcare. IT's product portfolio includes materials for wound care derived from alginates and other bio-polymers; breathable hydrophilic polyurethanes, ideal for thin films used in wound care, gloves, condoms, and waterproof breathable textiles; hydro-phobic polyurethanes in solution or pellets for latex rubber or nylon; bioactive pressure-sensitive and moisture-activated adhesives applicable for wound care and drug delivery; and speciality materials and coatings for catheters and guidewire products.

Stratagems

The founders realised at the company's inception that there would be many applications for IT's products but the demand from its customers has far exceeded their most optimistic forecasts. Its leading edge technology and proven capacity to deliver – rapidly – has led to a range of commercial opportunities. This has promoted a speedy growth in the company's size, particularly in terms of facilities and personnel. The challenge which has emerged from this promising expansion is the effective management of the company's growth.

Size and shape

Employees: 130   Locations: 2

Geographical income split (projected): Europe 35%, USA 40%, RoW 25%

To cope with increasing demand and to ensure that the group does not lose focus, it has been restructured into six operating groups: woundcare, matrix precision converting, dipped products, cubing and moulded products, tex-tiles, and biomaterials. The strategic development of each of these divisions will be different and so the focus of its strategy will be through these operations. Wound care, which was the original heart of the business, operates in a market worth $6 billion. It has a high-tech segment valued at $2 billion and which is expanding by more than 20 per cent a year. IT is well positioned to exploit the potential in the market because it has a fully integrated manufacturing capacity for films for polymer to finished product in-house. This division is one of the lowest cost producers in the sector.

Future prospects

- break-even reached in early 1997;
- US manufacturing facilities to open in late 1997;
- the launch of a series of new businesses in late 1997 to 1999: dipping technology and waterproof breathable and technology.

The US market, excluding drug delivery patches, for the custom conversion of non-woundcare medical devices alone is estimated to be more than $50 million. No other equivalent facilites exist in Europe, so Matrix has a major opportunity in this region and also in the expanding North American market. Dipped products are largely gloves and condoms. The global gloves market is 20 billion pairs, of which one billion are premium quality. The worldwide condom market is assessed at two billion units. This group also sees potential in nuclear biological chemical warfare and ski gloves. IT's new polyurethane gloves could command ten per cent of the high value segment of the market or 10 million pairs a year. The company hopes to take up to three per cent of the condom market, where it is developing products with a Japanese partner.

Cubing and moulded products include melt polymerisation from a licensed strategic partner, screw and barrel designs and a DTI LINK programme to develop a low-cost heart assist device. The LINK programme has helped substantially to broaden the company's technology base. In textiles and biomaterials, IT is pursuing markets worth $2.5 billion and $12 billion respectively. A joint venture in the former with Advanced Materials Group, a US business, was in discussion.

Outlook

Says Gilding 'In a few short years IT has created a base of materials and processing technology which has brought exceptional growth potential.' The company sees major possibilities for its technologies in a wide range of applications in a multiplicity of sectors.

Address:

Road Three, Industrial Estate, Winsford, Cheshire CW7 3PD. Tel: 01606 863500. Fax: 01606 863600

Inspec

Hythe, Southampton

Turnover			
1993	1994	1995	1996
£49M	£74.1M	£199.5M	£301M

Summary: Inspec supplies high margin chemicals into niche markets. It has bought several peripheral operations from blue chip chemical companies, made the plant work better and given local staff profit and loss responsibility. This approach has enabled it to grow into the eighth biggest chemicals company in the UK, by market capitalisation, in a little more than three years. Inspec's management predicts that profits growth and margins will rise rapidly. In 1996 they virtually doubled after the acquisition of the Shell Five Chemicals businesses.

The Business

The plan was a bold idea. A retired chemical company boss and a venture capitalist would buy the underperforming speciality chemical subsidiaries of blue chip companies. They would forge them into a group, concentrating on niche markets worldwide where the barriers to entry were high. The concept was not new in the wider business world. Many of the diversified conglomerates – especially the low-tech variety – had pioneered the formula in the late 1980s. But applied specifically to chemical companies, here was something new.

By mid-year 1996 it had risen from nowhere to the eighth largest UK chemicals company by market capitalisation. Since the business was conceived only in 1992, founders Dr John Hollowood and James Ratcliffe have a compelling story to tell. In 1992 Dr John Hollowood, retired from the chemical company he had run successfully before selling out to Laporte, and joined forces with James Ratcliffe, from venture capitalist Advent. They developed a business plan to buy subsidiary speciality chemical operations and run them as businesses in their own right.

This led to negotiations with BP about its fine chemicals business. The main site was at Hythe, near Southampton, with a smaller site in South London. Hollowood and Ratcliffe invited members of the Hythe management to join them in a combined buy-in, management buy-out or BIMBO scheme. The purchase was completed in October 1992 for £40 million after lengthy and detailed negotiations. Hollowood became Inspec chairman with Ratcliffe as MD.

BP closed the South London site down and concentrated on Hythe. Fine chemicals recorded losses of £2.5 million for BP in 1991. BP had invested in the Hythe site which, Hollowood recalls, had turned the corner but BP had not yet seen the results. Inspec got them instead. The staff were invited to purchase shares in the operation in March 1993. Most did. Hollowood says, 'It had always been our intention to get the people involved as shareholders. It does mean they are committed.'

Distinctive features

- buys low performing chemicals subsidiaries;
- transforms their structure and cost control;
- achieves outstanding PBT/sales growth;
- rapid rise in profitability.

Inspec searches for companies which were peripheral operations of blue chip chemical companies. They had to operate in niche speciality markets with high barriers to entry, thus having good and sustainable margins. A blue chip owner meant the highest safety standards on the sites. Safe, efficient plants are effective, long-lasting production units. The Hythe site has become the first UK chemical site to win the highest level on an international safety rating system and Inspec's Antwerp site is on the next level.

Inspec bought Allco in the USA in September 1993 and floated in March 1994 in order to repay a loan and free itself for further acquisitive activity. Management bought Imi-Tech in the USA in 1994 and gained a site producing fire-resistant foam. Next on the list was BP's Antwerp site which produced a synthetic rubber component on top of a commodity ethylene oxide and Glycol operation thus stepping outside Inspec's speciality chemical area. Inspec needed ethylene oxide as a raw material and the existing supply was not assured. The company reckons to have both secured its own supply and gained a cash generating ability – the upturn in the Glycol cycle means the plant's entire output will be needed by the market over the next few years. BP Antwerp became Inspec Belgium and contributed enormously to the 1995 results – £100.26 million of turnover and £17.12 million operating profit, more than the rest of Inspec combined.

Later purchases, including a part of Allied Signal in the USA in 1995 and a polyimide fire resistant fibre operation in Austria which complemented Imi-Tech foam, were not run as entities in their own right before. 'The old product sites never had their own P and L ... the people didn't feel as if they were running their own business, as if they had a stake. Now they do and, that's been the transformation really.'

In July the size of Inspec virtually doubled with the purchase of Shell's Five Chemicals businesses. These provided a valuable complement to its existing Speciality Chemicals Operation.

Stratagems

The strategy of the company follows a straightforward approach. It aims to secure further acquisitions to enhance the performance of the entire enterprise. These purchases are general operations which are non-core for existing owners and so can be sold. Given the prevailing management theory about sticking to core, Inspec has entered the market at an ideal time.

Size and shape

Employees: 900   Locations (manufacturing): 6
Geographical income split: UK 60%, mainland Europe 30%, USA 10%

There are several factors which the Inspec acquisitions team look for in a prospective addition to the group:

- underperforming speciality subsidiary company;
- capable of rapid transformation;
- strong but undermotivated staff;
- its markets/products will complete existing holdings.

Inspec's immediate strategy is to invest to get its plants working better. Removing bottlenecks from plant is a very effective use of money. Dr Hollowood says 'We generate two to three units of sales for every unit of capital. It's a much more efficient return on capital than building new plant.' It is investing up to £8 million in Hythe, £10 million in the USA and £20 million in Belgium. The 1996 financial year shows excellent growth over 1995 with 1997 being a really good year as the investment benefits feed through.

Over the medium term Inspec aims to extend its geographic spread. Currently it has no office in Canada and it aims to have a manufacturing facility in China and the Far East within five years. No suitable existing plant exists and, since Inspec is not keen on joint ventures, it is obliged to build a new plant. In all its acquisitions Inspec takes a year to get to know the operation and carry out any rationalisation needed – to reduce costs and understand the detailed potential. It then invites the existing staff to subscribe to private shares. After three years these shares are converted into tradable Inspec shares at a valuation obtained from an independent adjudicator. The aim is to get local staff committed to running their business.

Outlook

Future prospects

- good earnings growth;
- market leadership;
- further acquisitions.

Inspec's management intends to grow the company from its present £400 million market capitalisation to £750 million by the year 2001, when Hollowood would be 65. Inspec would rank number four in the UK chemical sector and number one in the UK speciality chemicals market. Its approach is simple and effective. The results bear testimony to the massive potential for the group. It is currently on target for its five year objective to be the UK's largest speciality. This is an impressively managed enterprise which will be a core stock in years to come.

Address:

Charleston Industrial Estate, Hardley, Hythe, Southampton SO45 3ZG. Tel: 01703 894666. Fax: 01703 243113

Jacobs Holdings plc SHIPPING, TRANSPORT, PROPERTY

London

Turnover				
1992	1993	1994	1995	1996
£2.2M	£2.8M	£8.6M	£23M	£41.7M

Summary: Jacobs Holdings is a diversified holding company with interests in shipping, transportation, property and harbours. Under new management since 1994, the group has grown in leaps and bounds and is poised to capitalise on a series of opportunities in each of its key markets. Although well known as John I. Jacobs, an established shipping company founded in 1881, the group has broadened the range of its activities and is now making exceptional progress in each of its new divisions. The group will continue to grow organically as well as by acquisition. Its aim is to be a substantially larger operation within a few years.

The Business

Jacobs Holdings is a business in the process of metamorphosis. Its achievements since July 1994 when Michael Kingshott took over as a transformative CEO have been outstanding and the group's potential for profits growth is exceptional. Kingshott's vision was to create a broadly based group out of the old shipping company John I. Jacobs. The new Jacobs Holdings business would feature only companies with the capacity to realise early and substantial return on capital. Also each business within the new company would fit into a corporate jigsaw, providing intra-group synergies and opportunities for selling a range of services to clients. In the summer of 1994 it drew a line under its earlier, often distinguished, life as John I. Jacobs, and began to forge a new identity in three diverse sectors of shipping, transportation and property, and harbours. A new strategy combining rapid acquisition and wholesale organic improvement was initiated by its management team of CEO Kingshott, FD Stuart Bridges and MD of its transportation subsidiary

267

Colin Parry-Williams. They are supported by chairman Sir Wilfrid Newton, ex-boss of London Underground, and as non-executive direct the former MD of Rover Group, Kevin Morley.

Kingshott wanted to create balance in its collection of holdings. Each of the three divisions would be strong performers in their own right and all three would be promoted with equal vigour. His first move was to eliminate those businesses which did not provide an excellent return on capital. The focus of the company which the team inherited was shipping. He sold off its fleet of 17 coastal tankers for £10.5 million but retained its shipping brokerage and its activity in shipping statistics with its publication, the *World Tanker Fleet Review*. Both had the capacity to provide substantially improved revenues.

Mark Hitchins, group public relations manager, says 'Michael Kingshott wanted to make the group considerably larger and he created the three divisions we know today. The process of diversification began with purchase of Sheertrucks and the operation of Thames Europort at Dartford.' The port is the central axis around which some of the businesses are based. Although it is managed in the property and harbours division of the group, it is the base for the transportation business and the home port for Jacobs' nascent freight shipping line. Dartford is the closest facility of its kind to London and though not yet as well known as many of the more established ports in the UK it is set to grow rapidly. It will be useful for both the outward and inward movement of cars via contracts gained by Sheertrucks.

Kingshott recalls that the first area for development was the property division. 'We paid £22 million for the Embassy Property Group in December 1994. The largest asset in its portfolio is the Kingsway Retail Park in Derby. When we bought it it was 60 per cent occupied, now every site is let. Another major asset, the Thorncliffe Industrial Estate in Sheffield, is experiencing rapid improvement in lettings.' Embassy also includes Skillion, a company which specialises in the management of commercial centres for light industrial use. The extensive skills of the Skillion management are also being put to good use in developing facilities at Thames Europort.

Distinctive features

- high degree of synergies between divisions;
- UK top four vehicle transportation company;
- growing port facility;
- major earnings potential.

The transportation and storage division of the business feeds into the port through vehicle distribution contracts from Land Rover, Hyundai, Honda, Ferrari and Volvo. In March 1995 the port management signed an agreement with United Car Carriers for reception, storage and distribution of motor vehicles at Dartford for shipping to Spain. Sheertrucks expanded with the purchase of BRS Car Delivery from NFC which led to construction of a fleet of 100 car transporters. This aspect of the business also provides storage facilities for car companies both on site in Dartford and at Thames Europort.

The group's roots in shipping have not been lost and it has launched the Dart Line, a joint venture with RMT, the Belgian state-owned ferry company. The line provides an unaccompanied freight route from Dartford to Vlissingen in the Netherlands. The division also controls Jacobs shipping brokerage which handles vessels from 20,000 tonnes to ultra large crude carriers.

Size and shape

Employees: 189   Locations: 20
Geographical income split: UK 100%

Stratagems

The Jacobs Holdings approach since 1994 has been to create and strengthen its three core divisions. This has been done by three key strategies – eliminating poorly performing activities, acquiring new businesses to add critical mass and extent of service provision, and enhancing the organic performance of existing companies. Several of the crucial purchases were made in the first year when the new management team attacked its new role with a spirit of determination. Kingshott sold the coastal vessels and two non-core businesses within the Embassy Property Group. A further property disposal in February 1995 made another contribution to the group's balance sheet. The property division is now shaping up based around retail centres, commercial parks for light industrial units and the development of select residential sites. 'We are particularly keen on the residential exploitation of oasthouses at the moment,' says Kingshott. The Skillion team is also applying its expertise to the creation of storage facilities for the transportation division and also on site at Thames Europort. He says that the rationale for including a property division within the group is twofold: the returns from optimum management of retail, commercial and residential sites where

Embassy can add value, and the application of property skills across the group – through Skillion.

Future prospects

- substantial profits and turnover growth in all sectors;
- actively seeking a new port to buy or manage;
- further cross-functional synergies.

The transportation division is based on Sheertrucks which continues to win significant orders from internationally reputed vehicle companies. Its recent contract with Land Rover was secured partly because Jacobs could provide construction facilities through the property division. 'We were able to provide a total solution for Land Rover which would not have ordinarily been there with other transportation companies,' says Hitchens. Kingshott is enthusiastic about Thames Europort. 'It is a 70 acre site with significant potential for development. Unlike many traditional ports, everything is laid out simply for efficient use. It is immediately adjacent to the M25 and close to the new international terminal at Ebbsfleet for rail links to mainland Europe. We are also actively seeking further ports – either to buy or to manage.'

The spearhead for development in the shipping division is the Dart Line. The group plans to increase the number of trailers using the route from 35,000 to 50,000. In January 1996, Simon Taylor, previously managing director of the Sally Line, joined the company to develop the potential of this route.

Outlook

Jacobs is set for rapid expansion. The group has been reshaped to take full advantage of the potential for expansion in three key divisions. Kingshott and his team have made early inroads into previous structural weaknesses and created a platform from which Jacobs can grow. The recent accent on high and rapid returns, and a strong internal drive for success will serve the group well.

Address:

6 Stratton Street, London W1X 5FD. Tel: 0171 408 0123. Fax: 0171 408 2122

Jarvis plc

Romford, Essex

Turnover			
1993	1994	1995	1996
£70.7M	£71.8M	£76.4M	£119M

Summary: Jarvis plc has experienced a dramatic shift both in the nature of its business and in its profitability. In early 1996 this was a broad based group in design, construction, finance and facilities management. The acquisition of NIMCo, which became Jarvis Facilities, became the focus of a series of Railtrack contracts which have since been increased and developed. The contracts embrace the maintenance of Railtrack infrastructure in the north of England. Although the rest of the group has strengthened, it is the activities of Jarvis Facilities which have radically transformed the shape and strength of the group.

The Business

Jarvis plc is a classic example of a business which found a completely new direction through acquisition and transformed its profile. As recently as 1994 the group, which embraced a wide range of interests in the construction sector, was still suffering poor financial results. The board announced a group-wide strategy for reforming the business which involved a rationalisation away from its traditional contracting activities to the management of construction services, the development of niche markets through Jarvis Projects which would emphasise education and healthcare, the continuation of the profitable property business and a reduction in the fixed cost base of the group.

It was able to report that by early 1996 it had made significant progress. It had become much more selective in the contracts which it undertook, it reduced the number of offices which it operated, and it ensured that the remaining tally of locations were fully integrated into the group. This meant that fixed costs were reduced and Jarvis management had greater flexibility in running the business.

The real advance, however, came when it proposed the purchase of NIMCo (the Northern Infrastructure Maintenace Company). This was one of the seven British Rail internal management companies which were responsible for the maintenance of the infrastructure of the railway. NIMCo covered an area from Holyhead to Grimsby and from Macclesfield to the Scottish border. The original contract excluded the east and west coast main lines but work on these two key arteries were added later.

Only three months after the integration was achieved, chairman Roger Payton said 'The major part of the revenues of Jarvis Facilities relate to the term maintenance contracts with Railtrack. However, this company has been successful in securing new project and facilities management contracts for both Railtrack and other customers within and outside the railway with £40 million worth of contract awards since the acquisition.'

The growth anticipated as a result of the Railtrack contracts prompted brokers Peel, Hunt to comment that it forecast that pretax profits would rise to £21 million in 1997 after languishing at £290,000 in 1995. Payton reported in September 1996 that the new division drew 70 per cent of its revenues from infrastructure maintenance, 20 per cent from facilities management and 10 per cent from other rail projects. Since acquisition the new business had generated £31 million in turnover and £3.4 million in operating profit.

Distinctive features

- change to facilities management business;
- thriving new Railtrack/maintenance activities;
- strategic improvements to the rest of the group;
- growth in construction.

On the construction side the rationalisation of the group's activities has paid off. It is now reporting £42 million in new contracts, a growth in contract values and opportunities for repeat business. The division looks certain to benefit from the widespread recovery of the construction industry which was hard hit by the recession and the period which followed.

Stratagems

The Jarvis strategy for bringing greater coherence to the business has brought the company back on target. Its directors realised that the company relied for too long on its traditional home in construction and they need to restructure the group to explore new opportunities. As well as taking a scalpel to parts of the group, some new management was infused and new targets were set to bring the organisation back to profitability.

After doing this the NIMCo opportunity arose. The projected benefits of the purchase were outlined in its proposal document: it would enhance earnings per share, reduce gearing from 128 per cent to 49 per cent and secure a strong underlying cashflow; it would provide further significant growth in maintenance and facilities management work; it pointed to a major proportion of future earnings coming from maintenance work – margins in maintenance are higher than in construction; it would add geographic spread and provide management with detailed experience of railways maintenance.

Size and shape

Employees: 601   Locations: 14
Geographical income split: UK 100%

The construction division has also experienced a resurgence in business and Jarvis management is cautiously confident that returns in the group will add to its increasing list of construction industry contracts.

Outlook

Future prospects

- more FM work;
- greater prosperity for its construction division;
- enhanced profitability.

Analysts appear united in the view that Jarvis plc is set for better times. The transformation wrought by strategic change and the creation of Jarvis Facilities has turned this group into one of the most tipped stocks in the City. There has been a cultural change in the company and it has moved from a construction-led business into a more flexible facilities management house.

Address:

Jarvis plc, Jarvis House, Southend Arterial Road, Romford, Essex RM3 0NU. Tel: 01708 718000. Fax: 01708 718100

JBA Holdings plc

Birmingham

Turnover				
1992	1993	1994	1995	1996
£56M	£75M	£91M	£125M	£162M

Summary: JBA is one of the fastest growing companies in the West Midlands. As a major supplier to IBM worldwide, it concentrates on software applications. In 1995 the company made major enhancements to its software products to maintain a world class position for a wide range of industry sectors. It is strong in the clothing, footwear, food, drink, automotive, business equipment sales and service disciplines. Now JBA is continuing to concentrate on providing new functionality in its software. But it is also delivering, in version three of its System 21, a new infrastructure architecture which will allow corporations to start to customise their software to fit exactly their changing business transaction process.

The Business

For a company which started life as an afterthought, JBA has done remark-ably well. The business now spans the world, it advises industry giant IBM on software applications for its mid-range computers and it aims to grow at a remarkable 40 per cent every year. It continues to argue that it is a niche player – but what a niche! It operates from 45 offices worldwide and has set its sights on being a billion dollar company. JBA was set up in 1981 by a group of businessmen who saw the potential to establish a management consultancy. This was later expanded to include IBM's A/S400 series of computers. They wanted to establish a foothold in Britain. In 1981, its first year of operation, the turnover was barely £600,000. But the seed was sown. JBA is now a leading international software solutions provider with more than 15 years experience of fully integrated solutions for more than 3500 clients in almost every industry and country in the world.

The annual turnover now stands at almost £125M and growth is 20 per cent a year with existing installations ranging from £50,000 to in excess of £5M. Products are accepted as leading in both business function and security of investment. Now, with an open door initiative, JBA is looking to build successful working relationships with information technology management consultants who can offer additional and complementary services of an equally high standard to company clients and user groups seeking independent advice on the company's products.

JBA's main product range is System 21, a complete, integrated information service infrastructure for business. Manufacturing, financial, customer services and logistics and service management modules fully interlock over a single database to provide the facilities and information businesses need in a uniquely adaptive and evolutionary manner. It has been re-engineered to run on Unix as well as the AS/400 system. The aim is to support businesses into the next century. There is particularly strong growth in Europe and the Americas.

David Williams, finance director and company secretary was involved in setting up the group in 1981. He became a director four years later. Williams joined from a senior executive position in Cavalier Tableware. But there is nothing cavalier about him. 'What we are about is evolution – not revolution.' System 21 is a development of its successful Business 400 product set. But the beauty of the current flagship is that it can run on different platforms and it has the flexibility to move with IT markets and not be buried in a long forgotten rut. System 21 can run in big or small businesses.

Distinctive features

- world leader in its sector;
- five-year plan on target;
- global support provision;
- massive earnings potential;
- IBM business asssociate;
- runaway growth.

Stratagems

JBA is a company which makes a science of forward planning. Its expansion in geographical and technological terms has been deeply researched and extensively considered. In 1993 the company launched its first five-year plan, which has been a crucial tool in achieving broader-based targets for its future. Guided by this central strategic instrument, the business has met all of its targets. Its global scope – and the prominence of Europe and the

Americas – was anticipated. These two continents are the stronghold of JBA but the business has also identified the potential growth markets of the next few years. Although it will continue to expand its scope within Europe and the Americas, it will also emphasise Asia and the former Eastern bloc in its marketing budgets.

Traditionally when companies talk about America they refer to the USA and Canada but JBA see central South America as equally important in building new business. Business in the UK and the rest of Europe is progressing powerfully, but on mainland Europe, France, Germany and Italy are critical markets which JBA intends to address further. It is absolute in designating Europe as a single entity. No division between the UK and the mainland is envisioned. The company argues that Britain is inseparable from its continental partners and should not be considered separately.

Size and shape

Employees: 1850   Locations: 45
Geographical income split: Europe 47.1%, Americas 46.1%, Asia 5.3%, Africa 1.5%

Asia and the Pacific region also offer scope for expansion of the company's established expertise. China is, in particular, in its sights. Projected growth patterns for Pacific Rim countries are around 35 per cent a year which means that JBA has huge potential pickings. At present Asia accounts for only five per cent of its annual sales but as the USA and Europe are more established markets, the contribution of the Far East to turnover should rise dramatically.

JBA asserts as a matter of policy that it is active in niche markets but this does not embrace the usual concept of a niche market. Indeed Williams may be tongue in cheek. His goal is a billion dollar company and staff are already working on a replacement for System 21, although it has a long life. He insists the process is continuous: business strategies and helping customers make their own operations more profitable. A major objective is to provide solutions to problems. That is the key to maximum growth.

Future prospects

- rapid growth in all markets;
- significant upgrades to core System 21 products;
- hard drive into Asia and former Eastern bloc;
- continued 40% growth yearly.

Outlook

Projected growth is twofold: JBA is looking for an annual increased turnover of between 30 and 40 per cent with a rapid short-term target of £200 million. The ultimate aim is to become a billion dollar turnover company.

It considers it was justified to float two years ago so that the markets could effectively monitor market capitalisation. That move raised JBA's profile and increased business from all quarters. The general expansion plan which the listing funded, means that customers buy JBA services and software because they like what they see.

It foresees growth every year in all spheres of operation with Europe leading the buying initiative and Asian markets opening up to take advantage of growing expertise and efficiency. A particular target is China but JBA will continue to develop Poland, Czechoslovakia and other former Iron Curtain countries.

Address:

28 Calthorpe Road, Edgbaston, Birmingham B15 1TS. Tel: 0121 627 5151. Fax: 0121 627 0032

Kewill Systems plc

Walton on Thames, Surrey

Turnover			
1994	1995	1996	1997
£32M	£34M	£35M	£43Me

Summary: Kewill Systems specialises in the provision of computer software and services to small and medium sized enterprises. Following a series of acquisitions over recent years, the group is now focused into four divisions, while its activities generate a substantial level of recurring income which is used for continuing product development. Kewill is establishing itself as a major player in a number of growth markets and has an increasing international presence. Its strong cashflow and balance sheet suggest that further acquisitions are likely.

The Business

Kewill was formed initially as a management consultancy in 1972. Eight years later it launched its principal manufacturing control system, Micross, which remains the company's most profitable product. The group was floated in 1985 and, following a series of acquisitions, is now structured in four divisions – manufacturing, design, accounting and logistics.

The group's manufacturing activities currently account for slightly more than 40 per cent of turnover and are centred around four main products; Micross, Micromax, Trifid and Xetal. Micross (or Micro Scheduling System) is designed to handle all aspects of a manufacturing production life-cycle – including estimating, job costing, material scheduling, and works order processing – and is aimed principally at small engineering companies. During the last 16 years, it has established a market-leading position with more than 2000 systems having been sold. Micromax is similar to Micross but is a US product. A new Windows-based version has recently been well received and the company is currently recruiting more staff to cope with the demand. This product will shortly be launched in the UK. Trifid is smaller in revenue terms and is aimed at companies with mid-range systems, while Kewill-Xetal sells specialist systems to the garment manufacturing industry.

The second largest division, representing around 27 per cent of group turnover, comprises the computer aided design operations. Kewill has focused on the mechanical and architectural markets for more than ten years, but has more recently introduced products aimed at building services and building management businesses. Its HAN Dataport subsidiary operates principally in Germany and Austria and targets smaller mechanical designers, building managers and architectural users. Kewill also has entered into a joint venture with IBM Germany, selling to larger users. This has proved highly successful and it seems likely that the relationship with IBM will be extended further across Europe in the near future. Kewill considers that the area of facilities management offers significant growth potential.

Kewill's accounting division had been built around its Omnicron Power-systems accounting package, which currently has more than 6000 users. However, in 1995 Kewill introduced its Windows-based Dynamics product, a new accounting package for the small and medium sized user. Dynamics is considered to be the first truly cross-platform, multi-user modular accounting package to appear in the UK. It is sold under licence from Great Plains Software Inc. of the USA and Kewill has exclusive distribution rights in the UK.

The fourth division, logistics (including electronic data interchange – EDI), is possibly the most exciting in terms of growth potential. EDI is a mechanism which allows suppliers to link their ordering and processing systems directly to their major retail customers and, as supply chains shorten throughout industry, offers considerable opportunities. Kewill has enjoyed 30 per cent sales growth in this activity in recent years. In February 1996, Kewill acquired Process Computing, a leading provider of warehouse management systems, to strengthen its position in the logistics market and in May purchased Meadowhouse Bar-Laser, a supplier of EDI systems.

Distinctive features

- leading position in growing markets;
- high level of recurring income;
- continuous product development;
- strong financial position.

Stratagems

The history of the computer services industry is littered with examples of companies which have expanded rapidly only to fail shortly thereafter. Kewill is conscious of avoiding the pitfalls which these companies fell into and has made a virtue of its risk-averse approach and solid success over a period of 20 years. Kewill's strategy is to develop and acquire stable and proven businesses. As a group of companies it is committed to lasting customer relationships based on solid products and services, all delivered with a long-term outlook and great care.

Another of the group's strengths is that several of its businesses occupy leading positions in the markets in which they operate. All of its companies are dedicated to the provision of superior products and services and are recognised as such by industry participants. The high level of recurring income which the firm receives provides an ideal platform for continuing product development – for example, a Windows version of Micross is currently under development. Kewill spends around £3M on developing new products as well as keeping existing ones up to date.

Size and shape

Employees: 460 Locations: 17
Geographical income split: UK 50%, mainland Europe 30%, USA 17%, RoW 3%

Kewill believes in allowing its local management a considerable amount of operational autonomy. Each group company is encouraged to be a thriving, independent entity and is expected to contribute consistently to the overall health and profitability of the group. Staff and management are remunerated appropriately if this is the case. The role of the group's head office is to provide detailed financial planning and monitor costs. However, as the group's activities become increasingly integrated, the centre will play a greater role in ensuring that potential synergies are identified and exploited.

Much of the group's development over the last ten years has been the consequence of acquisitions and this seems likely to continue, particularly if they widen the product range or increase Kewill's geographic presence. However, future acquisitions will all fall within Kewill's general area of expertise and will be characterised by a good product base and strong management. The group has learnt from a disastrous acquisition of a

German manufacturing systems company (subsequently disposed) in 1991 and is not keen to repeat its mistakes.

Future prospects

- strong growth in a range of key markets;
- forecasts of even higher margins;
- widespread expansion in international markets.

Kewill's capacity to make successful acquisitions is considerably enhanced by the strong cashflow which the group enjoys and its solid balance sheet. Furthermore, its high level of recurring revenue from annual support contracts, additional software, training and consultancy confer on the company a higher quality of earnings than its competitors. It fully expects the contribution made by added-value services such as consultancy to increase further over time.

Outlook

Kewill's prospects are excellent with strong growth predicted in a number of its markets. In particular, there is considerable potential within the EDI market – which should grow at around 30 per cent a year for the foreseeable future – while HAN Dataport is well-placed to exploit its relationship with IBM. The launches of revised Micross and Micromax products should also increase market share. Much of the company's success in the past has been the result of its ability to derive exceptional profitability from steady turnover growth. The group currently enjoys a gross margin of 75 per cent on its activities and believes that this is sustainable in the long term. As the product range widens and the group expands internationally, even higher levels of profitability should be achievable.

Address:

Case House, 85–89 High Street, Walton-on-Thames, Surrey KT12 1DL. Tel: 01932 248328 Fax: 01932 221662

Logica plc

Central London

Turnover				
1992	1993	1994	1995	1996
£183M	£197M	£210M	£250M	£285M

Summary: Logica is a UK computer consultancy, systems integrator and software developer, established in 1969, which has developed into a world-class information business. It sells applications and software development skills to blue chip clients in the finance, telecommunications, utilities, government and industrial markets. The company has enjoyed outstanding growth since the early 1990s and is anticipated to continue this progress. Brokers estimate that Logica will be turning over £325 million by the end of 1997 when it will achieve pretax profits of nearly £30 million.

The Business

Logica was founded in 1969 by Philip Hughes and Len Taylor, one of a clutch of UK software houses founded at the time, such as CAP and Software Science. Logica is the only one still independent and has expanded from its UK base into mainland Europe and the USA. Today it is a FTSE Top 250 company active in computer consultancy, systems integration and software development. Hughes and Taylor resigned in 1995 after 26 years of growing the company and steering it past obstacles that defeated its UK rivals.

The MD and CEO is Dr Martin Read who joined in 1993 and characterises the company's ability to bring in senior management from outside and so avoid the somewhat closed and in-grown management tendencies of its UK competitors.

The company earns revenue from three sources. One is selling its staff on time and materials-based contracts. The second is through developing and selling software applications. Thirdly, it carries out system integration – installing computer systems, developing linking software, writing applications and integrating it all together with components such as IBM's MQ Series messaging product. Typically some 66 per cent of its revenues come from system integration contracts, 20 per cent from consultancy and 15 per cent from products. Like all major systems houses it looks for long-term relationships with blue chip clients.

The majority of its key clients were customers more than twenty years ago. It also aims to operate internationally and across industry. Logica has always been careful to spread its business across focused sectors; finance, telecommunications, energy and utilities, defence, industry (manufacturing, pharmaceuticals), government, transport, computing, electronics and space, and to amass expertise in each. This has enabled it to withstand over-reliance on government business which is subject to delay and general decline.

Logica has reshaped its business continually to improve performance when conditions become unfavourable. There have been two severe downturns; one in 1985 and another in the 1990–92 period. As a people-based business it has found it difficult to prune costs when large contracts end and there is a downturn in the market. It has also been prone to low margins and low profitability. The US operation has been particularly susceptible to this cycling between losses and insignificant profits. Current management seems able to avoid such troughs.

Distinctive features

- reshaped company is moving forward and improving its margins;
- expanding global infrastructure serving finance, telecommunications, energy and utilities;
- heavy emphasis on quality management;
- strong relationships with blue chip corporate and public sector clients.

There was a UK reorganisation in 1993 and 1994 which removed layers of management, increased focus and, as a result, boosted margin, revenues and profit. In 1995 Logica UK sold off a 49 per cent interest in Speedwing Logica, its joint venture company with British Airways as Logica found the relationship somewhat limiting. It continues to do business with British Airways and work in the airlines sector outside the UK more effectively since the disposal. Across the channel Logica's Belgium subsidiary was combined with The Netherlands operation to improve low profitability levels in Belgium. In 1996 the mainland European business grew by 35 per cent with strong performances in the Netherlands and Germany. Finance, government, industry and transport were the key business sectors.

In America, where profits have been eclipsed by losses, investments have been made to strengthen the application portfolio and management is firmly focused on margin ahead of revenue growth. Logica has a strong focus on quality and has gained a category A supplier quality certificate from IBM UK five times. ISO 9001 registration applies to 90 per cent of its worldwide operations.

Stratagems

Logica's aim is to become a global business. To help it achieve this goal Read's team has three objectives. One is to improve margins and profitability. Secondly, the company wants to increase sales throughout their international network of products and services that have been successful in part of it. Thirdly it aims to expand its activities internationally into the growth markets of finance, telecommunications, energy and utilities.

Size and shape

Employees: 4800 Locations: 20
Geo. income split: UK 48%, mainland Europe 28%, North America 12%, RoW 12%

To bring this into being Logica has been expanding into fresh geographic territories and buying software businesses with applications pertinent to its focused markets. Purchases in the USA such as Precision Software in late 1993 and Synercom Software in 1994 have helped it improve its US operation but performance is not as good as desired with see-sawing profits and losses. It is now into profit and looks set to continue. Focus has been improved and management re-jigged with margin improvement being the current focus there, even to the extent of lower revenue growth. European operations were enhanced with a Swiss subsidiary being opened in 1993 and a small acquisition in The Netherlands in the same year which increased Logica's government business in Holland. A minor acquisition was completed in the UK in April 1996 involving a workflow business.

Future prospects

- organic sales projected to increase at about 15 per cent a year;
- North American business is anticipated to grow more rapidly than the rest;
- Logica is expected to pursue a policy of selective acquisition.

A New Zealand subsidiary was established in 1995 as well as one in the Czech Republic. The management team in the German operation was overhauled in the same year to reverse previous poor results. Logica's current strategy includes aggressive building up of its operations in these three territories. It is still looking for acquisitions considering that, 'this is an important avenue for development', but has not been able to conclude any at acceptable prices recently.

The board was strengthened in 1995 and a number of senior marketing staff and consultants have been recruited. The company is also looking to expand into new areas adjacent to its current business. Thus it has moved into multimedia as that technology is becoming pervasive and has opened an application outsourcing subsidiary in London, Logica Support Services, focused on investment portfolio management systems. Margin improvement is a continuous focus with overall margins heading towards eight per cent from the current year. The target is 10 per cent.

Outlook

Logica has strong potential in three areas: significant growth in the USA and Canada where it has historically under-performed, outsourcing, and acquisition of complementary businesses. A combination of any of these three would add significantly to the company's performance.

Address:

Stephenson House, 75 Hampstead Road, London NW1 2PL. Tel: 0171 637 9111. Fax: 0171 872 8994

London Industrial plc

Whitechapel, East London

Turnover			
1993	1994	1995	1996
£5.8M	£6.9M	£9.8M	£14M

Summary: London Industrial is the largest provider of light industrial, studio and office workspace for small businesses in the south-east. Its philosophy is to offer accommodation on flexible and affordable terms and, unlike most landlords, the company places great emphasis on developing close relationships both with its tenants and the community as a whole. Low capital values have enabled the company to acquire a series of further properties at attractive prices, while London Industrial's property management expertise has allowed it to maintain high levels of occupancy. With changes in working practices making small units increasingly popular, London Industrial is ideally placed to benefit from a fast-growing, specialist market.

The Business

London Industrial plc was formed in 1986 as a vehicle to acquire and manage a portfolio of 18 small-unit light industrial estates – predominately located in the east end of London – representing part of the former Greater London Council's industrial property portfolio. Since that time the company has expanded considerably. Its portfolio now comprises more than 68 estates with a total floorspace of some 3.3M square feet. In recent years, in particular, it has been able to take advantage of the stability of secondary property values by continuing to buy multi-tenanted estates cheaply.

London Industrial should not be regarded as a property company in the traditional sense. It rents almost exclusively to new and emerging businesses. Its 2450 lettable units have an average size of only just over 1200 square feet. Historically, property companies have tended to avoid small businesses because of their high incidence of business failure and a generally poor quality of covenant. Although London Industrial recognises that these weaknesses continue to exist, it argues that it is possible to mitigate against them by taking a more proactive approach.

Accordingly, whereas most property companies assume a largely passive property management role, the company sees itself as a 'retailer' of work-space, constantly revising its prices, terms and conditions to maintain high levels of occupancy. The company believes that by using such techniques, an occupancy rate of more than 90 per cent is sustainable in the long-term. Furthermore, the company's large portfolio means that when tenants do decide to move it is frequently to another London Industrial site.

One of the company's most significant acquisitions came in December 1994 with the purchase of a portfolio of 17 industrial estates from A. & J. Mucklow Group. The portfolio consisted of 12 properties in the Birmingham area, one each at Stoke, Derby and Daventry and two in West Sussex. The rationale for the acquisition was twofold: firstly, the units represented high quality stock which was ideal for the group's active management techniques. Secondly, it gave London Industrial critical mass in a second important economic region of the country. Following the acquisition, the company has opened a management office in Birmingham.

A series of further acquisitions in London and the south-east has followed. These include the Aberdeen Studios in Highbury Grove, North London, the Maritime Industrial Estate in Charlton SE7 and Leroy House, also in North London. Outside central London, the company has also purchased units in Newbury, Feltham, Reading, Southall and Rainham. At the same time, London Industrial has continued to invest heavily in refurbishing its existing stock. By the end of 1995, it had spent nearly £2M upgrading the Leather-market complex in Bermondsey, and is now focusing on the Three Mills complex in Stratford, East London.

Distinctive features

- strong tenant relationships;
- leader in growing, specialist market;
- able to exploit economies of scale;
- no direct competition.

The company is also looking to generate additional sources of income. At the end of 1995, it introduced Enerjet, a service designed to obtain the advan-tages of bulk purchasing of energy requirements. By purchasing energy in bulk, London Industrial is able to negotiate significant discounts from major suppliers. It can then resell the energy to its tenants at prices significantly below those they are presently paying. The company expects to introduce more of these services, possibly in the areas of insurance and equipment leasing, in the near future.

Stratagems

London Industrial's strategy is quite straightforward. It believes that its own interests are best served if its tenants and the local community also prosper. It therefore aims to offer accommodation on the most affordable, flexible and user-friendly terms possible. As MD Harry Platt puts it, 'We aim to offer the best deal for a new business in any area where we operate'.

Size and shape

Employees: 70   Locations: 68
Geographical income split: UK 100%

Its philosophy of being a good landlord is underpinned by a range of initiatives designed to foster its relationship with its tenants. Firstly, and unusually for a property company, it has a policy of direct contact with its tenants. It encourages tenants to keep the company informed of any problems and promises a quick response on all issues raised. Its tenancy agreements are designed to be simple and are written clearly in plain English so that tenants do not need to obtain legal advice. All services such as rent collection are performed in-house, rather than through an agent.

By such measures, London Industrial attempts to engender a spirit of community on its estates. As well as helping its tenants to prosper, these actions also give the company an extremely detailed knowledge of market conditions in any area. This is critical to the success of the company's proactive property management approach. London Industrial also believes in devolving as much operational responsibility to individual estates as possible although, as a matter of policy, rents are set centrally. London Industrial's immediate growth will be focused in London and the South-east and the West Midlands. The company feels there is still considerable growth potential in both of these regions, given the present level of coverage and the increasing level of demand. However, it does not rule out the possibility of opening up new regional operations if properties of sufficient critical mass become available.

Outlook

Future prospects

- more acquisitions;
- higher rates of occupancy;
- further enhancement of tenant relationships.

London Industrial has established a pre-eminent market position in a neglected sector of the property market. More importantly, it has developed an expertise in maintaining occupancy and growing rental income in difficult market conditions. As the nature of work changes in favour of smaller business units, the company is ideally placed to meet an increasing level of demand. The company is now of a sufficient size where future acquisitions can be assimilated at a relatively low marginal cost. However, it would be wrong to think that the company's growth is primarily acquisition-driven. It will see continuing improvements in occupancy which, together with rental growth as the market hardens and the increasing provision of services such as Enerjet, will mean higher profits from the existing business.

Address:

Magenta House, 85 Whitechapel Road, London E1 1DU. Tel: 0171 247 7614. Fax: 0171 247 0157

Madge Networks

High Wycombe

Turnover				
1992	1993	1994	1995	1996
£79M	£145M	£213M	£402M	£482M

Summary: Madge Networks has successfully designed, built, sold and supported Token Ring adapter cards for connecting PCs together in local area networks (LAN) together with hubs to link LANs. The company progressed to providing switching and fibre optic technology to make faster LAN connections and has now expanded to Ethernet and ISDN switching and promoting ATM as the future local area networking 'pipe' since it can carry voice, video and data and thus save costs. Madge was floated on the NASDAQ exchange and is a near half billion dollar company.

The Business

Businesses supplying connections between computers, the networking suppliers, have found their market growing very quickly during the 1980s and 1990s. Their customers, especially the larger and more international ones, need to interconnect all their staff PCs to host or server computers in the same building or campus. This is local area networking. IBM has promoted its own Token Ring scheme for this which has built up a sizable market niche alongside the more popular Ethernet concept. Increasingly customers want to add more users to LANs, inter-connect LANs and send video and other multimedia traffic to computers on these LANs as well as carry traffic across wide area networks.

Against this background there has been large scale consolidation in the industry as suppliers went on a feeding frenzy to gain technologies, sales channels and manufacturing efficiencies. Unsurprisingly American companies are dominant. But the fifth largest local area networking company in the world is British. This is Madge Networks, which was founded by Robert

Madge in 1986. Madge is both chaiman and CEO. Token Ring is, historically, Madge's market. And it is now providing products to interconnect LANs, of both types, and to support multimedia.

Madge floated on the American NASDAQ exchange in 1993 in a demonstration of commitment to American customers and partners. The parent company is registered in the Netherlands as Madge Networks NV. Networking is a boom market with a prolonged life and Madge says the strategy is to become the number one switched networking vendor for large organisations. It has grown rapidly.

Madge's company designed and built Token Ring Adapter cards for PCs. He realised in the early 90s that local area networks (LANs), ones that connect groups of PCs, were becoming over-burdened. By switching messages direct to their destination rather than sending them all over the network his company produced faster networks that could carry more messages. Competitors did the same thing but Madge had a major presence in the Token Ring niche of this market. Competitors concentrated on the larger Ethernet niche. Madge saw that ATM was the future for networking because of its scalability, high speed and quality of service in carrying networked voice, video and data to the desktop, thus enabling corporations to benefit from new multimedia applications. Also ATM's ability to carry all these kinds of traffic on one wire promises to simplify overall communications and to save significant amounts of money.

Distinctive features

- rapidly growing and highly profitable networking business;
- only company offering Token Ring, Ethernet and ATM switching at desktop PC level;
- co-author of the industry standard for LAN emulation;
- high emphasis on product and service quality.

Madge promoted the idea of transparently inserting ATM links or backbones between local area networks and combining switching with this. Since then Madge has been implementing a 'switch to ATM' strategy and buying its way into technologies needed to bring ATM to existing customers. It bought LANNET Communications in 1995 and gained Ethernet technology. Teleos Corporation was acquired in February 1996 and brought it ISDN and wide area access switching technology. The company is now demonstrating voice telephone traffic being carried with data across ATM networks. The potential here is for customers to combine data and voice traffic on to ATM and save potentially huge sums on their annual voice telephony costs.

Stratagems

In a fast-growing market companies need leading products, widespread sales coverage, the ability to keep up in the technology race, revenues to fund this and a good interpretation of market trends to avoid going down blind alleys. Madge has been able to do these things.

Size and shape

Employees: 2000   Locations: 54
Geographical income split: Europe 36%, Americas 39%, RoW 35%

The company view is that networking is getting more pervasive and that customers want to deal with suppliers who can offer an end-to-end solution, not just component pieces in the chain. Secondly networks are being asked to carry more and more and different kinds of traffic. Hence there is a need for more capacity and for a migration to that new capacity which does not involve throwing out existing network technology. So technology leadership requires capabilities in both kinds of local area networking (Token Ring and the more popular Ethernet), and in campus and wide area networking where fast telephone links (ISDN), fibre-optic links (FDDI) and the new all-purpose ATM links which can carry data, voice and multimedia traffic down one wire.

Future prospects

- major potential through desktop ATM technology;
- expanding global sales network;
- extension of its technological range.

Madge expertise extends down into the design of specialised silicon chips (ASICs) and software needed to build its products. It is reinforcing its overall expertise through building up its internal R&D facilities in the UK by opening a new 44 acre site in Buckinghamshire and concentrating efforts there. This internal expertise enables it to build faster products compared to others that use commodity off-the-shelf components.

The company sells to Global 1000 customers, mainly in the finance, manufacturing, insurance, transportation and government sectors, through its own sales force, resellers and through other companies that take or license Madge technology. These include some of the biggest networking and computer companies in the world, e.g. Cisco, Newbridge, Fore and others. Such deals extend Madge's coverage and also, through cross-licensing, improve its own product range.

Madge aims to provide 'best of breed products' through a global sales organisation backed up with truly excellent support. It has built up a worldwide sales and support organisation spanning more than 60 countries with major business and support centres in Hong Kong, London, San Jose, Tel Aviv and Tokyo.

Outlook

Madge is on course to pass the half billion dollar turnover mark this fiscal year and break the billion dollar barrier in 2001 or thereabouts. The company's future is tied to ATM and particularly Desktop ATM. If this becomes a successful networking technology then Madge will grow with it.

Address:

Knaves Beech Business Park, Loudwater, High Wycombe, Buckingham-shire HP10 9QZ. Tel: 01628 858000. Fax: 01628 858011

MAID plc

London

Turnover				
1992	1993	1994	1995	1996
£3.5M	£5.7M	£8.9M	£13.6M	£21.4M

Summary: MAID is a leading on-line supplier of business information. From daily news updates from more than 190 countries to in-depth market and brokers reports, MAID's information is used daily by thousands of corporate customers worldwide. Formed in 1985, MAID has grown rapidly since its 1994 London stock market flotation and the launch in mid-year 1995 of Profound™, its flagship service. Profound sources from more than 4000 publishers of business information but its key selling point is the way in which the information is organised. The company's proprietary indexing and search mechanism software, InfoSoft™, organises the entire portfolio of company reports and news services and allows users to access across the database and extract information at will according to predetermined criteria. The company is expanding rapidly and has established several blue chip joint ventures and badge arrangements with other information suppliers.

The Business

The genesis of MAID can be traced back specifically to one meeting in 1984. Around the table were executives of the advertising agency WCRS who were being briefed by BT. The telecommunications giant wanted the agency to develop a campaign which linked into many of the industry's emerging products. A two-page document was passed to young Daniel Wagner, who worked on research for a new business team at WCRS. The paper focused on local area networks (LANs), wide area networks (WANs) and other techno-logical wonders which meant nothing to the creative team. 'The paper was a product of deep research done by BT on the long-term direction of the industry,' recalls Wagner, now CEO of MAID. In those days an agency

294

generally had two weeks to come up with a proposal. The time could be spent fairly evenly on research and ideas development. It occurred to Wagner that his research would be greatly facilitated if information was available at a central point – on-line. This would save the agencies a great deal of time and expense which could be used more profitably on generating ideas.

The concept intrigued him. In early 1985 he left WCRS to establish Market Analysis and Information Database (MAID). The next two years were to follow a nightmarish round of chasing accounts, developing the technology, winning new clients and keeping the wolf from the door. Two significant positive developments took place in this period; the first was technological. After an abortive relationship with Thorn EMI's Datasolve, Wagner structured a partnership with Pergamon to act as host for the database. 'I spent six months working with their programmers explaining how I wanted the database to function. Databases were not user friendly. I was determined that the MAID product should be easy to access. I wanted to be able to key in a subject and source from the entire pool of data. The programmers told me that was not possible but I was determined.' His determination paid off because that philosophy remains at the heart of the company today. 'No-one else has yet opened a database which is organised like ours and given the high degree of development which has gone into the product the barriers to entry are high.' The second step forward came when Wagner brought on board professionals from banking, publishing, information science and marketing. A business plan was prepared and Hoare Octagon, the venture capitalists, put in £187,000 to relieve outstanding debt. Business expansion scheme investors gave the company additional capital.

Distinctive features

- unique product;
- ease of access;
- rapidly rising client base;
- blue chip partnerships;
- huge potential market.

Datasolve had launched its own product at a considerable discount even though it was traditionally configured and did not have the same ease of access. However, MAID won three of the four major information suppliers willing to deliver data. Then Pergamon suggested that MAID should exhibit in New York at a major on-line show. Sharing Pergamon's stand, he made sufficient contacts to win five blue chip clients, including Citibank and Colgate Palmolive. The next two years were spent in New York operating from a hotel room making cold calls from Yellow Pages. While he was away Datasolve slashed its price to £100. Wagner's response was to increase his to £4250. 'We succeeded in winning the psychological battle. Clients thought Datasolve had been forced to cut its price. We sent out a letter saying we were proud to announce that we were rapidly extending our client base and our service quality so we needed to increase our price.' McGraw-Hill and Dun & Bradstreet both offered to buy the company. 'The IT revolution was happening and we were at the heart of it.' From 1989 to 1994 MAID gathered pace and made pretax profits which were increasing by 100 per cent year-on-year.

Stratagems

The London float was a dramatic turning point in the history of MAID. Its recent meteoric growth in sales and subscriptions stem from the funding which was released by the listing. That money, and more, went into the development of Profound. This is available through a range of media including by a modem connection or through MAID's home page on the Internet. For example, Colgate Palmolive may have as many as 90 users each with separate subscriptions but MAID counts this as one client. The system includes access to material supplied by more than 4000 publishers. In addition, it carries a daily news service, broker reports, company statements, and newspaper and magazine articles. The presentation is enhanced by leading edge graphics made possible by an enhanced version of Adobe Acrobat. MAID has also developed its *Incremental Viewer*, which allows the viewer to read the first part of a document while the rest is being downloaded. The company's client list has now expanded to 50 FTSE 100 companies in the UK and 40 of the *Fortune 100* in the USA.

Size and shape

Employees: 460   Locations: 23
Geographical income split: UK 40%, USA 33%, mainland Europe 18%, Asia 9%

   A key element of the company's approach is the involvement of the staff. After six months every employee is given shares in the company. The business is structured in teams with high degrees of enthusiasm. Staff attrition rates are negligible, which in a company of its type is a remarkable phenomenon. Wagner says the initial collapse in the share price after listing caused some motivational problems but when it swung up again the employees knew their investment was safe. The growth in employee numbers since January 1995 has been outstanding, from 120 to 460. The number of offices worldwide has risen to 23 – 22 of which have been opened since the end of 1995.

The big push in the next few years will be America. In 1994 the number of on-line subscribers generally in the USA was eight million as opposed to 250,000 in Europe. Market forecasts suggested that the US subscriber base would grow to 11.8 million in 1995 and experience similar levels of annual growth. 'At the moment despite some excellent client names we are only scratching the surface.' During 1995 and 1996 MAID has signed agreements with Microsoft, NCM for badged software, Netscape, Easynet, IBM and Forte.

Outlook

Future prospects

- greater US penetration;
- higher mainland European business;
- further blue chip alliances;
- more badging operations.

The remarkable pace of MAID's growth since early 1995 looks set to be merely a foundation for the potential in the future. The range and scope of the joint ventures and partnerships which the company has forged in the two years since flotation elevates MAID's business into a new commercial arena. Its numbers of corporate subscribers rose by more than 1000 in only four quarters in late 1995 and early 1996. The influence of Profound as a generator of income and new business should not be underestimated. Also the increase in subscriptions from badge operations will certainly multiply. This is most decidedly a business for the new century which will become preferred supplier to other leading blue chips. And still no-one else has managed to come up with an indexing system to challenge InfoSort.

Address:

The Communications Building, 48 Leicester Square, London WC2H 7DB. Tel: 0171 930 6900. Fax: 0171 930 6006

Mayborn Group plc

London

Turnover				
1992	1993	1994	1995	1996
£36M	£40M	£43M	£49M	£54M

Summary: Mayborn is a diversified group of companies operating in the household goods sector. Its two principal divisions are consumer dyes and baby products. Since the early 1980s Mayborn has been on an intensively acquisitive path, seeking businesses which complement its existing strengths. Its potential purchases tend to be underperforming companies with similar structures and distribution channels, in retail, to its current portfolio and which generally own well-respected brand names. Although Mayborn is not well-known outside the City and its markets, this is an impressively managed business with an impressive catalogue of high performing brand name products.

The Business

The grey, austere days immediately after World War 2 gave birth to a company which brought a dash of colour into many lives. Dylon produced small tins of household dyes which shoppers purchased to change the colour of dresses or shirts. It rapidly became a brand leader with sales in the wider world as important as the UK. The founders of the business, Luca Purbeck and Peter Samuel, gave way to the current management team in 1980 and a new era for the company was forged. The principals of the group are MD The Hon Michael Samuel, the founder's son, and FD Norman Crausay. On taking control of the enterprise, the pair made a thorough reassessment of the business and its prospects.

'The first thing we did was to install a series of internal controls to ensure the proper functioning of the business. We made a full analysis of overheads and operating procedures, and made substantial improvements to the running and the management of the dyes business. Our next step was to introduce a planning process, including a database, to establish market opportunties and identify where we wanted to go,' says Samuel.

Crausay adds 'We planned for growth, which was something we had not done before. A main aim was to reduce our gearing and relieve the family of its exposure to personal guarantees.' Until 1983 Mayborn and Dylon were one and the same thing, but in that year a plan was made to grow by acquisition as well as organically and Mayborn became a distinct and separate entity. The first purchase came in August 1983, when Mayborn bought Jackel International. 'This was a peripheral interest for Guinness, which had decided to concentrate on its core business, but for us it was a major acquisition,' comments Samuel. 'We had examined the business in some depth before we bought and we knew what we wanted to do with it. We were lucky that the second half for Jackel was generally profitable and we enjoyed six months of good results as soon as we stepped in.' Mayborn cut the sales force by 50 per cent, slashed overheads, eliminated products which were not profitable and relaunched the business. It came with the Tommee Tippee brand of mugs and other baby products, which was and remains the distinctive market leader.

At first glance there appears to be little similarity between baby products and household dyes but in practice there were considerable factors in common. They were both dominant forces in niche markets, the structures of the businesses were similar, and there were production processes in common. The Mayborn management had recently been through a comparable reorganisation with Dylon and so were charged up to repeat the exercise with Jackel. The strategic objectives of the Jackel purchase became the format for future acquisitions.

Distinctive features

- leads in profitable niche markets;
- low cost production;
- growing world markets;
- major earnings potential.

The pattern of acquisitions continued with the 1984 purchase of US baby goods maker Stahlwood. A range of factors, not least cultural differences between the USA and Europe, condemned this initiative and, despite intense activity to support the company, it is now regarded as a learning exercise. Vastly more successful was the creation of Product Marketing

Mayborn (PMM) in Hong Kong, initially to source products for the division and subsequently to sell into the Far East.

In 1987 to supplement its rapidly expanding baby products division it acquired the licence to Pur, the teat manufacturer. Pur pioneered silicon teats as opposed to the more traditional latex variety. The acquisition could not have been better timed. The previous owner had invested heavily in this superior technology but was unable to make the necessary breakthrough. Mayborn already sold into the best outlets – independent chemists, Boots and the supermarkets. It was the marketing leap which the product needed. In November 1995 the baby products division acquired the Maws Group Ltd, which manufactures a range of long established products and distributes others, including infant sun cream. Since then the division has adopted a strategy of focusing on two principal brands, Tommee Tippee and Maws, which are now mainly manufactured in-house. As a consequence, an agreement was reached to discontinue the distribution of the Pur range of products from March 1997. During the 1990s in addition the group has added through acquisition Rainbow Acrylics, Brookline Delta and Big D.

Stratagems

Dylon was an international operator from day one and Mayborn Group is a top class manufacturer with markets all over the globe. Its brands such as Dylon, Big D (starch, polish and air freshener aerosols), Tommee Tippee, Disney (Rainbow Acrylics), and Maws are sold throughout the world. The group's sales and marketing approach is geared to global brands and its markets are tightly defined.

Size and shape

Employees: 963   Locations: 17
Geographical income split: UK 73%, mainland Europe 14%, Far East/Australasia 10%, RoW 3%

Another key factor in the Mayborn strategy is low cost manufacturing, as an increasing proportion of such manufacturing will take place in China, under the auspices of PMM. 'Automated production takes place in the UK but our Far East plants handle manufacturing which is more labour intensive', says Samuel. In 1995 Mayborn's baby products division opened a factory in China and in future further cost reductions will be achieved.

The core strategy for the group is to grow by acquisition and improve the performance of the divisions. Broker Panmure Gordon says 'Dylon dominates the UK market for household fabric dyes and has high market shares in mainland Europe, Japan and Australasia. The division exports 50 per cent of its sales.' It experienced problems in the mid-1980s but management effort was focused from 1990 and it has added to the portfolio of companies and products. Sales increased by only 27 per cent from 1989 to 1994 but profits quadrupled over the same period to £2.8M. In the baby products division, although the UK market is not growing rapidly, the spend per baby is going up significantly. The European market is relatively mature but the Far East offers extensive opportunities for growth. The investment in China will scale down return in 1996 and 1997 but the cost savings from full capacity production in the Far East and the integration of facilities in the UK will be substantial.

'The quality of our design is outstanding. Especially in our baby products division, we set the standard for the industry. All of our design work is done in the UK,' says Crausay. Mayborn argues that quality is a key plank of its strategy. This extends beyond design and manufacture to sales and marketing, and the management of the group. The business is nevertheless a low capital expenditure enterprise with high returns and strongly cash generative. The group also owns a small florists' sundries cash and carry business which has caused some problems but where losses have been eliminated.

Outlook

Future prospects

- household products growth;
- profitability for Maws and China facility;
- integration of UK production facilities.

The group intends to tread cautiously until 1997. In Dylon, household products can expect most growth but some of these are in direct competition to industry majors. The baby products division wants to transfer production of certain outsourced products to China and to eliminate existing losses from Maws. But after a short period of consolidation, group businesses will make further purchases and seek to enhance market shares and geographical spread. This is an exciting business and one which demonstrates a clear vision for a successful future.

MAYBORN GROUP PLC

Address:

Mayborn Group plc, Dylon House, Worsley Bridge Road, Lower Syden-
ham, London SE26 5HD. Tel: 0181 663 4801. Fax: 0181 650 9876

Merlin Publishing International plc

Milton Keynes

Turnover				
1991	1992	1993	1994	1995
£5.6M	£7.4M	£14.8M	£20.3M	£34.5M

Summary: Merlin Publishing International is the largest UK publisher of sticker collectables. Its main products, including the Premier League and Euro 96 football series, are, by far, the strongest brands in this sector in the world. Customers buy a sticker album and sealed packets of stickers. They collect sufficient stickers, normally around 180 per volume, to complete their albums. Although boys from about age seven onwards are a key market for these products, the upper age limit can reach the late teens or early twenties. Merlin has experienced substantial turnover and pretax profits growth since the late 1980s, and is poised to expand its business into new markets. Merlin is also planning to launch a series of collectable cards, after its takeover in 1995 by the US company Tops.

The Business

Merlin's story might easily have been cast from the old wizard's book of spells. The tale contains enough enterprise, vision, spirit, determination and inspiration to enchant even the most jaded weaver of magic. Behind it all is a formidable force – thousands of collectors who form the company's customer base. These are the groups of young people – mainly but not exclusively boys – who pay £1.25 for each sticker album and 25p for a package of six stickers. Merlin sells 1.5 million albums and more than 70 million sticker packages of its Premier League football collection every year. But they are more than customers; they are rather a huge extended family. Collectors are quietly passionate people who attend Merlin's regional sticker swap shops in their tens of thousands. The collection may be the mammoth Premier League set including 530 individual plates or licensed characters such as Batman, Gladiators, Power Rangers, World Wrestling Federation or My Little Pony.

Sticker collections started in 1967 and from the outset the UK market leader was the Italian family-owned business Panini. Distribution of the product to small newsagents and sweetshops was handled by W.H. Smith Distributors and the relationship between the Italians and the British grew so close that most of Panini's UK business was planned jointly by the two companies. But in the late 1980s, the family sold out to Robert Maxwell. Two of Panini's UK directors, Kelvyn Gardner and Peter Dunk, were horrified. They decided to set up their own business and invited two W.H. Smith Distributors' leading lights, Peter Warsop and Mark Hillier, to join them. In 1989 they opened Merlin in Milton Keynes, which they chose because it was halfway between where they lived (Panini was based in London, W.H. Smith Distributors in Leicester). They prepared for a September 1989 launch of Soccer Team 90 and The Magic of the Beano.

Second mortgages were taken out to fund the infant venture. But Maxwell had other plans. 'He wanted us out of the markeplace and launched wholly spurious legal actions against us. He thought he would frighten us. It did take time, effort and funds which should have been spent on the business. When his legal actions were thrown out, he tried to buy us out but that did not work either,' says managing director Peter Warsop. The Merlin directors won their battle but the development of the new company in its first crucial months was held back. Nevertheless Merlin was destined to be be a success from the outset. The company was led by four people who thoroughly understood every element of the market.

Distinctive features

- UK market leader;
- innovative design approach;
- publisher of largest collections in the world;
- high quality management.

The company has now grown into the UK market leader with a stream of notable achievements. It has secured highly favourable licensing deals on well known television and film series and feature films. Merlin's soccer collections are also major contributors to the company's profitablity. Its Premier League set is the largest collection of its type ever published. Peter Warsop says that the company now provides substantial added value through its swap shop meetings and service where customers can buy nominated stickers direct from the company to complete their collections.

'The extent of the interest in our collections has grown rapidly since we started. Our first swap shop was a key development. We had not realised how many enthusiasts there were. The event was held in Southampton. We sent 15 people because we thought we might perhaps see a maximum of 2000 people. In fact between 14,000 and 15,000 attended the convention. I received a telephone call from the *Southampton Echo* asking why our convention had brought the city to a standstill. Now we typically get more than 10,000 people at our swap shops. People come with their duplicate stickers and trade them. Such is the demand that we often carry as many as one million stickers to these meetings.'

Stratagems

The core of Merlin's strategy is the introduction of innovative new, high volume stickers and to roll these out to yet wider audiences. In recent years the company has opened offices in Italy, France, Spain and the Benelux countries and plans further mainland European expansion. A design centre has been opened in Italy but Merlin had planned to shift this back to the UK. Both mainland offices have been staffed by ex-Panini people so the tradition of drawing on proven industry expertise has been extended. Warsop says that the motivation of people is a key factor in his strategy and he has little problem in recruiting people to what is a fun culture.

Size and shape

Employees: 100   Locations: 5
Geographical income split: UK 45%, mainland Europe 40%, RoW 15%

Mainland European markets share some similarities with the UK but they also produce collections which are suitable only for their domestic markets. For example, a set such as Batman or Power Rangers would have universal applicability but in the Netherlands Merlin's local company produced a collection based on the successful Dutch television series *Goede Tijden, Slechte Tijden*. Merlin's management team is planning to extend its formula to Germany, Spain and France.

Merlin conducts intensive research into new market possibilities and discusses licensing opportunities with film makers, publishers and toy markets. 'We attend all the relevant fairs to seek out the latest characters with widespread appeal. Our licensing director assesses which of the new launches will be sufficiently successful to issue a new sticker collection with mass appeal.' Around a third of Merlin's collection are major profitmakers, while the other two thirds make a small return. The company currently makes around ten per cent return on sales, which can be expected to grow with the portfolio of impressive new titles which it is expected to launch in the UK and in mainland Europe.

Future prospects

- major growth in mainland Europe;
- higher returns from new and existing sticker collections;
- significant investment in UK headquarters facilities;
- launch of collectable cards.

The initial investment in the business came from the four founders plus some help from Merlin's printer Redwood Press. In the early 1990s US investor Pat Klugy bought an investment stake in the business. The sale of the equity delivered capital for the partners to move closer to the business. And in July 1995 the founders sold out completely to Tops, a US collectable cards company which had been trying to make headway in Europe. The deal is a very good one because the founders retain their role in the business and they were able to see some return on their years of patient hard work. The arrangement gives Merlin even greater strength and it will allow longer term penetration of the USA, but with the added advantage of using the Tops infrastructure, and networks. Equally, Tops is keen to sell its collectable cards – popular in the USA – in Europe.

Outlook

Merlin's prospects are rosy. Its rapid ascent to UK market leadership, the quality of its products management, its healthy financial position and the huge market opportunties which lie ahead make this business very attractive. The company is poised for remarkable growth.

Address:

18 Vincent Avenue, Crownhill, Milton Keynes MK8 0AW. Tel: 01908 561588. Fax: 01908 565406

Microvitec plc

Bradford, West Yorkshire

Turnover				
1992	1993	1994	1995	1996
£50M	£35M	£44M	£55M	£65M

Summary: Microvitec is a company which rose from the ashes. After a successful float in 1984, the company lost direction until the current chairman James Bailey and his management team revitalised the business. Originally Microvitec made PC monitors, but it has now broadened out into a range of innovative and leading edge products in the networking and software sectors. Key current initiatives include flat panel LCD displays, significant new developments in video conferencing technology, and a laser based networking product which allows the transmission of data and voice between buildings without the need to lay a cable. This is a business which has seen its heavy investment in research and development pay off in substantial measure.

The Business

James Bailey concludes that he probably would not have taken on the task if he had known in 1990 what he now appreciates. But he is a man who likes a challenge and he transformed Microvitec from an ailing PC monitor maker into a thriving growth company. The enterprise was founded in 1979 and showed considerable promise. Sales of PCs were destined to increase rapidly in the 1980s. The company enjoyed a successful float on the London Stock Exchange in 1984 but shortly afterwards internal wrangling undermined previous good work and the business began a steady decline.

Bailey joined as chairman and chief executive after a management buy-in in May 1990. He was headhunted from a leading Canadian networking company. 'The business was in dire straits. We had to fight for survival.' He realised that the corner would not be turned for some time but that Microvitec needed a series of strategic steps to move it from ever-deepening losses to polished performer. The company had lost £1.5 million in the four months prior to his joining, so the initial programme involved measures to stem the losses. These included: cutting staff numbers, closing a French subsidiary and signing a ten-year marketing alliance with a North American company.

One of the key reasons for the failure of the product was limited and out-of-date ranges. But Bailey was fortunate to have among the technical staff some good people who could be reorientated to develop new product ranges capable of reaching high volumes. Bailey and his team realised that IT customers were becoming increasingly demanding and that if Microvitec was ever to make the quantum leap from ailing outfit to leading edge company then it would need to invest heavily in research and development. The first result from this decision was an improved and extended range of PC displays. But the company faced a further two years of losses before it moved into the black.

As a second step, Bailey wanted to improve the credibility of the business. Customers of computer industry companies have consistently said that after-sales service is a key factor in repeat purchases. He knew that Microvitec's reputation among buyers for its continuing care was low. So immediately he set to work to construct a company culture where customer service, technical excellence and flexibility of approach are paramount.

This was an early victory. He found that his team, once motivated, were keen to be associated with a high performing company and he managed to instil the new approach comparatively quickly. Instead of a sloppy, strife-riven and lossmaking business, Bailey had begun to create a leading edge, broadly-based, innovative and profitable growth company. The transformation has achieved many plaudits. Another major part of the recovery was an acquisitions programme. In 1990, Microvitec bought SilCom Manufacturing Technologyy Inc., a Canadian networking business. Since Microvitec's return to profits in 1994 it has spent £5.4 million on five other purchases to strengthen and grow its networking and software activities.

Distinctive factors

- heavy R&D spend;
- innovative, flexible approach;
- diversification in high growth markets;
- capacity to forecast trends.

Stratagems

Bailey's medium term vision sought to reduce the company's reliance on PC monitors and to extend the base of the company. When he took over the business its sole source of income was display technology. By 1995, the management team diversified sufficiently to show results where the display division accounted for 60 per cent of sales and 44 per cent of operating profits. Two new areas – network products and services, and software – had begun to make an impact on the figures. The network division claimed 29 per cent of turnover and 41 per cent of profits. The software section achieved 11 per cent of sales and 15 per cent profits.

In the longer term, the company intends these shares of the corporate financial cake will shift such that networks, which Bailey believes has outstanding potential, and software will increase their portions and displays will, relatively speaking, decline. At the heart of Microvitec's ambitious plan is Bailey's over-riding philosophy: staying ahead of the game. 'It is vital to get a product which a customer will buy in the future – but does not know it yet. You need to master that. The trick is staying ahead of the game.'

Size and shape

Employees: 810   Locations: 12 (including 2 in Germany and 1 in Canada)
Geographical income split: UK 52.2%, USA 12.8%, Americas 13.7%, Germany 14.8%, RoEur 5%, RoW 1.2%

Bailey is determined to take advantage of the high growth potential in networking. Local area networks (LANs) are expected to grow by at least 30 per cent a year in both the UK and the USA. But the biggest potential lies in remote networking – also known as SOHO (small office, home office). Now more and more people are working from home using a PC and sending and receiving information through a modem or an ISDN line. This is mushrooming at 200 per cent a year, while the Internet outstrips even SOHO with a rise in users of 300 per cent a year.

Niche markets in networking and communications are high on the company's priority list. A laser developed by Microvitec is in use at York where it connects two council departments – on opposite banks of the River Ouse – for speech and data communication. R&D spend is also going into multimedia. Video on demand is in the vanguard of Microvitec's programme with a conference facility and links with four different windows in four different locations. Bailey anticipates that this will be a fiercely contested market and Microvitec needs to be in the forefront of the technology to win a critical share.

Flat panel LCDs are another weapon in the company's armoury. They save space, are cheap to run and do not emit the high levels of heat produced by traditional PC monitors. 'In my view, if you do not undertake R&D you cannot develop new products. We are Britain's 1700th company in terms of size but when measured by R&D spend, we are the 250th. I invest as much as I can in capital equipment to be competitive and as much as I can in R&D to give us growth.'

The company also plans to expand its sales and after-sales operations to give greater geographical spread and to improve the quality of, and access to, good customer service. Bailey's achievement to date is remarkable but he recognises that the last five years were the limbering up for a really tough competitive match.

Outlook

Future prospects

- exciting new products;
- improving management;
- strong profitability;
- lucrative new markets.

Microvitec still has its gaze firmly set on both organic and acquisitional growth in its determination to identify and exploit profitable niche markets. The challenge remains but Microvitec has radically revitalised its competitive position. It now has a strong base from which to fight for markets which will stretch all the participants in terms of innovation, marketing, product design and delivery. Microvitec will still go for opportunities rejected by the bigger players because of their high operational costs. As a spirited entrepreneur, Bailey knows that he needs to keep his company light on its feet to be a world class company.

Address:

Futures Way, Bolling Road, Bradford, West Yorkshire BD4 7TU. Tel: 01274 390011. Fax: 01274 734944

ML Laboratories plc PHARMACEUTICALS

Wavertree Technology Park, Liverpool L13

Turnover				
1992	1993	1994	1995	1996
£604K	£823K	£811K	£1.14M	£10.43M

Summary: The corporate objective of ML Laboratories is to become a major European based healthcare company principally focused on the research and development of treatments for serious diseases where therapy is initiated in hospital and continued in a homecare environment. The company is comprised of small groups of dedicated individuals who demonstrate the flexibility necessary to keep pace with the dynamics of a rapidly evolving industry. The progress of the company has been enhanced by combining a sound understanding of the development of scientific discovery with business know-how. Innovative ideas from researchers and inventors are identified, funded and brought to market on what is a long-term rather that an immediate basis.

The Business

ML's overriding philosophy is to bring quality to the life of those who suffer serious illness and who might otherwise have to spend a large proportion of their lives in hospital undergoing constant treatment. And the success of its operation is a tribute to a man who saw the long-term potential and was willing to risk cash to support the vision of the now deceased Jerry Milner. Kevin Leech is probably best known as an entrepreneur who made a fortune from his family's funeral directors' business in Manchester and who bought both Land's End and John O'Groats. But he made £50,000 available in 1983 when banks refused Milner financial backing. Now ML is fully listed with £350 million of market capital.

But it is a high risk business as deputy chief executive Stuart Sim readily admits. Current industry figures show that it takes £200M and 12 years of rigorous investigation before a new medical treatment is registered and put on the market. ML spends an average of just £6 million because the company puts most of its research out to leading experts in both universities and teaching hospitals. Sim puts it like this: 'It means we don't have 250 people, all with PhDs, and in white coats trying to re-invent the wheel. But we can go to the best experts in the world.' He adds, however: 'The risk to reward ratio is huge because we are in the global marketplace. It is like drilling for oil without the benefit of a geological survey which can predict the chances of success.'

There have been plenty of successes for ML and more are in the pipeline. Icodial, the company's patented dialysis solution continues to demonstrate substantial benefits over traditional glucose solutions in continuous ambulatory peritoneal dialysis (CAPD). The drug has the potential to extend significantly the average CAPD treatment life of patients were it to be prescribed in place of the strong glucose solution from the beginning of the treatment. Should this prove the case, the impact on the size of the CAPD market would be dramatic. Dry powder inhalers are making an impact on respiratory problems. ML is well on the way to marketing its own brand. Improved cancer treatments are in the stages of advanced research. So are anti-viral agents used in the treatment of AIDS.

Other key areas of activity include a palatable lipid lowering agent and a potential new treatment for endometriosis. The in-house design and development centre has produced prototypes of new devices to improve renal dialysis therapy and delivery of drugs to the lung. Progress is being made towards taking Icodial into the global marketplace. The development of a variety of other products conceived to enhance patient lifestyles are all showing encouraging results.

Distinctive features

- concentration of effort and resources;
- use of world experts in research;
- minimalisation of risk/reward ratio;
- determination to achieve world wide sales.

Stratagems

ML regards itself as primarily as a company seeking niche markets. To that end it refuses to even consider appointing sales teams which can only add to the burden of expense. Sim sees its strength as getting the right product on sale in the quickest possible time and as cheaply as possible. He and his fellow executives calculate that the timescale from lodging a patent to the market place is ten years, which leaves just ten years to fully exploit a product's potential and reward.

On expiry big rivals with low profit margins and high sales volumes can take 40 per cent of the market in the first year and another 25 per cent in the second. But ML precludes this by the depth of research. Other companies may know what is in the product, but lack the expertise to produce at once. This is to be a key element of ML's tactics of market share. The fact that most of the company's research is undertaken by outside experts, who then share profits, leads to a more efficient *modus operandi*, according to Sim.

But the key to success is a determination to get a licence as quickly as possibly and at the lowest possible cost. That gives ML an open door to contract their drugs to bigger companies and use of their sales teams for bigger and more rapid market penetration. Sim says: 'Our strategy is to take our own ideas, or ideas we may buy in from other inventors, and convert them as economically as possible into new products in the quickest possible time.'

Size and shape:

Employees: 90   Locations: 4 (head office and 3 research centres)
Geographical income split: UK 75.71% Europe 17.26% North America 7.03%

Outlook

There is huge potential. But Sim says, with utter candour: 'It is not an investment for widows and orphans. Don't put survival money on it. But the further along the line, the further research progresses, the less risk.' ML is putting great store and faith in a new design of drug delivery for cancer which streams medication straight into the abdominal cavity. This, it insists, will be more effective than traditional chemotherapy. The delivery system can also be used in the treatment of MDS and other serious diseases.

Future prospects

- long-term penetration of USA and European markets as a staging post to worldwide sales;
- increasing markets for peritoneal dialysis, cancer and AIDS.

ML is planning to mount an aggressive export campaign and have enough secure financial backing to be more than a bit part player in the global marketplace. If the product is right, it is immensely saleable.

Address:

ML Laboratories plc, Rutherford Close, Wavertree Technology Park, Liverpool L13 1EN. Tel: 0151 228 0984/5. Fax: 0151 228 4847

Morse Group

Brentford, Middlesex

Turnover				
1992	1993	1994	1995	1996
£21M	£24M	£48M	£65M	£88M

Summary: Morse Group is Europe's largest open systems integrator and one of the UK's fastest growing companies. It is a fully accredited partner for Sun, Hewlett-Packard, Compaq and Oracle systems and has developed a blue-chip customer base. In addition to its function as a reseller, Morse is increasingly offering a range of value-added services through its applications centre. It has experienced rapid and extensive growth, both in turnover and pretax profits. The company opened separate sales offices in Edinburgh and Frankfurt in 1996 and in January 1997 in Manchester.

The Business

Morse Group was initially formed, in 1984, as a division of a photographic retailing company. Operating out of a single sales office in Holborn, it soon began to appreciate the enormous potential of the PC market and in 1988, having established a solid core of business, the company was bought out from its parent and new capital was injected.

The other key decision which the company took at that time was to venture into the then embryonic Unix market. This made Morse the first UK company to take Unix systems into the general marketplace, and the company chose as its partner the US computer giant Sun Microsystems. Both these choices proved inspired, as Unix platforms quickly grew in popularity, and soon this part of the company's business began to outstrip its existing activities. Four years later, Morse entered into a similar arrangement with Hewlett-Packard to sell its systems to corporate customers. In 1995, following Microsoft's launch of its NT platform, Morse decided that it was essential

315

also to have a presence in this market. Having reviewed various products, it chose Compaq as its NT reseller partner.

Consequently, Morse is now structured in three sales divisions: Morse Computers, which acts as a Sun Microsystems authorised reseller, and is accredited to the highest level under Sun's Competency 2000 scheme; MorseData, the Hewlett-Packard corporate reseller; and MorseNT, the Compaq and Microsoft NT reseller. Within each of these sales divisions, staff are divided into specialist industry groups. Each division also has pre-sales technical specialists and sales support staff.

While Morse Computers currently represents around 60 per cent of total turnover, it should be recognised that it is operating in a relatively mature market and growth is beginning to tail off. The fastest growing division is MorseData which is fully expected to double its turnover within the next 12 months. MorseNT is also expected to produce substantial levels of growth once the market as a whole develops.

A key aspect of Morse's activities is its applications centre. This comprises a platform-independent team of consultants offering a range of value-added services. Principal among these are cross-platform integration, Oracle and Oracle Financials, systems resilience, systems and network management, storage and backup and Internet technologies. Morse confidently expects that the contribution made by the applications centre will steadily increase over time. The company also has a group services function which provides customers with delivery, installation, maintenance, evaluations and demonstrations and a 24-hour on-call service.

Distinctive features

- strong relationship with manufacturers;
- sustained financial strength;
- reputation for high quality service;
- operates in fast growing markets.

Approximately 60 per cent of Morse's business is derived from customers in the banking and finance industry, principally investment banks. The company is also strong in the telecommunications, energy, utilities and education sectors. Partly in order to capitalise on its expertise in finance, Morse last year opened an office in Edinburgh offering Sun, Hewlett-Packard and NT specialist sales and support. The company also opened an office in Frankfurt, which concentrates on Sun systems.

Stratagems

Morse has established, and intends to maintain, a pre-eminent position as a provider of open systems integration solutions. Its success can be attributed to a range of factors, but principal among these is its understanding of key trends within the computer industry, the strength of the relationships which it has established with manufacturers and the quality of service it provides to customers.

Morse first demonstrated its ability to discern the direction of developments in the computer industry in the late 1980s with its support of the then relatively unknown Unix software and the selection of Sun Microsystems as its partner. The company estimates that by moving into the Unix market so early it gained a competitive advantage measurable in years. It has been similarly successful with its choice of other partners. With developments in the computer industry now favouring smaller and more flexible systems, Morse believes that NT products are becoming increasingly important.

Size and shape

Employees: 150   Locations: 6
Geographical income split: UK 95%, mainland Europe 5%

The company is acknowledged as having especially strong relationships with its manufacturing partners. As systems become more sophisticated such close partnerships are becoming increasingly important. In particular, support from manufacturers can be of considerable assistance during the selling process. The company is a fully accredited partner of all its major suppliers, and the strength of its relationship with Oracle is demonstrated by the fact that it is Oracle's biggest reseller in the UK.

Future prospects

- major push in UK and mainland Europe;
- MorseData to double turnover by mid-1997;
- expansion in the product range.

Morse places considerable emphasis on the quality of service which it provides to customers. Its customer base includes companies, which although they are interested in value for money are buying on criteria other than cost. The range of ancillary services which Morse can provide through

317

its applications centre therefore gives it an important competitive edge over rival firms. Furthermore, its sectoral structure allows the business to develop particular skills and expertise which can be applied across a range of clients.

Morse has invested heavily in its own internal infrastructure. Much of this was made possible by a substantial capital injection which accompanied a management buy-out in 1995. In order to attract the highest quality of staff, the company is acknowledged as offering remuneration packages which are among the best in the industry, and is keen to provide employees with a good working environment.

Outlook

Morse has enjoyed extremely impressive growth over recent years, and it is fully anticipated that this will continue in future. In particular, its Hewlett-Packard and NT divisions should perform strongly as users move towards more flexible platforms. The company has now established a respected brand name and acquired a strong corporate client list which provide it with an important source of recurring revenue. Morse is also continuing to expand the range of products and services which it offers. It now has the financial strength to carry out major expansion in the UK and mainland Europe.

Address:

Brentside Executive Centre, Great West Road, Brentford, Middlesex TW8 9HE. Tel: 0181 380 8000. Fax: 0181 560 7700

Mulberry Company (Design) Ltd

Shepton Mallett

Turnover		
1994	1995	1996
£22.4M*	£20.6M	£22.7M
*1994 covers 16 months		

Summary: Mulberry represents the spirit of English style. This highly successful lifestyle brand is characterised by rural life, tradition and quality of craftsmanship. Many people might think that Mulberry is a Victorian venture, or even earlier. In fact it was started 26 years ago by a London designer called Roger Saul in the middle of one of the most flamboyant periods of UK fashion. The company has expanded and is now an international designer brand with product ranges encompassing accessories, ready-to-wear and home interiors. It has shops and corners in substantial stores around the globe. Most of its products are still made in Somerset to maintain tight quality control and to remain faithful to its English country roots.

The Business

When Roger Saul started producing leather chokers and belts on the kitchen table in his London flat in 1969, he probably had little sense of the extent to which his business would grow. In 1997 Mulberry is represented throughout the world in high quality stores – either wholly-owned, franchised or in corners in the major department stores such as Harrods and Harvey Nichols. The original concept has now broadened out into ready-to-wear items and home furnishings. The company has developed a mission statement to be the best accessories, clothing and interiors business in the world. It says that it will achieve this by offering perfect quality and a customer service which is second to none, by innovating, by creating a caring working environment and by increasing sales and market share and thus profitability.

Managing director John Rogers says that the company's goals are currently focused on building share in existing markets, penetrating new markets and expanding its product lines. 'Mulberry is more than a collection – it is a lifestyle concept. With the clothes, accessories and furnishings come a distinctively English approach. It is traditional, rural, reliable and carries an aura of quality,' he comments.

The catalogue includes 2700 items. Accessories still make up the largest number – more than 1000 are in this category. There are 950 home products and 750 in the ready-to-wear category. The expansion from accessories came in the early 1980s. 'It seems that we open a new division each decade,' he remarks. The linkage between accessories and ready-to-wear is obvious but it takes a leap to embrace home furnishings. 'People were coming to the stores and buying clothes but they also wanted to take away the props which we used to display the items. These would include traditional desks and tables, chairs and sofas.' The surprisingly high level of interest encouraged Roger Saul to investigate broadening the concept to include home interiors.

Distinctive features

- original and distinctive lifestyle brands;
- global reputation;
- broadening product portfolio;
- award-winning designs.

Stratagems

Mulberry's strategy embraces several key points. The company argues that it is selling a lifestyle concept rather than solely individual products; it emphasises not only the quality of the image but also of the craftsmanship which goes into the products, and its philosophy of a global brand. In strictly business terms, the enterprise has grown from a small factory in Somerset to a producer of goods to meet international demand and standards. Part of its success has been the opening of Mulberry shops and corners, some of which are company-owned and others which are franchised. Rogers says that the importance, and number, of franchises will grow.

At present the company is active in 65 Mulberry shops worldwide and its products are represented by 536 wholesalers around the globe. Rogers hopes for further expansion in the Far East and North America.

Licensing is another major step forward for the business. It has already launched a range of ladies perfumery and watches. He expects that sunglasses and writing equipment such as high class pens may be next on the list. In May 1996, Mulberry launched on the Alternative Investment Market of the London Stock Exchange, and this next step in Mulberry's development has proved successful, giving the company a far higher profile and greater awareness to the public.

Size and shape

Employees: 594   Locations: 1
Geographical income split: UK 35%, RoW 65%

Product quality is a key aspect of business for the company and it will assume the status of a priority objective in the next two years. In the early part of 1997 the company anticipated putting in new technology on to the production floor at a cost of £100,000. This would further enhance quality standards and allow for diversification of product lines. It has already begun this process by becoming the first company in Britain, and the third in Europe, to install a water-jet cutting machine to cut all its leather components. This has been a true marriage of tradition and technology, combining craftsmanship with computerised cutting. But emphatically new machinery is not to replace people but rather to help them do their job better. This business has astonishingly high employee morale and many of its people have been with the company since the early days.

Rogers is straightforward about what he regards as success in strictly financial terms. 'I look for a 20 per cent growth in the bottom line each year,' he says. In the clothing and fabrics sector this is a tough target but it tends to focus the attention of everyone in the business. 'We cannot afford to stand still. If we increase our market penetration, stay innovative in our designs, and invest in our people and systems we can meet our profitability targets.'

But Mulberry will not start manufacturing in the low cost economies of the Far East to reduce expenses. 'Our name is synonymous with England and we are absolute about retaining control over the quality of the production process.'

Outlook

Future prospects

- expansion in licensing;
- growth in the Far East and North America;
- investment in systems and people.

MULBERRY COMPANY (DESIGN) LTD

Where will Mulberry be in the first decade of the next century? Rogers says that it is unlikely to create a fourth division but rather concentrate on extending product range and quality in its existing structure. However, licensing will become an additional source of revenue. He foresees more franchised outlets around the world and a centrally directed expansion programme in North America and Japan. 'We are very cautious about the US but only because we want to get it right when we go there.'

Address:

Mulberry, Kilver Court, Shepton Mallet, Somerset BA4 5NE. Tel: 01749 340500. Fax: 01749 345532

On Demand Information plc

Leeds, West Yorkshire

Turnover			
1993	1994	1995	1996
£2.3M	£5.9M	£8.8M	£11.4M

Summary: On Demand Information develops and markets networked multimedia information systems which are transmitted to customers via BT's digital ISDN network and communications products. Apart from text documents, such database systems can involve colour stills, video images and audio. Custom-developed software allows rapid data access and retrieval, and complex interaction between database and a recipient's own PC is often built in to the network. A London Stock Exchange listing in 1993 produced an additional £10M in project finance. Continuing investment in product development, infrastructure and staff meant a 1996 pretax loss of £2.9M, but the company anticipates considerable growth and profits within three years, given a clear sector lead and a valuable contract with BT to distribute the first two of ODI's published information products.

The Business

Whatever its other attractions, and there are many, the Internet or so called 'global superhighway', is of little practical use as an information source for industry and commerce. The 'Net's' unstructured architecture and reaction speed usually makes it irritatingly slow and rambling. A better way of harnessing the power of digital technology to the speed of modern communications is a dedicated system, bringing instant information to companies, who can use it to sharpen and enhance their business activities.

On Demand Information believes it has the key to this, through custom-made databases, with modern search technology, and BT's digital ISDN2 network. Although less than five years old, the company has now sold two of its first information products – covering the construction industry and personnel professionals – to BT and is applying similar technology to other sectors of industry.

ODI founder Graham Poulter operated a marketing services business in Leeds. By 1990, he was frustrated at the 'totally inefficient' way of disseminating information via the printed page or by video tape. Despite the fact that such techniques were costing his own, and other companies, vast amounts of money in publishing costs, there was, then, little alternative but to accept the built-in obsolescence of printed information. He wanted to retain all the advantages of both text and videotape – colour images, voice communication, traceable records – but transfer them to a computer. Then, by linking the ODI central computers to desktop PCs, communicate that information quickly and effectively.

Despairing of software houses, he brought in his own software engineers to develop a solution that delivered both quality and speed. They eventually succeeded despite the demands he placed on them – 'I can turn over a full colour screen faster than you can turn over a full colour page in a book,' says Poulter. The software solution arrived at a time when digital information was being seen as an industrial timesaver and when BT, for instance, was searching for added value products, rather than being simply a service provider. Since taking over as exclusive distributor of two ODI information packages, BT says it has generated more than 1700 enquiries for the products in five months. ODI were paid, initially, over £1M for those rights and revenue is now flowing in.

Distinctive features

- commanding blue chip relationships;
- high technical competence;
- highly focused on information dissemination.

There is also additional cash to be earned in distributing non-core information, within such established packages, on products available, for instance, from sector manufacturers – which makes them the digital equivalent of newspaper or magazine advertising. Further products are currently under development; some are nearing completion.

Stratagems

Graham Poulter carried his dissatisfaction with traditional methods of information dissemination to an extreme when he launched a company to develop the distribution of digital information technology. This development was funded to the tune of more than £3M before it was ready for a market launch and could begin serious revenue earning. Now, despite an annual turnover of more than £11M in 1996, he feels that even with today's proven technology, as opposed to still-being-tested developments, and over the horizon advances, ODI has barely begun to scratch the surface of digital information processing, distribution and sales and allied communications products.

The next package, for the independent financial adviser (IFA) market will be launched soon, with substantial interest being shown from companies currently handling analysis of financial products by traditional paper, or PC techniques. 'A structured network is important in getting people to use a service. Go on the Internet and try to find the information you need and you

Size and shape

Employees: 190   Locations: 1
Geographical income split: UK 100%

realise why.' The majority of businesses, he said, are also suspicious of the Internet, of its slow download speed and the temptations of non-commercial use by staff. Increasingly, ODI's services are becoming available to better quality office PCs. As in any technology-based industry, advances are now being made at a faster rate than they can be applied, and Poulter regards it as an essential part of the chairman's job to attempt to look and plan ahead.

Future prospects

- growing range of sector-focused information systems;
- highly able technology base underpins future potential;
- thorough understanding of its market opportunities.

'I am a marketing man, but I know enough about technology not to be side-tracked and I have key technical experts working with me. Remember, the object of all this was to create something I wanted.' ODI's software engineers are increasingly coming to terms with needs that extend well beyond simple information transmission. 'Our system makes it impossible to work with outdated information,' he says.

'The index on a PC connected to our system performs an automatic check with the host when you switch on in the morning and is updated.' ODI goes further. 'One system has a job file built in, which is also checked and updated where necessary.' The scope and scale of the information which can be held in a digital system is almost limitless. Such a database removes the need for conventional record keeping and updating, and search technology is now so sophisticated that speed of access is startling to the new user. It is not, as some rashly suggested a year or two back, the forerunner of the paperless office. It is a high speed, high convenience method of handling large amounts of information which can quickly and easily be updated centrally as frequently as necessary. There is no reason why electronic data distribution and conventional publishing techniques cannot work together today; the forthcoming ODI database for financial advisers will incorporate daily headline news items, supplied by an industry magazine. Eventually, the entire text of such a magazine, stretching back years, could be incorporated, for instant reference.

Outlook

ODI has spent a great deal of money developing state of the art electronic information systems and communications packages. Its task now is to continue to translate that technology into sector-relevant packages which offer real benefits and revenue-earning assistance to professionals. The Stock Exchange obviously believes ODI can deliver; its market launch nearly three years ago was highly successful and the current valuation of the company is now 50 per cent higher than the £40M price tag put on it at flotation.

Address:

2 Burley Road, Leeds LS3 1NJ. Tel: 0113 233 0000. Fax: 0113 244 8796

Pace Micro Technology plc

Shipley, West Yorkshire

Turnover			
1993	1994	1995	1996
£80.1M	£77.4M	£99.9M	£195.8M

Summary: Pace Micro Technology has moved into a commanding position in the supply of satellite and cable decoder boxes – a sector which is experiencing burgeoning market demand. It is the dominant player in UK and European markets and its confident ambitions to be recognised as world market leader appear promising. Pace licences conditional access technology from conditional access providers. CA is used by broadcasters to restrict access to its services. This technology allows selected TV viewers to decode encoded TV signals to view them in intelligible form. Pace sees considerable opportunities in markets for digital cable, satellite and terrestrial broadcasting and believes that it is well placed to exploit them.

The Business

The dawning of the age of satellite and cable television has been the launching pad for the gathering success of Pace Micro Technology. Based in Saltaire in the heart of industrial West Yorkshire, the company has grown rapidly as the uptake of non-terrestrial television has mushroomed. Its primary business is the design, manufacture and distribution of analogue and digital receivers and decoders for receiving pay televison.

Pace employs more than 1000 people in the UK and overseas in the design and manufacture of more than 50 products for 80 countries worldwide. It sees rapid expansion in demand for its products since the number of satellite television channels will expand dramatically before the turn of century and, in addition, the introduction of digital terrestrial and satellite television should create – over the long-term – an increase in its potential market of at least fourfold, according to industry projections. The company has made significant progress in the markets outside Europe. It has opened joint venture plants in Thailand and Hong Kong, and operates its own facilities in Australia and the Middle East. The company has created relationships with broadcasters in some of these new markets. In Australia, it has linked up with Foxtel for analogue and Galaxy for digital television. In the Middle East, South Africa, Indonesia and Mexico it works with Multichoice.

Pace was founded in 1982 by its former joint chief executive David Hood and initially made modems for computer communications. In 1987 it developed its first analogue receiver for satellite television, which was in the early stages of its development in the UK. But the following year it captured its first original equipment manufacturer (OEM) contracts. This was crucial in the development of the business. The recognition of the Pace technology by leading manufacturers allowed the company to make a major leap forward and it has established itself since as the UK and European industry standard. Relationships with broadcasters, regulators and standard-setting bodies are key facets of the Pace approach to building business.

The early 1990s saw its first receiver decoder in the marketplace, which again reinforced its position as technical innovator in a business which is responsive to the needs of its sector. In 1993 it opened its state-of-the-art manufacturing facility in Shipley, and in 1994 came sales offices overseas. Pace opened offices in Scandinavia, Germany, the Middle East and Hong Kong.

A crucial development for the company was the conclusion of an agreement with NTL's advanced products division to develop and market MPEG2 digital products (NTL is a subsidiary of News Corporation which owns 40 per cent of BSkyB). Within a year it had emerged as the first volume manufacturer worldwide to make MPEG2 digital satellite receivers for the consumer market and it started to supply MPEG2 compliant digital satellite receivers for the first time to the Australian, South African, and Thai markets. In mid year 1996 Pace won contracts to supply digital receivers to Italy and the Middle East. During 1996 Pace manufactured 500,000 digital receivers and won a contract for £25 million from Canal+. Pace was already a player in the French analogue market and the new order at once made the company a force in digital. It acted as a catalyst to open a new production line at Shipley.

Distinctive features

- first to market;
- highly focused business model;
- key relationships with suppliers, broadcasters and standard-setting bodies worldwide.

Stratagems

The secret of the Pace achievement is that it spotted a major technical development at an early stage and identified clearly what needed to be done to secure a substantial position in that emerging market. First, Pace's directors realised that the number of television channels would rise quickly and substantially. Most of these new channels would come from satellite or cable operators and the viewer would require a decoder in order to be able to access these new channels.

Size and shape

Employees: 1000+   Locations: 12
Geographical income split: Europe 75%   RoW 25%

Industry reports looked to spiralling expansion in television stations in the United States as a forerunner to what would be likely to happen in Europe. Analysts argued – with justification as it turned out – that the eventual audience for these new stations would be many millions. Unlike the US where most major markets had dozens of stations, European broadcasting was heavily regulated. Observers said that once whetted, the appetite for satellite and cable would be extensive.

According to the television industry's TBI Yearbook, produced in association with KPMG, in 1995 around a fifth of the 909 million households receiving television watched pay-TV. By the year 2000, that number is expected to increase by around 50 per cent to 342 million. The growth will be fuelled, says the book, by the expansion in services.

Coupled with the growth of analogue satellite and cable is the whole new market of digital television which Pace set out to exploit at the end of the 1980s. Digital television increases sixfold the number of channels that can be broadcast in any given amount of radio spectrum. As digital technology is being used in both traditional broadcasting and pay-TV, Pace recognised that it could benefit by carefully positioning itself for these new opportunities.

Its strategy has also been marked by three other key characteristics. At an early stage, it planned to be a global company pursuing worldwide ambitions. And early in the 1990s, the company opened sales offices outside the UK. But its first development was to become the British market leader by supplying realistically priced but leading edge technology to the UK market. Its second development was to forge relationships with the blue chip broadcasters and suppliers in the field and thirdly to conclude joint venture agreements with companies in other expanding markets such as the Far East.

Pace has also obtained a series of conditional access licences such as Eurocrypt, NewsCrypt, VideoCrypt and News Digital to manufacture decoders for new broadcast systems. Also, the company invests heavily in design and manufacture to continue to refine products to extend their useful life.

Outlook

Pace has achieved considerable strength in a key marketplace of the future. It has established a significant market share in analogue pay-TV; and it has a leading role in the provision of pay-TV services worldwide. It has predicted with a high degree of focus the key changes in its sector and directed the company's business towards new broadcast and technical opportunities. The unparalleled growth in television services – both digital and analogue – offers the company extensive possibilities for increasing its returns. Its combination of market standing, relationship with the broadcasters/regulators and OEMs, technical quality, and joint venture manufacturing and sales network will present potential lucrative business.

Address:

Pace Micro Technology plc, Victoria Road, Saltaire, Shipley, West Yorkshire BD18 3LF. Telephone: 01274 532000. Fax: 01274 537096

Parity plc

Central London

Turnover		
1994	1995	1996
£20M	£89M	£128M

Summary: Parity has taken advantage of the rapidly increasing demand for a range of services linked to the information technology requirements of companies. Its clients include a broad selection of leading businesses and authorities in the UK and across mainland Europe. The company supplies consultancy, systems development, training and skills insourcing. Mainly through organic growth, but also via strategic acquisitions, it has experienced significant and sustained financial growth.

The Business

Parity is one of those companies which has been growing quietly, well known to its clients and the cognescenti of the markets and emerging businesses sector, but not well known outside. Like many others in this book, it saw a market opportunity and concentrated on its chosen sector with vision and a tight focus.

The results of Parity's efforts can readily be seen in many of the measures which denote a successful business. In the last three financial years alone its sales have climbed from £20 million to £128 million. Some of that sixfold expansion is due to acquisitions but the underlying performance is undeniable. Achievements in pretax profits present a mirror of the turnover picture. Profits of £600,000 in 1993 shot up £6.5 million two years later. Numbers of employees have risen from 159 to 582. Parity's directors have done this without gearing while at the same time increasing earnings per share from 3.73p to 10.34p over the same period.

The company's blue chip client base has expanded in tune with these results. It now includes BT, BZW, BNFL, Lloyds Bank, Nat West Bank,

Marks & Spencer, Swiss Life, the Department of Trade and Industry, the Foreign and Commonwealth Office and the DSS.

Parity operates three principal divisions from its Victoria headquarters. It states that it is first and foremost an information technology company, which conditions what activities it follows and the manner and style in which they are delivered. These divisions are: consultancy, systems development, training and skills insourcing. Around 89 per cent of the business is derived from the UK but the remainder – and an increasing part of the cake – is sourced in mainland Europe.

Parity plc is composed of Parity Solutions, CSS Trident and Eurosoft. Parity Solutions was formed in 1995 with the express aim of providing consultancy, systems development and training. It was the combination of four loss-making enterprises, purchased in the second half of 1994. These four companies – Class Limited, LBMS Consulting, ACT Business Systems and BIS Training – when brought together as Parity Solutions returned a profit in 1995. CEO Paul Davies says that it was a combination of the installation of experienced management and healthier trading conditions which were the key factors in the success – from day one – of Parity Solutions.

Distinctive features

- focused business approach;
- experienced management;
- flexible resourcing;
- high staff morale;
- organic and acquisitional growth.

CSS Trident opened in 1970 and is a market leader in the provision of temporary IT skills. It has achieved and retained this status by remaining true to both companies and freelancers. To the clients it aims to increase the value of its services while it makes a commitment to self-employed IT specialists to develop their careers.

Eurosoft was envisaged in 1995 as a consultancy providing project support services throughout mainstream mainland markets such as Germany, France, the Netherlands and Switzerland. It combined Parity's existing continental business IC Software and its then newly acquired companies Eurosoft Solutions SARL, Eurosoft Solutions GmbH and Software '92 plc. During 1996 Parity invested heavily in management skills, staff and systems in a bid to realise the commercial opportunities in these key territories.

Stratagems

Parity's management has forged a business which is only now achieving wider business public awareness. The concept of an IT company with principal operating divisions in key areas of customer demand was pivotal. A management team with substantial business and industrial experience was assembled to shape the company.

It has been driven by the market first and foremost. By clearly identifying market demand and trends within sectors, it has been able to shape a group which works well together and which makes perfect sense. Building the structure is a process which has been achieved by organic and acquisitional means. Davies says that management of the group is a straightforward process with direct communication links. There is tight financial control from the centre but great operational freedom for the managing directors to achieve their targets.

Size and shape:

Employees: 582   Locations: 18
Geographical income split: UK 89%, mainland Europe 11%

The strategies for the divisions are decided in consultation with the key players in the management team. Parity Solutions, for example, wanted to re-organise along vertical lines while retaining cross-functional skills. This approach, backed by the group's management team, facilitated new business in the utilities and finance sectors. So successful was it that it was extended to the health and pharmaceuticals sectors.

Parity's general ongoing commitment to providing added value to clients has helped win new assignments in the public sector where there is substantial demand for greater cost-effectiveness and efficiency. IT systems are at the sharp end of this work because they can be applied to achieve outstanding cost savings and high efficiencies. Parity's approach – and this is a major market advantage – has been to bridge the gap between corporate and IT strategies. In other words, its highly trained and motivated people can see the evolving commercial demands and apply the latest and appropriate technological solutions. The quality of Parity's managers as communicators is a strong factor in the group's success.

Another major distinctive feature in the Parity strategy has been the employment of more than 150 permanent technical staff supported by around 1900 freelancers. There is key investment in the upgrading of skills, software and systems. The management has developed a culture where managers in particular are very committed and this is shown in the extent of the repeat business which Parity is winning.

Outlook

Future prospects

- greater mainland European contribution;
- expanded blue chip business;
- further synergies from cross-functional work.

The case for a coherently managed IT company operating in systems, staffing and software is compelling. The key has been the creation of the core operating companies, a fusion of specialist knowledge, high quality customer service and flexibility. As the systems become more complex, the demand from client companies for logical and well grounded advice on their application to real business situations will expand rapidly.

Address:

Parity plc, 18 Grosvenor Gardens, Victoria, London SW1V 0DH. Tel: 0171 824 8008. Fax: 0171 259 0021

Probe Entertainment Ltd

Croydon

Turnover				
1991	1992	1993	1994	1995
£186M	£183M	£197M	£210M	£250M

Summary: Probe Entertainment was started by 17-year old Fergus McGovern in 1984 and supplied games for the first hand-held computer games consoles. Its revenues grew enormously and self-funded its growth to a business employing more than 90 people and producing in excess of 450 games that generated more than $1.7 billion of retail revenue as the games market went through a period of soaring growth. He sold out to a leading US games corporation in 1995 for a reputed £60 million and is now intent on owning the on-line gaming market where player machines are linked together.

The Business

Creating games software for the video game market is a business that can make miserable returns or take off like a rocket. Get the right game on the right platform and the results can resemble those which have made Probe Entertainment such a potent force in the industry. It has ridden succeeding waves of evolution in this arena as cartridge-based consoles grew more powerful, developed into CD-ROM-based systems and prompted the rise of the PC as a games platform. MD Fergus McGovern started the company in 1984 and developed games for the early consoles sold by Nintendo and Sega. Probe earned a dependable reputation and started converting arcade-style games to run on the consoles. It developed strong relationships with arcade machine manufacturers and became skilled at converting such products for the less powerful console machines. This turned into a booming business as console machines became more powerful. Film scenarios began to be incorporated in games and teenage boys could go and see the movie *Terminator 2*

335

and then play a *Terminator* game on their console. Forthcoming games in this genre include *Die Hard III* and *Judge Dredd*.

Probe generated new games mostly on a production fee and royalty basis. Sometimes it would launch an original product and then auction it to games distributors. This provided a higher percentage of the retail revenue to Probe as it had assumed more risk in the origination. Probe works as a development company for games publishers. For example, it has developed *Mortal Kombat* for Acclaim, which grossed $50 million in only three days. This sort of result is very reassuring for a publisher. Customers will pay millions for the rights to a game on a particular platform – SEGA, Nintendo, 3DO – and want a developer with a solid track record. Probe has consistently produced top quality output and kept licensees pleased with the results.

The skills needed to programme games for ever more powerful consoles meant Probe had to invest in state of the art computer workstations costing a quarter of a million pounds each. This has enabled the company to produce top ranked games for the latest CD consoles. Sony's Playstation, which has more graphics power than many desktop personal computers, is a prime example. Games now include acted sequences and video clips shot on location. These are very sophisticated multi-million pound projects.

Distinctive features

- timely delivery – a notable rarity in the computer games sector;
- attracting and keeping some of the best talents in the industry;
- keeping pace with the technological developments in the sector;
- superb financial performance.

Games development is very specialised. It is not at all like traditional software development or engineering. It requires developers in tune with games users, mainly adolescent males, and the average age of Probe's staff is only 27. McGovern says, 'We have some of the best people in the world. They want to work with the company. We give them the right environment, recognition – we do not pay them a great deal and we work them flat out. But there is a great buzz about the place.'

By 1995 Probe was the largest independent games developer in the world and had produced 450 games which generated $1.7 billion of retail revenue around the world. But the cost of producing video games, 'had taken a massive leap upwards with a major game costing up to £5 million to develop,' according to McGovern. Each advance in technology has meant a huge increase in the resources needed to develop games. Five people may have been needed for a typical game development in 1993. This has risen to more than 30 in 1996 with another 20 needed on a part-time basis to direct film shoots, do the sound recording and art direction. Consequently the industry is consolidating into major players who can afford this increasing financial risk.

Probe were acquired by the leading US games corporation Acclaim for a reputed £60 million in 1995. (The actual figure has never been made public.) McGovern's reason for selling, 'was access to proprietary technology and the ability to work in new fields. The time was right. It gives us new disciplines, new skills and the opportunity to jump to the next league. Acclaim had taken the next step forward. It was so far ahead that we could never dream of doing that.'

Stratagems

Probe has kept up to date with technology developments. Their are three main games platforms; arcade machines, specialised hand-held consoles connected to a television and the personal computer (PC). Probe specialised originally in developing games for the 8-bit consoles which loaded games from tape cartridges. These consoles became more powerful 16-bit machines and Probe began converting arcade games, which ran on very powerful arcade systems, to the less powerful hand-held console format. As the technology developed again to 32-bit consoles with highly specialised graphics chips and CD-ROM replacing the tape cartridges Probe converted and developed games for such systems from Sony, SEGA and Atari.

Size and shape

Employees: 92   Locations: 1
Geographical income split: company refuses to disclose

It also embraced the PC which had different characteristics from consoles but which has become steadily more powerful and now Probe don't distinguish between PCs or consoles; both are CD format. In 1995 20 per cent of their games were for cartridges and 75 per cent for CD formats. Now it is almost 100 per cent for CDs. Probe has invested to give its developers state-of-the-art graphics workstations and also extended its capabilities in the sound effects, music, location backdrops and video clips so that games like *Terminator 2* feature characters, voices, locations, even video sequences and music from the movie.

Probe has provided development services for many games owners and has been insulated from over-dependence on only one. This has helped prevent staff poaching as Probe would cease work for a games owner if that company hired Probe developers. Employee turnover has been minuscule, which has helped build up teamwork and a great mass of games expertise inside the company. Adolescent boys, the main users and buyers of games can be fickle and choose games partly on an intangible playability aspect. Probe has consistently shown that it can produce games that hit this bull's-eye and beat competing games which are technically similar but miss out on playability.

Probe has grown spectacularly with the computerised games market and rivers of cash have made it completely self-funding. McGovern says, 'We never had an overdraft in twelve years. It has all been financed by me.' As they have grown from one person to 92 McGovern has brought in professional managers to keep Probe's administration and management operating effectively whilst his teams of decidedly non-corporate games developers kept developing one blockbuster game after another.

Outlook

The hand-held console market is slowing as the meteoric sales seen in the 8 and 16-bit cartridge days have not been repeated with the 32-bit CD-based consoles. Nintendo is issuing a 64-bit cartridge for which Probe is developing games. The industry hope seems to be in networking players using consoles and/or PCs together. Probe is well-placed but as an in-house development shop for Acclaim. McGovern plans Grand Prix games where players race cars whose position on the computerised track is taken from satellite-transmitted telemetry off real Grand Prix cars on a real track. If the necessary networking bandwidth arrives such exciting concepts should power Probe on to ever higher earnings. As part of a US-quoted company it cannot provide outlook figures so the figures shown are external estimates.

Address:

Knollys House, First Floor, 17 Addiscombe Road, Croydon, Surrey CR0 6SR. Tel: 0181 680 4142. Fax: 0181 680 8847

Protean plc

High Wycombe, Buckinghamshire

Turnover				
1992	1993	1994	1995	1996
£22.7M	£33.6M	£42.2M	£54.5M	£74.2M

Summary: Protean is a high-quality industrial conglomerate encompassing a range of businesses primarily in the water purification and scientific equipment sectors. The group has grown significantly over recent years, both organically and by acquisition, and places considerable importance on the operational autonomy which it devolves to individual business units, albeit within the framework of rigorous financial discipline from the centre. Protean now occupies the leading position in a number of specialist markets and has developed a strong worldwide presence and customer base.

The Business

Protean's businesses are focused around the design, manufacture and supply of products and systems, together with the provision of related services, to a wide range of customers in three industries – water purification systems, scientific equipment and thermal technologies. The group's origins lie in its water purification activities. These are themselves based around the Elga group of companies, an international organisation which now has operations in the UK, France, Germany, Republic of Ireland and USA, with a network of agents and distributors in a further 50 countries. Elga supplies equipment which is designed to purify tap water to exacting levels of quality and serves a variety of scientific, medical and industrial customers. Elga is supported by a series of service businesses which ensure that the water remains at the specified quality and provide the requisite consumables and spares. In June 1995, Protean substantially increased its presence in Western Europe when it acquired DWA, a German company specialising in the production and service of water purification equipment designed for use in renal dialysis.

The second leg of Protean's business is the manufacture of scientific analysis equipment and it includes a range of diverse activities. Chromacol is the best known branded vial for chromatography autosamplers, while EGI is a market leader in converted glass tubing and LIP is involved in the design, manufacture and supply of a large range of single-use injection moulded sample containers. Techne designs and manufactures thermally controlled laboratory equipment for researchers working in life sciences. In September 1994, Protean acquired Jenway, an Essex-based company involved in the manufacture of analytical, metering and measurement products for laboratories and industry. This was followed in the following year by the purchase of HPLC Technology. HPLC supplies consumable items for use in high performance liquid chromatography and it is intended that this company will work in close co-operation with Chromacol.

Finally, Protean is also involved in thermal technology. Its two subsidiaries, Lenton and Carbolite, supply worldwide markets with ovens, furnaces, incubators and related products. These are designed to create a series of extremely complex heating and cooling conditions, while also providing the reliability and longevity demanded by increasingly cost-conscious customers. Both Carbolite and Lenton produce standard products, but are also able to provide a custom-built service.

Distinctive features

- market leadership;
- reputation for innovation and quality;
- strong financial controls;
- global sales;
- heavy R&D emphasis.

Protean is well-represented internationally. At present, approximately 40 per cent of its revenue is earned in the United Kingdom, a further 38 per cent is derived from Western Europe (with France and Germany being the principal markets), with the remainder coming from the Pacific Rim and North America. It is also worth noting that Protean has a well-balanced income stream, with around half the group's turnover being derived from after-market sales of service and consumables.

Stratagems

Although Protean has been aggressive in making acquisitions over recent years, it would be wrong to think of its growth as being acquisition-driven.

Indeed, the group has been very successful in continuing to generate organic growth from its existing businesses. Nevertheless, its acquisition criteria help to demonstrate the key points of the group's strategy. Protean is interested in companies which have a strong, niche position in a specialist market. The majority of its businesses are market-leaders with unrivalled track records and produce goods for which there is a clearly identified and steadily growing demand. Many businesses are also the most technologically advanced in their respective industries.

Protean places great importance on carrying out advanced research and development. For example, the Elga companies have taken a leading market position in ion exchange, reverse osmosis and ultra-filtration technologies, while Chromacol has a long-standing reputation as an innovator. The group's technological strengths are reflected in its record of product development. All group companies have undertaken a continuous programme of introducing new products to respond to changing customer requirements and advances in technology.

In making an acquisition, Protean looks only at companies and markets in which it already has some expertise. It will grow by sticking to what it knows best and, for this reason, remains the most tightly focused of conglomerates. At the same time, its spread of businesses means that poor performances in some sectors can generally be offset by strong performances in others. It is also looking for businesses involved in high-margin activities which have a significant consumable supplies content. This can provide a level of resilience when trading conditions are difficult.

Size and shape

Employees: 900   Locations: 20
Geographical income split: UK 40%, mainland Europe 38%, N. America 7%, Far East 7%, RoW 8%

Protean's management philosophy is to devolve as much operational autonomy to the individual units as possible. For example, all pricing decisions are the responsibility of local management. The role of the centre is to set tough, but achievable, targets and provide appropriate marketing – the group believes strongly in the branding of its products – and professional support.

Future prospects

- further organic growth in all existing businesses;
- possible future acquisitions;
- accelerating demand for Protean products.

Protean's activities have relatively little synergy, although there is some degree of commonality between many of the customers of the individual businesses. One area which a number of the Protean businesses are looking to attack, however, is the environmental market. Elga Environmental is responding to the ever increasing levels of efficiency and public safety demanded by both legislation and technological progress in servicing the water softener, chemical cleaning and water tank purity industries in the UK, while Jenway's measurement products are playing an important monitoring role in the environmental market. An increasing international presence has also been a strategic imperative for the group. With growth in domestic markets limited by competition, Protean has targeted the export market for sales growth. Its water purification products go well in the Far East and in 1995 Elga opened a new sales and distribution facility in North America. Protean has also invested in its French operations, moving to a single new industrial production facility near Paris.

Outlook

Given the standard competitive pressures in many of its business areas, the outlook for Protean is extremely healthy. It is strongly positioned in industries which have a steady and sustained growth in underlying demand. Furthermore, the group's technological skills and reputation for innovation should confirm its market leadership, both in the UK and overseas. Protean's strong central management team will continue to extract maximum added value from the group's businesses. While it is likely that there will be further acquisitions, these are not a necessary condition for future success. There is still considerable potential in the existing portfolio of businesses.

Address:

High Street, Lane End, High Wycombe, Bucks HP4 3JF. Tel: 01494 883366. Fax: 01494 882108

Psion plc IT

Central London

Turnover				
1992	1993	1994	1995	1996
£35M	£41M	£61M	£91M	£124M

Summary: Psion plc develops, designs, manufactures, distributes and markets palmtop computers, industrial terminals, PC card modems and peripherals and it licenses its software platforms. It was founded in 1980. Psion launched the first hand-held computer in 1984 and, amazingly for a British company, is the worldwide leader in the sector commanding a 32.7 per cent market share, compared to Hewlett-Packard's 28 per cent. It is the only British company that is a global leader in any full computer system sector whatsoever. An energetic expansion of its American retail outlets and aggressive product development should enable it to grow with this emerging market, as computing, radio and communications technologies converge, to become a significantly larger company. In June 1996 it announced that it was planning to takeover Alan Sugar's Amstrad businesses, but the deal did not go ahead after Psion withdrew its offer. Psion nevertheless continues to make outstanding progress with pretax profits rising in 1996 to £16 million from £11.7 million the previous year.

The Business

It was a surprise. Few observers anticipated Psion's announcement in June 1996 that it was bidding £234 million for the companies contained in Alan Sugar's Amstrad group. For David Potter, chairman of the hand-held computer company Psion, Amstrad – despite problems in its consumer electronics division – could add critical mass and a new diversity of products.

Potter wanted control of Amstrad's growth businesses: Dancall, a cellular phone manufacturer, and Viglen, a profitable computer operation. Also Beatcom, a cordless telephone company, which is 66 per cent owned by Amstrad, would absorb Amstrad Consumer Electronics (Ace) to eliminate the losses in the most famous element of the Sugar businesses. But it was not to be. Psion – after intensive discussions with Amstrad – withdrew its offer.

Potter admitted that at the time of the proposal, he had not appreciated the scope of Amstrad and the potential synergies between it and Psion. They apparently represented different ends of the market but Amstrad has transformed itself from the image of a consumer and popular marketing-driven enterprise into something which approaches the style of Psion. Psion is the supreme palmtop computer business, with a third of all global hand-held computer sales. It is a high quality, technology-based company. But Potter could see that the skills which had been applied in its rapid rise – leading to substantial profitability – could be applied to the Amstrad combination. However no agreement could be reached on the value of the Amstrad businesses.

Potter Scientific Instruments (Psion) was founded in 1980 and within two years had its first big hit – a flight simulator game which sold one million units. In 1984 he launched the Organiser, the first palmtop computer. Hand-held computers do things like storing address lists and phone numbers, word-processing memos and small documents, acting as electronic organisers and otherwise functioning as small data reference and capture devices. As they are very small portable devices they do not have rotating disk storage, separate keyboards and TV-style screens as personal computers do. Instead they are battery-powered with an expanded calculator-style keyboard and small monochrome LCD screen – just the thing the Japanese are so good at making.

Psion has beaten them at their own game by providing devices that are more capable than Sharp and Casio personal information managers but going nowhere near the grandiose optimism exemplified by Apple's ill-starred Newton. Psion recognised early that truly portable computers needed to be hand-held and have a battery life measured in weeks, not hours. American computer manufacturer Hewlett-Packard, with its scientific calculator product line, has developed the strongest competition to Psion with a similar device but, so far, Psion is still ahead.

The later Series 3 palmtop, introduced in 1991, sold more than a million units. This device pulled Psion out of the loss it had made in 1991. It earned a reputation as the best personal organiser product on the market. The Series 3a followed in 1993 with twice the memory, speed and screen resolution. And new models have followed since.

> **Distinctive features**
>
> - world market leader in hand-held computers;
> - UK and European leader in portable modems;
> - very strong retail channel and established brand name;
> - world leader in hardware and software technology for its markets.

Psion also makes specialised and rugged industrial models – the HC and Workabout range – plus data communications products such as plug-in modem cards for notebook computers. The Organiser is now classed as a corporate terminal and is sold into the industrial sector along with the HC and Workabout. The Series 3 sells into the retail market as well as into corporate markets in finance, banking and insurance. Each product range features several models with additional software and peripherals. All manufacturing is done in the UK and about half the company's revenues come from exports. In fact, Psion has won the Queen's Award for Export Achievement twice.

The group's Psion Dacom subsidiary is the European market leader in plug-in modems. It has successfully entered mainland Europe with a range of fast fax/modem, GSM communications and, in a technical breakthrough, combined GSM/Fax/modem cards. Overall sales doubled in 1995 compared to 1994. Potter took Psion public for the second time in April 1995 and a non-executive director was added to the board in May of the same year.

Stratagems

> **Size and shape**
>
> Employees (UK): 651   Locations: 6
> Geographical income split: UK 75%, mainland Europe 13%, USA 12%

Potter is one of the industry's deepest thinkers about strategy and he has seen the connection between his hand-held computers and the emerging telecommunications technologies. Amstrad's Dancall would have been a highly suitable partner with which to develop palmtop products with a telecommunications component. Potter told the *Sunday Times*, 'Dancall is fundamental because of the fusion between palmtop computers and digital telephony.' In his more traditional markets, Potter is concerned about suffering a fate similar to Apple – being marginalised – and wants to deliver products which predict market demand.

Psion designs, manufactures, markets and sells its products; it is not a 'computerless' computer company. Manufacturing investments were made in 1995 to expand capacity at its Greenford plant which now has three lines with more capacity capable of being added if needed. Psion Dacom kit is built at a separate plant in Milton Keynes which now has two lines. Potter had reorganised the company prior to the Amstrad issue. Psion plc is the holding company with two sets of subsidiaries: trading companies and manufacturing operations. The sales strategy has emphasised retail outlets on the one hand and systems integrators and value-added resellers on the other. The latter sell Psion products as part of an overall solution for specialised customer requirements.

Future prospects

- bigger broader-based company;
- new palmtop products with digital telephony facilities;
- increasing share of overseas business from world-leading technology.

The portable computer market is expanding rapidly through new markets opening up around the world and existing markets broadening as more customers see the benefits of the products. The geographical income split figures indicate that the USA, representing only 12 per cent of revenue could grow hugely. There is a view that, so far, hand-held computers have been bought by gadget buffs and status seekers. If they can become more capable and less expensive then they could sell in the tens of millions. On the modem front the notebook computer market is also growing rapidly.

Outlook

Psion's perspective changed radically in the spring of 1996. Potter had planned without the type of merger proposed by Sugar. But the logic inherent in the combination was already present in his thinking. Psion was planning to achieve revenues of more than £500 million shortly after the millennium without Amstrad; but a merger would have brought that target much closer to realisation. Psion has come out of the other side of the transaction with its confidence and self-esteem intact, and it is on course for growth organically. There may, however, be other opportunities around the corner for a takeover.

Address:

Alexander House, 85 Frampton Street, London NW8 8NQ. Tel: 0171 262 5580. Fax: 0171 258 7340

Radius plc

Hull

Turnover			
1994	1995	1996	1997
£24.9M	£26.1M	£27.3M	£30Me

Summary: Radius was among the earliest of the computer services companies to be listed, and apart from a small blip in the early 1990s it has continued to make strong and steady commercial and financial progress. Radius has substantially improved profitability and growth in many of the company's principal market sectors, especially original software for the printing and retail sectors. It also enjoys a comprehensive reputation for the development, implementation and support of computer systems. Radius has an impressive client list including many blue chip companies.

The Business

Radius was created in 1976 as a supplier of internal data processing activities and to provide bureau facilities to outside customers. Within a couple of years a management buy-out led to its selling and installing computer systems for the wider UK market. This was a springboard for an expansion into its own software products. The Radius directors realised that with the advent of personal computer systems within companies the need for bureaux would diminish and the demand for software packages would grow rapidly. But the company also appreciated that specialist skills inside companies would be thin on the ground and it could have a genuine market advantage by offering systems and software.

It became one of the earliest computer services companies to float by joining the Unlisted Securities Market in 1985. Elevation to the full market came in April 1995. Since the early 1980s Radius has pursued a strategy of growth through both acquisition and organic means. It has added a range of businesses in complementary market sectors so that in early 1997 it conducts business through five operating companies: Radius Computer Maintenance, Radius Computer Services, Radius Solutions, Radius Professional and Radius Retail. Core to the groups' activities is software, where it employs more than 300 technical and support staff out of a total headcount of 430.

Most of its work is carried out in Open Systems, using an established range of fourth generation languages (4GLs). Radius also boasts considerable expertise in COBOL, which is still the industry's dominant language. Some 60 engineers work on integrated hardware and software systems. The largest part of its revenue comes from support services and software services, which together account for 71 per cent of turnover.

The company concentrates on industry sectors where it has gained substantial disciplinary expertise. It defines these as: commerce (30.2 per cent), retail (23.8 per cent), printing (23 per cent), public sector (14 per cent) and professional (nine per cent). The company refocused itself in the early 1990s to emphasise its areas of greatest strength and this strategy has paid off excellently in terms of enhanced profitability.

Distinctive features

- strong industry orientation ;
- focused strategy;
- high technical expertise;
- good client base.

The two business areas where Radius is doing extremely well are retail and printing. 'The company is steaming ahead in both these markets. It has developed software products in the UK and is selling them to major businesses in the United States. One example is K-Mart, the large supermarket chain in the US,' says Charles Mathias, at the company's broker Credit Lyonnais Laing. These are key sectors for Radius, he comments, and they will be in the vanguard of the business as it progresses through the next few years.

Stratagems

Radius is now a finely honed operation which has defined its strategic direction clearly and succinctly. 'The central strategy of the group is the development or acquisition of software products and associated services concentrating on niche markets within commerce, utilities, central and local government, within the UK and overseas,' says a spokesman for the company.

This has been refined into four central objectives. The first is to maintain and extend its position as one of the leading systems houses in the UK. Secondly, it aims to provide high quality software products, ancilliary services and related hardware to its key markets. The company in practice rather downplays its role as a hardware supplier, emphasising instead its work in the software and applications sectors.

Thirdly, Radius aims to build on its track record in the development of new, technically and functionally advanced software products. As a structural objective, it plans to acquire, selectively, computer services companies or related products to enhance the group's market position. It has bought a range of businesses including MGB Computer Services, Slinn Computer Group, Systemsolve Computer Services, Merit Health, Novar Computer Maintenance, Avalon Systems and IT Professional Limited.

Size and shape

Employees: 430   Locations: 13

Geographical income split: Europe: 70%, N. America: 25%, RoW 5%

Chairman Michael Roberts told shareholders 'Growth in revenues is particularly marked in relation to the supply of our software packages. Initial licence values have risen 40 per cent ahead of last year. We have made a strategic commitment to overseas markets by opening offices in Canada and the United States. North America now accounts for 25 per cent of group revenues.

'We recognise the need to acquire the detailed knowledge required in different markets, so we need a very focused approach. We believe that is something which can only be achieved by developing a close working partnership with our customers. The relationships which we have with our customers are long term investments and we believe that this approach is the best guarantee of an appropriate return.'

This strategy is certainly working in its key divisions because Radius is now working with, among others, IBM, Rexam, BBC, BAA, British Printing Corporation, SmithKline Beecham, Ernst & Young, KLM, Pizza Hut, Body Shop, and the Smurfit Group. In September 1996, at interims presentation, Roberts indicated rapid expansion in print and retail and the creation of a new sales force in Chicago to exploit new opportunities.

At the time of the interims statement, the company reported that hardware equipment sales and bureau work were steady which reflects the renewed emphasis in Radius on the supply of software to key markets. Combined with its commercial approach, the company tightened its financial and administrative control within the business to warrant greater efficiencies.

Outlook

Future prospects

- growth in retail and printing sectors;
- widespread increase in software sales;
- more revenue from overseas, especially North America.

Radius now sees itself as a premier UK software house supplying original software to a multiplicity of geographical markets within defined industry specialisms. External observers are enthusiastic about the company's warm reception in the USA and suggest that the inroads which Radius has made in North America are highly promising for the future. Its approach appears to have struck a chord with the Americans. Without doubt, Radius will move steadily away from its traditional hardware vending role though it is obliged to keep up its service contracts with clients. The real drive will go into retail and printing where the applications generated by Radius are producing better than anticipated results.

Address:

Wykeland House, 47 Queen Street, Hull HU1 1UU. Tel: 01482 227181. Fax: 01482 325660

Ramco Energy plc

Aberdeen

Turnover				
1992	1993	1994	1995	1996
£5.4M	£4.8M	£7.6M	£6.9M	£8.2M

Summary: Ramco Energy is one of the UK's leading oil independents. It was the first western oil company into the lucrative fields in Azerbaijan. Ramco was the small but influential operator which was invited by the government of Azerbaijan to put together a multinational consortium to open up its Caspian Sea fields. After initial reservation by the big players, this has now become perhaps the most exciting development in the history of the oil industry and the majors are now prepared to pay a premium to get in on the action. The original Ramco business was a pipe cleaning and pipeline coating company which remains market leader in the field.

The Business

The early oil pioneers were motivated by a mixture of adventure and profits. Steve Remp, the American CEO of the UK's Ramco Energy, was born into an oil family and for years he nursed an ambition to run his own upstream oil business. His market leading oil services company went from strength to strength but still there was an unmet challenge. Few new business ventures – however charged for the originators – can match the thrill of being the first western oilman to open up the world's last great oilfields. Remp was the first western oil company boss to set foot in Baku for over 70 years. The Azeri capital is buzzing with activity for what may be the biggest development in the history of the industry. Some of the former Soviet Union countries are rich in oil and gas reserves which the communist machinery never had the capacity to exploit.

The Ramco oil services company

In 1977 the pipe cleaning and pipeline coating business was established. It rapidly became world market leader and throughout the succeeding years it has taken quantum leaps forward. It is used by all the oil majors and is in partnership with leading world calibre steel makers to coat pipes before they are sold. It is based at a purpose-built site at Badentoy, Aberdeen and operates from mobile pipe care units (PCUs) worldwide.

As the fences and walls dividing east from west came clattering down in the late 1980s, Steve Remp could smell the potential for oil development. He set off around the capitals of the former Soviet Union and established a strong relationship with the Azeri government. The Azeris knew the potential of their oil fields but recognised that they needed western help to make best use of their opportunity. Remp was invited to construct a consortium including the government oil company. For its stake, Pennzoil agreed to cover Ramco's costs, which means that the business risk for the Aberdeen-based organisation is negligible. The original three Caspian fields have merged into one and Ramco is at the heart of the BP-led consortium. When Ramco first went into the region, the majors were sceptical. Now like Exxon they are paying a premium to get in. The first oil is expected to be on stream at the end of 1997. Ramco's stake is two per cent – effectively three cent of the return – and Ramco's share is 83 million barrels or $332M. Not bad for a small oil services business. The dogged determination with which Ramco – and Remp – has pursued the Caspian Sea contracts is a role model of commitment, business acumen and personal vision. But the deal has not only put Ramco at the top table in a key project; it has provided an entry visa to many other projects in the region. Ramco's talent for constructing partnerships, and attracting the world's senior oil companies, has not gone unnoticed in the area.

Distinctive features

- innovative services business;
- capacity to build strong relationships;
- foresight to be in the FSU before western majors;
- great dealmakers.

As the project has achieved enhanced credibility in the eyes of western industrial and political leaders, each of the key players such as BP, Amoco and Exxon has put in a local manager. Only Ramco has chosen an Azeri to do the job. Apart from being an individual appropriate to the task, he also has strong contacts in government and the state oil company. The Azeri government is keen to develop other fields and Ramco is the first western oil company to explore major onshore reserves at Muradhandli. There are also other opportunities in Kazakhstan where Ramco would have to bid but where it comes highly recommended. Ramco has also appointed a Russian national to run its Moscow operation.

Stratagems

Ramco's strategy is spelled out on page one of its 1995 annual report and accounts. It aims to become a leading independent oil and gas production company focusing on the former Soviet Union. Ramco also plans 'to build a portfolio of world class oil and gas development projects, maximising our financial rectums through partnering major oil companies.' This encapsulates the distinctiveness of its approach. Remp says that Ramco's influence in the Caspian – in the wider geopolitical arena – far exceeds its relatively small stake in the Azerbaijan International Oil Company. It is a company which has built impressive links with regional governments and with the oil majors.

'The World Bank has told the Azeri government that it should have a spread of western interests. Not only the majors but also medium-sized and smaller companies for economic balance. But Ramco is the only western medium-sized oil independent in the region,' says Remp. His analysis is

Size and shape

Employees: 108   Locations: 5
Geographical income split: UK 48.8%, former Soviet Union 22.9%, Asia 16.8%, Norway 11.5%

supported by countless broker reports. At first the City was unconvinced but after five years of watching the hurdles overcome and the milestone payments from Pennzoil drop into Ramco's bank account many brokers are keen on its potential earnings. This has been reflected in a share price which lifted from 32.5p in 1992 to 638p in early 1996.

During 1996 the board has been strengthened – under Cadbury corporate governance rules – to bring in heavyweight players, including an ex-Shell UK

MD and a leading US businessman with formidable links with the American investment banking community. The management team has also been enhanced. Ramco was always a very lean ship and that has not changed. But Remp was always the front man. Now there is more of a team presence. Steven Bertram, the group finance director, who used to deputise for Remp at headquarters is now in the front line as much as the CEO, and a new financial controller has been appointed for Aberdeen. Long-standing oil and gas leader Mike Burchell is in the field, especially assessing the opportunities in onshore production. New managers have been chosen for Baku and Moscow.

Remp and Bertram are acutely aware that the potential opportunities for Ramco Energy in the FSU are extensive and they will need to select carefully to see which ones suit the shareholders' interests. Still, they are confident that as the AIOC project in the Caspian goes on-line at the end of 1997, so too will the onshore development at Muradhandli. 'We are looking for other international partners in this project as at present we own 100 per cent of the rights. The majors are less certain about onshore development in Azerbaijan than the Caspian Sea enterprises but this is familiar ground for us and I would not be surprised if they become more excited. Potentially this is worth more to us – in strict revenue terms – than the return from the AIOC.'

Ramco has already proved proficient at constructing consortia with leading international players. For Steve Remp this has been the realisation of a dream. But his skills as a negotiator and a dealmaker have pulled off a financial package for the company which could not have been achieved by determination alone.

Outlook

Future prospects

- significant future revenues from the Caspian;
- low risk and substantial upside at Muradhandli;
- new FSU opportunities;
- strengthening of management and board.

The FSU is probably the last big oil and gas development in the world. The western oil companies were not really sure what they were letting themselves in for when they first put their toes in the water. Now it is clear. Remp went into the Soviet Union as it crumbled and made the key contacts. He stayed with the idea throughout and now Ramco is reaping the benefit. The figures do not yet reflect direct income from the Caspian but it will go into substantial and sustained profit shortly after the tap is tuned on.

Address:

Ramco Energy plc, 4 Rubislaw Place, Aberdeen AB10 1NX. Tel: 01224 626224. Fax: 01224 625425

Regent Inns plc   BREWERIES, PUBS AND RESTAURANTS

Whetstone, North London

Turnover				
1992	1993	1994	1995	1996
£11.9M	£13M	£15.3M	£22M	£32M

Summary: Regent Inns is one of the leading independent pub operators in Greater London. Since its formation the company has pursued a vigorous expansion policy, while at the same time managing to maintain like-for-like profit growth which is among the best in the industry. Regent specialises in larger than average outlets in good locations with a strong emphasis on customer focus, and much of its expansion has been due to the development of previously unlicensed sites. The company's strong management team is now looking to employ its retailing expertise outside London.

The Business

When Regent Inns was acquired by its current managing director David Franks, in 1980, its portfolio consisted of six pubs. By 1988, it had grown to 17 outlets and this rose to 27 following a merger with Lockton Inns, a loss-making Business Expansion Scheme company. Regent's flotation in 1993 and a share placing two years later provided funds for further expansion. The company now has 58 trading outlets in its portfolio, with several more sites under development or awaiting planning permission, with another two outlets under a management contract.

Approximately three-quarters of Regent's outlets are located in London postal districts. Among its most famous names are The Fire Station in Waterloo, The Princess Louise in High Holborn, and the Jongleurs Comedy Clubs in Battersea and Camden. Of the remainder, the majority are located in the Home Counties. However, it is the company's intention to expand the portfolio outside the M25 in the near future. Offers have been made and accepted on sites in Walsall, Nottingham, York, Barnsley, Liverpool and

Leicester and, to underpin this expansion, Regent Inns is planning to open a regional office.

The company's most profitable outlet at the moment is the Outback Inn, an Australian theme pub and sports bar based in Covent Garden. Such is its popularity that it is now obliged to charge an entrance fee on busy evenings. A second Outback Inn has now opened in Islington and more are planned. Regent is also intending to expand its Harvey Floorbangers trading concept.

Regent has been very successful at consistently improving its operating margins, which are now, at nearly 26 per cent, among the highest in the industry. A variety of factors lie behind this success. Firstly, outlets have enjoyed strong turnover growth due to an improving sales mix (with less draught beer and more bottled beer, wines and spirits being sold) and retail prices generally exceeding inflation. Regent's status as being free of tie is undoubtedly important here since it allows pubs to offer the increasingly wide range of products which the public is demanding.

Also, the company has implemented strong controls over costs. It recently signed long-term supply agreements with major brewers, including a five year agreement with Bass, designed to protect the level of its free trade discounts and promote the good relationships Regent has with its suppliers. In addition, as the group has expanded, its head office costs as a percentage of total turnover have fallen. Finally, rents have also continued to fall as a percentage of sales – a development assisted by Regent's preference for unlicensed sites which are currently in plentiful supply.

Distinctive features

- strong retailing skills;
- independent status;
- good cashflow – to fund future acquisitions;
- motivated management;
- improving margins.

The company's strong underlying cashflow also means that acquisition and refurbishment costs can also be met without putting an undue strain on Regent's balance sheet. However, this does not mean that the company is prepared to pay over the odds for acquisition opportunities. Its tight control on costs also applies to its acquisition strategy. In 1995, after making an initial offer for Unicorn Inns, Regent allowed the offer to lapse rather than match the substantially increased terms offered by a rival bidder.

Stratagems

One of the main reasons for Regent's success has been its astute acquisition and site selection strategy. It is interested only in outlets which are situated in prime, urban locations. In particular, they must be close to high levels of pedestrian traffic. The search for new outlets has been greatly helped by the increased availability of high street premises, including former banks, building societies and post office branches. Much of Regent's expansion has come from the purchase of previously unlicensed sites which can generally be purchased at large discounts. Often, buildings are superior quality – 40 per cent of its pubs are Grade II listed.

Size and shape

Employees: 550   Locations: 65
Geographical income split: UK 100%

Having selected the site, Regent will undertake extensive refurbishment with the intention of producing a modern bar. The company recognises the importance of the surrounding environment and, for this reason, does not impose any type of group-wide branding. However, when it refurbishes a pub there are certain key features which it will always bear in mind. It will seek to generate a smart and family-friendly ambience. All pubs will have no-smoking areas and disabled toilets. The decor will be light, with no dark or imposing corners, in order to make the pub more attractive to female customers. According to Franks, 'Regent's philosophy is to create the best bar in the area.'

Future prospects

- strong profit growth;
- multiple opportunities for expansion;
- extension of the formula to other sites;
- strengthening of management.

Regent is then in a position to exercise its strong retailing skills. Significantly, its pubs will generally be liquor-led rather than food-led. Although gross profit margins on food are similar to those on drink, the net margin is lower because of the higher staff costs involved in the service and preparation of food. As a result, since 1994, the company has disposed of a number of food-led pubs. Alcohol currently accounts for around 80 per cent of the company's turnover compared to food's 15 per cent (the balance is made up by gaming machines and the hire of function rooms) and this is not expected to change significantly in the future. Another of the company's key strengths is its management and staff. Regent's senior management is one of the most experienced in the industry and the management structure has recently been strengthened to enable it to accelerate the development of the retail estate while still maintaining tight control over the company's day-to-day operations. All staff are included in a generous bonus scheme. The impact on employee motivation is a key reason why Regent is able to deliver high service standards to its customers. Regent gained a top award in the 1995 National Innkeeping Training Awards.

As indicated earlier, Regent is expected to continue to develop its geographical presence in the UK. As well as the traditional pub, it anticipates opening more sports bars and comedy clubs (it has targeted university towns for the further expansion of this concept), and ultimately may move into other sectors of the leisure industry.

Outlook

Notwithstanding Regent's rapid expansion over recent years, there is still an enormous potential market to be tapped. Regent's portfolio currently represents a small percentage of the majors and there remain plenty of prime sites available for development. The company has perfected a highly successful retail-led pub management policy which is capable of replication (subject to local market conditions) elsewhere. Regent's strong management team – assisted by healthy cashflow, a modest level of gearing and the current low interest rates – should be able to continue to deliver strong profit growth into the foreseeable future.

Address:

Northway House, 1379 High Road, Whetstone, London N20 9LP. Tel: 0181 445 5016. Fax: 0181 446 0886

Rolfe & Nolan plc

Central London

Turnover				
1994	1995	1996	1997	1998
£12.7M	£14.3M	£17Me	£20Me	£24Me

Summary: Rolfe & Nolan is the market leader in systems to support trading, clearing and settlement for financial institutions dealing in exchange-traded derivatives worldwide. It also supplies systems to support front, middle and back-office for the complete range of treasury and capital markets products for major banks and corporates. In addition to its nine bureau services worldwide, R&N also offers facilities management and in-house services. It operates in more than 20 countries and is ideally placed to benefit from the continued growth in derivatives trading in both developed and emerging markets. Its state-of-the art Lighthouse risk management system is in place at Credit Suisse and is expected to become a leading product in this key, fast-growing market. R&N's technology base for all products has progressed towards a C++ object-oriented, class library-based client/server architecture.

The Business

The last 20 years has seen an explosive growth in the volumes of derivatives trading on exchanges worldwide. Many dealing houses, under pressure to make substantial returns, allowed their front offices to flourish, leaving the back-office creaking under the strain of reconciliation and reporting. Step forward Rolfe & Nolan. The specialist provision of back-office support, accounting, settlement and risk management, is where R&N is king. The company provides computer bureau services, in-house computer installations and facilities management to financial institutions. With financial products becoming ever more exotic, and the risks associated with their use potentially unlimited, many houses are unable to incur the systems development and overhead costs necessary to support derivatives trading activities.

Historically, the core of R&N's business has been computer bureau services. The company has implemented nine bureau services across the globe and now supports more than 270 clients, ranging from global clearers, bank treasuries and commodities houses through to fund management and life assurance groups. Its systems provide trade support, clearing, reconciliation and settlement functions, as well as performing margin calculations and producing risk management and accounting information. For global players, import and export modules can be added to link all their sites and achieve the level of integration and consolidation they need. The systems run on Digital's high-performance Alpha-AXP technology, as well as IBM's AS/400 platform, and is capable of handling extremely high levels of throughput. It is not uncommon for some users to enter more than 10,000 trades a day. R&N also provides in-house computer installation under licence and, increasingly, full-scale facilities management services. For major institutions wishing to integrate core business functionality within their existing systems rather than implement a complete system, R&N offers libraries of C++ object-oriented toolkit products to address margining, exchange links and reconciliation activities.

All its services are provided under long-term contracts, usually between one and five years, and, to date, it has a 100 per cent success rate in contract renewals across the globe. Furthermore, as the income under these deals is mainly a function of market volumes (especially for bureau services), R&N has benefited from record levels of exchange-traded derivatives activity. Since 1993, it has developed a major new treasury and capital markets system called Lighthouse. Using high performance technology, this product is aimed at the investment banks and large corporates. Lighthouse introduces greater control over the risks inherent in trading and gives a consistent view of dealing positions across an organisation. Lighthouse operates at Credit Suisse in Zurich, London, New York, Frankfurt and is being instituted in a number of banks in Europe and the USA. Rolfe & Nolan is marketing Lighthouse to more institutions, and industry commentators suggest that, through its data warehousing techniques and the toolkit approach, the system is destined to become a leading product in the market.

The company is well represented in both Europe and North America and recently opened a seventh office, in Singapore, to take advantage of opportunities in Asia-Pacific. As well as an existing client base, this office will also service the 40 members of the Kuala Lumpur Options and Financial Futures Exchange (KLOFFE) which opened in 1995.

Distinctive features

- pre-eminent status in growing markets;
- technological edge over rivals;
- reputation for integrity, delivery, performance;
- strong revenue flow;
- innovative products.

Stratagems

At the heart of the company's strategy is a determination to retain its market superiority and its technical lead over rivals by constantly upgrading systems, creating a cohesive, open systems-based product range and increasing its value-added services. This in turn has increasingly allowed R&N to satisfy global clients' needs for comprehensive integrated services. R&N recognises that a number of large players in the market are already wedded to existing systems, so straightforward replacement of functionality is not a realistic option. Instead these customers are looking for services to be integrated with contemporary systems.

R&N's products are designed to be flexible and portable so that they can be adapted to suit any customer's specific requirements. For example, Lighthouse is intended as either a primary system or an additional element in an established architecture, while the Rolfe & Nolan System has been created in a series of modules. Also R&N's large client base offers great ongoing marketing opportunities for additional products and allows the business to defray development costs.

Size and shape

Employees: 270   Locations: 7
Geographical income split: UK 39%, mainland Europe 31%, N. America 24%, Asia/Pacific 6%

The company's strong revenue flow from bureau activities has been the engine of its expansion. Nevertheless, R&N is keen to convert clients from bureau services and in-house licences to complete facilities management. Current FM client numbers are strong in relation to the rest of the business and strategic policy – by customers – to outsource IT functions is expected to make FM contracts even more commonplace in the next few years. This must favour Rolfe & Nolan, which is at the forefront of this service approach in terms of quality and presence. Other factors – some economic, others corporate – will probably work to R&N's advantage. Uncertain markets, coupled with rapidly changing technology and increasing regulatory burdens, indicate that companies will look to outside providers for support. Rolfe & Nolan is well-placed to benefit from the nervousness among traders and end-users about the risk profile and resultant exposure from derivatives products. For users of many of the complicated derivatives products, to adequately monitor their exposure they are better off using an outside agency, like R&N, than trying to master the complexity of the technology.

A further plank of the company's policy is intimacy both with clients and the world's exchanges. Like many businesses which have been successful in recent years, R&N maintains a continuous dialogue with these organisations in order to enhance existing and future service quality. In addition to its enviable technical reputation R&N has recognised the need to be respected for its service quality.

Outlook

Future prospects

- further far east growth;
- expansion in Eastern Europe;
- treasury management and capital markets growth;
- developing FM business sales increase in:
  - derivatives systems
  - exchange-traded toolkit libraries.

Rolfe & Nolan enjoys a position of esteem in its industry. It is market leader in exchange-traded derivatives, where underlying demand continues to be strong and significant business opportunities still remain. Lighthouse continues to underscore this reputation. R&N's size, track record and technological record remain unrivalled. Growth opportunities continue to exist in the UK and North America but the real challenge for the company is to exploit fresh opportunities in the Far East and Eastern Europe. Bureau operations and Lighthouse sales will be the generators for these markets and R&N is continuing to expand its market-leading position in facilities management. R&N's cashflow from core areas of the business will provide support to build new areas of business and strengthen existing disciplines.

Address:

Lowndes House, 1–9 City Road, London EC1Y 1AA. Tel: 0171 374 4841.
Fax: 0171 374 0732.

The Roxboro Group plc

Cambridge

Turnover				
1992	1993	1994	1995	1996
£36M	£42M	£70M	£94M	£108M

Summary: The Roxboro Group comprises three separate divisions – electronic components, sensors and instrumentation – which are driven from a very lean group HQ in Cambridge. The group started with an MBO and an MD with a personal ambition to build an international group of specialist world-leading suppliers bringing technically advanced products into emerging markets. The group is succeeding through energetic organic growth and carefully selected acquisitions. It has experienced rapid and sustained growth throughout the 1990s and its prospects are strong for the future.

The Business

Harry Tee has turned Roxboro into a £100 million plus turnover company since leading an MBO from Graseby plc in 1990. Group MD Tee recalls 'I set out to build a strong subsidiary in the UK, and a strong one in the US. And then to build the basis of a strong group of companies.' Roxboro began life with Dialight Corporation in the USA, making light-emitting diodes (LEDs), and a trio of component businesses in the UK making connectors and solenoids which were merged to form BLP.

There were 1200 employees in 1990 who had been whittled down to 721 by November 1993 when the group was floated. Tee says floating was 'a crucial part of our strategy'. Now, through growth and acquisitions there are 1500 employees generating £108 million a year compared with the approximate £42 million that would have been earned by the original 1200.

The group is composed of three pillars, the original electrical and electronics components business having had sensors and instrumentation businesses

366

established through the acquisition of, Solartron in May, 1994, a major addition to the group. Pressure Systems Inc., a supplier of pressure sensors was acquired in January 1996 and will go into the sensors division.

Group members are autonomous with development, manufacturing and marketing resources in-house. Tee says they have a very open management structure with a team approach across the whole group. When he visits member businesses 'I, effectively, am part of their management team. When I go into their businesses I do not chair the meetings; the MD does.' The group's strategy is 'identifying emerging markets and investing heavily to be a world leader when these markets really start to grow'. Group businesses specialise in developing solutions to specific customer problems, as well as providing a wide range of standard products in their chosen area. They will happily supply product to OEM customers who may badge it for their own purposes. They are also driven to partner OEMs in producing specialist products for customers and thus build up long-term business relationships.

Distinctive features

- focus on speciality electronic products in international growth markets;
- a lean central group manages and encourages autonomous subsidiaries;
- aims to be world leader in each of its core businesses;
- strong organic growth enhanced by carefully selected bolt-on acquisitions.

Stratagems

The group grows by energetic organic growth. Component businesses are rationalised and pointed away from commodity products towards higher margin specialist products and emerging markets. Tee says 'We're not going to be a huge worldwide player in a large area. Rather we're addressing niche markets with very powerful brand identities.' Since Roxboro operates in largely niche businesses it can command high margins and, once these companies are operating effectively, become strongly cash-generative. This cash helps improve earnings and fund the acquisition of niche 'bolt-on' businesses in allied areas.

Tee believes that the group must grow by acquisition because the cost of entry into new niche markets with good margins is too high. The group has shown that it can swallow and digest its acquisitions and both enhance earnings and generate more cash.

Acquisitions are given the Roxboro treatment and enlarge group revenues still further. Their cost base is reduced, gross margin increased, working capital better managed to improve return on capital, low margin products eliminated and sales channels expanded through other group members. Product development is driven towards innovative, technically advanced products that can provide better solutions to existing requirements or build new markets. An important aspect of improving member businesses is to concentrate their focus.

Tee says group HQ is the catalyst for the subsidiaries. He and his fellow directors conceive of the group as a series of circles that overlap each other as they form a ring around and overlap the circle representing group HQ. The headquarters' function is carried out by just nine people whose function is to encourage subsidiary performance and synergy.

Each subsidiary is intent on becoming a world leader in its field and close constant attention is paid to improving product technology and quality. For example, Dialight has developed high-intensity LEDs which can replace incandescent bulbs used in indicative vehicle and traffic lights. They are as bright as a bulb, use a tenth of the power, and last thirty times longer.

Size and shape

Employees: 1500   Locations: 13
Geographical income split: UK 27.6%, USA 38.7%, RoEur 18.4%, RoW 15.3%

Outlook

The Dialight advanced LED technology is at the very beginnings of its growth. Initial trials have been successful and the first sales have shown that the market responds to the message of similar luminance, greater longevity and much better value for money. This technology should bring in significant revenues.

With the constantly growing need for better measurement, both of solid objects and of gas and liquid states, the sensors division is also in a very strong position. The components business has a good position in metering switches which also has a healthy outlook. All in all, the Roxboro Group should show pronounced earnings growth over the next few years. This growth could accelerate if, as seems likely, more acquisitions occur. We could be looking at the prospect of a £100 million revenue company by the turn of the century.

Address:

The Roxboro Group plc, Byron House, Cambridge Business Park, Cambridge, CB4 4WZ. Tel: 01223 424626 Fax: 01223 424692. E-mail: roxboro@roxboro.com. Website: LHp://www.roxboro.com

The Sage Group plc

Tyneside

Turnover				
1992	1993	1994	1995	1996
£27M	£41M	£51M	£102M	£136M

Summary: **The Sage Group is one of Britain's most impressive software companies and is regularly cited as a definitive example of a well-managed growth company. Started in 1981, Sage was born out of a specific market need – to fashion some estimating software for the print industry. Chairman David Goldman and his colleagues moved out of their original printing business and within five years became the UK market leader in small business accounting software. The company listed in 1989 and is around number 220 by market capitalisation. Its 1996 turnover reached £136 million. The group aims to extend its impressive position in mainland Europe and the USA.**

The Business

When commentators seek to identify exciting growth companies which symbolise the inherent strength of the UK economy, the Sage Group is often quoted. Sage has risen in 15 years from start-up to be the world's largest supplier of accounting software and services to small business. It is not only market leader in the UK and France but is making impressive headway in other mainland European countries and in the USA. Year on year Sage is improving sales by 49 per cent and profits by 34 per cent compound. It operates to a distinctive business model which favours brand leadership and building on initial sales to supply other packages and support services to existing customers.

Chairman David Goldman was operating a Tyneside printing business in the late 1970s when the government offered incentives to install micro-processors. The business discovered that there was no software available to

369

provide estimating for printing products, so technical director Graham Wylie devised a package for estimating. 'We provided a full turnkey service including the hardware. And within two years we had sold 80 systems,' says Goldman. In 1983 Sage launched a basic bookkeeping package for small businesses. Venture capitalists became interested in the company for investment purposes and Thorn-EMI, which was building a group of software houses, made a £2 million bid for Sage. 'For a company which had barely traded this was a remarkable sum and we very nearly accepted it. But our venture capitalists encouraged us to stay independent,' comments Goldman.

He says that the company did not need venture capital for working capital but wanted funds to establish its credibility. Its principal competitor was much bigger and better known. Sage sold its original printing software business and put the money on deposit for a year. Then it used this capital to build dealer channels and poured cash into advertising. 'At one time we were spending 40 per cent of sales on advertising,' remarks Goldman.

The company experienced its great lift upwards in October 1985 after Goldman attended a computer show. Goldman recalls 'Alan Sugar introduced his PCW machine and we knew that this was the point when cost-effective software packages would take off. I had always believed that our products would be high volume but we would need to wait for PCs to sell in large numbers. We took an old CPM accounting package off the shelf and repackaged it at £100 including VAT. By the following January we had moved five to six thousand units a month.'

In 1989 Sage floated. 'At that time it was generating £3 million pretax profits on £9 million sales. Now the group makes £30 million on £126 million sales,' says a leading City analyst. By market capitalisation Sage is rated around number 220 and after the publication of its 1996 figures, the company hopes to improve its share price sufficiently to enter the *Sunday Times Top 200*. Its outstanding annual growth is based on active acquisition, both in the UK and overseas, and thriving organic growth. Each year Sage adds substantially to its core group customers to whom it aims to sell extra products and services.

Distinctive features

- strong organic growth in niche markets;
- positive French and US acquisitions;
- 25% annual sales and profits growth;
- success through brand leadership.

Stratagems

There are three key elements to the Sage strategic approach: strength through brand leadership, selling further products and services to its key group of customers, and growing the business through acquisition. The buying trail began in 1988 when Sage took over Sky Software – a smaller accounting package rival in the UK. Two years after the flotation, the group acquired its first overseas purchase – Daceasy, a Dallas, Texas-based accounting software company.

1992 was a busy year. During the course of 12 months, Sage made three acquisitions: Ciel in Paris; Telemagic, a US west coast software house; and Dataform, a printing business. These acqusitions broadened the product and geographical scope of the group. Collectively, these businesses also elevated the quality of the Sage offering and gave the group a series of upmarket brands.

Size and shape

Employees: 1700   Locations: 10
Geographical income split: UK 40%, mainland Europe 45%, USA 15%

Two years later, three more purchases were made: Multisoft in the UK; Timeslips, which created billing software for lawyers and accountants; and Saari, another French buy. The latest purchase was Sybel, the second largest accounting software company in France. The entire collection of companies gave Sage three UK businesses, three in France and three in the USA. It also now has operations in Spain and Portugal.

Finance director Aidan Hughes says that the philosophy has been to retain the independent identities of the subsidiary companies. 'We believe strongly in brand leadership – it is a major factor in our business approach. And although the subsidiary companies will retain an individual identity, our objective is to build Sage as a global brand.'

Chairman Goldman says that the subsidiary companies have provided an effective platform for the exploitation of the group's other key strategic tenet. This is selling other products and services to the core customer base. 'We established this as an early business priority and now around half of our turnover comes from selling initial packages to companies. The other 50 per cent is derived from providing other packages, supplying service contracts such as maintenance. This approach has been applied to all group companies and is one of the main secrets of the Sage success story.

Early software packages for Sage tended to be fairly basic in composition.

The original Sage accounting packages were designed to appeal to smaller companies on tight budgets. Several of the corporate acquisitions have allowed the business to upgrade its product packages and to give the enterprise an upmarket profile. It has also achieved market leadership in the UK and France, and begun to create a presence in Germany and in the highly lucrative American market.

Outlook

Future prospects

- overseas expansion, especially Germany;
- further acquisition in the United States;
- sustained high levels of sales and profits growth.

The Sage Group is extending its overseas operations and has already targeted Germany as its next large mainland European territory for expansion. Goldman says that the company wants to grow in the United States and further acquisitions should be expected. He says that the rates of growth in sales and profits should continue and there is plenty of room in its existing companies for more organic expansion. Its brand leadership in small business accounting packages will broaden out in both geographical and product initiatives to give the company a wider customer and service base.

Address:

Benton Park Road, Newcastle upon Tyne NE7 7LZ. Tel: 0191 255 3000. Fax: 0191 255 0308

Sheriff Holdings plc

Nottingham

Turnover				
1992	1993	1994	1995	1996
£10.6M	£12.8M	£20.2M	£23.8M	£26.6M

Summary: Sheriff Holdings, an East Midlands-based, and central England concentrated plant hire company has, during the 1990s, built up a strong position in the highly fragmented UK plant hire sector. Its share of the overall UK market, at 0.5 per cent of construction plant and two per cent in terms of tools and other plant, may appear modest. But it puts the company into the top tier of market players and, more than most, has provided the financial and management strengths needed to extract some benefit from a trading climate which has been soured by five years of recession in the British construction industry. Turnover at the company has nearly trebled in five years, with pretax profits climbing from a modest £300,000 to £3.6M over the same period.

The Business

Market fragmentation in the plant hire business has been caused by a plethora of local businesses, each serving its own immediate area, usually with a well-established position and loyal customer support. Many of these smaller businesses have suffered badly through the recession in construction. Some are now more than usually inclined to consider realistic offers for their businesses. This has opened up an expansion route which Sheriff has not been slow to exploit.

The nature of the plant hire business, and skilful management of the changing factors that can distort dogmatic plans – rapid changes in technology, unexpected quirks of industrial taste – have been handled so well that cash generation at Sheriff has been sustained, even dramatic by most industry standards, almost doubling, to £11.2M, in 1993–96. This has clearly been of considerable benefit to a company which has made 13 acquisitions, in addition to organic growth, since flotation on the USM in 1989 and a total of 25 acquisitions since the company was established. Indeed, given that 50 hire sites are now in operation, the company is almost unrecognisable from the 1983 infant business with only three local sites.

Such an expansion programme can often impose strains on management strengths, but not at Sheriff. Using a 'ripple-out' advance from its Nottingham base, the company has been able to quietly extend its boundaries by around 100 miles to south Lancashire, the Home Counties and the North East. Each acquisition provides an additional link in a chain than never strides too far, too quickly. There are now initial, if barely perceptible, indications that the construction industry, long the major customer for plant, tool and portable cabin hire, is beginning to emerge from its long and painful recession. This can only strengthen performance at Sheriff, which reported that it had been able to maintain, significantly, pretax profits at £3.6M in December 1996, despite heightening pressure on margins throughout the plant hire sector.

Distinctive features

- cautious, well-timed expansion;
- diversity of operations;
- big player in fragmented market;
- strong financial management;
- powerful service ethos.

Stratagems

It is foolish to insist that a successful new business needs a new product, a niche, if it is to demonstrate sustained growth over almost twenty years. Sheriff does nothing revolutionary in its operation of plant hire centres. It simply does most things very well indeed in an industry where customer service, brand loyalty and thus repeat business can vary. Founded in 1977 as part of a family-owned building group wanting to expand external hire options to make better use of its own equipment, the new activity was large enough, and performing well enough – unlike the cyclical building business – to be demerged for a USM float after little more than 10 years of trading. The erstwhile parent building group was later sold in an MBO.

Chairman Richard Dunn is now convinced that part of Sheriff's success was the decision to move well beyond only building plant and equipment at the start of the hire business. The broad range of hire products – from portable buildings to tools and to giant dump trucks – that has resulted from this conservative philosophy sets the company apart from many of its market rivals and provides some degree of protection against construction industry cycles. But those cycles are not necessarily anathema. They can be turned to a hirer's advantage; when times get tougher, capital spending falls and plant hire can benefit. This is borne out, says Dunn, by figures from JCB, the British plant manufacturer known and respected throughout the world, which suggested that 75 per cent of its output was sold to hirers last year, compared with about half a few years ago.

Size and shape

Employees: 500   Locations: 50
Geographical income split: UK 100%

Size is proving of added importance to Sheriff as overall industry rationalisation influences buying power that is, or should, be reflected in margins. This puts even greater pressure on smaller businesses which are often over-borrowed, and unable easily to fund their way through a tight, barren market phase. Sheriff's energetic management continues to seek out such opportunities of acquisition; in such a market climate these are more easily identified. But Dunn and his team don't snatch at every potential bargain that is sniffed out. 'Because the hire service is, in general terms, fairly local, we feel that it is safer to ripple out from our existing hire construction and plant hire centres.

Future prospects

- rippling expansion programme;
- earnings expansion from sector growth;
- excellent and continuing cashflow;
- further strengthening of management.

Fewer but bigger competitors are emerging, with increased centres. If we can find acquisitions that are on the perimeter of our existing operations we can get the benefit of overlap marketing, targeting new customers who already know of us. It is always tempting to leap about the map on the wall, and it is lovely to see little company flags in Inverness and Land's End. But they cost an awful lot of money to service and gobble up valuable management energy in travelling time,' he says.

Management of the business is divided into divisional teams to make the maximum use of specialist knowledge, experience gained and market intelligence that can play such a part in judging short and medium term equipment demand. Customer service also benefits from such concentration of expertise, insists Dunn. It is, however, interesting that in the case of such items as the large and expensive dump trucks for earth moving or portable buildings which are, invariably, medium to long term hire propositions, Sheriff is happy to offer national coverage. Testing the water?

Outlook

With tenfold growth by most measures in the last ten years despite a relatively cautious acquisition philosophy, the Sheriff management seems keenly aware that over-rapid expansion can, if only temporarily, slow even the swiftest mover. But there is no reason why recent organic and acquisition growth should not continue, given the inner strengths of this business. Diversity has provided a partial shield against the volatile construction industry but the company knows it must continue to improve overall turnover and increase depots if margins are not to begin to wither. Training and motivation of management, so far exemplary, will therefore be of even greater importance if current strength and flair is not to be spread too thinly. Plant hire is better established in Britain than in other parts of Europe or America. In the UK plant hire philosophy, technique and management is now a part of the industrial culture. As the pressure for more efficient use of assets affects Europe as a whole, then opportunities for a well managed, mature hire professional will undoubtedly emerge across the Channel and Sheriff is only too aware of the future potential there. But given the way the company has progressed in the UK market, there are plenty of expansion opportunities closer than Calais.

Address:

Wilford Industrial Estate, Ruddington Lane, Nottingham NG11 7ET. Tel: 0115 945 5544. Fax: 0115 945 5588

Shield Diagnostics

Dundee

Turnover				
1992	1993	1994	1995	1996
£0.45M	£1.6M	£2.3M	£4.7M	£5.8M

Summary: Shield Diagnostics specialises in the manufacture of kits for the detection of autoimmune, infectious and cardiovascular diseases, and neonatal screening. The company's leading product range of autoimmune diagnostics brings in revenues of almost £2.0 million a year. Shield aims to become a leading recognised international *in vitro* diagnostics company within the next two to three years. The results of clinical trials on the Activated Factor Twelve (AFT) test, which identifies personal susceptibility to heart attacks, were presented in March 1997. The results confirmed Shield's belief that AFT has significant potential. Market interest in the company has therefore risen sharply on the expectation that the commercialisation of AFT will generate significant profits.

The Business

Shield Diagnostics is on the verge of a major leap forward. A consolidation of the results of the current clinical trials for AFT were presented in March 1997. The results were very positive and should carry the business into a highly promising future which will revolutionise the company from a small, but effective supplier of diagnostic kits into a major market player. Today Shield is an established diagnostics company that recognises that to compete effectively it must work with the big market players and it has cultivated a strong OEM (original equipment manufacturer) strategy, working alongside majors such as Sanofi, Baxter and Behring. Its product portfolio has expanded from five products in 1990 to the current range of over 60 products, with plans to launch an additional six products annually for the foreseeable future.

The principal market opportunity for Shield Diagnostics lies in its AFT test which, it is anticipated, will accurately predict an individual's susceptibility to heart attacks and strokes. Its currently strong but niche performance in diagnostic kits is the result of accurate analysis of the business opportunity for the company at its launch in 1982 and its reformation in 1987. Initially Shield emphasised science over business. But in 1990 the company recognised this and appointed experienced marketeer and ex-Abbott general manager Gordon Hall as CEO to oversee the transition to a tougher commercial regime. Prior to 1990, the company was making a loss of £250,000 a month with sales of £100,000 a year. In the 1980s Shield devised a technically superior antibody test for urinary tract infection, which cost between £1.20 and £1.50 per test to produce against a market expectation of no more than 8p per test. Hall demonstrated that selling products is paramount for the future vitality of the business and significant management changes were implemented and turnover increased considerably. This was the turning point in the company when the true commercial potential started to unfold.

Hall and his colleagues devised a financial strategy to strengthen the company by acquisition. In 1992 the infectious diseases product line from Northumbria Biologicals Limited was acquired, instantly turning Shield into a company with a turnover approaching £2 million a year. Shield floated on the London Stock Exchange in September 1993, raising over £5.4 million, and hard on the listing the company made two more strategic acquisitions. These were: the medical division of the UK oral drug delivery company, Cortecs International, and, in May 1994, Porton Cambridge Limited, which cost Shield £2.5 million but doubled sales. In November 1996, Shield acquired Guardian Laboratories and Plasmatec Laboratories, adding infectious disease product lines to its portfolio, as well as additional manufacturing and distribution capabilities.

Distinctive features

- strong OEM culture;
- direct management style;
- market driven approach;
- capacity to read markets and deliver innovative products.

The leading product range of autoimmune diagnostics brings in revenues of almost £2.0 million and is growing strongly.

Competition comes from a variety of sources – in the fast growing autoimmune sector, Elias of Germany and Inova of the USA are Shield's biggest competitors. Through carefully chosen acquisitions, control of key analytes and a very active R&D effort, Shield maintains its position in the infectious diseases market. This market is large enough to support many small operators as well as major multinational companies.

Stratagems

The Shield strategy centres on its aim to become a leading recognised international *in vitro* diagnostics company within the next two to three years. As a central plank of this approach, the company plans to maintain a good stream of new products in its existing and new target areas.

To ensure that its research is focused and adequately funded, Shield set up Discovery, as a separate operating unit during 1996. Discovery will be responsible for identifying new technologies appropriate for near patient testing and developing them to commercialisation. Discovery is also charged with bringing existing development projects to completion more rapidly and adding new analytes to existing product ranges. Currently, its most exciting development is its programme on AFT. It is this project which drove the company's share price performance during the early part of 1997 and has been subject of much press attention, says Hall.

Blood clotting is a finely balanced process that must prevent a person bleeding to death when they are injured, but must allow blood to flow normally in the rest of the body. The activation of factor XII (AFT) is part of the process for switching on blood clotting and it has been shown that this activation can be increased by fat circulating in the blood stream. When this gets out of control, the balance is upset and clots are formed where they can cause severe problems, for example, heart attack or stroke. Measurement of AFT in the blood may give an indication of how much at risk a person is of this happening to them in the future.

Size and shape

Employees: 92   Locations: 1
Geographical income split: UK 30%, mainland Europe 39%, N.America 11%, RoW 20%

Shield has developed a proprietary test which measures, specifically, levels of AFT and is currently sold around the world into the 'research-only' market.

Patents have recently been granted for the test in Europe and the USA giving patent protection on the AFT test until 2010. Shield is involved in a number of clinical trials aimed at establishing the relevance of elevated levels of AFT to clinical outcomes. A major UK study, begun in 1990, is looking at thrombotic events and the corresponding levels of AFT. An interim analysis of the data has been carried out and is due for publication in the summer of 1997. The data from this study and other supporting studies showed that: AFT levels increased with increasing relative risk of cardiovascular disease. There was also more than a 30 per cent higher level of AFT in patients with coronary artery disease compared to healthy controls. This compared to around 7 per cent difference for cholesterol and 14 per cent for fibrinogen, in the same patients. In addition, day to day variation of AFT in individuals was much less than with cholesterol.

Future prospects

- major potential for its AFT tests;
- rapid growth of its existing businesses;
- direct selling opportunities in mainland Europe.

Shield's other product developments are:

- **Rapid testing:** the development of novel rapid technologies to take testing as near to the patient as possible. This will include neonatal screening tests to cover syndromes such as respiratory distress, with the aim of producing tests for neonatal intensive care units ensuring that the correct therapeutic intervention can occur as rapidly as possible.
- **Probe technology:** a longer term project looking at the use of DNA probes and probe technology for the identification of infectious diseases and other disease states in the body.
- **New areas:** new market opportunities such as osteoporosis and neural disease identification, for example Alzheimer's disease.

Shield aims to increase the market penetration for its existing product ranges, in particular by making its autoimmune product range compatible with a wider range of instruments and creating additional OEM opportunities. Shield has expanded its direct-selling activities through the acquisition of Guardian and will look at direct selling in Europe where appropriate.

Outlook

AFT is clearly Shield's main hope for major league success. A test to identify which patients are most at risk from cardiovascular diseases has major implications for the health of nations. But even without AFT, Shield is poised for worthwhile growth. Shield is working on strategies to allow the development and funding of the technologies required to remain up-to-date with trends within the diagnostics industry. The company currently invests around 10–15 per cent of turnover in development: 'We don't go beyond our means, but if a real opportunity arrives, we will seek ways to fund it,' says Hall.

Address:

Shield Diagnostics Group, The Technology Park, Dundee DD2 1SW. Tel: 01382 422000. Fax: 01382 561201

Skillsgroup

Haslingden, Lancashire

Turnover				
1992	1993	1994	1995	1996
£223M	£217M	£264M	£342M	£344M

Summary: Skillsgroup is a business on the verge of major change. A collection of specialist technology businesses, it has provided hardware, software and communication products along with a comprehensive range of consultancy, implementation and support services. It has a strong track record in supplying computer solutions to a broad range of clients and has built a reputation for quality and expertise. In May 1997 the group changed its name to Skillsgroup which it believes better reflects the nature of its activities. It boasts a large portfolio of customers including many FT 500 companies, public sector organisations and computer businesses in the UK and in Europe. A dip in turnover and profits in 1991 has been overcome to put Skillsgroup on course to take a bigger share of a specialist market.

The Business

Skillsgroup was started as a sideline by a husband and wife social worker team in 1980. This 'peripheral interest' has grown into a multi-million-pound concern with limitless prospects. Peter Fisher, currently deputy chairman, and his American born spouse Pam spotted the potential of personal computers on their many visits to the USA. They used their initials to name the company (originally P&P) and gave up their full time jobs to concentrate on the sale of PCs and associated product ranges. Skillsgroup is now a major player in the UK market with a strong and effective management structure whose aim is more expansion and financial growth.

As Skillsgroup it will build on the success of P&P. The new business will operate through a strong and flexible business structure. The new business will be divided into three sectors: Acuma, QA and Skillsgroup. QA is people-based solutions, Acuma is mid-range technology and Skillsgroup focuses on the desktop environment. Before the shareholders' meeting in late May 1997, the new structure took effect.

Customers draw on the specialist core skills through the three divisions. Each of these businesses focuses on providing 'best of breed' solutions for their specialism and is backed by the resources and personnel required to meet clients' demands. This approach ensures that Skillsgroup is able to offer a high level of specialism across the spectrum of PC to mid-range computing.

Each of these operating businesses functions in a selected specialist sector of IT. And while the strategy of Skillsgroup has evolved over the past few years to reflect rapid changes in the market place, the fundamental objective is to be a financially strong group aiming to constantly develop solutions for the client/server market, working with partners where appropriate. Throughout 1996 the company broadened its involvement with a number of major corporations. It worked with Glaxo, ICI, Nuclear Electric and BNFL on major projects. In addition long-term major contractual relationships have recently been concluded with the BBC, Marks and Spencer, and Westland.

Distinctive features

- employs more than 1400 IT professionals from offices in the UK and in mainland Europe;
- twelve specialist lines integrated into total business solutions;
- long-term financial strength boosting customer confidence;
- more than 15 years of providing IT solutions.

Stratagems

Successful strategies have been the cornerstone of Skillsgroup's development. Effective planning has created a financially strong group of IT businesses which are closely linked to common strategies. Since 1992, Skillsgroup has transformed its activies and the way the group is represented in the market place, producing a substantial change of approach which is allowing the company to focus on and be competitive in market areas where a clear differentiation is needed in order to succeed.

Group MD David Southworth, headhunted from a leading accountancy firm 11 years ago to take the company forward, believes that trends in the IT market highlight why the key success is specialisation rather than generalisation. He is convinced the specialist path being successfully followed ensures that Skillsgroup is ideally placed for the future and can introduce new business areas and expertise as the demand arises.

Routes to market are determined by the use of specialist brands backed by a service led culture based on qualitative delivery processes. The aim is to constantly develop solutions for the client/server market place, working, where appropriate, through strategic alliances and with leading blue chip commercial partners.

Size and shape

Employees: 1406   Locations: 25
Geographical income split: UK 73.2%, mainland Europe 26.1%, RoW 0.6%

Southworth is certain that PC to mid-range technology is reaching a position of maturity in which certain platforms and manufacturers are showing signs of dominance. Suppliers of the calibre of IBM, Hewlett-Packard, Digital and Microsoft will be, he is convinced, in the strongest positions.

Skillsgroup has formed alliances with these companies to address specific areas of the market, adding to the experience the company has already gained. But the most important thing is to match costs to revenues. Significant to the company's expansion and turnover surge has been a series of acquisitions since 1994. QA Training, a leading technical training and consultancy company joined the stable in 1994. The Technology Training Centre followed a year later along with Space Consultancy. And during 1996 the acquisition of Myriad strengthened the group's position in the IT and outsourcing services market.

Future prospects

- further strategic alliances with leading suppliers to address specific market needs;
- responsive and dynamic approach to needs of target markets;
- enhanced development of four core strands which encompass the Skillsgroup businesses;
- more organic growth and possible acquisitive expansion.

Outlook

Projected business with IBM could be 'huge', according to Southworth. And he has recently negotiated a prestigious three-year deal with Marks and

Spencer. Skillsgroup will continue to play to its strengths, one of the most important of which is developing and maintaining close relationships with customers. This in itself has led to the addition of a host of products and services which support the changing needs of the market. The MD insists: 'We are now recognised as a serious player in the market place.'

Address:

Todd Hall Road, Haslingden, Rossendale, Lancashire BB4 5HU. Tel: 01706 830400. Fax: 01706 832383

Spectrum
Computer Services plc

Bradford, West Yorkshire

Turnover				
1992	1993	1994	1995	1996
£15M	£26M	£33M	£45M	£53M

Summary: Spectrum Computer Services is a broadly-based computer services company based in Bradford. Started in 1979, it recently reported its 13th successive year of record sales growth and profitability. It is composed of four service divisions selling to a range of major market clients, in both the public and commercial sectors. Spectrum is founded on an unquenchable belief in financial stability and the provision of dependable service to customers. It has grown largely through organic approaches to the market but is nevertheless in search of suitable acquisitions to add critical mass to the company.

The Business

Spectrum's current chairman Barry Burns and a co-director came to a similar conclusion in the early 1970s – the deployment of computers would become commonplace for both business and personal users. They correctly judged that many companies would find the implementation of computer systems a major operational issue, demanding time and consideration. In many cases, these businesses would need external help to assist their implementation of systems which were the most appropriate for their requirements.

Burns, with a maths background, wanted to create a company with inherent financial stability. He had seen sector companies come and go; some had collapsed because they lacked a sufficiently strong business grounding. 'I did not want to repeat these failures. So I concentrated on achieving stability and reliability. I believed that we could win repeat business by generating high levels of confidence in our services among our clients,' he says. The

386

over-riding philosophy of business practice in Spectrum is that stability is an absolute requirement for organisations which demand total reliability. This extends beyond a current order into future enhancements, new market innovations, confidentiality and comprehensive professional advice. 'Reliability manifested itself in a desire among clients for a long term relationship of total integrity with a preferred supplier,' he comments.

The chairman was – and remains – committed to an approach of building business through creative marketing, developing relationships with customers and, as an essential element, achieving such high quality work that assignments are won through customer recommendation. The spread of businesses are: computer supplies, computer systems, data services and software services. The core of the company is computer supplies, which earns the majority of Spectrum's sales. The focus for this business is large commercial organisations, discrete government sectors, mail order, resellers, retailers and purchasing departments. The business is being built by increasing direct sales capacity and greater use of direct mail, including mail order catalogues. Its expanding product range is being sold aggressively, complemented by substantial service support. Computer supplies has experienced a 25 per cent year-on-year expansion and proven approaches have been put in place for this division to achieve an even greater market share. Burns and his team have paid close attention to ensure seamless growth in all business units, including suitable training for personnel to attain expert specialist status in identified client market sectors. Computer supplies is the heart of the company but Burns sees the other divisions as equally important to its operation and future profitability as part of an impressive commercial family.

Distinctive features

- consistent financial stability;
- high orientation towards customer satisfaction;
- emphasis on cost control;
- to remain competitive;
- continuous improvement processes operate.

The second largest aspect of the business is computer systems. The key markets for this business are public sector financial management disciplines in local government, health and education. The company has commissioned the development of a new general ledger product using the latest relational database techniques, completing a range of products which cater for every financial need in the public sector. An innovative lifetime concept has been introduced to positively encourage newcomers to view their licence as an ongoing investment in the company's products.

Data services is increasing sales rapidly. Clients draw on its skills to provide consistently high quality and reliable services using specialist PC-based data capture software which enables sophisticated, complex and integrated data processing. Software services is extending the scope of its financial applications and development services at client locations. Among its current portfolio of assignments are: product and service planning for the millennium and the implementation of client/server document image processing and workflow management solutions.

Stratagems

Spectrum was founded and thrives on its main commercial objective – identifying and exploiting new markets of high potential which have synergies with existing businesses. Key to the strength of the enterprise is a concerted and sustained profits ploughback. Burns reinvests return to develop the expansion of new markets, technologies and approaches to client service. The company is rock solid financially and the chairman uses this as a technique to create new business.

Size and shape

Employees: 200   Locations: 2
Geographical income split: UK 100%

So far Spectrum's drive has been concentrated in using a series of opportunities for organic growth. Acquisitions continue to be examined and Burns believes that the company, which is strong enough to fund its own purchases, should follow a course of prudent acquisition on the right terms. This would give the company a greater range of services, access to more clients or a toehold in complementary markets. The decision to pursue a buying policy causes him to reconsider his previous approach to seek a listing for Spectrum. 'We have been victims of our own success and so we have not needed to float. But a significant acquisition could change that. The company does not need a cash injection but I have not ruled out a listing,' Burns remarks. He currently owns and controls the vast majority of the shares in the company.

Future prospects

- substantial potential growth in domestic markets;
- expansion, possibly by acquisition;
- continuing development of activities and growth in turnover and profits.

He is determined not to repeat the mistakes made by other IT companies which have gone to market. 'After floating they discovered they did not have the most appropriate infrastructure to carry out their development plans.' In the meantime, Spectrum will continue to increase its share in all four operating divisions. He believes there is plenty of potential for each of the divisions to build on their current positions. Burns comments that it is a fragmented sector and Spectrum's approach of total reliability will secure further advances.

Cost control is a key factor in improving services. The company will continue to offer its catalogue of services on competitive terms. This does not mean that it is the cheapest but, he suggests, it is the most effective. Spectrum's management keeps a tight watch on routine costs and redirects expenditure into customer service. Burns says there is no dominant player which favours his company's philosophy of its markets.

Outlook

The business intends to expand its personnel and office premises to strengthen its determined offensive to build on its niche specialisms. Spectrum believes that there is considerable scope for growth in the UK and possibilities of expansion in the wider world.

Address:

PO Box 199, East Parade, Bradford BD1 5RJ. Tel: 01274 308188. Fax: 01274 307264

Stalbridge Linen Services Limited

Shaftesbury, Dorset

Turnover				
1991	1992	1993	1994	1996
£5M	£5.9M	£5.7M	£5.9M	£7.4M

Summary: Stalbridge Linen Services is one of the leading laundry companies operating in the catering and hospitality sectors. It handles more than a quarter of a million items of catering workwear and table linen every week. Stalbridge offers key benefits over rival operations and ranks among the top ten industrial laundry operations in the UK. In its sector it is in the top three and is probably the most progressive. Changes in ownership have adversely affected its financial results but it is now soundly based and well positioned for growth. The company has expanded its operations through the opening of a second facility and is on course for a major improvement in margins.

The Business

The rapid growth in the catering and hospitality sectors – see our reports on Checkout, Eldridge Pope, Regent Inns and J.D. Weatherspoon – has created a direct benefit for its suppliers. But like the companies engaged in retail management of pubs, restaurants and hotels, suppliers have needed to demonstrate unique cost and client service advantages. Stalbridge offers outstanding service to the operators of catering and hospitality outlets. It has invested heavily in technology to enhance its service quality and the company has expanded the range of facilities which are available to its customers. The impact has been a 50 per cent increase in profitability since 1991 despite changes in ownership.

Founder and former MD David Coulter puts down the success of Stalbridge to its dialogue with its customers. 'We listen very carefully to requirements of our customers and communicate these messages to our workforce. This process enables us to be in the forefront of service provision in our sector.' The core business focuses on the cost-sector and catering event niches of the industry. It provides, uniquely, hire and laundry services for table linen and catering workwear. It is a tenet of faith for Stalbridge that it responds flexibly to the changing demands of its customers. For example it does not insist on fixed term contracts for standard items, no penalties are levied when the size of clothes are changed and it does not make residual charges when staff changes means that the customer needs to return items.

Coulter opened the business in 1975, meeting contracts by laundering pub teatowels and bar mats himself in the washers of an everyday launderette. The operation started with zero cash investment and a maximum of entrepreneurial zeal. In 1988 he sold out to Cannon Street Investments for £3.5 million but he stayed at the helm. In 1990 Cannon Street hit problems and the Bank of Scotland encouraged Coulter to lead a management buy-out. He dismissed the senior management, who he believed were holding the company back, and installed a flatter structure to expedite decision-making and innovation.

Distinctive features

- strong leadership;
- heavy investment;
- locates fresh niche markets;
- high customer service;
- commitment to training;
- strong growth despite structural changes.

In 1995, the MBO was dissolved and Coulter sold out again; this time to Johnson Group Cleaners for £6.5 million. The money was welcome because it ensured investment for future development of the business. Johnson is a larger player and synergies from the acquisition are potentially numerous. A sophisticated state-of-the-art factory has been opened. Hampers arrive from all over the country and all catering workwear is bar coded to ensure that stocks can be traced. In all support offices, a high tech electronic data interchange system reduces paperwork. In 1996 around £800,000 has been spent on new machinery and a further £400,000 has been allocated for a factory extension.

Although the company is based in Dorset, distance is no barrier, with clients throughout the UK regularly serviced by a fleet of delivery vehicles. Radio control links to head office control means that drivers can be contacted easily and all the vans carry back-up stock, in case of emergency. Collected soiled goods are dropped back in Shaftesbury for overnight sorting, washing, pressing, folding and can be back on the road for use again the next morning.

Stratagems

The strategic direction of the company has been refined since the March 1995 purchase by Johnson. Coulter has confirmed the key role of his people in the success of the business. Before the sale, he gave each member of staff with the company for more than two years a bundle of shares, as part of a £250,000 handout. His own personality has been the key motivational factor in Stalbridge but he has created an egalitarian culture. The company has grown the skills and responsibilities of team leaders and managers – ensuring that it does not become a one-generation operation. All members of the workforce, now numbering around 260, are encouraged to develop their talents and leadership skills through work assessment and external training. Earning an Investors in People Award in 1994 underlined Stalbridge's achievement in focusing on the advancement of employees.

Size and shape

Employees: 260   Locations: 2
Geographical income split: UK 100%

On the commercial side, Stalbridge has begun the search for new markets. The company has concentrated on the catering sector of the laundry market-place. Stalbridge is now a familiar regular at some of the UK's most prestigious outdoor sporting events, from Royal Ascot to Aintree, Wimbledon to the Henley Regatta. The rapid growth in business will come from expanding service lines, securing more business from current customers, and adding more clients. Stalbridge and Johnson both see the potential for further growth by exploitation of mutual client bases.

The traditional Stalbridge values will continue to predominate. Coulter states that the company has prospered because it pays great attention to the needs of its clients. Service quality is enhanced year-on-year and the commitment to leading edge technology offers further opportunties for efficiencies. Stalbridge has achieved accreditation under BS5750 which means that customers can be confident that its processes are second-to-none.

Future prospects

- strong growth in market share;
- second outlet opened;
- expansion of existing customer service.

One key sign that the business is doing well is that it has opened a second factory. The aim would be to offer an enhanced service to customers in Manchester, Leeds and the north-east. The company is adding new lines as a standard feature of its operation. In 1994, it introduced the first coloured chef's jackets in the UK. This was a popular move, despite being seen by some observers as a controversial step away from traditional white. Another niche service launched recently was the introduction of round white table-cloths. This has been further expanded by the addition of coloured round tablecloths.

Outlook

Stalbridge can expect to experience a major period of growth. Its acquisition by Johnson has given the company a platform from which to build. In the next five years it should be UK market leader, assisted by high investment in systems and service, strong employee motivation, outstanding leadership and responsive customers. Coulter comments 'Our philosophy is dedicated to client service, supported by a belief that we can always improve. We recognise the route to competitive advantage is through the development of our people, backed by management, technology and systems innovation.' Clients have reacted warmly to each of the Stalbridge new services – and the quality of these relationships will be the bedrock on which it builds in the future.

Address:

Christy's Lane, Shaftesbury, Dorset SP7 8PH. Tel: 01747 851585. Fax: 01747 851155

Taylor Nelson AGB plc

West London

Turnover				
1991	1992	1993	1994	1995
£18M	£47M	£56M	£62M	£80M

Summary: Taylor Nelson AGB is the leading UK company in the market research industry. The company is focused on four principal business sectors – consumer goods, healthcare, media and business services – and is continuing to report major contract wins and widen the range of services it offers. It has recently been investing heavily in database and direct marketing services, which it believes will be the fastest-growing area of the industry, and is looking to replicate its domestic success internationally.

The Business

Taylor Nelson AGB stands at the head of a market sector which has thrived in recent years as companies need to target their customers and potential customers with pinpoint accuracy. TN AGB provides a range of services of increasing sophistication which its clients use to accurately plan likely demand for new products or services or make quality enhancements to existing packages. The company's core activity is the collection and provision of accurate market information. This is achieved using a variety of techniques, ranging from face-to-face interviews to sophisticated technology such as barcode scanning devices. The market information collected is then either sold as part of a standard package to a group of customers or can be customised for individual users.

Taylor Nelson AGB's largest division generates research on consumer goods. Its flagship product is the Superpanel service, which provides a continuous measurement of household purchases of fast moving consumer goods. The service is sold to more than 200 clients, including manufacturers, retailers and distributors, and is finding an increasing audience among retail and other professional analysts. It is the leading service in the household panel sector with more than 85 per cent of the market. In 1995 TN launched TVSpan, a major innovation offering a service which measures television viewing in 750 Superpanel homes and is designed to measure the effectiveness of television advertising on consumer behaviour. The division's Impulse service has established a strong presence in the niche market of measuring more casual purchases such as confectionery, snacks and soft drinks. Its success has prompted the launch of Fashion Trak, a specialist product for the clothing and footwear markets.

Distinctive features

- steady growth forecast for core markets;
- potential for major international expansion;
- high quality customer base;
- market leadership in key industrial and commercial sectors.

In recent years, Taylor Nelson AGB's best performing division has been healthcare. The company works for all top 40 drug companies and has developed an outstanding reputation for performing multi-country projects, conducting research in more than 50 countries during 1995. It has also developed a range of new multi-client services such as Scriptcount, a service that monitors the dispensing of prescriptions through pharmacies.

The company's media division is best known for its impressive work on the collection of TV viewing figures. Its contract with the Broadcasters' Audience Research Board (BARB) was extended last year until 2000, and its panel of 4500 homes is among the largest TV viewing measurement panel in the world. Of equal importance is the fact that this contract provides a significant base from which to expand into overseas markets, and earlier this year Taylor Nelson agreed a six year deal with Telewijza Polska, the public broadcasting company, to provide a similar service in Poland. The division is also strong in the national and regional press market.

The business services and finance division offers market research and related consultancy to clients operating principally in financial services, telecommunications, IT and other business-to-business markets. Its principal activity is customer satisfaction surveys and other service quality projects. Taylor Nelson's FOQUS brand, which is designed to identify and measure key service issues is now being marketed on a world-wide basis, and a number of overseas licences have already been granted. The company also has extensive fieldwork, telephone research and telemarketing capabilities.

Internationally, Taylor Nelson has established a European toiletries and cosmetics database, a pan-European panel of 7000 individuals in more than five countries, which is installed on more than 35 user sites. The company's French operation, which currently focuses on consumer and healthcare work, will also be expanded. Taylor Nelson has also opened in Moscow – the base for a syndicated pricing and distribution service in 20 cities across Russia and the Czech republic.

Stratagems

Taylor Nelson's strategy is to be world leader in the provision of market information services and a leader in the main market sectors of consumer goods, healthcare, media and business services. It aims to achieve this both by expanding its range of continuous syndicated contracts (which can be sold simultaneously to a number of customers at minimal marginal cost) and by offering bespoke services to address specific marketing needs. The company has recognised that IT is playing an increasingly important role in the market information industry – in particular, customers are demanding more sophisticated and timely information – and has been investing heavily in this direction. It has developed a new computer assisted personal interviewing system, which should improve the accuracy and turnaround times of face-to-face surveys. TN is also the first market research company looking at the use of speech recognition systems and was recently awarded an EU grant in connection with this work. In the long-term, the company's transfer of data processing from a mainframe to a Unix platform should improve operational flexibility and performance.

Size and shape

Employees: 1,050   Locations: 15
Geographical income split: UK 80%, mainland Europe 13%, North America 6%, RoW 1%

Taylor Nelson is also responding to the trend towards the greater targeting of marketing effort and this is reflected in its movement into database and direct marketing services. In January 1995, the company purchased MPM, one of the leading providers of distribution and promotional services in the UK. The acquisition should enhance Taylor Nelson's capabilities in the door to door distribution of promotional materials and product samples and in coupon processing.

Given the company's existing strengths in the UK, international expansion is necessarily a key part of its strategy. It has deliberately eschewed moving into the North American market since it believes it would lack the critical mass to make much of an impression in what is already a mature market. The current focus of its ambitions is Central and Eastern Europe where markets are developing fast. Closer to home, in August 1995 Taylor Nelson acquired AGB Attwood, a leading Irish market research company previously owned by the AGB Group. In the long-term, the company is expected to expand into the Pacific Rim where market growth is running at the rate of 20 per cent a year. However, the UK market research industry is continuing to grow at 10 per cent and the company will still be able to generate substantial growth from its core activities into the foreseeable future.

Outlook

Future prospects

- world market leadership;
- margin improvements from effective IT application;
- reduced competition due to high entry barriers.

With market growth in Europe running at the rate of 10 per cent a year, TN's core business will continue to grow steadily, while its investment in IT should contribute margin improvements. Also, its position will be strengthened as the market research industry becomes more sophisticated since higher service standards will effectively create barriers to entry to lesser competitors. TN's expansion into database marketing is already generating substantial contracts and opening up a large and fast-growing sector of the market. Finally, Taylor Nelson is beginning to export its expertise overseas and the benefits of this should be feeding through shortly.

Address:

Westgate, London W5 1UA. Tel: 0181 967 0007. Fax: 0181 967 4060

Telspec plc

Rochester, Kent

Turnover			
1993	1994	1995	1996
£18M	£36M	£59M	£64M

Summary: Telspec is a telecoms engineering company with a broad range of international sales to blue chip PTT companies throughout the world. It produces leading edge components used by suppliers and users of most telecommunications networks. The quality of its output and the ever-increasing catalogue of clients has ensured that the business has grown substantially since the outset in 1975. As the demand for telecoms services grows rapidly Telspec is well-positioned for a major expansion in sales.

The Business

Any high quality, well managed manufacturer in the telecommunications sector can look forward to rapid growth in the next decade. Telecoms is one of the premier growth industries of the world economy. Demand for a wide variety of telecommunications services by personal and corporate users is mushrooming. Even by these exacting standards Telspec is special. A glance at its performance since flotation in London in 1993 shows the dynamic growth which the company has enjoyed. Focused on national telecoms providers, Telspec has increased sales from £18 million to £64 million. Operations have spread from the UK with some mainland European and Australian business to a significant presence in all five continents and new manufacturing joint ventures in Slovakia and Turkey. Major new markets have opened since 1993 in Eastern Europe and the former Soviet Union countries, Spain, and Latin America including Brazil.

The company was founded by its current chairman Frank Hackett-Jones, who opened its first facility in Maidstone in 1975. Today it operates from nine sites in England, Scotland, Germany, Turkey, Slovakia, Spain and Australia.

The majority of its business is in access to the network. This is the part between the telephone exchange and the subscribers. The market is all the copper, fibre optic, and radio links – the pipeline between the exchange and the customer. One of the main product areas is pair-gain, which allows the user to get more than one conversation down a single pair of wires. At present pair-gain accounts for 64 per cent of sales. Telespec sells this all over the world to the telephone operating companies; BT, Deutsche Telekom and Telefonica are among its clients for this system. With pair-gain, the provider can use the network more efficiently at a very low price.

The vast majority of Telspec's products are designed and manufactured in-house and sold through agents or the Telspec marketing and distribution network. Occasionally, the company also installs and repairs products. It has international patent coverage for its products and the business commands an enviable reputation for the quality of its work. It has achieved ISO 9000 accreditation both in the UK and its manufacturing facilities elsewhere. The company is adamant that a quality approach is key to its success. The general philosophy is that the only way to conduct long term business is on the essential quality of the products and services.

Distinctive features

- high quality and sophisticated product portfolio;
- worldwide blue chip customers;
- highly skilled professional management and employees;
- dedicated in-house research and development facilities;
- proven track record, based on long term commitments.

In a highly competitive market, Telspec needs to combine its quality approach with innovation in design and the efficiency in its support network to succeed. 'We cannot afford to be delinquent in any of these areas. I would say that our biggest asset is that we are very responsive and fast-moving. That is partly a function of our size and our management structure, which allows us to make rapid decisions. We make our global regions as autonomous as possible. It would be impossible, for example, to run Australia from the UK on a day-to-day basis' says one of its directors.

Telspec invests strongly in R&D to stay ahead of the market. It faces few UK-based competitors but around the world Telspec needs to compete with some extensively able businesses. Despite the challenges, Telspec has succeeded in winning substantial new assignments and extensive follow-on work. One of the main reasons for its achievements in new markets is its aggressive approach to marketing. 'We do our homework. On tender work, there is a price window within which our competitors and ourselves will pitch. We have become very good at predicting at what level our rivals will pitch. We do this by studying their operations and their approaches to the market – whether they are price or quality driven,' he continues.

Stratagems

The choice of Telspec's place in the market has proved inspired. 'In the developing world, putting in telephone exchanges is comparatively cheap. The real investment is in the links with the subscribers which is the market in which we operate. So demand is very high. It is a different picture in the developed world. There is a huge growth in fibre optics. Telspec is also highly active in ISDN terminals. We are currently UK market leader in this, we are a big supplier to Deutsche Telekom and also to the PTT in Australia. The expansion in Internet access and in data transfer between companies are markets where we are well represented.' Telspec is now placed in some of the fastest growing sectors of the fastest growing industry in the world.

> **Size and shape**
>
> Employees: 766   Locations: 8
> Geographical income split: UK 62.5%, mainland Europe 9.8%, Australia 18.2%, RoW 9.5%

To enhance its market share, the company has adopted a customer-focused strategy. 'It sounds like jargon but customer relationships really do matter. We have taken a long term approach to building business. This means attention to cost, support services, timely delivery, quality products and design, speed of decision-making and actively responding to what the customer says.' This appears to be paying off because Telspec, faced with intelligent and well-managed competitors, wins 90 per cent repeat business from the world's top telecoms providers. 'Flexibility is an essential component of our success. This is a risk business and although we have laid plans we need to be able respond and to take a risk.'

Future prospects

- growth in the developing world through links from new exchanges;
- expansion in developed countries through fibre optics, ISDN and data transfer;
- increased presence in new markets through joint venture manufacturing and sales offices.

Its plans include a phased movement into new markets. The company serves markets initially with local sales offices using local people to market the technology. Where demand is high the company will open a manufacturing facility for semi-finished products. The opening of a plant in Slovakia followed its initial sales and marketing presence. Telespec says that it did not want to go to Russia because of political uncertainty.

Outlook

Telspec aims to increase its penetration of global markets through deepening of relationships with existing and new clients. It places great emphasis on its state-of-the-art engineering and product development, aggressive marketing and quality procedures. The company says there is plenty of scope in territories such as North America and China, and for its new products across the world. 'We can meet our growth expectations by purely organic means so we have no need for acquisitions.' The next ten years will see rapid expansion of its core markets and so the challenge for Telspec is to provide innovative products to tap demand.

Address:

Lancaster Parker Road, Rochester Airport, Rochester, Kent ME1 3QU. Tel: 01634 687133. Fax: 01634 684984

Tinsley Robor plc   PAPER, PRINTING AND PACKAGING

Chichester, West Sussex

Turnover				
1992	1993	1994	1995	1996
£23.5M	£27.5M	£29.5M	£35.1M	£47.1M

Summary: Although involved in a full range of printing and packaging activities, Tinsley Robor is reputed for its work in the multimedia sector. As a major supplier to the music industry, the company enjoys a reputation for designing innovative solutions to increasingly complex customer requirements. TR has recently undergone a substantial capital investment programme and the technological lead which it has now established, together with its strong marketing skills, should ensure that it is a major beneficiary of the multimedia revolution.

The Business

The development of the CD, in all its myriad versions, could not have come at a better time for the south coast printer and packager Tinsley Robor. This established group of sector companies has stamped out a reputation as printer and packager to the music and software markets at precisely the moment where these industries are set to experience remarkable growth. Music and software are only two of the markets where TR has targeted its services. It supplies a range of services to customers in a number of defined market sectors throughout the UK and mainland Europe. These include labelling, commercial printing, design and origination, and standard and specialist packaging for the music and multimedia industries. But during recent years, the group has become the leading supplier to the music and multimedia publishing industries in the UK.

The compact disc has now evolved from simple music carrier to all-purpose data carrier (in a variety of formats), and consensus exists that this high rate of industry growth will continue as CD-ROM hardware penetrates the market. Through its James Upton subsidiary, Tinsley Robor's track record in the music industry has enabled it to establish a pre-eminent position in the production of the printed package that every compact disc must have, whether it is a standard 'envelope' or a complex book or box designed to add perceived value to the product. Instrumental to its success has been its position as the sole UK supplier of the popular *Digipak® cardboard CD case, a form of packaging that is now proving particularly suitable for the growing number of CD-ROM products on the market.

In 1995, partly in order to satisfy the growing demand for special packaging for CD-ROM and Interactive CD, the company transferred the bulk of its standard CD packaging production to a new, state-of-the-art plant in Swindon – close to Thorn EMI's huge CD operations. By improving the efficiency of job-scheduling, the multi-batching technology which is on offer at this new site offers the firm a considerable competitive advantage in an environment where music companies are constantly reducing turnaround times. Two years ago, the company launched TRACS Multimedia.

Formed out of a merger of TR Audio and Computer Services and TR Displayprint, this is a 'one-stop shop' operation which is designed to offer independent computer and music companies a complete production package – packaging construction, design, reproduction, printing and fulfilment. In Howards, the group has established a successful labelling business by identifying particular market sectors where it can develop a niche position. Individual markets earmarked for growth are self-adhesive labels and 'no-label-look' labels, especially in the drinks, toiletries and confectionery sectors. In November 1995 the group acquired Arun Labels, based in Rustington, West Sussex – a supplier of on-roll labels to FMCG companies. Sonicon is a design-led creative communications company able to handle design and reproduction work from clients anywhere in the world. The increased demand for pure design work has led the company to open a specialist design unit in West London, close to many of the major record companies.

Tinsley Robor is increasingly targeting the European market. Its factory in Uden in the Netherlands has been expanded to twice its previous size to allow the company to widen its product offer and customer base in Europe. In addition, last year's acquisition of Printing Resources Limited (trading as IPR) in Dublin allowed the company to offer a factory gate service in one of Europe's major software and CD processing centres. In August 1996, Austrian printer Reischl Druck was acquired with the object of supplying Sony pressing operations in Salzburg.

---

*Digipak is a registered trademark of AGI Inc.

Distinctive features

- high quality management;
- strong position in growth markets;
- able marketeers;
- technological lead over rivals.

Stratagems

Tinsley Robor's strategy is to offer a turn key service for every possible market opportunity and this is manifested in the wide range of services which it offers. It aims to offer a complete service to the customer right from the initial concept through to the delivery of the packaged product ready for distribution. As a consequence, although individual operating subsidiaries are allowed considerable autonomy so as to foster initiative, synergies between them are encouraged and rewarded. Advanced technological links also make close working relationships between group companies easy to manage. Many of the group's customers operate in markets where product differentiation can be critical to commercial success or failure. In the music and multimedia industries, in particular, the quality of shelf-space which a product can demand is vital, and design and packaging are becoming increasingly important to its success.

Size and shape

Employees: 500   Locations: 10
Geographical income split: UK 80%, mainland Europe 20%

Future prospects

- growing critical mass;
- rapid growth in its multimedia assignments;
- extensive mainland European growth.

To meet its clients' quest for product differentiation, Tinsley Robor has invested heavily in technology. It can now not only handle higher volumes and reduce cycle times, but also produce extremely high quality product. In a ground-breaking move last year, for example, the company produced more than two million CD packs of Pink Floyd's album *Pulse* which contained a light emitting diode. Considerable emphasis has been placed on quality and this has been reflected by BS5750 awards at all its major manufacturing plants.

After an uncertain period following flotation (when the group was excessively focused on traditional packaging activities), Tinsley Robor now has a comprehensive understanding of the market. The business has now developed sufficient critical mass to deter potential new competitors. With customers often staking large sums of money on having their product in the right place at the right time, they need to know that their packaging provider will be able to deliver. Tinsley Robor now has the track record and sufficiently strong customer relationships to satisfy these concerns.

Marketing strategy is a key area of focus. By exhibiting widely at shows both in the UK and mainland Europe, TR has created a comprehensive database covering an enormous range of current and potential CD publishers. This offers significant advantages which the company will aim to exploit over time as the market develops. Furthermore, TR aims to change its mix of accounts to concentrate on higher-margin work. Tinsley Robor aims to build on its established position in a number of key markets both by organic growth and acquisition. This has already been seen in the acquisitions of IPR and Arun Labels (a Sussex-based specialist flexographic printer, which is intended to give Tinsley Robor greater access to the food labelling market). In particular, it will pursue overseas expansion in order to mirror the trend on the part of many of its customers towards a more European and international approach to manufacturing and distribution.

Outlook

The European multimedia market will double by 2000. Tinsley Robor is ideally placed to exploit this trend by providing printing and packaging services to this market. The critical mass which the company already commands, together with the strength of its existing customer base, will make it increasingly hard for other companies to enter the industry. However, it is not simply its multimedia activities which are expected to flourish. The move towards 'one-stop shopping' should mean that all Tinsley Robor's businesses will benefit. In addition, the company's technical skills should prove equally attractive to European customers as it expands the size and scope of its activities.

Address:

Drayton House, Drayton, Chichester, West Sussex PO20 6EW. Tel: 01243 774000. Fax: 01243 774567

TrafficMaster plc

Milton Keynes

Turnover				
1992	1993	1994	1995	1996
£0.5M	£0.8M	£1M	£2.5M	£5Me

Summary: TrafficMaster has developed what is believed to be the world's first commercially available in-car, real-time traffic monitoring system. Following major investment in its information gathering infrastructure and product development, the company is now looking to build revenues. TrafficMaster occupies a pre-eminent position in the fast-emerging international arena of intelligent transport systems (ITS) and the marketplace for its products is potentially huge. Furthermore, given that the company's cost base is relatively fixed, additional revenue will flow directly through to the bottom line.

The Business

The science of ITS has developed over the last five years in an effort to help society use motor vehicles more efficiently and safely on a finite amount of road space. For motorists, this not only means avoiding getting stuck in traffic jams, but also other benefits such as more accurate definition of journey times prior to departure and better scheduling of journeys.

TrafficMaster is the clear market leader in the UK in the ITS market. Indeed, it has no directly comparable competitors – its closest rivals are the traditional methods of disseminating traffic information such as motorway signs and national and local radio broadcasts. However, none of these latter methods provides real-time information covering a large geographical area which is available at the push of a button to motorists in their cars or prior to commencing a journey, or in fleet control rooms.

The heart of TrafficMaster's business is the network of more than 2400 traffic sensors installed across the British motorway and trunk road network.

These are located at approximately two mile intervals and normally over one lane of each direction of traffic flow. When the traffic flow in either direction falls below a predetermined average of 30 miles per hour, a micro-processor triggers a radio transmission to the TrafficMaster control centre. The control centre processes the information received from the sensor sites and generates a signal to update the TrafficMaster units, which then display the approximate speed of the traffic. After making enquiries, usually from the police, as to the cause of the congestion, the control room can then relay a further explanatory text message to subscribers to provide them with more information about the situation.

TrafficMaster provides a wide range of products and services. In 1995 it launched its two volume in-car products, TrafficMaster YQ and TrafficMate. The YQ model offers national coverage and is aimed principally at the high-mileage motorist. TrafficMate is a cheaper, speech-based product which provides only local coverage (within ten miles) and is intended for the mass market. Both YQ and TrafficMate have been officially approved by the RAC.

The company considers the original equipment marketplace – the installation of traffic information systems as original equipment in new vehicles – to be especially attractive. The most significant new product to be launched in 1996 is TrafficMaster Oracle, which allows drivers to receive information from the network through car radios. This product is important because it provides significant opportunities without having to wait for vehicle manufacturers to install screens in their dashboards.

Distinctive features

- unique technology;
- no comparable competitors;
- enormous potential market;
- infrastructure in place.

In addition, specially designed systems are being installed on BMW's own on-board monitor screen as standard on the BMW 750 model and as an option on the 730 and 740 models. The same unit is available as an option on the new 5 series launched in 1996. Traffic congestion is a major international problem and TrafficMaster sees considerable potential overseas. During November 1995 the company signed an exclusive option agreement with Mannesmann Autocom to develop a TrafficMaster network throughout Germany.

Stratagems

TrafficMaster's strategy from the time of its flotation in February 1994 to date has been to consolidate its pre-eminent position in the marketplace. Its information gathering infrastructure is now largely completed and its major products have been launched – the company's objective is now to build product awareness and grow the revenue stream.

Its potential marketplace is immense. There are currently some 25 million drivers on UK roads, around half of which regularly use motorways and main trunk roads, and it is these drivers which form the target market. Research from Japan, where the market is more highly developed although technology is behind that in Europe, suggests the potential for the product. There are already more than one million in-vehicle display-based navigation systems in the Japanese marketplace and up to 15 per cent of certain models are now leaving the factory with in-vehicle displays fitted as standard equipment. Independent research has indicated that an explosion of ITS products is almost certainly going to occur in Europe within the next two to five years.

> **Size and shape**
>
> Employees: 60   Locations: 1
> Geographical income split: UK 98%, RoW 2%

TrafficMaster uses a variety of sales and marketing techniques. It has invested heavily in joint initiatives with retailers to install innovative in-store displays and has developed relationships with paging and motor vehicle distributors. Both TrafficMaster YQ and TrafficMate are being marketed to the RAC's membership base. The company's relationship with the RAC has been further cemented by an agreement to provide traffic information for its forthcoming radio station service. Brand awareness is also being built through the company's TV-based Monitor product which is being installed in hotels and service stations.

Having its units fitted as original equipment is obviously the most effective way of promoting brand awareness. In addition to its relationship with BMW, the company is currently in discussion with a number of other manufacturers which are considering the integration of TrafficMaster information into in-car navigation systems. The company estimates that, within the next five years, one-quarter of all new cars will be produced with units fitted as standard.

One of the principal benefits of TrafficMaster's strategy has been to create substantial barriers to entry to the industry. As well as its existing infrastructure, technological lead and strong industry relationships, the company is in receipt of the requisite Department of Transport licence. Traffic-Master's current licence was recently extended through to 2006 and, while it is not exclusive, any potential competitor would be expected to undergo extensive testing in order to receive one. The company estimates it would have a three-year lead time on any potential entrants to the industry.

TrafficMaster does not see itself as a manufacturer, but rather as an information provider, and for this reason much of its production is sub-contracted. Furthermore, since it is primarily a subscription business, most of the revenues which are generated do not have any directly attributable marginal costs. This will allow the company to become extremely profitable once a critical mass of sales have been achieved. Overseas, the company's chosen method of expansion is by granting licences to use its technology. As well as the agreement with Mannesmann, TrafficMaster is in negotiations with two companies in other European countries with regard to establishing TrafficMaster systems.

Outlook

TrafficMaster is well placed to profit from the growth of the ITS market. Department of Transport figures suggest there will be significantly greater levels of traffic congestion across the UK in the very near future, with 10 per cent of the network suffering at peak hours. The company has barely scratched the surface of potential demand – only 15,000 units of the YQ have been sold, for example, out of an estimated possible market of two million. As congestion worsens and awareness of TrafficMaster's products grows, the upside for the company is enormous both at home and overseas.

Address:

Marlborough Court, Sunrise Parkway, Linford Wood, Milton Keynes MJK14 6DX. Tel: 01908 249800. Fax: 01908 200330

Trinity Holdings plc

Coventry

Turnover				
1992	1993	1994	1995	1996
£82M	£110M	£136M	£164M	£208M

Summary: Trinity Holdings is a highly successful manufacturer of specialist motor vehicles. Its eight operating companies design and make fire engines, buses, coaches, waste disposal trucks, and airport handling vehicles. Trinity entered the market in 1989 at a time of comprehensive industry reorganisation and established its market leadership positions through a combination of modern design, performance efficiencies and deep appreciation of customer need. The group has benefited from a market need for more new buses and coaches, and the inability of competitors to meet its quality standards.

The Business

In the early 1980s the core group of companies which now form Trinity Holdings were key elements of the Hestair engineering conglomerate. At that stage 75 per cent of the group's income came from Dennis fire engines, buses, coaches and other engineering products. By 1988, 75 per cent of the group's income was derived from services, especially employment bureaux. 'The engineering companies tried to get investment from the Hestair board for new products but were consistently turned down,' says Trinity CEO Steve Burton. The outcome was an MBO proposal which Hestair was pleased to accept. The new business was launched in January 1989 with £25 million from Citicorp and Bankers' Trust.

'It was the best thing that could have happened for our companies. The philosophy at Hestair was copycat – or me too. In other words, we followed slavishly what competitors did. When we launched Trinity we adopted a fresh approach which has remained at the heart of the group ever since.' In the bus and coach markets, its designers started from scratch. They talked to potential customers about what their requirements would be. 'We had no presence in the bus and coach markets so we had no reputations to lose or baggage to take with us. We asked the question "What should a bus or coach do?" We started with a clean sheet of paper. For the coach market we designed a coach which was one ton lighter, offered a 12 per cent saving in fuel costs and a new simpler configuration,' he remarks.

Trinity was helped by the radical nature of the change which faced the bus and coach sectors. Grants for bus purchase had been phased out and widespread privatisation was underway. Burton also points out that traditional market leaders Leyland and MCW had disappeared because they had failed to adapt to the new demands of the industry. At that time only 350 new buses were being ordered each year. Trinity had long viewed that position as unsustainable and in 1995 commissions returned to the levels of subsidy days – 2285 registrations.

The group has never looked back. It has reported continuous sales and profit growth, which it has achieved through a combination of acquisitional and organic methods. Seven years after the MBO, Trinity enjoys commanding leads in its domestic markets and is an emerging world player.

Distinctive features

- niche markets leadership;
- innovative and speedy design;
- quick decision-making;
- rapid production throughput;
- skilful financial management.

The group has six UK businesses and two overseas. The biggest contributor to sales is Dennis Specialist Vehicles which makes bus, coach and fire engine chassis. The next largest is Dennis Eagle which concentrates on refuse vehicles and utility and airport vehicle chassis. Two companies focus on airport ground support vehicles and cargo handling – Reliance Mercury and Douglas. Duple Metsec builds bus bodying kits for export. Carmichael International deals in fire bodies and crash tenders. Schopf in Germany makes airport ground support vehicles and cargo handling units. In Malaysia, the UMW-Dennis joint venture manufactures complete buses and coaches for the domestic market and for export to the rest of the region.

Stratagems

As one might expect from a tightly managed company, Trinity's strategy is precisely defined. Its first tenet is that the group operates in specifically designated niche markets. These are fire engines, buses, coaches, airport vehicles and waste disposal trucks. 'We emphatically do not enter high volume markets such as cars and lorries. Trinity is active in specialist vehicle markets,' says Burton. Its second core principle is that it designs leading edge vehicles, manufactures the distinctive parts, buys in the most appropriate components for such parts as the engines and gearing, and then assembles the units. 'One of our key distinctive factors is that we are able to choose the most suitable engineering components unlike the larger motor companies like Volvo or Renault which are obliged to draw on, say, in-house engines which are expressly designed for cars or lorries. If we are building buses, we can pick the best engines for buses.'

Trinity then gives customers a reason to buy. It is insufficient to display exciting new technology. In the example of its first coach, the company was able to show that average users could save £5000 a year from the reduction in fuel consumption which would ultimately pay for the coach. The group also set out a three phase plan for the development of the business. In the first phase it aims to achieve market shares in the UK of between 40 and 50 per cent in each of its key disciplines. This has already been done. In phase two Trinity expands the range of products and sectors in the UK and launches its export penetration initiative with full vigour. The company already has plants in Malaysia and China and aimed to be up and running in Nigeria by the end of 1996. Burton says that the group is presently engaged in phase two with two new sectors opening up in the UK and the facilities in the Far East and Africa beginning to make a contribution.

Size and shape

Employees: 1500   Locations: 8
Geographical income split: UK 59%, Pacific Rim 26%, Africa 6.5%, mainland Europe 4%, Asia 2.5%

Phase three is the establishment of operations worldwide. Europe is virtually untouched. It is a harder market to crack than the UK was at the outset but its technology is superior to anything available on the mainland. However, subsidies still exist in many European countries and this will favour indiginous operators. The Far East and Africa hold countless possibilities. As countries in these regions develop more industrial sites the demand for public transport, airport facilities and waste disposal units will grow rapidly.

The return on capital in this business is remarkably high. Two key approaches help the financial management of the group. Each of the businesses runs autonomously but the lean headquarters facility offers guidance on cross-functional marketing opportunities and agrees annual targets. Equally the central decision-making process is immediate. Second, there is no warehousing, throughput in assembly is rapid, and components arrive at the line precisely when they are needed. Speed, as well as quality, is a major driving force. The Trinity culture permeates all the subsidiaries and can be characterised as innovative, confident, straightforward but cautious and considered.

Outlook

Future prospects

- further joint ventures overseas;
- penetration in mainland Europe;
- new domestic sectors.

Trinity has achieved 40–50 per cent market share in all of its domestic markets. As it continues to expand its product range this will rise but the group does not want to command substantially greater proportions domestically. It is currently in the next phase of its programme, which is export penetration via joint ventures in Malaysia, China and Nigeria. It has recently moved into two new market sectors and in the medium term it expects to broaden its role in mainland Europe, the Far East and Africa. Managing the growth is the key challenge for the future.

Address:

5 Elm Court, Copse Drive, Coventry CV5 9RG. Tel: 01676 523211. Fax: 01676 532828

Vanguard Medica Group plc   PHARMACEUTICALS

Guildford

Fund raising				
1991	1993	1994	1995	1996
£0.25M	£6M	£3.5M	£11.3M	£49.5M

Summary: Vanguard Medica is a development stage pharmaceutical company which was set up in 1991 by a group of R&D experts from the pharmaceutical industry. The management team and the founders led by CEO Robert Mansfield have steered a course for the business which is at once highly commercial and at the leading edge of the development of new drugs. Vanguard has five compounds in development including three in clinical trials. Four of these are due to reach the market around the year 2000 – if they achieve regulatory approval. this company is extremely astute in identifying both prospective partners and new compounds which will make a contribution to the improvement of healthcare and make a profit.

The Business

When Vanguard Medica floated on the London Stock Exchange in May 1996, its outstanding success was due as much to the commanding weight of its founders and management as to the concept of the company. The founding team, which today makes up the company's project advisory board, is drawn from former top drawer management at SKB, Wellcome, Glaxo, Upjohn and ICI (now Zeneca). Professor Erik Anggard of Bristol Myers and Professor Sir John Vane, of Wellcome (their surnames have been combined to make Vanguard) brought together Dr Roger Brimblecombe of SKB, Dr William Duncan of SK&F, ICI and Johnson & Johnson, Sir David Jack of Glaxo and Dr Charles Smith of Upjohn, Squibb and Revlon.

Their concept was straightforward. Pharmaceutical multinationals need new compounds to design fresh pharma products. At the same time there are hundreds of tiny pharmaceutical and biotechnology research organisations which cannot afford to go beyond discovery stage and are unhappy about dealing with the industry giants. Vanguard Medica was created to take new ideas through the financially onerous stages of development, clinical trials and regulatory approval. It understands the process of trials and also the hurdles which products need to go through before they can win the regulatory go-ahead.

The company was formed in 1991 but the first stage in its commercial operation was in late 1992 when Robert Mansfield was recruited from SmithKline Beecham where he had occupied senior management posts for 14 years. Among these roles were MD Australia and head of new product development. 'We spent a long time finding someone who could display suitable credentials for moving the business forward commercially,' says chairman Dr Roger Brimblecombe. This quiet lion-tamer has a reputation for making teams work which is absolutely vital in the identification of new research, the development of products in the clinic and negotiating the most beneficial deals for suppliers of compounds, prospective development partners and for Vanguard itself.

Mansfield says that he spent the first six months in the job looking for appropriate funding. Potential backers needed to be aware that profits are anticipated over a longer duration than with many emerging companies. The long period of clinical trials and the subsequent regulatory challenges are highly expensive and before developing pharmaceutical companies can make money their pipeline products need to win approval and be taken up for marketing purposes. But if these new compounds have been selected carefully when they pass through the clinic and the regulator they will be highly profitable.

Vanguard Medica (VM) has five products in development. VML 251 is an anti-migraine compound being developed with SKB; VML 252 is a new treatment for renal patients with hyperphosphataemia which is a partnership with BTG and Kings College; VML 295 with Eli Lilly is targeted at diseases with an inflammatory component; VML 262 is at a pre-clinical stage and is a partnership with Strathclyde University to combat psoriasis; and VML 275 is a long lasting skin protection for exposure to ultra-violet radiation. If VM's plans work out on target, the final products will be available to their markets between the years 2000 and 2003.

Distinctive features

- five mainstream compounds in development;
- formidable development team;
- strong capacities for selection and planning;
- extensive sector links.

Stratagems

The commercial instincts of VM were honed in some of the best run pharmaceutical multinationals in the world. What has emerged is a business with the accent on planning, quality of personnel and superb skills in selecting new compounds. 'In some ways we are like the Japanese; we do not go forward with any projects until we have evaluated them thoroughly. The Japanese say that thorough pre-planning facilitates faster execution. We are very similar,' says Mansfield.

Size and shape

Employees: 40   Locations:1
Geographical income split: too early to tell

The strategy has been to add to the formidable qualities on the board and then to staff the organisation with highly skilled people for selection, development and ultimately marketing of compounds. One of VM's great capacities is to identify markets and then to select appropriate technologies for addressing market need. It aims to draw its compounds from five sources: multinational pharma companies, local pharma businesses, emerging bio-techs, emerging biopharma research companies and academic teams. So far the five compounds in development have come from two – multinationals and academia. But since VM intends to have six to eight compounds in development before the end of 1998, the balance of probabilities suggests that it will have compounds from the other three sources as well.

Mansfield says that VM is determined to be an early commercial success and so has focused its attention on those compounds which meet readily identifiable, clinical needs. He summarises the selection criteria for compounds as: commercial viability, clearly identified clinical need, strong patent position, acceptable development costs, and what the company calls well defined clinical endpoints. This means that VM can address a major clinical need where the objectives are widely agreed by practitioners. With drugs for mass markets, the most sensible marketing and production options are to link with a multinational partner but with niche opportunities the company will handle its own sales and marketing opportunities.

Financial director Peter Worrall says that the company went for a listing in 1996 to raise funds for clinical development. 'We plan to have several compounds going through different stages of the development process at any one time. The valuation of compounds – and therefore the company – rises steeply during phases one, two and three of trials. I have told the City and our shareholders that we will be back for more funds. The sooner this happens, the better our clinical results will have been.'

Outlook

Future prospects

- rapid profitability;
- further exciting new drugs in the pipeline;
- more blue chip partnerships.

Vanguard Medica is anticipated to be in profit at a far earlier stage of development than many other companies of its kind. Brokers are projecting rocketing share prices for the company, because even if all five compounds in the pipeline failed, VM's strategy and approach would still be right. The failure of all five is a remote possibility – developing new compounds is a risky business – but it is more likely that at least two will be major international successes. At the heart of the VM success is the quality of its founders and management, and the meticulous care which is taken in identifying markets and compounds.

Address:

Chancellor Court, Surrey Research Park, Guildford, Surrey GU2 5SF. Tel: 01483 787878. Fax: 01483 787811. E-mail: Admin@vanguardmedica.com

VideoLogic plc

Kings Langley, Herts

Turnover				
1992	1993	1994	1995	1996
£7M	£10M	£9M	£12M	£14M

Summary: VideoLogic is a graphics and multimedia performance accelerator company that develops graphics technology and supplies add-in cards for personal computers to display video, TV pictures, and other two-dimensional (2D) scenes faster. This is a worldwide technology leader which has not yet been able to translate its product superiority into profits. Its world-leading 3D PowerVR (virtual reality) display technology, joint-development partnership with NEC, contract with Compaq, the global PC leader, and support from third party games developers together with a change in management is leading to a turnaround in the business.

The Business

Tony Maclaren founded VideoLogic with his father, Derek, in 1984. They became MD and chairman respectively and were part of Avesco plc until a demerger in mid-1994. At this time they had developed and were selling the 928Movie add-on graphics accelerator cards for PCs. However the competition moved to technology that was inherently more powerful and it took VideoLogic a while to catch up with its GrafixStar range which commenced sales in 1995.

VideoLogic has had a history of failing to translate its outstanding technical superiority into market success. The reasons have been strong competition which reduces the shelf-life of products, wild swings in component pricing and availability causing supply problems, and the lack of an industry standard causing development costs to be higher than they would otherwise be. A new management team formed in the first half of 1996 when

Derek Maclaren and FD Bruce Powell stepped down. Geoff Shingles, ex-head of Digital UK, was promoted from deputy chairman to chairman and Trevor Selby was appointed as the replacement FD. Graphics expert Hossain Yossaie was promoted to become technical director and a new non-executive director completed the board strengthening.

The new board has got a grip on the business and reduced both its cost base and its susceptibility to component pricing and supply swings through better purchasing arrangements. The development of its 3D PowerVR technology spawned a joint-development agreement with Japanese giant NEC to develop chips that could go into PCs, arcade machines and games consoles. Compaq is taking the chips for its PCs, Namco is converting arcade games for the chips and many other games developers are supportive. NEC has signed a second development agreement to develop multimedia and interactive TV set-top box chips using VideoLogic's technology. Its *Highlander* programme positions the company to take advantage of the looming convergence between PC and TV. Shingles believes that, 'PC's and TVs are, without doubt, converging. By the year 2000 you will not be able to tell which you have got.'

VideoLogic has had such promising technology that it has not found financing a problem although it has been cash-negative in recent years. An investment from NEC in 1995 was followed by an additional share issue in early 1996. Shingles does not think any more interim financing will be needed as the cash outflow has ceased; 'This financial year we have become cash-neutral. If things go according to the current plan we will start to see cash flowing in from royalty sales in the first three months of 1997.' Christmas is a peak selling season for consumer PCs and the Compaq deal should come good then.

Distinctive features

- global technological leadership;
- joint development contract with NEC;
- capacity to attract blue chip investors;
- new and talented management team.

The company is moving to become a technology developer and licensee as well as a manufacturer, through sub-contracting arrangements, of its own technology. This should remove a lot of volatility from its results, 'de-risking the company,' according to Shingles, and enabling it to show its real potential.

Stratagems

The company has three objectives; to make PowerVR a market leader, to move the company into profitability and to have excellent control of working capital and resources. It also wants to retain its key staff and, longer term, to be a market leader in the consolidated computing, communications and multimedia market. Shingles says, 'We want to see VideoLogic become recognised as a centre of excellence in the current merging of the communications, PC, media and content industries that is going on right now.'

The company needs to show a profit. Market leadership requires Video-Logic to have technology leadership. R&D spending will remain high as the PowerVR and *Highlander* programmes are implemented. Shingles says the new team has, 'cut overheads by 40 per cent by March 1996 on March 1995. We are taking a very active set of steps to increase our control of working capital.' Its cost base reduction efforts are limited by the necessity to continue a relatively high level of R&D spend. Thus it needs to share selling and marketing costs and broaden its channels to market.

Size and shape

Employees: 116　　　　　　　　　　Locations: 3
Geographical income split: Europe 46%, North America 33.3%, RoW 20.7%

Typically it has developed technology, implemented it in add-on cards that it has had manufactured through sub-contractors and then sold the cards either to PC manufacturers or through the retail channel against strong American and German competition. Neither PC manufacturers nor retail customers have bought the cards in enough numbers to compensate for the effects of component price/supply swings and fast competitive responses. Under Shingle's guidance the company is opening up a technology business separate from the existing systems business. Revenues will come from royalties through licensing. The company will look to earn revenues from royalty streams utilising both its own and NEC's sales channels as well as from its traditional systems business. VideoLogic is talking to all the main consumer PC and games console manufacturers about PowerVR, and third party card vendors like Diamond are also showing an interest.

Future prospects

- massive increase in turnover by 1997;
- profitability in 1996 and high margin in 1997;
- further blue chip alliances.

Videologic is also broadening its market and adding general games machines – both hand-held consoles and arcade systems – as well as TVs to its target platforms. It believes it has the right technology with PowerVR to lower games developers' costs significantly. Secondly, by combining its existing technology to play TV, video and sound on PCs with PowerVR-class technology it aims to develop industry-leading graphics chips for interactive TV through set-top boxes and for general/consumer PCs. The add-on card market will still be addressed by VideoLogic but through an OEM and value-added distributor route rather than through direct involvement with the retail channel. They will also sell direct to large corporates. Existing GrafixStar cards which use third party chips, will probably have their technology uprated and become 3D cards using PowerVR chips.

Outlook

The company's ability to attract world class partners such as NEC and Compaq means that, at least, its promise could equal profits. Other suppliers in the consumer PC market have to follow in Compaq's footsteps. Also, a significant console supplier must sign up. This means Sony, Nintendo or SEGA. Its NEC partnership could work in VideoLogic's favour as NEC is linked with all these suppliers already. Thirdly, games have to flow through that use PowerVR technology. Longer term, the *Highlander* initiative has to show similar results with set-top box manufacturers incorporating the resulting technology. All this has to happen without GrafixStar retail sales being demolished by unanticipated competitive responses.

Address:

Home Park Estate, Kings Langley, Herts WD4 8LZ. Tel: 01923 260511. Fax: 01923 268969

J.D. Wetherspoon plc

Watford

Turnover				
1991	1992	1993	1994	1995
£13M	£21M	£31M	£47M	£69M

Summary: Wetherspoon has spearheaded a retail revolution in the pub industry. The straightforward concept of moderately-priced beer, no music and basic but affordable food has helped the chain become the largest quoted managed pub company in the UK. By adopting a strategy of converting unlicensed premises into pubs, it has been able to expand rapidly, firstly across London and now around the country. Generally, the pubs are on high streets and some – of at least 4,500sq ft – so called superpubs. A policy of music-free outlets, no-smoking areas, almost all day food, and minimal presence of slot machines has rapidly found favour among the public.

The Business

The pub sector has experienced rapid and total change during the last half-decade. The majors have been threatened by nimble footed, younger and more vibrant competitors. J.D. Wetherspoon is among the leaders of the new wave. Its dynamic and positive approach has won the company a range of friends – not least among its clientele. The concept for the company's outlets was based on George Orwell's vision of the ideal pub. All the chain's pubs are managed, that is directly controlled, from head office via site managers rather than let to tenants. The majority of turnover comes from the sale of drinks, primarily beer. It floated on the London Stock Exchange in October 1992, the first of a new breed of pub chains to do so.

The company has grown from a single pub owner by Tim Martin. After qualifying as a barrister, Martin decided to quit the law to set up his own pub in North London in 1979. He considered that the pubs in his area were poor and believed he could do better. When Wetherspoon started, the pub industry was in the hands of the big brewers. Vertical integration was how the brewers maintained their grip – they controlled the production and distribution of beer and owned most of the retail outlets for it. With only £10,000 of capital, raised through the profit on the sale of his flat, Martin began building a pub empire to take on the monopoly and created the estate which has developed into the business which is so successful in mid-year 1996.

The start was slow and by 1983 there were still only four pubs. But by the end of the summer of 1996, the estate had mushroomed to more than 150 Wetherspoon outlets. But turnover has climbed rapidly in response to the significant increase in number of pubs. In 1991 the 13 pubs in the group produced £28M of sales but the 110 trading outlets at the year end in 1995 generated a turnover of £69M. Analysts confidently predict sales should be in excess of £170M by 1998. Profitability has shown similar major advances, and in 1995 pretax profits grew 50 per cent to reach £9.7M.

Distinctive features

- well-managed sites;
- larger than average pubs;
- effective operational systems;
- traditional format.

Stratagems

Founder Martin took George Orwell's vision of the ideal pub and turned it into reality. The Moon Under Water, as envisioned by Orwell, would have no music, good beer and conversation. Martin could do little about the latter but he tries to supply the first two in all his pubs. Along the way he has won many supporters, including consumer pressure group the Campaign for Real Ale (CAMRA). Consumers like being offered a selection of beers, particularly from breweries which did not own any pubs locally and therefore did not have outlets for their beer.

The company's policy of selling beer cheaper than rival pubs has also found favour with the public. Hardly a revolutionary business concept but it has yielded spectacular results. Wetherspoon has cheered its customers but struck fear in the hearts of rivals. It is a compliment to the company that when it proposes to open a new pub, other pub landlords in the area will often campaign against the Wetherspoon outlet being granted a licence, often citing unfair competition as the reason.

Music – or its absence – is a major factor in the Wetherspoon success story. Not piping music throughout the premises is again hardly revolutionary but few other pubs even today have chosen to scrap the jukebox. Other simple, easily implemented ideas still mark out Wetherspoon outlets. The menu is short but sufficient; more importantly the food is served from the morning until 10 p.m. in every pub. Like the beer and other drinks, the food is competitively priced. The rapid growth of the chain is helping to keep prices low. It has the critical mass needed to extract good discounts from suppliers and is believed to have some of the best beer supply deals in the industry.

The pubs were among the first to be equipped with a full electronic point of sale system. It was not the only area where the skills and expertise used by leading retailers on the High Street were brought into the pub environment. The establishment of successful operating systems was supported by a stress on service standards. Although the vast majority of Wetherspoon pubs are based in England, the company has recruited throughout the UK and Ireland for the best personnel to staff its outlets.

Size and shape

Employees: 5100   Locations: 170
Geographical income split: UK 100%

Straightforward procedures – like insisting the bar staff inspect the toilets every hour and then sign a notice publicly displayed in the conveniences to ensure the inspection is carried out – have helped main high standards. The single most important factor contributing to the group's success is probably its site selection. High Street locations with a heavy passing pedestrian traffic are chosen.

Rather than rely on buying licensed pubs – which would have meant virtual stagnation for the company given other operators' hostility to selling it pubs – Wetherspoon has pioneered the acquisition of unlicensed sites. In its estate there are former car showrooms, cinemas and host of other buildings with no history of selling alcohol. Martin has often been forced into court battles to obtain licences but perhaps because of his legal background he has fought and won.

Future prospects

- continued rapid expansion;
- strong and building management culture;
- further acquisitional and organic growth.

Rather than tie-up valuable capital in property the bulk of the pubs are held
on leases – another feature common for High Street retailers but, until
recently, rare among pub chains. this change means the company is focused
on retailing rather than property management like so many of its competitors. The acquisition of previously unlicensed sites has meant the group
could build bigger than average pubs. The fixed costs of each site – such as
the management couple – could be spread over a higher turnover. Wetherspoon has driven this trend in the industry towards the so-called superpub.

Outlook

Rumours of bigger companies wanting to takeover Wetherspoon have been
running for years. It is no surprise and a compliment to the management. But
the group has an exceptionally high market capitalisation – each pub is
valued at almost £3M – that predators have so far stayed away. USA-based
investors, who have a better understanding of the hospitality sector than
their UK counterparts, have built-up a sizeable stake. There is still some
room for the chain to expand, believes Martin. It was only this year the chain
opened its first outlet in Scotland and most Wetherspoon pubs are still in
Greater London.

Address:

Wetherspoon House, Central Park, Reeds Crescent, Watford WD1 1QH.
Tel: 01923 477777. Fax: 01923 219810

Xenova Group plc

Slough

Turnover				
1994	1995	1996	1997	1998
£2M	£1.8M	£1.5M	£2M	£3Me

Summary: Xenova is a well-established drug discovery group concentrating on the identification of new products from natural raw materials. It operates the world's largest library of source materials. These are all derived from nature – which optimises the chances of the ultimate success of the resultant drug compounds. The company has attracted a growing bank of blue chip partners, some of whom are so convinced of the long-term success of Xenova that they have taken stakes in the company.

The Business

Biotechnology is one of the buzz words of the commercial world. The City and corporate investors have been attracted to the huge potential for profit which biotech businesses promise. If one of these companies succeeds with a blockbuster drug then its share price will rocket. The long-term future for such enterprises is compelling. they are partnered by some of the leading names in the corporate environment and with proven capability in drug discovery they will be seen as the stars of the future. But the task for them lies in the often onerous process in getting from concept to a marketable product. This is why the biotechs need the financial muscle and regulatory/clinical experience of the blue chips.

Xenova is one of the biotechs which is starred for success. It was founded in 1987 by its current CEO Dr Louis Nisbet and now embraces drug discovery, preclinical development and a therapeutics division in Slough. The company also has a 70 per cent stake in MetaXen, A Californian-based business which applies combinational chemistry and software applications to preclinical development.

426

A key distinguishing factor of Xenova is its library of raw chemicals – all drawn from natural sources – which is believed to be the largest in the world. Brokers Yamaichi comment 'This raw chemicals library provides a more directed autosynthesis of chemicals than random autosynthesis. Their natural origin means that they have a much better chance of exhibiting any biological activity than chemicals chosen at random and promises to speed up early lead discovery. Six of the world's top 25 drugs are sourced from naturally-occurring materials – generating annual sales of $8 billion. Finding semi-relevant starting chemicals is emerging as the main process bottleneck. Xenova's library addresses just this bottleneck. Its R&D pipeline also has at least two potentially major anti-cancer drugs in early stage clinical development.'

The company focuses on drugs derived from naturally-occurring chemicals in extracts from micro-organisms such as fungi and bacteria, and from plants. This mixed chemical library is called NatChem and it is based on 25,000 microbes and 6000 plant extracts. It has built a collection of 64,000 partially purified samples available for rapid screening. Xenova's directors believe that it has developed one of the world's leading independent capabilities to discover natural chemical drug leads, based on a group of integrated technologies. To extend its capacity to develop these leads it has joined in alliances and partnerships with companies such as Bristol-Myers Squibb, Zeneca, Warner-Lambert, Suntory, Genentech, Genzyme and Pharma-Genetics.

Distinctive features

- emphasis on naturally occurring sources;
- world leading library of more than 30,000 sources;
- blue chip relationships;
- two potential blockbusters in the clinic.

The company's drugs in early clinical trials both have the potential to be anti-cancer blockbuster treatments. These are XR5000 and XR9051. Both address the core problem of resistance to cytotoxic drugs – a market currently worth $5bn. XR5000 is a dual action inhibitor which, says the brokers, could challenge the market for an existing product – Taxol – which is worth $700 million annually. XR9051 is a drug resistance blocker which is designed to overcome the resistance by cancers to cytoxics.

The company has its own proprietary high-throughput screening system called ASSET and its own RAPIDD information handling system. The support given by MetaXen which should strengthen Xenova's capacity to deliver lead candidates in the process of designing new drugs. It has seven discovery programmes in operation. Two embrace XR5000 and XR9051. The rest cover thrombosis, tumour supressors, cancers which are resistant to several treatments and solid cancers.

Stratagems

Xenova's strategic direction has been straightforward from the outset. It has employed people of extremely high calibre to work in its laboratories. The group employs 114 people of whom 43 hold PhD degrees and 94 work in research and development. Its board and senior management read like a Who's Who in the commercial and academic research fields of the pharmaceutical sector.

The company has committed itself to a concentration on medical and therapeutic needs where these are presently poorly served. Its emphasis has lain heavily on cancer drugs and also on thrombosis. Six out of its seven programmes currently focus on drugs which will limit resistance to cancer.

Size and shape

Employees: 114   Locations: 2
Geographical income split: UK 25%, North America 40%, RoW 35%

Like many biotechs, Xenova has identified relationships with major pharmaceutical, research and academic organisations as vitally important to its work. Among these collaborations are assignments with the Cancer Research Campaign, Auckland Cancer Laboratory, Academic Medical Centre in Amsterdam, the Department of Haematology at the University of London and the Memorial-Sloan Kettering Cancer Center, New York.

Xenova also exploits its technologies commercially by undertaking collaborative research for, and providing high value services to, major pharmaceutical and biotech companies for research and milestone payments and future royalties on drug sales. The company focuses solely on small molecule drugs which have the potential to be administered orally and also by injection. In 1995, according to the publication Pharma Business, some 23 of the top 25 selling drugs were based on small molecules.

In meeting such demand the company argues that the combination of its wholly natural source material and its inventive use of technology and systems will give it a substantial advantage in what is a highly competitive and risky marketplace.

Outlook

The future for biotech companies is always difficult to predict. Some with apparently attractive prospects fail to stay the course during the intensive period of clinical trials. Others by expertise and original thinking hit on compounds which will save lives and give relief from suffering to thousands of people. The overall health care market is booming and the demand for high quality drugs with fewer side-effects is increasing rapidly. So the potential is extensive.

Future prospects

- further blue chip alliances;
- early results from the clinic on compounds with huge potential;
- a strong contribution from MetaXen;
- a deep pipeline of future drug prospects.

By mid year 1998, Xenova expects the early clinical results from its two key products and its other prospects will have entered the clinical process. This is a testing time for the company. But the quality of its partners and the international recognition which it is steadily building will contribute to its growth.

Address:

Xenova Group plc, 240 Bath Road, Slough, Berkshire SL1 4EF. Tel: 01753 692229. Fax: 01753 692613

Groundbreakers 100 list

Sector analysis

Agriculture/horticulture

Cranswick plc
Hozelock

Biotechnology/pharmaceuticals

Azur
British Biotech
Cambridge Antibody Technology
Celsis International
Chiroscience
Cortecs
ML Labs
Shield Diagnostics
Vanguard Medica
Xenova

Chemicals

Inspec

Construction/plant

Allen plc
Bruntcliffe Aggregates

Sherriff Plant Hire

Distribution

Abacus Polar
Azlan Group plc
Chernikeeff Group
Dagenham Motors
European Telecom
Finelist Group
Flying Flowers
Ideal
Morse

Energy

Cairn Energy
Ramco Energy

Engineering

AES Engineering
Critchley Group plc
Domnick Hunter
IES
Protean plc

Financial services

Brockbank Group
Close Brothers
DBS Management

Healthcare

Ashbourne plc
Biocompatibles
Huntleigh Technology
Innovative Technologies

IT/systems

ARM
Bookham Technology
Card Clear
Checkout Computers
Compel Group
Datrontech Group
Epitaxial Products International
Filtronic Comtek
Forward Group
Madge Networks
MAID plc
Microvitec plc
On Demand Information
Pace Micro Technology
Parity
Skillsgroup
Psion
Radius
Rolfe & Nolan
The Roxboro Group
Spectrum Computer

Leisure

Bluebird Toys
Eldridge Pope
Mulberry
Probe Entertainment
Regent Inns
Tinsley Robor
VideoLogic
JD Wetherspoon

Media

Brann Limited
Colleagues Group
Demon Internet
Dorling Kindersley

GWR Group
Howell, Henry, Chaldecott, Lury
Merlin Publishing International
Taylor Nelson

Property

London Industrial

Outsourcing

Admiral plc
Capita Group
CMG
F I Group
Jarvis
Logica plc

Retailing

The Carphone Warehouse

Services

BTG
Corporate Services Group
Havelock Europa
Stalbridge Linen Services

Software

Cedardata
Coda Group
DCS Group
JBA Holdings
Kewill Systems
Sage Group plc

GROUNDBREAKERS 100 LIST

Telecoms

Telspec PLC

Transport

Jacobs Holdings
TrafficMaster
Trinity Holdings

Others

Headlam Group
Mayborn Group

Index by Sector

INDEX BY SECTOR

INDEX BY SECTOR

Printed and bound by CPI Group (UK) Ltd, Croydon, CR0 4YY

Printed and bound by CPI Group (UK) Ltd, Croydon, CR0 4YY

23/04/2025

14660974-0001